ILTS 106 Science: Chemistry
Teacher Certification Exam

By: Sharon Wynne, M.S.

XAMonline, INC.
Boston

Copyright © 2013 XAMonline, Inc.

All rights reserved. No part of the material protected by this copyright notice may be reproduced or utilized in any form or by any means, electronic or mechanical, including photocopying, recording or by any information storage and retrievable system, without written permission from the copyright holder.

To obtain permission(s) to use the material from this work for any purpose including workshops or seminars, please submit a written request to:

XAMonline, Inc.
25 First Street, Suite 106
Cambridge, MA 02141
Toll Free 1-800-301-4647
Email: info@xamonline.com
Web www.xamonline.com

Library of Congress Cataloging-in-Publication Data

Wynne, Sharon A.
    Science: Chemistry 106: Teacher Certification / Sharon A. Wynne. -2nd ed.
    ISBN 978-1-58197-979-4
    1. Science: Chemistry 106.   2. Study Guides.   3. ILTS
    4. Teachers' Certification & Licensure.   5. Careers

Disclaimer:

The opinions expressed in this publication are the sole works of XAMonline and were created independently from the Pearson Corporation, National Education Association, Educational Testing Service, or any State Department of Education, National Evaluation Systems or other testing affiliates.

Between the time of publication and printing, state specific standards as well as testing formats and website information may change that is not included in part or in whole within this product. Sample test questions are developed by XAMonline and reflect similar content as on real tests; however, they are not former tests. XAMonline assembles content that aligns with state standards but makes no claims nor guarantees teacher candidates a passing score. Numerical scores are determined by testing companies such as NES or ETS and then are compared with individual state standards. A passing score varies from state to state.

Printed in the United States of America   œ-1

ILTS: Science: Chemistry 106
ISBN: 978-1-58197-979-4

TEACHER CERTIFICATION STUDY GUIDE

Table of Contents

SUBAREA I.   SCIENCE AND TECHNOLOGY

COMPETENCY 1.0   UNDERSTAND AND APPLY KNOWLEDGE OF SCIENCE AS INQUIRY 1

Skill 1.1   Recognize the assumptions, processes, purposes, requirements, and tools of scientific inquiry 1

Skill 1.2   Use evidence and logic in developing proposed explanations that address scientific questions and hypotheses 4

Skill 1.3   Identify various approaches to conducting scientific investigations and their applications 5

Skill 1.4   Use tools and mathematical and statistical methods for collecting, managing, analyzing, and communicating results of investigations .. 8

Skill 1.5   Demonstrate knowledge of ways to report, display, and defend the results of an investigation 9

COMPETENCY 2.0   UNDERSTAND AND APPLY KNOWLEDGE OF THE CONCEPTS, PRINCIPLES, AND PROCESSES OF TECHNOLOGICAL DESIGN 10

Skill 2.1   Recognize the capabilities, limitations, and implications of technology and technological design and redesign 10

Skill 2.2   Identify real-world problems or needs to be solved through technological design 10

Skill 2.3   Apply a technological design process to a given problem situation ... 10

Skill 2.4   Identify a design problem and propose possible solutions, considering such constraints as tools, materials, time, costs, and laws of nature 11

Skill 2.5   Evaluate various solutions to a design problem 11

SCIENCE: CHEMISTRY

TEACHER CERTIFICATION STUDY GUIDE

COMPETENCY 3.0 UNDERSTAND AND APPLY KNOWLEDGE OF ACCEPTED PRACTICES OF SCIENCE 12

Skill 3.1 Demonstrate an understanding of the nature of science and recognize how scientific knowledge and explanations change over time 12

Skill 3.2 Compare scientific hypotheses, predictions, laws, theories, and principles and recognize how they are developed and tested 13

Skill 3.3 Recognize examples of valid and biased thinking in reporting of scientific research 15

Skill 3.4 Recognize the basis for and application of safety practices and regulations in the study of science 15

COMPETENCY 4.0 UNDERSTAND AND APPLY KNOWLEDGE OF THE INTERACTIONS AMONG SCIENCE, TECHNOLOGY, AND SOCIETY 18

Skill 4.1 Recognize the historical and contemporary development of major scientific ideas and technological innovations 18

Skill 4.2 Demonstrate an understanding of the ways that science and technology affect people's everyday lives, societal values and systems, the environment, and new knowledge 25

Skill 4.3 Analyze the processes of scientific and technological breakthroughs and their effects on other fields of study, careers, and job markets 26

Skill 4.4 Analyze issues related to science and technology at the local, state, national, and global levels 26

Skill 4.5 Evaluate the credibility of scientific claims made in various forums 34

TEACHER CERTIFICATION STUDY GUIDE

COMPETENCY 5.0 UNDERSTAND AND APPLY KNOWLEDGE OF THE MAJOR UNIFYING CONCEPTS OF ALL SCIENCES AND HOW THESE CONCEPTS RELATE TO OTHER DISCIPLINES 35

Skill 5.1   Identify the major unifying concepts of the sciences and their applications in real-life situations 35

Skill 5.2   Recognize connections within and among the traditional scientific disciplines 36

Skill 5.3   Apply fundamental mathematical language, knowledge, and skills at the level of algebra and statistics in scientific contexts 36

Skill 5.4   Recognize the fundamental relationships among the natural sciences and the social sciences 40

SUBAREA II. LIFE SCIENCE

COMPETENCY 6.0 UNDERSTAND AND APPLY KNOWLEDGE OF CELL STRUCTURE AND FUNCTION 41

Skill 6.1 Compare and contrast the structures of viruses and prokaryotic and eukaryotic cells 41

Skill 6.2 Identify the structures and functions of cellular organelles 43

Skill 6.3 Describe the processes of the cell cycle 46

Skill 6.4 Explain the functions and applications of the instruments and technologies used to study the life sciences at the molecular and cellular levels 51

COMPETENCY 7.0 UNDERSTAND AND APPLY KNOWLEDGE OF THE PRINCIPLES OF HEREDITY AND BIOLOGICAL EVOLUTION 52

Skill 7.1 Recognize the nature and function of the gene, with emphasis on the molecular basis of inheritance and gene expression 52

Skill 7.2 Analyze the transmission of genetic information 52

Skill 7.3 Analyze the processes of change at the microscopic and macroscopic levels 55

Skill 7.4 Identify scientific evidence from various sources, such as the fossil record, comparative anatomy, and biochemical similarities, to demonstrate knowledge of theories about processes of biological evolution 56

TEACHER CERTIFICATION STUDY GUIDE

COMPETENCY 8.0 UNDERSTAND AND APPLY KNOWLEDGE OF THE CHARACTERISTICS AND LIFE FUNCTIONS OF ORGANISMS 59

Skill 8.1 Identify the levels of organization of various types of organisms and the structures and functions of cells, tissues, organs, and organ systems 59

Skill 8.2 Analyze the strategies and adaptations used by organisms to obtain the basic requirements of life 59

Skill 8.3 Analyze factors that influence homeostasis within an organism 61

Skill 8.4 Demonstrate an understanding of the human as a living organism with life functions comparable to those of other life forms 61

COMPETENCY 9.0 UNDERSTAND AND APPLY KNOWLEDGE OF HOW ORGANISMS INTERACT WITH EACH OTHER AND WITH THEIR ENVIRONMENT 63

Skill 9.1 Identify living and nonliving components of the environment and how they interact with one another 63

Skill 9.2 Recognize the concepts of populations, communities, ecosystems, and ecoregions and the role of biodiversity in living systems 63

Skill 9.3 Analyze factors that influence interrelationships among organisms .. 63

Skill 9.4 Develop a model or explanation that shows the relationships among organisms in the environment 65

Skill 9.5 Recognize the dynamic nature of the environment, including how communities, ecosystems, and ecoregions change over time 65

Skill 9.6 Analyze interactions of humans with their environment 66

Skill 9.7 Explain the functions and applications of the instruments and technologies used to study the life sciences at the organism and ecosystem level 67

SCIENCE: CHEMISTRY

TEACHER CERTIFICATION STUDY GUIDE

SUBAREA III.   **PHYSICAL SCIENCE**

COMPETENCY 10.0 UNDERSTAND AND APPLY KNOWLEDGE OF THE NATURE AND PROPERTIES OF ENERGY IN ITS VARIOUS FORMS 68

Skill 10.1   Describe the characteristics of and relationships among thermal, acoustical, radiant, electrical, chemical, mechanical, and nuclear energies through conceptual questions 68

Skill 10.2   Analyze the processes by which energy is exchanged or transformed through conceptual questions 71

Skill 10.3   Apply the three laws of thermodynamics to explain energy transformations, including basic algebraic problem solving 73

Skill 10.4   Apply the principle of conservation as it applies to energy through conceptual questions and solving basic algebraic problems 74

COMPETENCY 11.0 UNDERSTAND AND APPLY KNOWLEDGE OF THE STRUCTURE AND PROPERTIES OF MATTER 75

Skill 11.1   Describe the nuclear and atomic structure of matter, including the three basic parts of the atom 75

Skill 11.2   Analyze the properties of materials in relation to their chemical or physical structures and evaluate uses of the materials based on their properties 75

Skill 11.3   Apply the principle of conservation as it applies to mass and charge through conceptual questions 78

Skill 11.4   Analyze bonding and chemical, atomic, and nuclear reactions in natural and man-made systems and apply basic stoichiometric principles 79

Skill 11.5   Apply kinetic theory to explain interactions of energy with matter, including conceptual questions on changes in state 80

Skill 11.6   Explain the functions and applications of the instruments and technologies used to study matter and energy 80

TEACHER CERTIFICATION STUDY GUIDE

COMPETENCY 12.0 UNDERSTAND AND APPLY KNOWLEDGE OF FORCES AND MOTION 81

Skill 12.1   Demonstrate an understanding of the concepts and interrelationships of position, time, velocity, and acceleration through conceptual questions, algebra-based kinematics, and graphical analysis 81

Skill 12.2   Demonstrate an understanding of the concepts and interrelationships of force, inertia, work, power, energy, and momentum 81

Skill 12.3   Describe and predict the motions of bodies in one and two dimensions in inertial and accelerated frames of reference in a physical system, including projectile motion but excluding circular motion 83

Skill 12.4   Analyze and predict motions and interactions of bodies involving forces within the context of conservation of energy and/or momentum through conceptual questions and algebra-based problem solving 86

Skill 12.5   Describe the effects of gravitational and nuclear forces in real-life situations through conceptual questions 88

Skill 12.6   Explain the functions and applications of the instruments and technologies used to study force and motion in everyday life 89

COMPETENCY 13.0 UNDERSTAND AND APPLY KNOWLEDGE OF ELECTRICITY, MAGNETISM, AND WAVES 90

Skill 13.1   Recognize the nature and properties of electricity and magnetism, including static charge, moving charge, basic RC circuits, fields, conductors, and insulators 90

Skill 13.2   Recognize the nature and properties of mechanical and electromagnetic waves 92

Skill 13.3   Describe the effects and applications of electromagnetic forces in real-life situations, including electric power generation, circuit breakers, and brownouts 93

Skill 13.4   Analyze and predict the behavior of mechanical and electromagnetic waves under varying physical conditions, including basic optics, color, ray diagrams, and shadows 94

SCIENCE: CHEMISTRY

TEACHER CERTIFICATION STUDY GUIDE

SUBAREA IV.   **EARTH SYSTEMS AND THE UNIVERSE**

COMPETENCY 14.0 UNDERSTAND AND APPLY KNOWLEDGE OF EARTH'S LAND, WATER, AND ATMOSPHERIC SYSTEMS AND THE HISTORY OF EARTH 97

Skill 14.1   Identify the structure and composition of Earth's land, water, and atmospheric systems and how they affect weather, erosion, fresh water, and soil 97

Skill 14.2   Recognize the scope of geologic time and the continuing physical changes of Earth through time 98

Skill 14.3   Evaluate scientific theories about Earth's origin and history and how these theories explain contemporary living systems 100

Skill 14.4   Recognize the interrelationships between living organisms and Earth's resources and evaluate the uses of Earth's resources 101

COMPETENCY 15.0 UNDERSTAND AND APPLY KNOWLEDGE OF THE DYNAMIC NATURE OF EARTH 103

Skill 15.1   Analyze and explain large-scale dynamic forces, events, and processes that affect Earth's land, water, and atmospheric systems, including conceptual questions about plate tectonics, El Nino, drought, and climatic shifts 103

Skill 15.2   Identify and explain Earth processes and cycles and cite examples in real-life situations, including conceptual questions on rock cycles, volcanism, and plate tectonics.. 104

Skill 15.3   Analyze the transfer of energy within and among Earth's land, water, and atmospheric systems, including the identification of energy sources of volcanoes, hurricanes, thunderstorms, and tornadoes 108

Skill 15.4   Explain the functions and applications of the instruments and technologies used to study the earth sciences, including seismographs, barometers, and satellite systems 109

SCIENCE: CHEMISTRY

COMPETENCY 16.0 UNDERSTAND AND APPLY KNOWLEDGE OF OBJECTS IN THE UNIVERSE AND THEIR DYNAMIC INTERACTION 110

Skill 16.1 Describe and explain the relative and apparent motions of the sun, the moon, stars, and planets in the sky 110

Skill 16.2 Recognize properties of objects within the solar system and their dynamic interactions 111

Skill 16.3 Recognize the types, properties, and dynamics of objects external to the solar system 112

COMPETENCY 17.0 UNDERSTAND AND APPLY KNOWLEDGE OF THE ORIGINS OF AND CHANGES IN THE UNIVERSE 113

Skill 17.1 Identify scientific theories dealing with the origin of the universe 113

Skill 17.2 Analyze evidence relating to the origin and physical evolution of the universe 113

Skill 17.3 Compare the physical and chemical processes involved in the life cycles of objects within galaxies 114

Skill 17.4 Explain the functions and applications of the instruments, technologies, and tools used in the study of the space sciences, including the relative advantages and disadvantages of Earth-based versus space-based instruments and optical versus nonoptical instruments 115

TEACHER CERTIFICATION STUDY GUIDE

SUBAREA V. MATTER, STRUCTURE, AND PRACTICAL KNOWLEDGE

COMPETENCY 18,0 UNDERSTAND AND APPLY KNOWLEDGE OF BASIC SCIENTIFIC AND MATHEMATICAL SKILLS, SAFE LABORATORY PRACTICES, AND ISSUES OF PUBLIC CONCERN RELATED TO THE FIELD OF CHEMISTRY.... 116

Skill 18.1 Apply appropriate mathematical skills and technology to collect analyze and report data and to solve problems in chemistry 116

Skill 18.2 Select appropriate experimental procedures and equipment for the measurement and determination of chemical reactions and properties 132

Skill 18.3 Recognize safety practices in the chemistry laboratory, including the characteristics and purposes of chemical hygiene plans 136

Skill 18.4 Evaluate the role of chemistry in daily life, including ways in which basic research and the development of new technology affect society 152

COMPETENCY 19.0 UNDERSTAND AND APPLY KNOWLEDGE OF PERIODIC RELATIONSHIPS AND THE NATURE OF MATTER 154

Skill 19.1 Demonstrate knowledge of the chemical constitution of matter as elements, compounds, and mixtures 154

Skill 19.2 Distinguish between physical and chemical changes 156

Skill 19.3 Demonstrate knowledge of basic techniques used to separate substances based on differences in properties 156

Skill 19.4 Analyze the periodic nature of the elements and the relationship between their electron configuration and the periodic table 160

Skill 19.5 Connect the chemical and physical properties of elements to electron configuration 172

Skill 19.6 Demonstrate proficiency at naming compounds and writing formulas 173

COMPETENCY 20.0 UNDERSTAND AND APPLY KNOWLEDGE OF THE DEVELOPMENT AND CENTRAL CONCEPTS OF ATOMIC THEORY AND STRUCTURE, INCLUDING THE QUANTUM MECHANICAL MODEL 188

Skill 20.1 Recognize the central concepts of atomic theory and atomic structure 188

Skill 20.2 Demonstrate knowledge of the historical progression in the development of the theory of the atom, including the contributions of Dalton, Thomson, Rutherford, and Bohr 188

Skill 20.3 Describe the energy of an electron in an atom or ion in terms of the four quantum numbers 194

Skill 20.4 Demonstrate a qualitative knowledge of the role of probability in the description of an orbital's size and shape 196

Skill 20.5 Analyze the properties of an atomic nucleus that affect its stability ... 197

Skill 20.6 Apply strategies for writing and balancing equations for nuclear reactions 198

COMPETENCY 21.0 UNDERSTAND AND APPLY KNOWLEDGE OF THE FORMATION OF BONDS AND THE GEOMETRY AND PROPERTIES OF THE RESULTING COMPOUNDS 202

Skill 21.1 Analyze electron behavior in the formation of various types of bonds and the polarity of compounds in terms of shape and electronegativity differences 202

Skill 21.2 Apply the concepts of Lewis structures, valence-shell electron-pair repulsion, and hybridization to describe molecular geometry and bonding 208

Skill 21.3 Demonstrate knowledge of the general features and properties of compounds of metals, nonmetals, and transition elements and the materials derived from them 215

Skill 21.4 Describe the hybridization of the central atom based on the geometry of coordination compounds 218

TEACHER CERTIFICATION STUDY GUIDE

COMPETENCY 22.0 UNDERSTAND AND APPLY KNOWLEDGE OF THE KINETIC MOLECULAR THEORY AND THE NATURE AND PROPERTIES OF MOLECULES IN THE GASEOUS, LIQUID, AND SOLID STATES 222

Skill 22.1 Demonstrate knowledge of the basic principles of the kinetic molecular theory 222

Skill 22.2 Explain the properties of solids, liquids, and gases and changes of state in terms of the kinetic molecular theory and intermolecular forces 223

Skill 22.3 Apply various laws related to the properties and behavior of ideal gases to solve problems 225

Skill 22.4 Demonstrate an understanding of the differences between real and ideal gases 230

Skill 22.5 Interpret phase diagrams and use them to explain the transitions between solids, liquids, and gases 231

Skill 22.6 Classify unknown solids as molecular, metallic, ionic, and covalent network solids according to their physical and chemical properties .. 235

COMPETENCY 23.0 UNDERSTAND AND APPLY KNOWLEDGE OF THE INTERACTIONS OF PARTICLES IN SOLUTION AND THE PROPERTIES OF SOLUTIONS 238

Skill 23.1 Describe the solution process, including the effects of temperature and pressure on the solubility of solids, liquids, and gases 238

Skill 23.2 Analyze the qualitative colligative properties of solutions, including the practical applications of these properties to technological problems 241

Skill 23.3 Demonstrate knowledge of how to prepare solutions of specific concentrations, including molality, molarity, normality, mole fraction, and percent by weight 248

Skill 23.4 Select appropriate solvents for the dissolution or purification of solid compounds 250

SCIENCE: CHEMISTRY

SUBAREA VI. STOICHIOMETRY AND CHEMICAL REACTIONS

COMPETENCY 24.0 UNDERSTAND AND APPLY KNOWLEDGE OF THE CONCEPTS AND PRINCIPLES OF CHEMICAL EQUATIONS AND STOICHIOMETRY 251

Skill 24.1 Classify types of chemical reactions and balance equations to describe chemical reactions 251

Skill 24.2 Use mass and mole relationships in an equation to solve stoichiometric problems 257

Skill 24.3 Use gas laws and solution concentrations to solve stoichiometric problems 260

Skill 24.4 Demonstrate proficiency at converting between percent composition and the formulas of compounds 264

COMPETENCY 25.0 UNDERSTAND AND APPLY KNOWLEDGE OF THE CONCEPTS AND PRINCIPLES OF ACID-BASE CHEMISTRY 266

Skill 25.1 Compare the Arrhenius, Brønsted-Lowry, and Lewis concepts of acids and bases 266

Skill 25.2 Recognize the relationship between acid and base strength, pH, and molecular structure 270

Skill 25.3 Explain the characteristics of buffered solutions in terms of chemical equilibrium of weak acids 271

Skill 25.4 Demonstrate an understanding of how to prepare a standardized solution or a buffer of a specified pH, given the Ka of various acids and a standardized NaOH solution 272

Skill 25.5 Design and analyze the results of an acid-base titration 273

COMPETENCY 26.0 UNDERSTAND AND APPLY KNOWLEDGE OF THERMODYNAMICS AND THEIR APPLICATIONS TO CHEMICAL SYSTEMS 278

Skill 26.1 Recognize the relationships among enthalpy, entropy, Gibbs free energy, and the equilibrium constant 278

Skill 26.2 Evaluate the thermodynamic feasibility of various reactions and calculate energy changes during chemical reactions 279

Skill 26.3 Analyze the thermodynamics and kinetic dynamics that move a reversible reaction to a position of chemical equilibrium 286

Skill 26.4 Apply Le Chatelier's principle to analyze reversible reactions 286

COMPETENCY 27.0 UNDERSTAND AND APPLY KNOWLEDGE OF ELECTROCHEMISTRY 289

Skill 27.1 Demonstrate an understanding of oxidation/reduction reactions and their relationship to standard reduction potentials 289

Skill 27.2 Demonstrate an understanding of electrolysis reactions 292

Skill 27.3 Balance redox reactions 293

Skill 27.4 Demonstrate knowledge of devising and building electrochemical cells 300

COMPETENCY 28.0 UNDERSTAND AND APPLY KNOWLEDGE OF THE MECHANISMS OF CHEMICAL REACTIONS AND THE THEORY AND PRACTICAL APPLICATIONS OF REACTION RATES 302

Skill 28.1 Recognize the basics of collision and transition-state theories and the significance of the Arrhenius equation 302

Skill 28.2 Explain how various factors influence reaction rates 304

Skill 28.3 Analyze experimental data involving reaction rates, concentration, and/or time to determine kinetic parameters 306

Skill 28.4 Demonstrate an understanding of the relationship of rate laws to reaction mechanisms 312

TEACHER CERTIFICATION STUDY GUIDE

COMPETENCY 29.0 UNDERSTAND AND APPLY KNOWLEDGE OF MAJOR ASPECTS OF ORGANIC CHEMISTRY 314

Skill 29.1 Identify the functional group classification and nomenclature of organic compounds and the general characteristics and reactions of each group 314

Skill 29.2 Demonstrate an understanding of the concepts and mechanisms of substitution, addition, elimination, and other reactions of organic molecules 317

Skill 29.3 Demonstrate knowledge of appropriate separation, purification, and identification schemes for organic molecules 323

Skill 29.4 Recognize the general structure, properties, and uses of polymers, pharmaceuticals, pesticides, and other practical products 325

Skill 29.5 Demonstrate an understanding of the structure, properties, and function of common biological molecules and how these biomolecules are involved in life processes 327

Skill 29.6 Recognize the general features of three-dimensional structures, bonding, molecular properties, and reactivity of organic molecules .. 333

Sample Test 334

Answer Key 359

Rationales with Sample Questions 360

Sample Open-Response Questions 430

TEACHER CERTIFICATION STUDY GUIDE

Great Study and Testing Tips!

What to study in order to prepare for the subject assessments is the focus of this study guide but equally important is *how* you study.

You can increase your chances of truly mastering the information by taking some simple, but effective steps.

Study Tips:

1. Some foods aid the learning process. Foods such as milk, nuts, seeds, rice, and oats help your study efforts by releasing natural memory enhancers called CCKs (*cholecystokinin*) composed of *tryptopha*n, *choline*, and *phenylalanine*. All of these chemicals enhance the neurotransmitters associated with memory. Before studying, try a light, protein-rich meal of eggs, turkey, and fish. All of these foods release the memory enhancing chemicals. The better the connections, the more you comprehend.

Likewise, before you take a test, stick to a light snack of energy boosting and relaxing foods. A glass of milk, a piece of fruit, or some peanuts all release various memory-boosting chemicals and help you to relax and focus on the subject at hand.

2. Learn to take great notes. A by-product of our modern culture is that we have grown accustomed to getting our information in short doses (i.e. TV news sound bites or USA Today style newspaper articles.)

Consequently, we've subconsciously trained ourselves to assimilate information better in neat little packages. If your notes are scrawled all over the paper, it fragments the flow of the information. Strive for clarity. Newspapers use a standard format to achieve clarity. Your notes can be much clearer through use of proper formatting. A very effective format is called the *"Cornell Method."*

> Take a sheet of loose-leaf lined notebook paper and draw a line all the way down the paper about 1-2" from the left-hand edge.
>
> Draw another line across the width of the paper about 1-2" up from the bottom. Repeat this process on the reverse side of the page.

Look at the highly effective result. You have ample room for notes, a left hand margin for special emphasis items or inserting supplementary data from the textbook, a large area at the bottom for a brief summary, and a little rectangular space for just about anything you want.

SCIENCE: CHEMISTRY

3. **Get the concept then the details.** Too often we focus on the details and don't gather an understanding of the concept. However, if you simply memorize only dates, places, or names, you may well miss the whole point of the subject.

A key way to understand things is to put them in your own words. If you are working from a textbook, automatically summarize each paragraph in your mind. If you are outlining text, don't simply copy the author's words.

Rephrase them in your own words. You remember your own thoughts and words much better than someone else's, and subconsciously tend to associate the important details to the core concepts.

4. **Ask Why?** Pull apart written material paragraph by paragraph and don't forget the captions under the illustrations.

Example: If the heading is "Stream Erosion", flip it around to read "Why do streams erode?" Then answer the questions.

If you train your mind to think in a series of questions and answers, not only will you learn more, but it also helps to lessen the test anxiety because you are used to answering questions.

5. **Read for reinforcement and future needs.** Even if you only have 10 minutes, put your notes or a book in your hand. Your mind is similar to a computer; you have to input data in order to have it processed. *By reading, you are creating the neural connections for future retrieval.* The more times you read something, the more you reinforce the learning of ideas.

Even if you don't fully understand something on the first pass, *your mind stores much of the material for later recall.*

6. **Relax to learn so go into exile.** Our bodies respond to an inner clock called biorhythms. Burning the midnight oil works well for some people, but not everyone.

If possible, set aside a particular place to study that is free of distractions. Shut off the television, cell phone, and pager and exile your friends and family during your study period.

If you really are bothered by silence, try background music. Light classical music at a low volume has been shown to aid in concentration over other types. Music that evokes pleasant emotions without lyrics is highly suggested. Try just about anything by Mozart. It relaxes you.

7. Use arrows not highlighters. At best, it's difficult to read a page full of yellow, pink, blue, and green streaks. Try staring at a neon sign for a while and you'll soon see that the horde of colors obscure the message.

A quick note, a brief dash of color, an underline, and an arrow pointing to a particular passage is much clearer than a horde of highlighted words.

8. Budget your study time. Although you shouldn't ignore any of the material, *allocate your available study time in the same ratio that topics may appear on the test.*

TEACHER CERTIFICATION STUDY GUIDE

Testing Tips:

1. Get smart, play dumb. Don't read anything into the question. Don't make an assumption that the test writer is looking for something else than what is asked. Stick to the question as written and don't read extra things into it.

2. Read the question and all the choices *twice* before answering the question. You may miss something by not carefully reading, and then re-reading both the question and the answers.

If you really don't have a clue as to the right answer, leave it blank on the first time through. Go on to the other questions, as they may provide a clue as to how to answer the skipped questions.

If later on, you still can't answer the skipped ones . . . **Guess.** The only penalty for guessing is that you *might* get it wrong. Only one thing is certain; if you don't put anything down, you will get it wrong!

3. Turn the question into a statement. Look at the way the questions are worded. The syntax of the question usually provides a clue. Does it seem more familiar as a statement rather than as a question? Does it sound strange?

By turning a question into a statement, you may be able to spot if an answer sounds right, and it may also trigger memories of material you have read.

4. Look for hidden clues. It's actually very difficult to compose multiple-foil (choice) questions without giving away part of the answer in the options presented.

In most multiple-choice questions you can often readily eliminate one or two of the potential answers. This leaves you with only two real possibilities and automatically your odds go to Fifty-Fifty for very little work.

5. Trust your instincts. For every fact that you have read, you subconsciously retain something of that knowledge. On questions that you aren't really certain about, go with your basic instincts. **Your first impression on how to answer a question is usually correct.**

6. Mark your answers directly on the test booklet. Don't bother trying to fill in the optical scan sheet on the first pass through the test.

Just be very careful not to miss-mark your answers when you eventually transcribe them to the scan sheet.

7. Watch the clock! You have a set amount of time to answer the questions. Don't get bogged down trying to answer a single question at the expense of 10 questions you can more readily answer.

SCIENCE: CHEMISTRY

THIS PAGE BLANK

| SUBAREA I. | SCIENCE AND TECHNOLOGY |

COMPETENCY 1.0 UNDERSTAND AND APPLY KNOWLEDGE OF SCIENCE AS INQUIRY

Skill 1.1 Recognize the assumptions, processes, purposes, requirements, and tools of scientific inquiry.

Modern science began around the late 16th century with a new way of thinking about the world. Few scientists will disagree with Carl Sagan's assertion that "science is a way of thinking much more than it is a body of knowledge" (Broca's Brain, 1979). Thus science is a process of inquiry and investigation. It is a way of thinking and acting, not just a body of knowledge to be acquired by memorizing facts and principles. This way of thinking, the scientific method, is based on the idea that scientists begin their investigations with observations. From these observations they develop a hypothesis, which is extended in the form of a predication, and challenge the hypothesis through experimentation and thus further observations. Science has progressed in its understanding of nature through careful observation, a lively imagination, and increasing sophisticated instrumentation. Science is distinguished from other fields of study in that it provides guidelines or methods for conducting research, and the research findings must be reproducible by other scientists for those findings to be valid. It is important to recognize that scientific practice is not always this systematic. Discoveries have been made that are serendipitous and others have not started with the observation of data. Einstein's theory of relativity started not with the observation of data but with a kind of intellectual puzzle.

The Scientific method is just a logical set of steps that a scientist goes through to solve a problem. There are as many different scientific methods as there are scientists experimenting. However, there seems to be some pattern to their work.

While an inquiry may start at any point in this method and may not involve all of the steps here is the pattern.

Observations
Scientific questions result from observations of events in nature or events observed in the laboratory. An **observation** is not just a look at what happens. It also includes measurements and careful records of the event. Records could include photos, drawings, or written descriptions. The observations and data collection lead to a question. In chemistry, observations almost always deal with the behavior of matter. Having arrived at a question, a scientist usually researches the scientific literature to see what is known about the question. Maybe the question has already been answered. The scientist then may want to test the answer found in the literature. Or, maybe the research will lead to a new question.

Sometimes the same observations are made over and over again and are always the same. For example, you can observe that daylight lasts longer in summer than in winter. This observation never varies. Such observations are called **laws** of nature. Probably the most important law in chemistry was discovered in the late 1700s. Chemists observed that no mass was ever lost or gained in chemical reactions. This law became known as the law of conservation of mass. Explaining this law was a major topic of chemistry in the early 19th century.

Hypothesis

If the question has not been answered, the scientist may prepare for an experiment by making a hypothesis. A **hypothesis** is a statement of a possible answer to the question. It is a tentative explanation for a set of facts and can be tested by experiments. Although hypotheses are usually based on observations, they may also be based on a sudden idea or intuition.

Experiment

An **experiment** tests the hypothesis to determine whether it may be a correct answer to the question or a solution to the problem. Some experiments may test the effect of one thing on another under controlled conditions. Such experiments have two variables. The experimenter controls one variable, called the *independent variable*. The other variable, the *dependent variable*, is the change caused by changing the independent variable.

For example, suppose a researcher wanted to test the effect of vitamin A on the ability of rats to see in dim light. The independent variable would be the dose of Vitamin A added to the rats' diet. The dependent variable would be the intensity of light that causes the rats to react. All other factors, such as time, temperature, age, water given to the rats, the other nutrients given to the rats, and similar factors, are held constant. Chemists sometimes do short experiments "just to see what happens" or to see what products a certain reaction produces. Often, these are not formal experiments. Rather they are ways of making additional observations about the behavior of matter.

In most experiments, scientists collect quantitative data, which is data that can be measured with instruments. They also collect qualitative data, descriptive information from observations other than measurements. Interpreting data and analyzing observations are important. If data is not organized in a logical manner, wrong conclusions can be drawn. Also, other scientists may not be able to follow your work or repeat your results.

Steps of a Scientific Method

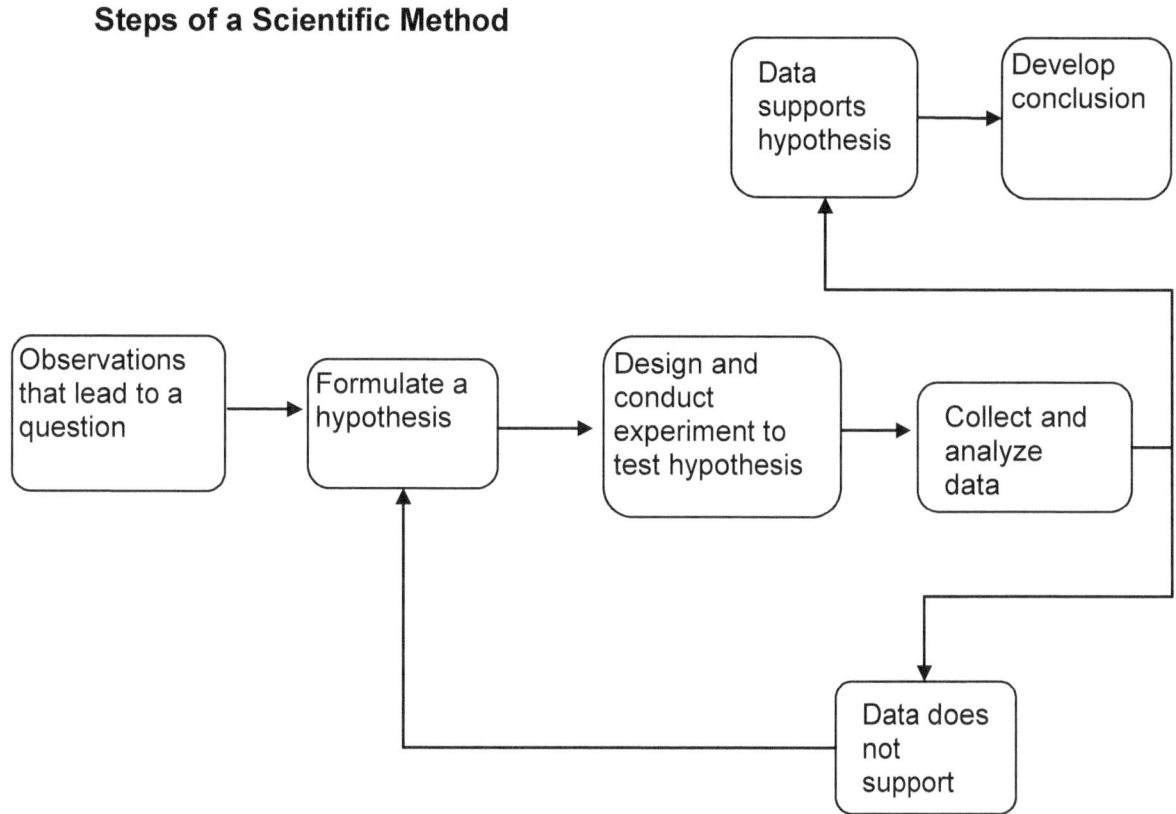

Conclusion
Finally, a scientist must draw conclusions from the experiment. A conclusion must address the hypothesis on which the experiment was based. The conclusion states whether or not the data supports the hypothesis. If it does not, the conclusion should state what the experiment *did* show. If the hypothesis is not supported, the scientist uses the observations from the experiment to make a new or revised hypothesis. Then, new experiments are planned.

Theory
When a hypothesis survives many experimental tests to determine its validity, the hypothesis may evolve into a **theory**. A theory explains a body of facts and laws that are based on the facts. A theory also reliably predicts the outcome of related events in nature. For example, the law of conservation of matter and many other experimental observations led to a theory proposed early in the 19th century. This theory explained the conservation law by proposing that all matter is made up of atoms which are never created or destroyed in chemical reactions, only rearranged. This atomic theory also successfully predicted the behavior of matter in chemical reactions that had not been studied at the time. As a result, the atomic theory has stood for 200 years with only small modifications.

A theory also serves as a scientific **model**. A model can be a physical model made of wood or plastic, a computer program that simulates events in nature, or simply a mental picture of an idea. A model illustrates a theory and explains nature. In your chemistry course, you will develop a mental (and maybe a physical) model of the atom and its behavior. Outside of science, the word theory is often used to describe someone's unproven notion about something. In science, theory means much more. It is a thoroughly tested explanation of things and events observed in nature.

A theory can never be proven true, but it can be proven untrue. All it takes to prove a theory untrue is to show an exception to the theory. The test of the hypothesis may be observations of phenomena or a model may be built to examine its behavior under certain circumstances.

Skill 1.2 Use evidence and logic in developing proposed explanations that address scientific questions and hypotheses.

A scientific model is a set of ideas that describes a natural process and are developed by empirical or theoretical objects and help scientists to focus on the basic fundamental processes. They may be physical representations such as a space-filling model of a molecule or a map, or they may be mathematical algorithms.

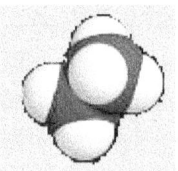

Whatever form they take, scientific models are based on what is known about the science systems or objects at the time that the models are constructed. Models usually evolve and are improved as scientific advances are made. Sometimes, a model must be discarded because new findings show it to be misleading or incorrect. How do scientists use models?

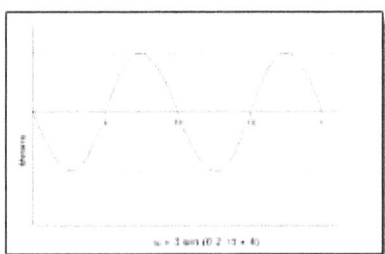

Models are developed in an effort to explain how things work in nature. Because models are not the "real thing", they can never correctly represent the system or object in all respects. The amount of detail that they contain depends upon how the model will be used as well as the sophistication and skill of the scientist doing the modeling. If a model has too many details left out, its usefulness may be limited. But too many details may make a model too complicated to be useful. So it is easy to see why models lack some features of the real system.

To overcome this difficulty, different models are often used to describe the same system or object. Scientists must then choose which model most closely fits the scientific investigation being carried out, which findings are being described, and, in some cases, which one is compatible with the sophistication of the investigation itself. For example, there are many models of atoms. The solar system model described above is adequate for some purposes, because electrons have properties of matter. They have mass and charge and they are found in motion in the space outside the nucleus. However, a highly mathematical model based on the field of quantum mechanics is necessary when describing the energy (or wave) properties of electrons in the atom.

Scientific models are based on physical observations that establish some facts about the system or object of interest. Scientists then combine these facts with appropriate laws or scientific principles and assumptions to produce a "picture" that mimics the behavior of the system or object to the greatest possible extent. It is on the basis of such models that science makes many of its most important advances, because such models provide a vehicle for making predictions about the behavior of a system or object. The predictions can then be tested as new measurements, technology or theories are applied to the subject. The new information may result in modification and refinement of the model, although certain issues may remain unresolved by the model for years. The goal, however is to continue to develop the model in such a way as to move it every closer to a true description of the natural phenomenon. In this way, models are vital to the scientific process.

Skill 1.3 Identify various approaches to conducting scientific investigations and their applications.

The design of chemical experiments must include every step to obtain the desired data. In other words, the design must be **complete** and it must include all required **controls**.

Complete design
Familiarity with individual experiments and equipment will help you evaluate if anything is missing from the design. For data requiring a difference between two values, the experiment **must determine both values**. For data utilizing the ideal gas law, the experiment **must determine three values of P, V, n, or T** in order to determine the fourth or one value and a ratio of the other two in order to determine the fourth.

Example: In a mercury manometer, the level of mercury in contact with a reaction vessel is 70.0 mm lower than the level exposed to the atmosphere. Use the following conversion factors:
$$760 \text{ mm Hg} = 1 \text{ atm} = 101.325 \text{ kPa}.$$
What additional information is required to determine the pressure in the vessel in kPa?

Solution: The barometric pressure is needed to determine vessel pressure from an open-ended manometer. A manometer reading is always a **difference** between two pressures. One standard atmosphere is 760 mm mercury, but on a given day at a given location, the actual ambient pressure may vary. If the barometric pressure on the day of the experiment is 104 kPa, the pressure of the vessel is:
$$104 \text{ kPa} + 70.0 \text{ mm Hg} \times \frac{101.325 \text{ kPa}}{760 \text{ mm Hg}} = 113 \text{ kPa}.$$

Controls: Experimental **controls** prevent factors other than those under study from impacting the outcome of the experiment. An **experimental sample** in a controlled experiment is the unknown to be compared against one or more **control samples**. These should be nearly identical to the experimental sample except for the one aspect whose effect is being tested.

A **negative control** is a control sample that is known to lack the effect. A **positive control** is known to contain the effect. Positive controls of varying strengths are often used to generate a **calibration curve** (also called a **standard curve**).

When determining the concentration of a component in a mixture, an **internal standard** is a known concentration of a different substance that is added to the experimental sample. An **external standard** is a known concentration of the substance of interest. External standards are more commonly used. They are not added to the experimental sample; they are analyzed separately.

Replicate samples decrease the impact of random error. A mean is taken of the results from replicate samples to obtain a best value. If one replicate is obviously inconsistent with the results from other samples, it may be discarded as an **outlier** and not counted as an observation when determining the mean. Discarding an outlier is equivalent to assuming the presence of a systematic error for that particular observation. In research, this must be done with great caution because some real-world behavior generates sporadically unusual results.

Example: A pure chemical in aqueous solution is known to absorb light at 615 nm. What controls would best be used with a spectrophotometer to determine the concentration of this chemical when it is present in a mixture with other solutes in an aqueous solution?

Solution: The other solutes may also absorb light at 615 nm. The best negative control would be an identical mixture with the chemical of interest entirely absent. Known concentrations of the chemical could then be added to the negative control to create positive controls (external standards) and develop a calibration curve of the spectrophotometer absorbance reading at 615 nm as a function of concentration. Replicate samples of each standard and of the unknown should be read.

Example: Ethanol is separated from a mixture of organic compounds by gas chromatography. The concentration of each component is proportional to its peak area. However, the chromatograph detector has a variable sensitivity from one run to the next. Is an internal standard required to determine the concentration of ethanol?

Solution: Yes. The variable detector sensitivity may only be accounted for by adding a known concentration of a chemical not found in the mixture as an internal standard to the experimental sample and control samples. The variable sensitivity of the detector will be accounted for by determining the ratio of the peak area for ethanol to the peak area of the added internal standard.

Experimental bias is when a researcher favors one particular outcome over another in an experimental setup. In order to avoid bias, it is imperative to set each experiment under exactly the same conditions, including a *control* experiment, an experiment with a known negative outcome. Additionally, in order to avoid experimental bias, a researcher must not "read" particular results into data.

An example of experimental bias can be seen in the classic example of the mouse in the maze experiment. In this example, a researcher is timing mice as they move through the maze towards a piece of cheese. The experiment relies on the mouse's ability to smell the cheese as it approaches. If one mouse chases a piece of cheddar cheese, while another chases Limburger, or so called "stinky" cheese, clearly the Limburger mouse has a huge advantage over the cheddar mouse. To remove the experimental bias from this experiment, the same cheese should be used in both tests.

Skill 1.4 Use tools and mathematical and statistical methods for collecting, managing, analyzing (e.g., average, curve fit, error determination), and communicating results of investigations.

The knowledge and use of basic mathematical concepts and skills is a necessary aspect of scientific study. Science depends on data and the manipulation of data requires knowledge of mathematics. Scientists often use basic algebra to solve scientific problems and design experiments. For example, the substitution of variables is a common strategy in experiment design. Also, the ability to determine the equation of a curve is valuable in data manipulation, experimentation, and prediction.

Understanding of basic statistics, graphs and charts, and algebra are of particular importance. In addition, scientists must be able to represent data graphically and interpret graphs and tables.

Scientists must be able to understand and apply the statistical concepts of mean, median, mode, and range to sets of scientific data. Modern science uses a number of disciplines to understand it better. Statistics is one of those subjects, which is absolutely essential for science.

Mean is the mathematical average of all the items. To calculate the mean, all the items must be added up and divided by the number of items. This is also called the arithmetic mean or more commonly as the "**average**".

The **median** depends on whether the number of items is odd or even. If the number is odd, then the median is the value of the item in the middle. This is the value that denotes that the number of items having higher or equal value to that is same as the number of items having equal or lesser value than that. If the number of the items is even, the median is the average of the two items in the middle, such that the number of items having values higher or equal to it is same as the number of items having values equal or less than that.

Mode is the value of the item that occurs the most often, if there are not many items. Bimodal is a situation where there are two items with equal frequency.

Range is the difference between the maximum and minimum values. The range is the difference between two extreme points on the **distribution curve**.

Error

There are many ways in which errors could creep in measurements.
Errors in measurements could occur because –

1. Improper use of instruments used for measuring – weighing etc.
2. Parallax error – not positioning the eyes during reading of measurements
3. Not using same instruments and methods of measurement during an experiment
4. Not using the same source of materials, resulting in the content of a certain compound used for experimentation

Besides these mentioned above, there could be other possible sources of error as well. When erroneous results are used for interpreting data, the conclusions are not reliable. An experiment is valid only when all the constants like time, place, method of measurement, etc. are strictly controlled.

Skill 1.5 Demonstrate knowledge of ways to report, display, and defend the results of an investigation.

Lab notebooks are commonly used in the laboratory to record data. This information is often then transferred into a computer file or spreadsheet once outside of the lab. Scientists use spreadsheets to organize, analyze, and display data. Use of spreadsheets simplifies data collection and manipulation and allows the presentation of data in a logical and understandable format. Models are another common way of portraying evidence. A model may be built to demonstrate an object too large or too small to otherwise visualize with ease. In the case of chemistry, computers and their simulations are often used to show the three dimensional structure of a molecule and to predict its possible chemical interactions.

It is the responsibility of the scientists to share the knowledge they obtain through their research. After the conclusion is drawn, the final step is communication. In this age, much emphasis is put on the way and the method of communication. The conclusions must be communicated by clearly describing the information using accurate data, visual presentation and other appropriate media such as a power point presentation. Examples of visual presentations are graphs (bar/line/pie), tables/charts, diagrams, and artwork. Modern technology must be used whenever necessary. The method of communication must be suitable to the audience.

Written communication is as important as oral communication. This is essential for submitting research papers to scientific journals, newspapers, other magazines etc.

COMPETENCY 2.0 UNDERSTAND AND APPLY KNOWLEDGE OF THE CONCEPTS, PRINCIPLES, AND PROCESSES OF TECHNOLOGICAL DESIGN.

Skill 2.1 Recognize the capabilities, limitations, and implications of technology and technological design and redesign.

Science and technology are interdependent as advances in technology often lead to new scientific discoveries and new scientific discoveries often lead to new technologies. Scientists use technology to enhance the study of nature and solve problems that nature presents. Technological design is the identification of a problem and the application of scientific knowledge to solve the problem.

While technology and technological design can provide solutions to problems faced by humans, technology must exist within nature and cannot contradict physical or biological principles. In addition, technological solutions are temporary and new technologies typically provide better solutions in the future. Monetary costs, available materials, time, and available tools also limit the scope of technological design and solutions. Finally, technological solutions have intended benefits and unexpected consequences. Scientists must attempt to predict the unintended consequences and minimize any negative impact on nature or society.

Skill 2.2 Identify real-world problems or needs to be solved through technological design.

The problems and needs, ranging from very simple to highly complex, that technological design can solve are nearly limitless. Disposal of toxic waste, routing of rainwater, crop irrigation, and energy creation are but a few examples of real-world problems that scientists address or attempt to address with technology.

Skill 2.3 Apply a technological design process to a given problem situation.

The technological design process has five basic steps:
1. Identify a problem
2. Propose designs and choose between alternative solutions
3. Implement the proposed solution
4. Evaluate the solution and its consequences
5. Report results

After the identification of a problem, the scientist must propose several designs and choose between the alternatives. Scientists often utilize simulations and models in evaluating possible solutions.

Implementation of the chosen solution involves the use of various tools depending on the problem, solution, and technology. Scientists may use both physical tools and objects and computer software.

After implementation of the solution, scientists evaluate the success or failure of the solution against pre-determined criteria. In evaluating the solution, scientists must consider the negative consequences as well as the planned benefits.

Finally, scientists must communicate results in different ways – orally, written, models, diagrams, and demonstrations.

Example:

Problem – toxic waste disposal
Chosen solution – genetically engineered microorganisms to digest waste
Implementation – use genetic engineering technology to create organism capable of converting waste to environmentally safe product
Evaluate – introduce organisms to waste site and measure formation of products and decrease in waste; also evaluate any unintended effects
Report – prepare a written report of results complete with diagrams and figures.

Skill 2.4   Identify a design problem and propose possible solutions, considering such constraints as tools, materials, time, costs, and laws of nature.

In addition to finding viable solutions to design problems, scientists must consider such constraints as tools, materials, time, costs, and laws of nature. Effective implementation of a solution requires adequate tools and materials. Scientists cannot apply scientific knowledge without sufficient technology and appropriate materials (e.g. construction materials, software). Technological design solutions always have costs. Scientists must consider monetary costs, time costs, and the unintended effects of possible solutions. Types of unintended consequences of technological design solutions include adverse environmental impact and safety risks. Finally, technology cannot contradict the laws of nature. Technological design solutions must work within the framework of the natural world.

Skill 2.5   Evaluate various solutions to a design problem.

In evaluating and choosing between potential solutions to a design problem, scientists utilize modeling, simulation, and experimentation techniques. Small-scale modeling and simulation help test the effectiveness and unexpected consequences of proposed solutions while limiting the initial costs. Modeling and simulation may also reveal potential problems that scientists can address prior to full-scale implementation of the solution. Experimentation allows for evaluation of proposed solutions in a controlled environment where scientists can manipulate and test specific variables.

COMPETENCY 3.0 UNDERSTAND AND APPLY KNOWLEDGE OF ACCEPTED PRACTICES OF SCIENCE.

Skill 3.1 Demonstrate an understanding of the nature of science (e.g., tentative, replicable, historical, empirical) and recognize how scientific knowledge and explanations change over time.

Probably one of the best examples of the progressive development of science would be the development of atomic theory. The ancient Greeks debated over the continuous nature of matter and two schools of thought emerged; matter is continuous or matter is not continuous. The continuous idea was promoted by Aristotle and due to his high regard among scholars that was the idea that flourished. However, there was no effort made by the Greeks to prove of disprove this idea. During the Dark Ages alchemists started experimenting and keeping records of their results, sending science on a pathway of experimentation and discovery. Robert Boyle and his famous J-tube experiment in 1661 gave the first experimental evidence for the existence of atoms. He even used words similar to Democritus to describe the results saying that the air consisted of atoms and a void between them. By increasing the pressure inside the J-tube, some of the void was squeezed out, decreasing the volume. Slowly, experimental evidence, including the work of Lavoisier and Priestly, to name a few, began to mount and in 1803 John Dalton proposed the Modern Atomic Theory which contained 5 basic postulates about the nature and behavior of matter. Ben Franklin's discovery of electricity in 1746 sent scientists to work to understand this new "thing"-electricity. J.J Thomson investigated a cathode ray tube and identified the negatively charged particle in the cathode ray in 1897. His work was closely followed by Robert Milliken who gave the electron a -1 charge in his oil drop experiment.

Experiments were under way to understand how electricity and matter interact when the discoveries of x-rays and radioactivity were announced. Scientists trying to understand this new phenomena radioactivity experimented day and night. Ernest Rutherford was one of the many. He tried to understand the nature of radioactivity and classified it into three basic types. While trying to find out more about radioactivity, he conducted his gold foil experiment that ultimately provided greater insight into the subatomic nature of the atom by discovering the nucleus. He also identified the proton present in the nucleus.

Rutherford's graduate student, Neils Bohr, made slight alterations to the model of the atom proposed by Rutherford to account for his experimental results. These changes helped Rutherford's model stand up to classical physics. However, scientists looking for other patterns and information proposed more changes to the planetary model of the atom. These changes seemed to fit with spectroscopy experiments and the quantum mechanical view of the atom was formed. About the same time as this new theory was emerging, James Chadwick, a collaborator of Rutherford's, announced in 1932 the discovery of the neutron found in the nucleus. This discovery, ultimately led to the discovery of fission and the development of the nuclear bomb. The technology the came from the Manhattan project has developed the fields of medicine, computing and provided entertainment from television.

Skill 3.2 **Compare scientific hypotheses, predictions, laws, theories, and principles and recognize how they are developed and tested.**

A Law is the highest-level science can achieve. Followed by laws and theories and hypothesis. The Scientific Method is the process by which data is collected, interpreted and validated.

Law is defined as: a statement of an order or relation of phenomena that so far as is known is invariable under the given conditions. Everything we observe in the universe operates according to known natural laws.

- If the truth of a statement is verified repeatedly in a reproducible way then it can reach the level of a natural law.

- Some well know and accepted natural laws of science are:

    1. The First Law of Thermodynamics

    2. The Second Law of Thermodynamics

    3. The Law of Cause and Effect

    4. The Law of Biogenesis

    5. The Law of Gravity

Theory is defined as: In contrast to a law, a scientific theory is used to explain an observation or a set of observations. It is generally accepted to be true, though no real proof exists. The important thing about a scientific law is that there are no experimental observations to prove it NOT true, and each piece of evidence that exists supports the theory as written. They are often accepted at face value, since they are often difficult to prove, and can be rewritten in order include the results of all experimental observations. An example of a theory is the big bang theory. While there is no experiment that can directly test whether or not the big bang actually occurred, there is no strong evidence indicating otherwise.

Theories provide a framework to explain the **known** information of the time, but are subject to constant evaluation and updating. There is always the possibility that new evidence will conflict with a current theory.

Some examples of theories that have been rejected because they are now better explained by current knowledge:

Theory of Spontaneous Generation
Inheritance of Acquired Characteristics
The Blending Hypothesis

Some examples of theories that were initially rejected because they fell outside of the accepted knowledge of the time, but are well-accepted today due to increased knowledge and data include:

The sun-centered solar system
Warm-bloodedness in dinosaurs
The germ-theory of disease
Continental drift

Hypothesis is defined as: a tentative assumption made in order to draw out and test its logical or empirical consequences. Many refer to an hypothesis as an educated guess about what will happen during an experiment. A hypothesis can be based on prior knowledge, prior observations. It will be proved true or false only through experimentation.

Scientific Method is defined as: principles and procedures for the systematic pursuit of knowledge involving the recognition and formulation of a problem, the collection of data through observation and experiment, and the formulation and testing of hypotheses. The steps in the scientific method can be found elsewhere in this text.

Skill 3.3 **Recognize examples of valid and biased thinking in reporting of scientific research.**

Scientific research can be biased in the choice of what data to consider, in the reporting or recording of the data, and/or in how the data are interpreted. The scientist's emphasis may be influenced by his/her nationality, sex, ethnic origin, age, or political convictions. For example, when studying a group of animals, male scientists may focus on the social behavior of the males and typically male characteristics. Although bias related to the investigator, the sample, the method, or the instrument may not be completely avoidable in every case, it is important to know the possible sources of bias and how bias could affect the evidence. Moreover, scientists need to be attentive to possible bias in their own work as well as that of other scientists.

Objectivity may not always be attained. However, one precaution that may be taken to guard against undetected bias is to have many different investigators or groups of investigators working on a project. By different, it is meant that the groups are made up of various nationalities, ethnic origins, ages, and political convictions and composed of both males and females. It is also important to note one's aspirations, and to make sure to be truthful to the data, even when grants, promotions, and notoriety are at risk.

Skill 3.4 **Recognize the basis for and application of safety practices and regulations in the study of science.**

All science labs should contain the following items of **safety equipment**. Those marked with an asterisk are requirements by state laws.

* fire blanket which is visible and accessible
*Ground Fault Circuit Interrupters (GCFI) within two feet of water supplies
*signs designating room exits
*emergency shower capable of providing a continuous flow of water
*emergency eye wash station which can be activated by the foot or forearm
*eye protection for every student and a means of sanitizing equipment
*emergency exhaust fans providing ventilation to the outside of the building
*master cut-off switches for gas, electric and compressed air. Switches must have permanently attached handles. Cut-off switches must be clearly labeled.
*an ABC fire extinguisher
*storage cabinets for flammable materials
-chemical spill control kit
-fume hood with a motor which is spark proof
-protective laboratory aprons made of flame retardant material
-signs which will alert potential hazardous conditions
-containers for broken glassware, flammables, corrosives, and waste. Containers should be labeled.

Students should wear safety goggles when performing dissections, heating, or while using acids and bases. Hair should always be tied back and objects should never be placed in the mouth. Food should not be consumed while in the laboratory. Hands should always be washed before and after laboratory experiments. In case of an accident, eye washes and showers should be used for eye contamination or a chemical spill that covers the student's body. Small chemical spills should only be contained and cleaned by the teacher. Kitty litter or a chemical spill kit should be used to clean spill. For large spills, the school administration and the local fire department should be notified. Biological spills should also be handled only by the teacher. Contamination with biological waste can be cleaned by using bleach when appropriate.

Accidents and injuries should always be reported to the school administration and local health facilities. The severity of the accident or injury will determine the course of action to pursue.

It is the responsibility of the teacher to provide a safe environment for their students. Proper supervision greatly reduces the risk of injury and a teacher should never leave a class for any reason without providing alternate supervision. After an accident, two factors are considered; **foreseeability** and **negligence**. Foreseeability is the anticipation that an event may occur under certain circumstances. Negligence is the failure to exercise ordinary or reasonable care. Safety procedures should be a part of the science curriculum and a well managed classroom is important to avoid potential lawsuits.

All laboratory solutions should be prepared as directed in the lab manual. Care should be taken to avoid contamination. All glassware should be rinsed thoroughly with distilled water before using and cleaned well after use. All solutions should be made with distilled water as tap water contains dissolved particles that may affect the results of an experiment. Unused solutions should be disposed of according to local disposal procedures.

The "Right to Know Law" covers science teachers who work with potentially hazardous chemicals. Briefly, the law states that employees must be informed of potentially toxic chemicals. An inventory must be made available if requested. The inventory must contain information about the hazards and properties of the chemicals. This inventory is to be checked against the "Substance List". Training must be provided on the safe handling and interpretation of the Material Safety Data Sheet.

The following chemicals are potential carcinogens and not allowed in school facilities: Acrylonitriel, Arsenic compounds, Asbestos, Bensidine, Benzene, Cadmium compounds, Chloroform, Chromium compounds, Ethylene oxide, Ortho-toluidine, Nickel powder, and Mercury.

Chemicals should not be stored on bench tops or heat sources. They should be stored in groups based on their reactivity with one another and in protective storage cabinets. All containers within the lab must be labeled. Suspect and known carcinogens must be labeled as such and segregated within trays to contain leaks and spills.

Chemical waste should be disposed of in properly labeled containers. Waste should be separated based on their reactivity with other chemicals.

Biological material should never be stored near food or water used for human consumption. All biological material should be appropriately labeled. All blood and body fluids should be put in a well-contained container with a secure lid to prevent leaking. All biological waste should be disposed of in biological hazardous waste bags.

Material safety data sheets are available for every chemical and biological substance. These are available directly from the company of acquisition or the internet. The manuals for equipment used in the lab should be read and understood before using them.

COMPETENCY 4.0 UNDERSTAND AND APPLY KNOWLEDGE OF THE INTERACTIONS AMONG SCIENCE, TECHNOLOGY, AND SOCIETY.

Skill 4.1 Recognize the historical and contemporary development of major scientific ideas and technological innovations.

Development of Modern Chemistry

Chemistry emerged from two ancient roots: **craft traditions** and **philosophy**. The oldest ceramic crafts (i.e., pottery) known are from roughly 10000 BC in Japan. **Metallurgical crafts** in Eurasia and Africa began to develop by trial and error around 4000-2500 BC resulting in the production of copper, bronze, iron, and steel tools. Other craft traditions in brewing, tanning, and dyeing led to many useful empirical ways to manipulate matter.

Ancient philosophers in Greece, India, China, and Japan speculated that all matter was composed of four or five elements. The Greeks thought that these were: fire, air, earth, and water. Indian philosophers and the Greek **Aristotle** also thought a fifth element—"aether" or "quintessence"—filled all of empty space. The Greek philosopher **Democritus** thought that matter was composed of indivisible and indestructible atoms. These concepts are now known as **classical elements** and **classical atomic theory**.

Before the emergence of the **scientific method**, attempts to understand matter relied on **alchemy**: a mixture of mysticism, best guesses, and supernatural explanations. Goals of alchemy were the transmutation of other metals into gold and the synthesis of an elixir to cure all diseases. Ancient Egyptian alchemists developed cement and glass. Chinese alchemists developed gunpowder in the 800s AD.

During the height of European alchemy in the 1300s, the philosopher **William of Occam** proposed the idea that when trying to explain a process or develop a theory, **the simplest explanation with the fewest variables is best**. This is known as **Occam's Razor**. European alchemy slowly developed into modern chemistry during the 1600s and 1700s. This began to occur after **Francis Bacon** and René **Descartes** described the scientific method in the early 1600s.

Robert **Boyle** was educated in alchemy in the mid-1600s, but he published a book called *The Skeptical Chemist* that attacked alchemy and advocated using the scientific method. He is sometimes called **the founder of modern chemistry** because of his emphasis on proving a theory before accepting it, but the birth of modern chemistry is usually attributed to Lavoisier. Boyle rejected the 4 classical elements and proposed the modern definition of an element. **Boyle's law** states that gas volume is proportional to the reciprocal of pressure.

Blaise **Pascal** in the mid-1600s determined the relationship between **pressure** and the height of a liquid in a **barometer**. He also helped to establish the scientific method. The SI unit of pressure is named after him.

Isaac **Newton** studied the nature of **light**, the laws of **gravity**, and the **laws of motion** around 1700. The SI unit of force is named after him.

Daniel **Bernoulli** proposed the **kinetic molecular theory** for gases in the early 1700s to explain the nature of heat and Boyle's Law. At that time, heat was thought to be related to the release of a substance called *phlogiston* from combustible materials

James **Watt** created an efficient **steam engine** in the 1760s-1780s. Later chemists and physicists would develop the theory behind this empirical engineering accomplishment. The SI unit of power is named after him.

Joseph **Priestley** studied various gases in the 1770s. He was the first to produce and drink **carbonated water**, and he was the first to isolate **oxygen** from air. Priestley thought oxygen was air with its normal phlogiston removed so it could burn more fuel and accept more phlogiston than natural air.

Antoine **Lavoisier** is called **the father of modern chemistry** because he performed **quantitative, controlled experiments**. He carefully weighed material before and after combustion to determine that burning objects gain weight. Lavoisier formulated the rule that **chemical reactions do not alter total mass** after finding that reactions in a closed container do not change weight. This disproved the plogiston theory, and he named Priestley's substance oxygen. He demonstrated that air and water were not elements. He defined an element as a substance that could not be broken down further. He published the first modern chemistry textbook, *Elementary Treatise of Chemistry*. Lavoisier was executed in the Reign of Terror at the height of the French Revolution.

Additional Gas Laws in the 1700s and 1800s
These contributions built on the foundation developed by Boyle in the 1600s.

Jacque **Charles** developed **Charles's law** in the late 1700s. This states that gas volume is proportional to absolute temperature.

William Henry developed the law stating that gas solubility in a liquid is proportional to the pressure of gas over the liquid. This is known as **Henry's Law**.

Joseph Louis **Gay-Lussac** developed the gas law stating that gas pressure is directly proportional to absolute temperature. He also determined that two volumes of hydrogen react with one of oxygen to produce water and that other reactions occurred with similar simple ratios. These observations led him to develop the **Law of Combining Volumes**.

Amedeo **Avogadro** developed the hypothesis that **equal volumes of different gases contain an equal numbers of molecules** if the gases are at the same temperature and pressure. The proportionality between volume and number of moles is called **Avagadro's Law**, and the number of molecules in a mole is called **Avagadro's Number**. Both were posthumously named in his honor.

Thomas **Graham** developed **Graham's Law** of effusion and diffusion in the 1830s. He is called the father of **colloid chemistry** .

Electricity and Magnetism in the 1700s and 1800s
Benjamin Franklin studied electricity in the mid-1700s. He developed the concept of **positive and negative electrical charges**. His most famous experiment showed that lightning is an electrical process.

Luigi **Galvani** discovered **bioelectricity**. In the late 1700s, he noticed that the legs of dead frogs twitched when they came into contact with an electrical source.

In the late 1700s, Charles Augustin **Coulomb** derived mathematical **equations for attraction and repulsion** between electrically charged objects.

Alessandro **Volta** built the first **battery** in 1800 permitting future research and applications to have a source of continuous electrical current available. The SI unit of electric potential difference is named after him.

André-Marie **Ampère** created a mathematical theory in the 1820s for magnetic fields and electric currents. The SI unit of electrical current is named after him.

Michael **Faraday** is best known for work in the 1820s and 1830s establishing that a moving magnetic field induces an electric potential. He built the first **dynamo** for electricity generation. He also discovered benzene, invented oxidation numbers, and popularized the terms *electrode*, *anode*, and *cathode*. The SI unit of electrical capacitance is named in his honor.

James Clerk **Maxwell** derived the **Maxwell Equations** in 1864. These expressions completely describe **electric and magnetic fields** and their interaction with matter. Also see Ludwig Boltzmann below for Maxwell's contribution to thermodynamics.

Nineteenth Century Chemistry: Caloric Theory and Thermodynamics

Lavoisier proposed in the late 18th century that the heat generated by combustion was due to a weightless material substance called **caloric** that flowed from one place to another and was never destroyed.

In 1798, **Benjamin Thomson**, also known as **Count Rumford** measured the heat produced when cannon were bored underwater and concluded that caloric was not a conserved substance because heat could continue to be generated indefinitely by this process.

Sadi **Carnot** in the 1820s used caloric theory in developing theories for the **heat engine** to explain the engine already developed by Watt. Heat engines perform mechanical work by expanding and contracting a piston at two different temperatures.

In the 1820s, Robert **Brown** observed dust particles and particles in pollen grains moving in a random motion. This was later called **Brownian motion**.

Germain Henri **Hess** developed **Hess's Law** in 1840 after studying the heat required or emitted from reactions composed of several steps.

James Prescott **Joule** determined the equivalence of heat energy to mechanical work in the 1840s by carefully measuring the heat produced by friction. Joule attacked the caloric theory and played a major role in the acceptance of **kinetic molecular theory**. The SI unit of energy is named after him.

William Thomson, 1st Baron of Kelvin also called **Lord Kelvin** recognized the existence of **absolute temperature** in the 1840s and proposed the temperature scale named after him. He failed in an attempt to reconcile caloric theory with Joule's discovery and caloric theory began to fall out of favor.

Hermann von **Helmholtz** in the 1840s proposed that **energy is conserved** during physical and chemical processes, not heat as proposed in caloric theory

Rudolf **Clausius** in the 1860s introduced the concept of **entropy**.

In the 1870s, Ludwig **Boltzmann** generalized earlier work by Maxwell solving the **velocity or energy distribution among gas molecules**. The final diagram in **Skill 6.4** shows the Maxwell-Boltzmann distribution for kinetic energy at two temperatures. Maxwell's contribution to electromagnetism is described above.

Johannes **van der Waals** in the 1870s was the first to consider **intermolecular attractive forces** in modeling the behavior of liquids and non-ideal gases.

Francois Marie **Raoult** studied colligative properties in the 1870s. He developed **Raoult's Law** relating solute and solvent mole fraction to vapor pressure lowering.

Jacobus **van't Hoff** was the first to fully describe **stereoisomerism** in the 1870s. He later studied **colligative properties** and the impact of temperature on equilibria

Josiah Willard **Gibbs** studied thermodynamics and statistical mechanics in the 1870s. He formulated the concept now called **Gibbs free energy** (see **Skill 8.4**) that will determine whether or not a chemical process at constant pressure will spontaneously occur.

Henri Louis **Le Chatelier** described chemical **equilibrium** in the 1880s using **Le Chatelier's Principle**.

In the 1880s, Svante **Arrhenius** developed the idea of **activation energy**. He also described the dissociation of salts—including **acids and bases**—into ions. Before then, salts in solution were thought to exist as intact molecules and ions were mostly thought to exist as electrolysis products. Arrhenius also predicted that CO_2 emissions would lead to global warming.

In 1905, **Albert Einstein** created a **mathematical model of Brownian motion** based on the impact of water molecules on suspended particles. Kinetic molecular theory could now be observed under the microscope. Einstein's more famous later work in physics on **relativity** may be applied to chemistry by correlating the energy change of a chemical reaction with extremely small changes in the total mass of reactants and products.

Nineteenth and Twentieth Century: Atomic Theory

The contributions to atomic theory of John **Dalton**, **J. J. Thomson**, Max **Planck**, Ernest **Rutherford**, Niels **Bohr**, Louis **de Broglie**, Werner **Heisenberg, and** Erwin **Schrödinger** are discussed later in this book.

Wolfgang **Pauli** helped to develop quantum mechanics in the 1920s by forming the concept of spin and the **exclusion principle**.

Friedrich **Hund** determined a set of **rules to determine the ground state** of a multi-electron atom in the 1920s. One particular rule is called **Hund's Rule** in introductory chemistry courses.

Discovery and Synthesis: Nineteenth Century:

Humphry **Davy** used Volta's battery in the early 1800s for **electrolysis of salt solutions**. He synthesized several pure elements using electrolysis to generate non-spontaneous reactions.

Jöns Jakob **Berzelius** isolated several elements, but he is best known for inventing modern **chemical notation** by using one or two letters to represent elements in the early 1800s.

Friedrich **Wöhler** isolated several elements, but he is best known for the chemical **synthesis of an organic compound** in 1828 using the carbon in silver cyanide. Before Wöhler, many had believed that a transcendent "life-force" was needed to make the molecules of life.

Justus **von Liebig** studied the chemicals involved in agriculture in the 1840s. He has been called the **father of agricultural chemistry**.

Louis **Pasteur** studied **chirality** in the 1840s by separating a mixture of two chiral molecules. His greater contribution was in biology for discovering the germ theory of disease.

Henry **Bessemer** in the 1850s developed the **Bessemer Process** for mass producing steel by blowing air through molten iron to oxidize impurities.

Friedrich August **Kekulé** von Stradonitz studied the chemistry of carbon in the 1850s and 1860s. He proposed the **ring structure of benzene** and that carbon was tetravalent.

Anders Jonas **Ångström** was one of the founders of the science of spectroscopy. In the 1860s, he found hydrogen and other **elements in the spectrum of the sun**. A non-SI unit of length equal to 0.1 nm is named for him.

Alfred **Nobel** invented the explosive **dynamite** in the 1860s and continued to develop other explosives. In his will he used his fortune to establish the **Nobel Prizes**.

Dmitri **Mendeleev** developed the first modern **periodic table** in 1869.

Discovery and Synthesis: Turn of the 20th Century

William **Ramsay** and Lord **Rayleigh** (John William Strutt) isolated the **noble gases**.

Wilhelm Konrad **Röntgen** discovered **X-rays**.

Antoine Henri **Becquerel discovered radioactivity** using uranium salts.

Marie **Curie** named the property radioactivity and determined that it was **a property of atoms** that did not depend on which molecule contained the element.

Pierre and Marie **Curie** utilized the properties of radioactivity to **isolate radium** and other radioactive elements. Marie Curie was the first woman to receive a Nobel Prize and the first person to receive two. Her story continues to inspire. See http://nobelprize.org/physics/articles/curie/index.html for a biography.

Frederick **Soddy** and William **Ramsay** discovered that **radioactive decay can produce helium** (alpha particles).

Fritz **Haber** developed the **Haber Process** for synthesizing ammonia from hydrogen and nitrogen using an iron **catalyst**. Ammonia is still produced by this method to make fertilizers, textiles, and other products.

Robert Andrew **Millikan** determined the **charge of an electron** using an oil-drop experiment.

Discovery and Synthesis: 20th Century

Gilbert Newton **Lewis** described **covalent bonds** as sharing electrons in the 1910s and the **electron pair donor/acceptor theory of acids and bases** in the 1920s. Lewis dot structures (see **Skill 4.3**) and Lewis acids are named after him.

Johannes Nicolaus **Brønsted** and Thomas Martin **Lowry** simultaneously developed the **proton donor/acceptor theory of acids and bases** in the 1920s.

Irving **Langmuir** in the 1920s developed the science of **surface chemistry** to describe interactions at the interface of two phases. This field is important to heterogeneous catalysis.

Fritz **London** studied the electrical nature of chemical bonding in the 1920s. The weak intermolecular **London dispersion forces** are named after him.

Hans Wilhelm **Geiger** developed the **Geiger counter** for measuring ionizing radiation in the 1930s.

Wallace **Carothers** and his team first synthesized **organic polymers** (including neoprene, polyester and nylon) in the 1930s.

In the 1930s, Linus **Pauling** published his results on **the nature of the covalent bond.** Pauling electronegativity is named after him. In the 1950s, Pauling determined the ☐-helical structure of proteins.

Lise **Meitner** and Otto **Hahn** discovered **nuclear fission** in the 1930s.

Glenn Theodore **Seaborg** created and isolated several **elements larger than uranium** in the 1940s. Seaborg reorganized the periodic table to its current form.

James **Watson** and Francis **Crick** determined the double helix structure of DNA in the 1950s.

Neil **Bartlett** produced **compounds containing noble gases** in the 1960s, proving that they are not completely chemically inert.

Harold Kroto, Richard Smalley, and Robert Curl discovered the **buckyball C_{60}** in the 1980s.

Skill 4.2 **Demonstrate an understanding of the ways that science and technology affect people's everyday lives, societal values and systems, the environment, and new knowledge.**

Society as a whole impacts biological research. The pressure from the majority of society has led to these bans and restrictions on human cloning research. Human cloning has been restricted in the United States and many other countries. The U.S. legislature has banned the use of federal funds for the development of human cloning techniques. Some individual states have banned human cloning regardless of where the funds originate.

The demand for genetically modified crops by society and industry has steadily increased over the years. Genetic engineering in the agricultural field has led to improved crops for human use and consumption. Crops are genetically modified for increased growth and insect resistance because of the demand for larger and greater quantities of produce.

With advances in biotechnology come those in society who oppose it. Ethical questions come into play when discussing animal and human research. Does it need to be done? What are the effects on humans and animals? There are not right or wrong answers to these questions. There are governmental agencies in place to regulate the use of humans and animals for research.

Science and technology are often referred to as a "double-edged sword". Although advances in medicine have greatly improved the quality and length of life, certain moral and ethical controversies have arisen. Unforeseen environmental problems may result from technological advances. Advances in science have led to an improved economy through biotechnology as applied to agriculture, yet it has put our health care system at risk and has caused the cost of medical care to skyrocket. Society depends on science, yet is necessary that the public be scientifically literate and informed in order to allow potentially unethical procedures to occur. Especially vulnerable are the areas of genetic research and fertility. It is important for science teachers to stay abreast of current research and to involve students in critical thinking and ethics whenever possible.

Skill 4.3 Analyze the processes of scientific and technological breakthroughs and their effects on other fields of study, careers, and job markets.

Scientific and technological breakthroughs greatly influence other fields of study and the job market. All academic disciplines utilize computer and information technology to simplify research and information sharing. In addition, advances in science and technology influence the types of available jobs and the desired work skills. For example, machines and computers continue to replace unskilled laborers and computer and technological literacy is now a requirement for many jobs and careers. Finally, science and technology continue to change the very nature of careers. Because of science and technology's great influence on all areas of the economy, and the continuing scientific and technological breakthroughs, careers are far less stable than in past eras. Workers can thus expect to change jobs and companies much more often than in the past.

Skill 4.4 Analyze issues related to science and technology at the local, state, national, and global levels (e.g., environmental policies, genetic research).

A baby born today in the United States is expected to live 30 years longer on average than a baby born 100 years ago. A significant cause of this improvement is due to chemical technology. The manufacture and distribution of vaccines and antibiotics, an increase in understanding human nutritional needs, and the use of fertilizers in agriculture have all played a significant role in improving the length and the quality of human life. But the benefits of these technologies are almost always accompanied by problems and significant risks.

Nutrition: general

Chemical technology helps **keep foods fresh** longer and **alters the molecules** in food. The thermochemistry of refrigeration helps food last longer without altering it. Other technologies such as pasteurization, drying, salting, and the addition of preservatives all prevent microbial contamination by altering the nutritional content of food. **Preservatives** are substances added to food to prevent the growth of microorganisms and spoilage. For example, potassium and sodium **nitrites** and **nitrates** are often used as a preservative for root vegetables and processed meats.

Physical separation techniques such as milling, centrifugation, and pressing give flour, oils, and juices that are used as ingredients. **Chemical techniques** give particular fatty acids, amino acids, vitamins, and minerals that are used in nutritional supplements or to fortify processed foods. Some molecules in processed foods are removed intentionally or as an unintended consequence of processing. Other molecules are added for a wide variety of reasons such as improving taste or decreasing the cost of production.

Eating too much processed food over time has a long history of **causing harm** because of the substances it lacks or contains. Whole, fresh food usually has a better nutritional value. For example, in the late 1800s many infants in the US developed **scurvy (vitamin C deficiency)** by drinking heat-treated milk that controlled bacterial infections but destroyed vitamin C. Local production of food with minimal time-to-market and proper preparation seem to be a more sensible approach to food safety than long-distance transport of both the food and the means to protect it, but processed food will remain popular for the foreseeable future because it is usually **cheaper** to buy, more **profitable** to sell, and more **convenient** to obtain, store, prepare and use.

Nutrition: hydrogenation

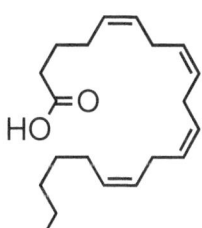

Hydrogenation uses a chemical reaction to convert unsaturated to saturated oils. Many plant oils are **polyunsaturated** with double bonds in the *cis-* form as shown at left. These molecules contain rigid bends in them. Complete hydrogenation creates a flexible straight-chain molecule that permits more area for London dispersion forces to form intermolecular bonds. The result is that **hydrogenation increases the melting point** of an oil. Semi-solid fats are preferred for baking because the final product has the right texture in the mouth. Unfortunately, saturated fats are less healthy than *cis-* unsaturated fats because they promote obesity and heart disease. Complete hydrogenation of the molecule above is shown here:

When the hydrogenation process does not fully saturate, it results in partially **hydrogenated** oil. Partial hydrogenation often creates a semi-solid fat in cases where complete hydrogenation would create a fat that is fully solid.

However, **partial hydrogenation** of cis-polyunsaturated fats results in a **random isomerization** creating a **mixture of *cis*- and *trans*-** forms. In the structure below, the molecule at the top of the page has been partially hydrogenated, resulting in the saturation of two double bonds. One of the two remaining *cis*-bonds has been isomerized to a *trans*- form:

Trans-fatty acids have a slight kink in them compared to *cis*- forms, and they rarely occur in the food found in nature. Campaigns against saturated fat in the 1980s led to the increased use of partially hydrogenated oils. The health benefits of **monounsaturated fat** were promoted, but labels made **no distinction between *cis*- and *trans*-** forms. As a result, there has been an increase in consumption of *trans* fat. Unfortunately, it is now known that ***trans* fat is even worse for the body than saturated fat**. Some nations have completely banned the use of partially hydrogenated oils. Food labels in the United States are currently (as of 2006) required to list **total, saturated, and *trans*-fat content**. Fatty acids with one or more *trans* nonconjugated double bonds are labeled as *trans* fat under this rule.

Nutrition: irradiation
Food may also be sterilized and preserved by **food irradiation**. **Gamma rays** from a sealed source of ^{60}Co or ^{137}Cs are used to **kill microorganisms** in over 40 countries. This process is less expensive than refrigeration, canning, or additives, and it **does not make food radioactive**.

Opponents of irradiation fear the risks involved in the **transport and use of nuclear materials** to build the facilities and to maintain them. A potential health risk in the food itself is the possibility that the radiation required to kill organisms may alter a biological molecule to produce a harmful by-product, but no evidence has been found of such a toxin. Another concern is that irradiation will lead to a permissive attitude about safe food-handling procedures that can lead to other types of contamination. Food irradiation is still under study in the United States to conclusively prove its safety, particularly for meats

Industry
The *chemical industry* usually refers to **industries that manufacture chemicals**. But it could be argued that the impact of those chemicals and of the ability to alter matter by chemical technology has **created tools that have improved the industrial production of nearly every substance**. Some divisions of the chemical industry are: petrochemicals (chemicals from petroleum), oleochemicals (chemicals from biological oils and fats), agrochemicals (chemicals for agriculture), pharmaceuticals, polymers, and paints. Chemical technology has impacted everything from testing and maintaining a clean water supply to the plastics used in cell phones.

These industries make up an entire **sector of the economy**. In the United States, about 900,000 people are employed in the chemical industry, and sales totaled about $500 billion in 2004 (http://pubs.acs.org/cen/coverstory/83/8302wcousa.html).

Chemical engineering is the **application of chemistry** along with mathematics and economics to the process of converting raw materials or chemicals into more useful forms. In the development of a new chemical, a chemist typically discovers or **designs the compound** and synthesizes it for the first time. A chemical engineer will then typically take that information and the **design the process** to manufacture the chemical in the amounts required. The individual processes used by chemical engineers (such as distillation or solvent extraction) are called **unit operations**. All chemical engineers are trained in process design, but most work in a variety of other disciplines.

Medicine
In the field of **medicinal chemistry**, scientists identify, synthesize, develop, and study chemicals to use for diagnostic tools and pharmaceuticals. **Pharmacology** is the study of how chemical substances interact with living systems. As biological knowledge has increased, the biochemical causes of many diseases have been determined and the field of pharmacology has grown tremendously.

Antibiotics are organic chemicals to **kill or slow the growth of bacteria**. Before antibiotics were available, infections were often treated with moderate levels of poisons like strychnine or arsenic. Antibiotics **target the disease without harming the patient**, and they have saved millions of lives. Unfortunately, some bacteria in **antibiotic resistant strains** have developed defenses against these chemicals since they first became available over 60 years ago. New antibiotics are developed every year in an effort to continue the suppression of bacterial diseases.

Biotechnology uses living organisms—often cells in a **fermentation tank** or **bioreactor**—to create useful molecules. The oldest examples are the use of yeast to make bread and beer. Since 1980, **genetic engineering** has been used to design **recombinant DNA** in order to produce **human protein** molecules in bioreactors using non-human cells. These molecules fight diseases by elevating the level of proteins made naturally by the human body or by providing proteins that are missing due to genetic disorders. Most tools in biotechnology originated from chemical technology.

Agriculture

Plants, like humans and animals, need adequate water, protection from disease, and certain chemical compounds to grow. Soil fertility where no agriculture occurs is maintained at an even level when the waste products derived from plants are returned to the soil. Human agriculture prevents this from occurring. **Fertilizers** are materials given to plants to **promote growth. Nitrogen, phosphorus, and potassium** are the most important elements in fertilizers.

There are many types of fertilizer, including natural materials like manure, seaweed, compost, and minerals from deposits. Plants that are able to utilize nitrogen from the atmosphere may also be grown some seasons so their nitrogen is added to the soil. Many of these technologies are thousands of years old. In the 1800s, studies by **von Liebig** and others resulted in the worldwide transport of a few minerals and by-products of the steel industry as fertilizer.

The major breakthrough in the use of fertilizers from chemical processes occurred with the development of the **Haber process for ammonia production** in 1910:

$N_2(g) + 3H_2(g) \rightleftharpoons 2NH_3(g)$ over Fe catalyst.

Millions of tons of ammonia are used worldwide each year to supply crops with nitrogen. Ammonia is either added to irrigation water or injected directly into the ground. Many other nitrogen fertilizers are synthesized from ammonia. Phosphorus in fertilizers originates from phosphate (PO_4^{3-}) in rock deposits. Potassium in fertilizers comes from evaporated ancient seabeds in the form of potassium oxide (K_2O).

Pesticides are used to control or kill organisms that compete with humans for food, spread disease, or are considered a nuisance. Herbicides are pesticides that attack weeds; insecticides attack insects; fungicides attack molds and other fungus. Sulfur was used as a fungicide in ancient times. The development and use of new pesticides has exploded over the last 60 years, but these pesticides are often poisonous to humans.

Farming designed to **maximize productivity** is called **intensive agriculture**. These methods of fertilizer and pesticide use in combination with other farming techniques decreased the number of farm laborers needed and gave a growing world population enough to eat in the last 50 years. Intensification of agriculture in developing countries is known as the **green revolution**. These techniques were credited with saving a billion people from starvation in India and Pakistan.

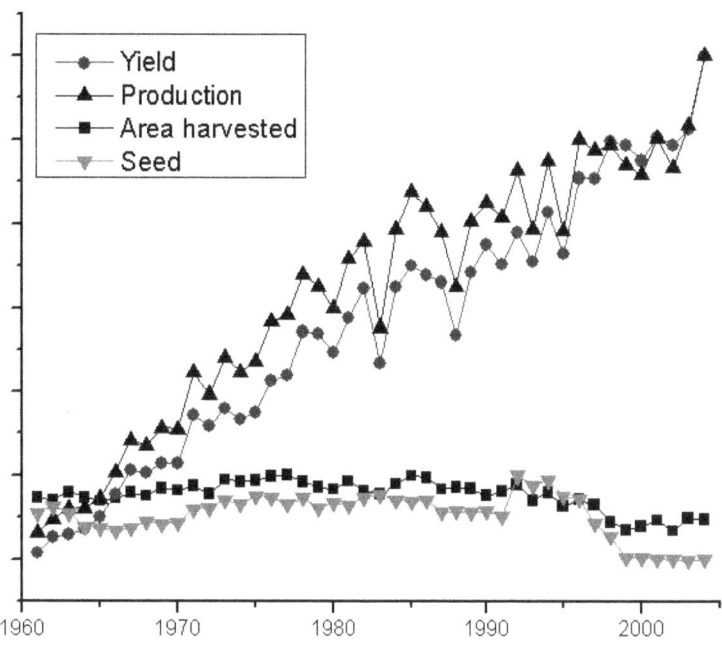

Source: Food and Agriculture Organization of the United Nations (http://faostat.fao.org/)

The **insecticide DDT** was widely used in the 1940s and 1950s and is responsible for **eradicating malaria from Europe and North America**. It quickly became the most widely used pesticide in the world. In the 1960s, some claimed that DDT was preventing fish-eating birds from reproducing and that it was causing birth defects in humans. DDT is now banned in many countries, but it is still used in developing nations to prevent diseases carried by insects. Unfortunately, its use in agriculture has often led to resistant mosquito strains that have hindered its effectiveness to prevent diseases.

The **herbicide *Roundup*** kills all natural plants it encounters. It began to be used in the 1990s in combination with **genetically engineeredcrops** that include a gene intended to make the crop (and only the crop) resistant to the herbicide. This combination of chemical and genetic technology has been an economic success but it has raised many concerns about potential problems in the future.

Environment

Many chemical technologies that save lives or improve the quality of life in the short term have had a negative impact on the environment. Chemical **pollution** is often divided into gas, liquid, and solid waste materials. Additional technologies often exist remediate these effects and improve pollution.

Most scientists believe the emission of **greenhouse gases** has already led to **global warming** due to an increase in **the greenhouse effect**. The greenhouse effect occurs when these gases in the atmosphere warm the planet by **absorbing heat** to prevent it from escaping into space. This is similar—but not identical—to what occurs in greenhouse buildings. Greenhouse buildings warm an interior space by preventing mixing with colder gases outside. Many greenhouse gases such as water vapor occur naturally and are important for life to exist on Earth. Human production of **carbon dioxide** from combustion of fossil fuelshas increased the concentration of this important greenhouse gas to its highest value since millions of years ago. The precise impact of these changes in the atmosphere is difficult to predict and is a topic of international concern and political debate.

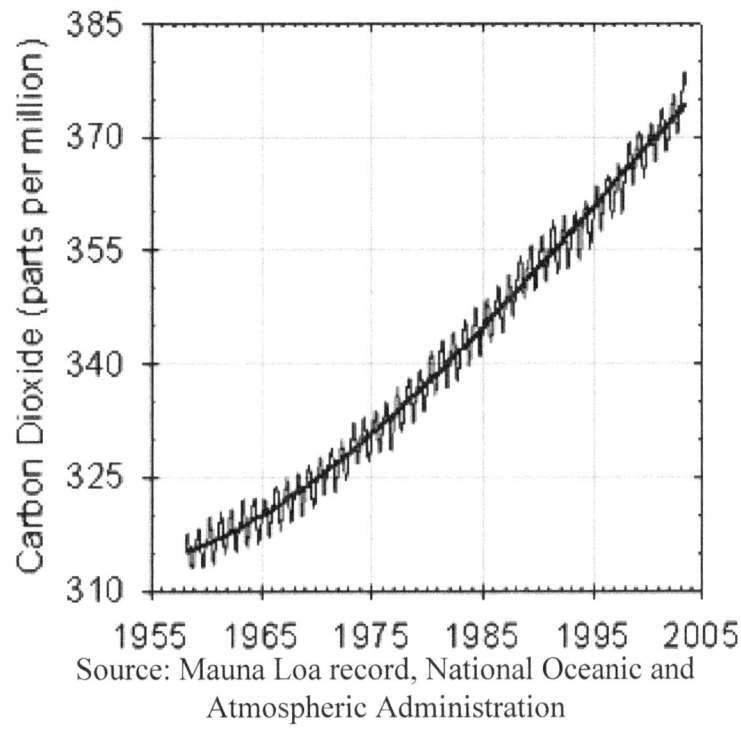

Source: Mauna Loa record, National Oceanic and Atmospheric Administration

Rain with a pH less than 5.6 is known as **acid rain**. Acid rain is caused by burning fossil fuels (especially coal) and by fertilizers used in intensive agriculture. These activities emit sulfur and nitrogen in gas compounds that are converted to sulfur oxides and nitrogen oxides. These in turn create sulfuric acid and nitric acid in rain. Acid rain may also be created from gases emitted by volcanoes and other natural sources. Acid rain harms fish and trees and triggers the release metal ions from minerals into water that can harm people. The problem of acid rain in the United States has been addressed in recent decades by the use of **scrubbers** in coal burning power plants and **catalytic converters** in vehicles.

Ozone is O_3. The **ozone layer** is a region of the stratosphere that contains higher concentrations of ozone than other parts of the atmosphere. The ozone layer is important for human health because it **blocks ultraviolet radiation** from the sun, and this helps to protect us from skin cancer. Research in the 1970s revealed that several gases used for refrigeration and other purposes were depleting the ozone layer. Many of these ozone-destroying molecules are short alkyl halides known as **chlorofluorocarbons** or **CFCs**. CCl_3F is one example. The widespread use of ozone-destroying gases was banned by an international agreement in the early 1990s. Other substances are used in their place such as CF_3CH_2F, a hydrofluorocarbon. Since that time the concentration of ozone-depleting gases in the atmosphere has been declining and **the rate of ozone destruction has been decreasing**. Many see this improvement as the most important positive example of international cooperation in helping the environment. The story of these new refrigerants is found at http://www.chemcases.com/fluoro/index.htm.

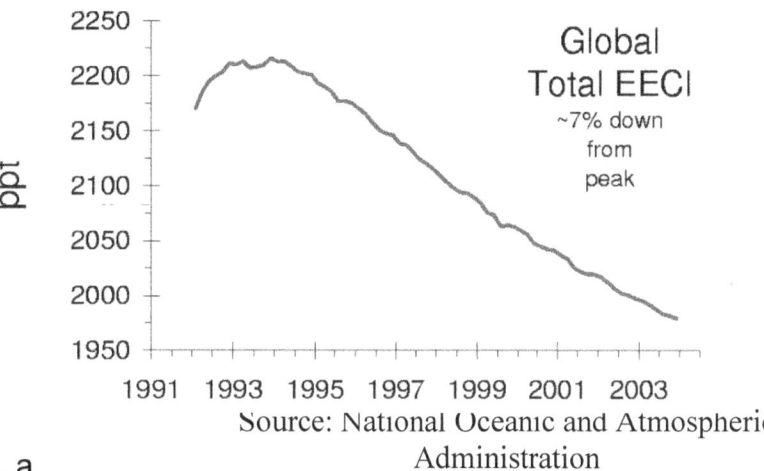

Source: National Oceanic and Atmospheric Administration

Skill 4.5 **Evaluate the credibility of scientific claims made in various forums (e.g., the media, public debates, advertising).**

Because people often attempt to use scientific evidence in support of political or personal agendas, the ability to evaluate the credibility of scientific claims is a necessary skill in today's society. In evaluating scientific claims made in the media, public debates, and advertising, one should follow several guidelines.

First, scientific, peer-reviewed journals are the most accepted source for information on scientific experiments and studies. One should carefully scrutinize any claim that does not reference peer-reviewed literature.

Second, the media and those with an agenda to advance (advertisers, debaters, etc.) often overemphasize the certainty and importance of experimental results. One should question any scientific claim that sounds fantastical or overly certain.

Finally, knowledge of experimental design and the scientific method is important in evaluating the credibility of studies. For example, one should look for the inclusion of control groups and the presence of data to support the given conclusions.

COMPETENCY 5.0 UNDERSTAND AND APPLY KNOWLEDGE OF THE MAJOR UNIFYING CONCEPTS OF ALL SCIENCES AND HOW THESE CONCEPTS RELATE TO OTHER DISCIPLINES.

Skill 5.1 Identify the major unifying concepts of the sciences (e.g., systems, order, and organization; constancy, change, and measurement) and their applications in real-life situations.

The following are the concepts and processes generally recognized as common to all scientific disciplines:

- Systems, order, and organization
- Evidence, models, and explanation
- Constancy, change, and measurement
- Evolution and equilibrium
- Form and function

Because the natural world is so complex, the study of science involves the **organization** of items into smaller groups based on interaction or interdependence. These groups are called **systems**. Examples of organization are the periodic table of elements and the five-kingdom classification scheme for living organisms. Examples of systems are the solar system, cardiovascular system, Newton's laws of force and motion, and the laws of conservation.

Order refers to the behavior and measurability of organisms and events in nature. The arrangement of planets in the solar system and the life cycle of bacterial cells are examples of order.

Scientists use **evidence** and **models** to form **explanations** of natural events. Models are miniaturized representations of a larger event or system. Evidence is anything that furnishes proof.

Constancy and **change** describe the observable properties of natural organisms and events. Scientists use different systems of **measurement** to observe change and constancy. For example, the freezing and melting points of given substances and the speed of sound are constant under constant conditions. Growth, decay, and erosion are all examples of natural change.

Evolution is the process of change over a long period of time. While biological evolution is the most common example, one can also classify technological advancement, changes in the universe, and changes in the environment as evolution.

Equilibrium is the state of balance between opposing forces of change. Homeostasis and ecological balance are examples of equilibrium.

Form and **function** are properties of organisms and systems that are closely related. The function of an object usually dictates its form and the form of an object usually facilitates its function. For example, the form of the heart (e.g. muscle, valves) allows it to perform its function of circulating blood through the body.

Skill 5.2 **Recognize connections within and among the traditional scientific disciplines.**

Because biology is the study of living things, we can easily apply the knowledge of biology to daily life and personal decision-making. For example, biology greatly influences the health decisions humans make everyday. Other areas of daily life where biology affects decision-making are parenting, interpersonal relationships, family planning, and consumer spending.

What foods to eat, when and how to exercise, and how often to bathe are just three of the many decisions we make everyday that are based on our knowledge of science.

This is true for chemistry as well. The chair you sit in to read this manual is made of carbon, and the shampoo you used this morning is a combination of useful chemicals, probably of a synthetic nature. Science is everywhere!

Skill 5.3 **Apply fundamental mathematical language, knowledge, and skills at the level of algebra and statistics in scientific contexts.**

The knowledge and use of basic mathematical concepts and skills is a necessary aspect of scientific study. Science depends on data and the manipulation of data requires knowledge of mathematics. Understanding of basic statistics, graphs and charts, and algebra are of particular importance. Scientists must be able to understand and apply the statistical concepts of mean, median, mode, and range to sets of scientific data. In addition, scientists must be able to represent data graphically and interpret graphs and tables. Finally, scientists often use basic algebra to solve scientific problems and design experiments. For example, the substitution of variables is a common strategy in experiment design. Also, the ability to determine the equation of a curve is valuable in data manipulation, experimentation, and prediction.

Modern science uses a number of disciplines to understand it better. Statistics is one of those subjects that is absolutely essential for science.

Mean: Mean is the mathematical average of all the items. To calculate the mean, all the items must be added up and divided by the number of items. This is also called the arithmetic mean or more commonly as the "average".

Median: The median depends on whether the number of items is odd or even. If the number is odd, then the median is the value of the item in the middle. This is the value that denotes that the number of items having higher or equal value to that is same as the number of items having equal or lesser value than that. If the number o the items is even, the median is the average of the two items in the middle, such that the number of items having values higher or equal to it is same as the number o items having values equal or less than that.

Mode: Mode is the value o the item that occurs the most often, if there are not many items. Bimodal is a situation where there are two items with equal frequency.

Range: Range is the difference between the maximum and minimum values. The range is the difference between two extreme points on the distribution curve.

Scientists use mathematical tools and equations to model and solve scientific problems. Solving scientific problems often involves the use of quadratic, trigonometric, exponential, and logarithmic functions.

Quadratic equations take the standard form $ax^2 + bx + c = 0$. The most appropriate method of solving quadratic equations in scientific problems is the use of the quadratic formula. The quadratic formula produces the solutions of a standard form quadratic equation.

$$x = \frac{-b \pm \sqrt{b^2 - 4ac}}{2a}$$

One common application of quadratic equations is the description of biochemical reaction equilibriums. Consider the following problem.

Example 1

80.0 g of ethanoic acid (MW = 60g) reacts with 85.0 g of ethanol (MW = 46g) until equilibrium. The equilibrium constant is 4.00. Determine the amounts of ethyl acetate and water produced at equilibrium.

$$CH_3COOH + CH_3CH_2OH = CH_3CO_2C_2H_5 + H_2O$$

The equilibrium constant, K, describes equilibrium of the reaction, relating the concentrations of products to reactants.

$$K = \frac{[CH_3CO_2C_2H_5][H_2O]}{[CH_3CO_2H][CH_3CH_2OH]} = 4.00$$

The equilibrium values of reactants and products are listed in the following table.

	CH_3COOH	CH_3CH_2OH	$CH_3CO_2C_2H_5$	H_2O
Initial	80/60 = 1.33 mol	85/46 = 1.85 mol	0	0
Equilibrium	1.33 − x	1.85 − x	x	x

Thus, $K = \dfrac{[x][x]}{[1.33-x][1.85-x]} = \dfrac{x^2}{2.46 - 3.18x + x^2} = 4.00$.

Rearrange the equation to produce a standard form quadratic equation.

$$\dfrac{x^2}{2.46 - 3.18x + x^2} = 4.00$$
$$x^2 = 4.00(2.46 - 3.18x + x^2) = 9.84 - 12.72x + 4x^2$$
$$0 = 3x^2 - 12.72x + 9.84$$

Use the quadratic formula to solve for x.

$$x = \dfrac{-(-12.72) \pm \sqrt{(-12.72)^2 - 4(3)(9.84)}}{2(3)} = 3.22 \text{ or } 1.02$$

3.22 is not an appropriate answer, because we started with only 3.18 moles of reactants. Thus, the amount of each product produced at equilibrium is 1.02 moles.

Scientists use trigonometric functions to define angles and lengths. For example, field biologists can use trigonometric functions to estimate distances and directions. The basic trigonometric functions are sine, cosine, and tangent. Consider the following triangle describing these relationships.

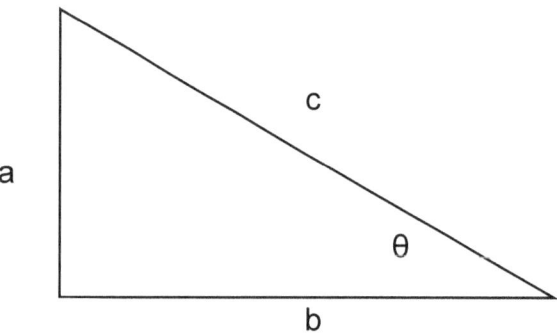

$$\sin \theta = \dfrac{a}{c}, \quad \cos \theta = \dfrac{b}{c}, \quad \tan \theta = \dfrac{a}{b}$$

Exponential functions are useful in modeling many scientific phenomena. For example, scientists use exponential functions to describe bacterial growth and radioactive decay. The general form of exponential equations is $f(x) = Ca^x$ (C is a constant). Consider the following problem involving bacterial growth.

Example 2

Determine the number of bacteria present in a culture inoculated with a single bacterium after 24 hours if the bacterial population doubles every 2 hours. Use $N(t) = N_0 e^{kt}$ as a model of bacterial growth where N(t) is the size of the population at time t, N_0 is the initial population size, and k is the growth constant.

We must first determine the growth constant, k. At t = 2, the size of the population doubles from 1 to 2. Thus, we substitute and solve for k.

$$2 = 1(e^{2k})$$

$\ln 2 = \ln e^{2k}$ Take the natural log of each side.

$\ln 2 = 2k(\ln e) = 2k$ $\ln e = 1$

$k = \dfrac{\ln 2}{2}$ Solve for k.

The population size at t = 24 is

$$N(24) = e^{(\frac{\ln 2}{2})24} = e^{12 \ln 2} = 4096.$$

Finally, logarithmic functions have many applications to science. One simple example of a logarithmic application is the pH scale. Scientists define pH as follows.

pH = $- \log_{10} [H_+]$, where $[H_+]$ is the concentration of hydrogen ions

Thus, we can determine the pH of a solution with a $[H_+]$ value of 0.0005 mol/L by using the logarithmic formula.

pH = $- \log_{10} [0.0005] = 3.3$

Skill 5.4 **Recognize the fundamental relationships among the natural sciences and the social sciences.**

The fundamental relationship between the natural and social sciences is the use of the scientific method and the rigorous standards of proof that both disciplines require. This emphasis on organization and evidence separates the sciences from the arts and humanities. Natural science, particularly biology, is closely related to social science, the study of human behavior. Biological and environmental factors often dictate human behavior and accurate assessment of behavior requires a sound understanding of biological factors.

TEACHER CERTIFICATION STUDY GUIDE

SUBAREA II.   **LIFE SCIENCE**

COMPETENCY 6.0   UNDERSTAND AND APPLY KNOWLEDGE OF CELL STRUCTURE AND FUNCTION.

Skill 6.1   Compare and contrast the structures of viruses and prokaryotic and eukaryotic cells.

The cell is the basic unit of all living things. There are three types of cells. They are prokaryotes, eukaryotes, and archaea. Archaea have some similarities with prokaryotes, but are as distantly related to prokaryotes as prokaryotes are to eukaryotes.

PROKARYOTES

Prokaryotes consist only of bacteria and cyanobacteria (formerly known as blue-green algae). The classification of prokaryotes is in the diagram below.

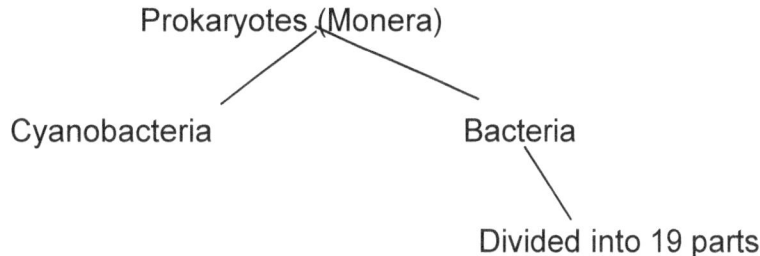

These cells have no defined nucleus or nuclear membrane. The DNA, RNA, and ribosomes float freely within the cell. The cytoplasm has a single chromosome condensed to form a **nucleoid**. Prokaryotes have a thick cell wall made up of amino sugars (glycoproteins). This is for protection, to give the cell shape, and to keep the cell from bursting. It is the **cell wall** of bacteria that is targeted by the antibiotic penicillin. Penicillin works by disrupting the cell wall, thus killing the cell.

The cell wall surrounds the **cell membrane** (plasma membrane). The cell membrane consists of a lipid bilayer that controls the passage of molecules in and out of the cell. Some prokaryotes have a capsule made of polysaccharides that surrounds the cell wall for extra protection from higher organisms.

Many bacterial cells have appendages used for movement called **flagella**. Some cells also have **pili**, which are a protein strand used for attachment of the bacteria. Pili may also be used for sexual conjugation (where the DNA from one bacterial cell is transferred to another bacterial cell).

Prokaryotes are the most numerous and widespread organisms on earth. Bacteria were most likely the first cells and date back in the fossil record to 3.5 billion years ago. Their ability to adapt to the environment allows them to thrive in a wide variety of habitats.

EUKARYOTES

Eukaryotic cells are found in protists, fungi, plants, and animals. Most eukaryotic cells are larger than prokaryotic cells. They contain many organelles, which are membrane bound areas for specific functions. Their cytoplasm contains a cytoskeleton which provides a protein framework for the cell. The cytoplasm also supports the organelles and contains the ions and molecules necessary for cell function. The cytoplasm is contained by the plasma membrane. The plasma membrane allows molecules to pass in and out of the cell. The membrane can bud inward to engulf outside material in a process called endocytosis. Exocytosis is a secretory mechanism, the reverse of endocytosis. The most significant differentiation between prokaryotes and eukaryotes is that eukaryotes have a **nucleus**.

VIRUSES

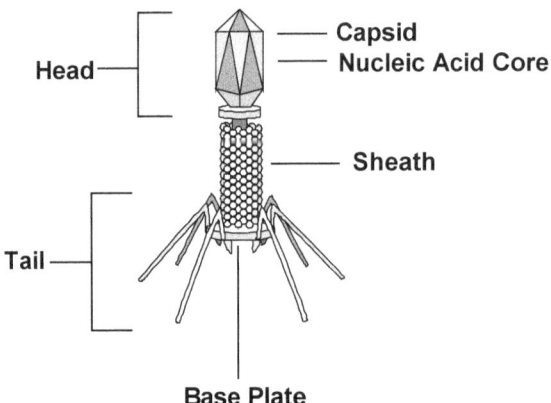

Bacteriophage

All viruses have a head or protein capsid that contains genetic material. This material is encoded in the nucleic acid and can be DNA, RNA, or even a limited number of enzymes. Some viruses also have a protein tail region. The tail aids in binding to the surface of the host cell and penetrating the surface of the host in order to introduce the virus's genetic material.

Other examples of viruses and their structures:

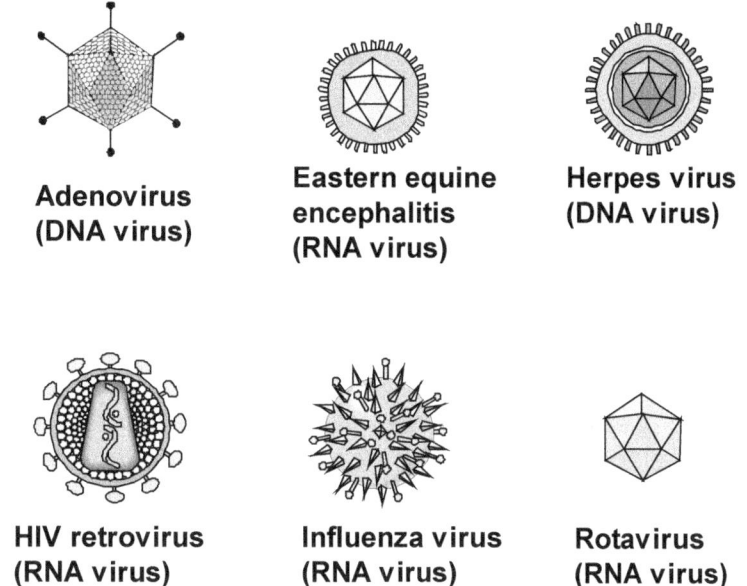

Skill 6.2   Identify the structures and functions of cellular organelles.

The **nucleus** is the brain of the cell that contains all of the cell's genetic information. The chromosomes consist of chromatin, which is a complex of DNA and proteins. The chromosomes are tightly coiled to conserve space while providing a large surface area. The nucleus is the site of transcription of the DNA into RNA. The **nucleolus** is where ribosomes are made. There is at least one of these dark-staining bodies inside the nucleus of most eukaryotes. The nuclear envelope is two membranes separated by a narrow space. The envelope contains many pores that let RNA out of the nucleus.

Ribosomes are the site for protein synthesis. Ribosomes may be free floating in the cytoplasm or attached to the endoplasmic reticulum. There may be up to a half a million ribosomes in a cell, depending on how much protein is made by the cell.

The **endoplasmic reticulum** (ER) is folded and provides a large surface area. It is the "roadway" of the cell and allows for transport of materials through and out of the cell. There are two types of ER. Smooth endoplasmic reticulum contains no ribosomes on their surface. This is the site of lipid synthesis. Rough endoplasmic reticulum has ribosomes on their surface. They aid in the synthesis of proteins that are membrane bound or destined for secretion.

Many of the products made in the ER proceed on to the Golgi apparatus. The **Golgi apparatus** functions to sort, modify, and package molecules that are made in the other parts of the cell (like the ER). These molecules are either sent out of the cell or to other organelles within the cell. The Golgi apparatus is a stacked structure to increase the surface area.

Lysosomes are found mainly in animal cells. These contain digestive enzymes that break down food, substances not needed, viruses, damaged cell components and eventually the cell itself. It is believed that lysomomes are responsible for the aging process.

Mitochondria are large organelles that are the site of cellular respiration, where ATP is made to supply energy to the cell. Muscle cells have many mitochondria because they use a great deal of energy. Mitochondria have their own DNA, RNA, and ribosomes and are capable of reproducing by binary fission if there is a greater demand for additional energy. Mitochondria have two membranes: a smooth outer membrane and a folded inner membrane. The folds inside the mitochondria are called cristae. They provide a large surface area for cellular respiration to occur.

Plastids are found only in photosynthetic organisms. They are similar to the mitochondira due to the double membrane structure. They also have their own DNA, RNA, and ribosomes and can reproduce if the need for the increased capture of sunlight becomes necessary. There are several types of plastids. **Chloroplasts** are the sight of photosynthesis. The stroma is the chloroplast's inner membrane space. The stoma encloses sacs called thylakoids that contain the photosynthetic pigment chlorophyll. The chlorophyll traps sunlight inside the thylakoid to generate ATP which is used in the stroma to produce carbohydrates and other products. The **chromoplasts** make and store yellow and orange pigments. They provide color to leaves, flowers, and fruits. The **amyloplasts** store starch and are used as a food reserve. They are abundant in roots like potatoes.

The Endosymbiotic Theory states that mitochondria and chloroplasts were once free living and possibly evolved from prokaryotic cells. At some point in our evolutionary history, they entered the eukaryotic cell and maintained a symbiotic relationship with the cell, with both the cell and organelle benefiting from the relationship. The fact that they both have their own DNA, RNA, ribosomes, and are capable of reproduction helps to confirm this theory.

Found in plant cells only, the **cell wall** is composed of cellulose and fibers. It is thick enough for support and protection, yet porous enough to allow water and dissolved substances to enter. **Vacuoles** are found mostly in plant cells. They hold stored food and pigments. Their large size allows them to fill with water in order to provide turgor pressure. Lack of turgor pressure causes a plant to wilt.

The **cytoskeleton**, found in both animal and plant cells, is composed of protein filaments attached to the plasma membrane and organelles. They provide a framework for the cell and aid in cell movement. They constantly change shape and move about. Three types of fibers make up the cytoskeleton:

1. **Microtubules** – the largest of the three, they make up cilia and flagella for locomotion. Some examples are sperm cells, cilia that line the fallopian tubes and tracheal cilia. Centrioles are also composed of microtubules. They aid in cell division to form the spindle fibers that pull the cell apart into two new cells. Centrioles are not found in the cells of higher plants.

2. **Intermediate filaments** – intermediate in size, they are smaller than microtubules but larger than microfilaments. They help the cell to keep its shape.

3. **Microfilaments** – smallest of the three, they are made of actin and small amounts of myosin (like in muscle tissue). They function in cell movement like cytoplasmic streaming, endocytosis, and ameboid movement. This structure pinches the two cells apart after cell division, forming two new cells.

The following is a diagram of a generalized animal cell.

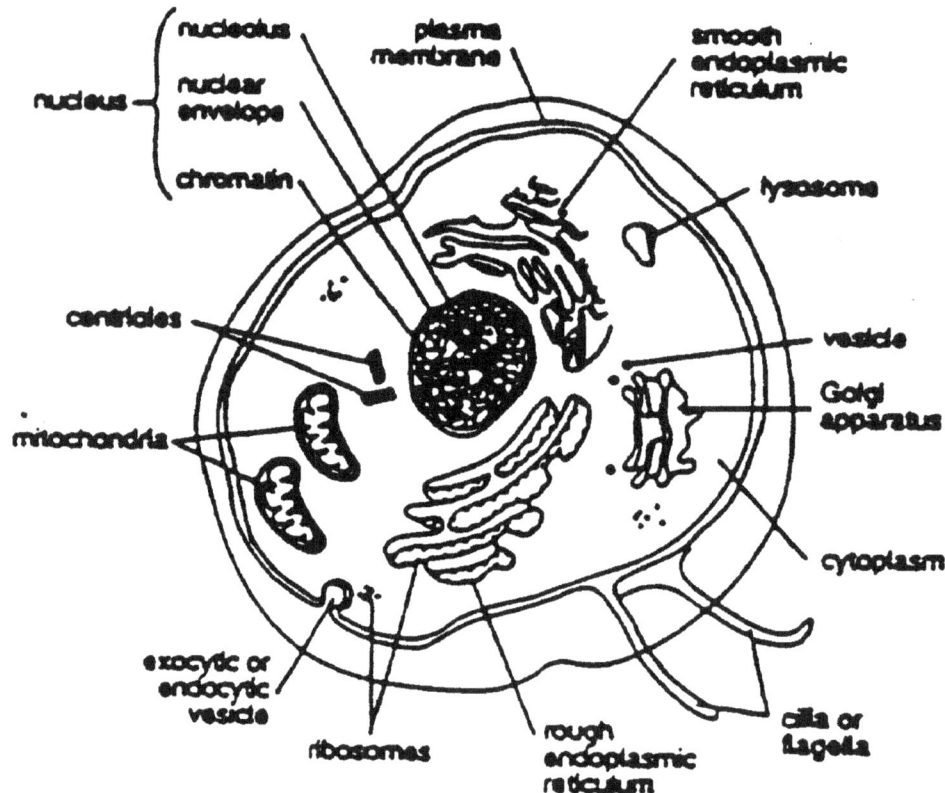

ARCHAEA

There are three kinds of organisms with archaea cells: **methanogens** are obligate anaerobes that produce methane, **halobacteria** can live only in concentrated brine solutions, and **thermoacidophiles** can only live in acidic hot springs.

Skill 6.3   Describe the processes of the cell cycle.

The purpose of cell division is to provide growth and repair in body (somatic) cells and to replenish or create sex cells for reproduction. There are two forms of cell division. **Mitosis** is the division of somatic cells and **meiosis** is the division of sex cells (eggs and sperm).

Mitosis is divided into two parts: the **mitotic (M) phase** and **interphase**. In the mitotic phase, mitosis and cytokinesis divide the nucleus and cytoplasm, respectively. This phase is the shortest phase of the cell cycle. Interphase is the stage where the cell grows and copies the chromosomes in preparation for the mitotic phase. Interphase occurs in three stages of growth: **G1** (growth) period is when the cell is growing and metabolizing, the **S** period (synthesis) is where new DNA is being made and the **G2** phase (growth) is where new proteins and organelles are being made to prepare for cell division.

The mitotic phase is a continuum of change, although it is described as occurring in five stages: prophase, prometaphase, metaphase, anaphase, and telophase. During **prophase**, the cell proceeds through the following steps continuously, with no stopping. The chromatin condenses to become visible chromosomes. The nucleolus disappears and the nuclear membrane breaks apart. Mitotic spindles form that will eventually pull the chromosomes apart. They are composed of microtubules. The cytoskeleton breaks down and the spindles are pushed to the poles or opposite ends of the cell by the action of centrioles. During **prometaphase**, the nuclear membrane fragments and allows the spindle microtubules to interact with the chromosomes. Kinetochore fibers attach to the chromosomes at the centromere region. (Sometimes prometaphase is grouped with metaphase). When the centrosomes are at opposite ends of the cell, the division is in **metaphase**. The centromeres of all the chromosomes are aligned with one another. During **anaphase**, the centromeres split in half and homologous chromosomes separate. The chromosomes are pulled to the poles of the cell, with identical sets at either end. The last stage of mitosis is **telophase**. Here, two nuclei form with a full set of DNA that is identical to the parent cell. The nucleoli become visible and the nuclear membrane reassembles. A cell plate is seen in plant cells, whereas a cleavage furrow is formed in animal cells. The cell is pinched into two cells. Cytokinesis, or division of the cytoplasm and organelles, occurs.

Below is a diagram of mitosis.

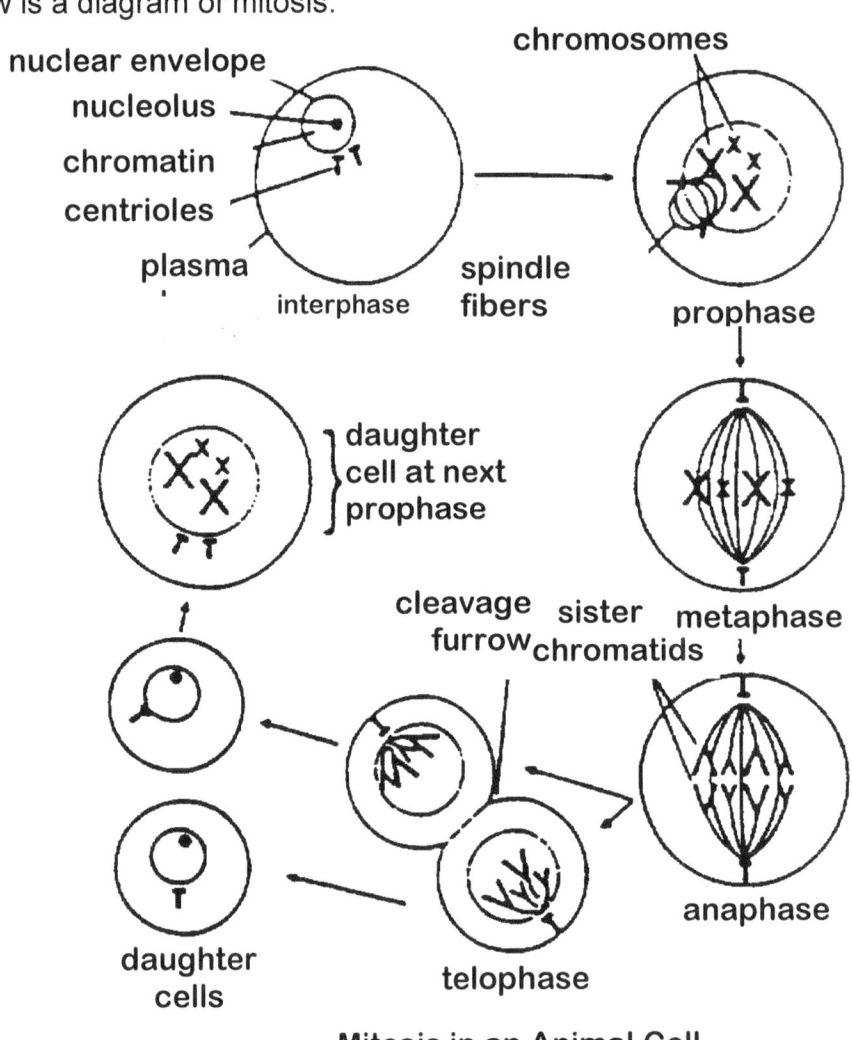

Mitosis in an Animal Cell

Meiosis is similar to mitosis, but there are two consecutive cell divisions, meiosis I and meiosis II in order to reduce the chromosome number by one half. This way, when the sperm and egg join during fertilization, the haploid number is reached.

Similar to mitosis, meiosis is preceded by an interphase during which the chromosome replicates. The steps of meiosis are as follows:

1. **Prophase I** – the replicated chromosomes condense and pair with homologues in a process called synapsis. This forms a tetrad. Crossing over, the exchange of genetic material between homologues to further increase diversity, occurs during prophase I.
2. **Metaphase I** – the homologous pairs attach to spindle fibers after lining up in the middle of the cell.
3. **Anaphase I** – the sister chromatids remain joined and move to the poles of the cell.
4. **Telophase I** – the homologous chromosome pairs continue to separate. Each pole now has a haploid chromosome set. Telophase I occurs simultaneously with cytokinesis. In animal cells, cleavage furrows form and cell plate appear in plant cells.
5. **Prophase II** – a spindle apparatus forms and the chromosomes condense.
6. **Metaphase II** – sister chromatids line up in center of cell. The centromeres divide and the sister chromatids begin to separate.
7. **Anaphase II** – the separated chromosomes move to opposite ends of the cell.
8. **Telophase II** – cytokinesis occurs, resulting in four haploid daughter cells.

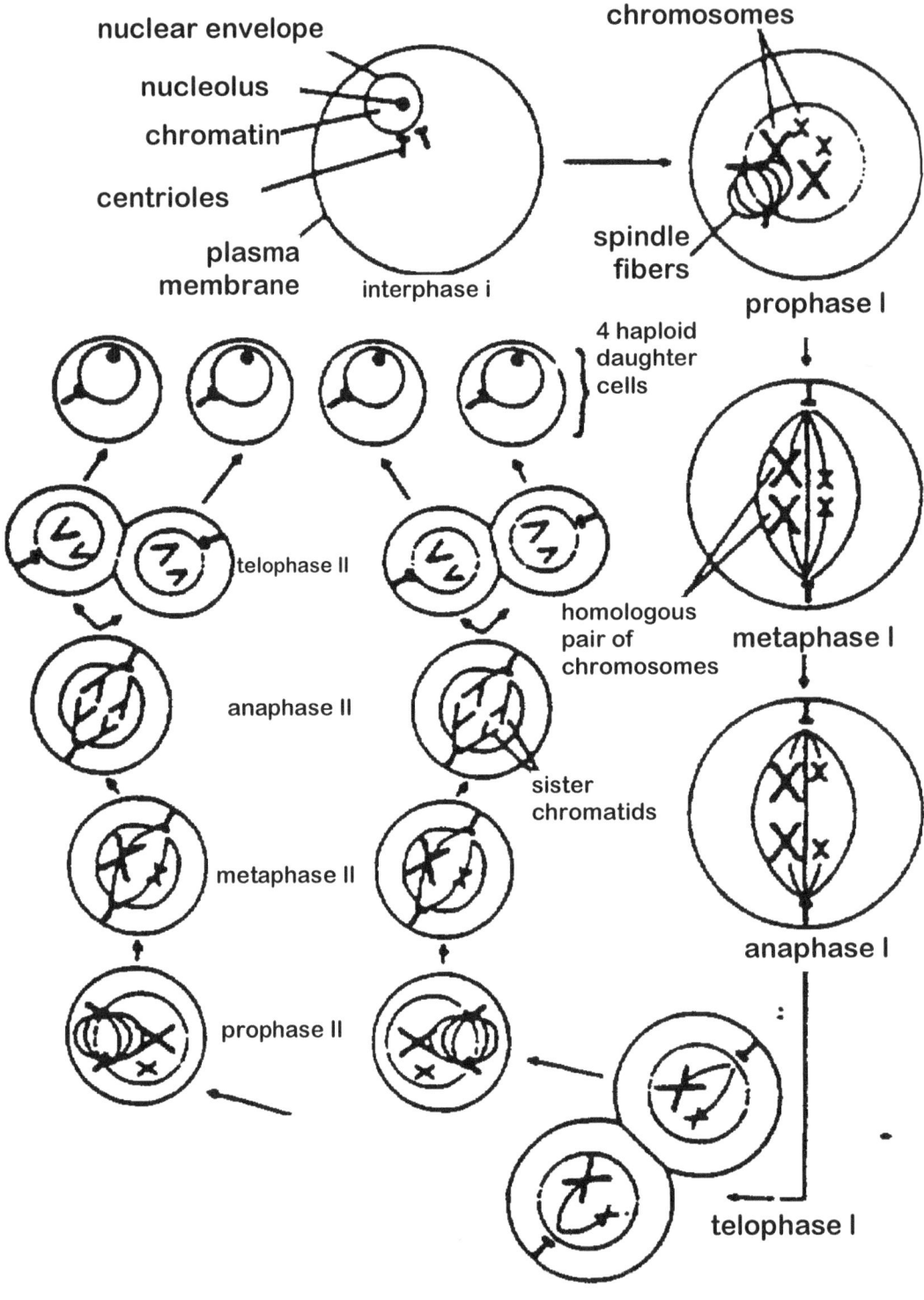

Skill 6.4 **Explain the functions and applications of the instruments and technologies used to study the life sciences at the molecular and cellular levels.**

Gel electrophoresis is a method for analyzing DNA. Electrophoresis separates DNA or protein by size or electrical charge. The DNA runs towards the positive charge as it separates the DNA fragments by size. The gel is treated with a DNA-binding dye that fluoresces under ultraviolet light. A picture of the gel can be taken and used for analysis.

One of the most widely used genetic engineering techniques is **polymerase chain reaction (PCR)**. PCR is a technique in which a piece of DNA can be amplified into billions of copies within a few hours. This process requires primer to specify the segment to be copied, and an enzyme (usually taq polymerase) to amplify the DNA. PCR has allowed scientists to perform several procedures on the smallest amount of DNA.

TEACHER CERTIFICATION STUDY GUIDE

COMPETENCY 7.0 UNDERSTAND AND APPLY KNOWLEDGE OF THE PRINCIPLES OF HEREDITY AND BIOLOGICAL EVOLUTION.

Skill 7.1 Recognize the nature and function of the gene, with emphasis on the molecular basis of inheritance and gene expression.

Gregor Mendel is recognized as the father of genetics. His work in the late 1800s is the basis of our knowledge of genetics. Although unaware of the presence of DNA or genes, Mendel realized there were factors (now known as **genes**) that were transferred from parents to their offspring. Mendel worked with pea plants and fertilized the plants himself, keeping track of subsequent generations which led to the Mendelian laws of genetics. Mendel found that two "factors" governed each trait, one from each parent. Traits or characteristics came in several forms, known as **alleles**. For example, the trait of flower color had white alleles (*pp*) and purple alleles (*PP*). Mendel formed two laws: the law of segregation and the law of independent assortment.

In bacterial cells, the *lac* operon is a good example of the control of gene expression. The *lac* operon contains the genes that encode for the enzymes used to convert lactose into fuel (glucose and galactose). The *lac* operon contains three genes, *lac Z*, *lac Y*, and *lac A*. *Lac Z* encodes an enzyme for the conversion of lactose into glucose and galactose. *Lac Y* encodes for an enzyme that causes lactose to enter the cell. *Lac A* encodes for an enzyme that acetylates lactose.

The *lac* operon also contains a promoter and an operator that is the "off and on" switch for the operon. A protein called the repressor switches the operon off when it binds to the operator. When lactose is absent, the repressor is active and the operon is turned off. The operon is turned on again when allolactose (formed from lactose) inactivates the repressor by binding to it.

Skill 7.2 Analyze the transmission of genetic information (e.g., Punnett squares, sex-linked traits, pedigree analysis).

The **law of segregation** states that only one of the two possible alleles from each parent is passed on to the offspring. If the two alleles differ, then one is fully expressed in the organism's appearance (the dominant allele) and the other has no noticeable effect on appearance (the recessive allele). The two alleles for each trait segregate into different gametes. A Punnet square can be used to show the law of segregation. In a Punnet square, one parent's genes are put at the top of the box and the other parent's on the side. Genes combine in the squares just like numbers are added in addition tables. This Punnet square shows the result of the cross of two F_1 hybrids.

SCIENCE: CHEMISTRY

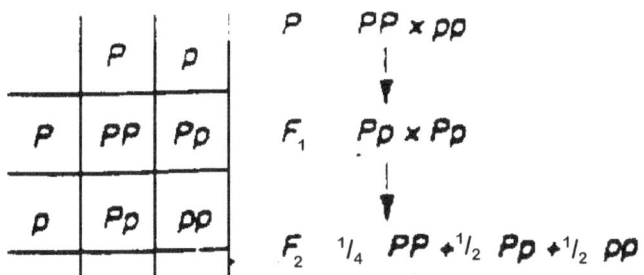

This cross results in a 1:2:1 ratio of F_2 offspring. Here, the P is the dominant allele and the p is the recessive allele. The F_1 cross produces three offspring with the dominant allele expressed (two PP and Pp) and one offspring with the recessive allele expressed (pp). Some other important terms to know:

Homozygous – having a pair of identical alleles. For example, PP and pp are homozygous pairs.
Heterozygous – having two different alleles. For example, Pp is a heterozygous pair.
Phenotype – the organism's physical appearance.
Genotype – the organism's genetic makeup. For example, PP and Pp have the same phenotype (purple in color), but different genotypes.

The **law of independent assortment** states that alleles sort independently of each other. The law of segregation applies for a monohybrid crosses (only one character, in this case flower color, is experimented with). In a dihybrid cross, two characters are being explored. Two of the seven characters Mendel studied were seed shape and color. Yellow is the dominant seed color (Y) and green is the recessive color (y). The dominant seed shape is round (R) and the recessive shape is wrinkled (r). A cross between a plant with yellow round seeds (YYRR) and a plant with green wrinkled seeds (yyrr) produces an F_1 generation with the genotype YyRr. The production of F_2 offspring results in a 9:3:3:1 phenotypic ratio.

	YR	Yr	yR	yr
YR	YYRR	YYRr	YyRR	YyRr
Yr	YYRr	YYrr	YyRr	Yyrr
yR	YyRR	YyRr	yyRR	yyRr
yr	YyRr	Yyrr	yyRr	yyrr

P   YYRR × yyrr

↓

F_1 YyRr

↓

F_2 YYRR – 1
       YYRr – 2
       YyRR – 2
       YyRr – 4 } 9 yellow round

       yyRR – 1
       yyRr – 2 } 3 green round

       YYrr – 1
       Yyrr – 2 } 3 yellow wrinkled

       yyrr – 1 } 1 green wrinkled

Based on Mendelian genetics, the more complex hereditary pattern of **dominance** was discovered. In Mendel's law of segregation, the F_1 generation have either purple or white flowers. This is an example of **complete dominance**. **Incomplete dominance** is when the F_1 generation results in an appearance somewhere between the two parents. For example, red flowers are crossed with white flowers, resulting in an F_1 generation with pink flowers. The red and white traits are still carried by the F_1 generation, resulting in an F_2 generation with a phenotypic ration of 1:2:1. In **codominance,** the genes may form new phenotypes. The ABO blood grouping is an example of codominance. A and B are of equal strength and O is recessive. Therefore, type A blood may have the genotypes of AA or AO, type B blood may have the genotypes of BB or BO, type AB blood has the genotype A and B, and type O blood has two recessive O genes.

A **family pedigree** is a collection of a family's history for a particular trait. As you work your way through the pedigree of interest, the Mendelian inheritance theories are applied. In tracing a trait, the generations are mapped in a pedigree chart, similar to a family tree but with the alleles present. In a case where both parent have a particular trait and one of two children also express this trait, then the trait is due to a dominant allele. In contrast, if both parents do not express a trait and one of their children do, that trait is due to a recessive allele.

Sex linked traits - the Y chromosome found only in males (XY) carries very little genetic information, whereas the X chromosome found in females (XX) carries very important information. Since men have no second X chromosome to cover up a recessive gene, the recessive trait is expressed more often in men. Women need the recessive gene on both X chromosomes to show the trait. Examples of sex linked traits include hemophilia and color-blindness.

Skill 7.3 Analyze the processes of change at the microscopic and macroscopic levels.

In order to fully understand heredity and biological evolution, students need to comprehend the material on both a smaller (microscopic) and a larger (macroscopic) scale. For example, smaller items would include molecules, DNA, and genes and larger items might include organisms and the biosphere.

The teaching of molecular biology is important to the understanding of the chemical basis of life. Students tend to associate molecules with physical science, not realizing that living systems are made of molecules as well as cells. At the macroscopic level, students learn species as a basis for classifying organisms; in order to understand species at the microscopic level, they need to comprehend the genetic basis of the species.

Microscopic Level:

Atoms, molecules, chemical processes and reactions, bacteria, viruses, protists, cells, tissues, chromosomes, genes, meiosis, mitosis, mutations, comparative embryology, molecular evolution.

Macroscopic Level:

Comparative anatomy, natural selection, convergent evolution, divergent evolution, taxonomy, organs, organisms, body systems, animal and plant structure and function, animal behavior, populations, communities, food chains and webs, biomes.

Skill 7.4 **Identify scientific evidence from various sources, such as the fossil record, comparative anatomy, and biochemical similarities, to demonstrate knowledge of theories about processes of biological evolution.**

The hypothesis that life developed on Earth from nonliving materials is the most widely accepted theory on the origin of life. The transformation from nonliving materials to life had four stages. The first stage was the nonliving (abiotic) synthesis of small monomers such as amino acids and nucleotides. In the second stage, these monomers combine to form polymers, such as proteins and nucleic acids. The third stage is the accumulation of these polymers into droplets called protobionts. The last stage is the origin of heredity, with RNA as the first genetic material.

The first stage of this theory was hypothesized in the 1920s. A. I. Oparin and J. B. S. Haldane were the first to theorize that the primitive atmosphere was a reducing atmosphere with no oxygen present. The gases were rich in hydrogen, methane, water and ammonia.. In the 1950s, Stanley Miller proved Oparin's theory in the laboratory by combining the above gases. When given an electrical spark, he was able to synthesize simple amino acids. It is commonly accepted that amino acids appeared before DNA. Other laboratory experiments have supported the other stages in the origin of life theory could have happened.

Other scientists believe simpler hereditary systems originated before nucleic acids. In 1991, Julius Rebek was able to synthesize a simple organic molecule that replicates itself. According to his theory, this simple molecule may be the precursor of RNA.

Prokaryotes are the simplest life form. Their small genome size limits the number of genes that control metabolic activities. Over time, some prokaryotic groups became multicellular organisms for this reason. Prokaryotes then evolved to form complex bacterial communities where species benefit from one another.

The **endosymbiotic theory** of the origin of eukaryotes states that eukaryotes arose from symbiotic groups of prokaryotic cells. According to this theory, smaller prokaryotes lived within larger prokaryotic cells, eventually evolving into chloroplasts and mitochondria. Chloroplasts are the descendant of photosynthetic prokaryotes and mitochondria are likely to be the descendants of bacteria that were aerobic heterotrophs. Serial endosymbiosis is a sequence of endosymbiotic events. Serial endosymbiosis may also play a role in the progression of life forms to become eukaryotes.

Fossils are the key to understanding biological history. They are the preserved remnants left by an organism that lived in the past. Scientists have established the geological time scale to determine the age of a fossil. The geological time scale is broken down into four eras: the Precambrian, Paleozoic, Mesozoic, and Cenozoic. The eras are further broken down into periods that represent a distinct age in the history of Earth and its life. Scientists use rock layers called strata to date fossils. The older layers of rock are at the bottom. This allows scientists to correlate the rock layers with the era they date back to. Radiometric dating is a more precise method of dating fossils. Rocks and fossils contain isotopes of elements accumulated over time. The isotope's half-life is used to date older fossils by determining the amount of isotope remaining and comparing it to the half-life.

Dating fossils is helpful to construct and evolutionary tree. Scientists can arrange the succession of animals based on their fossil record. The fossils of an animal's ancestors can be dated and placed on its evolutionary tree. For example, the branched evolution of horses shows the progression of the modern horse's ancestors to be larger, to have a reduced number of toes, and have teeth modified for grazing.

Comparative anatomical studies reveal that some structural features are basically similar – e.g., flowers generally have sepals, petals, stigma, style and ovary but the size, color, number of petals, sepals etc., may differ from species to species.

The degree of resemblance between two organisms indicates how closely they are related in evolution.

- Groups with little in common are supposed to have diverged from a common ancestor much earlier in geological history than groups which have more in common

- To decide how closely two organisms are, anatomists look for the structures which may serve different purpose in the adult, but are basically similar (homologous)

- In cases where similar structures serve different functions in adults, it is important to trace their origin and embryonic development

When a group of organisms share a homologous structure, which is specialized, to perform a variety of functions in order to adapt to different environmental conditions are called adaptive radiation. The gradual spreading of organisms with adaptive radiation is known as divergent evolution.

Examples of divergent evolution are – pentadactyl limb and insect mouthparts

SCIENCE: CHEMISTRY 57

Under similar environmental conditions, fundamentally different structures in different groups of organisms may undergo modifications to serve similar functions. This is called convergent evolution. The structures, which have no close phylogenetic links but showing adaptation to perform the same functions, are called analogous.

Examples are – wings of bats, bird and insects, jointed legs of insects and vertebrates, eyes of vertebrates and cephalopods.

Vestigial organs: Organs that are smaller and simpler in structure than corresponding parts in the ancestral species are called vestigial organs. They are usually degenerated or underdeveloped. These were functional in ancestral species but no have become non functional, e.g., vestigial hind limbs of whales, vestigial leaves of some xerophytes, vestigial wings of flightless birds like ostriches, etc.

COMPETENCY 8.0 UNDERSTAND AND APPLY KNOWLEDGE OF THE CHARACTERISTICS AND LIFE FUNCTIONS OF ORGANISMS.

Skill 8.1 Identify the levels of organization of various types of organisms and the structures and functions of cells, tissues, organs, and organ systems.

Life has defining properties. Some of the more important processes and properties associated with life are as follows:

*Order – an organism's complex organization.
*Reproduction – life only comes from life (biogenesis).
*Energy utilization – organisms use and make energy to do many kinds of work.
*Growth and development – DNA directed growth and development.
*Adaptation to the environment – occurs by homeostasis (ability to maintain a certain status), response to stimuli, and evolution.

Life is highly organized. The organization of living systems builds on levels from small to increasingly more large and complex. All aspects, whether it is a cell or an ecosystem, have the same requirements to sustain life. Life is organized from simple to complex in the following way:

Atoms ⑧ molecules ⑧ organelles ⑧ cells ⑧ tissues ⑧ organs ⑧ organ systems ⑧ organism

Skill 8.2 Analyze the strategies and adaptations used by organisms to obtain the basic requirements of life.

Members of the five different kingdoms of the classification system of living organisms often differ in their basic life functions. Here we compare and analyze how members of the five kingdoms obtain nutrients, excrete waste, and reproduce.

Bacteria are prokaryotic, single-celled organisms that lack cell nuclei. The different types of bacteria obtain nutrients in a variety of ways. Most bacteria absorb nutrients from the environment through small channels in their cell walls and membranes (chemotrophs) while some perform photosynthesis (phototrophs). Chemoorganotrophs use organic compounds as energy sources while chemolithotrophs can use inorganic chemicals as energy sources. Depending on the type of metabolism and energy source, bacteria release a variety of waste products (e.g. alcohols, acids, carbon dioxide) to the environment through diffusion.

All bacteria reproduce through binary fission (asexual reproduction) producing two identical cells. Bacteria reproduce very rapidly, dividing or doubling every twenty minutes in optimal conditions. Asexual reproduction does not allow for genetic variation, but bacteria achieve genetic variety by absorbing DNA from ruptured cells and conjugating or swapping chromosomal or plasmid DNA with other cells.

Animals are multicellular, eukaryotic organisms. All animals obtain nutrients by eating food (ingestion). Different types of animals derive nutrients from eating plants, other animals, or both. Animal cells perform respiration that converts food molecules, mainly carbohydrates and fats, into energy. The excretory systems of animals, like animals themselves, vary in complexity. Simple invertebrates eliminate waste through a single tube, while complex vertebrates have a specialized system of organs that process and excrete waste.

Most animals, unlike bacteria, exist in two distinct sexes. Members of the female sex give birth or lay eggs. Some less developed animals can reproduce asexually. For example, flatworms can divide in two and some unfertilized insect eggs can develop into viable organisms. Most animals reproduce sexually through various mechanisms. For example, aquatic animals reproduce by external fertilization of eggs, while mammals reproduce by internal fertilization. More developed animals possess specialized reproductive systems and cycles that facilitate reproduction and promote genetic variation.

Plants, like animals, are multi-cellular, eukaryotic organisms. Plants obtain nutrients from the soil through their root systems and convert sunlight into energy through photosynthesis. Many plants store waste products in vacuoles or organs (e.g. leaves, bark) that are discarded. Some plants also excrete waste through their roots.

More than half of the plant species reproduce by producing seeds from which new plants grow. Depending on the type of plant, flowers or cones produce seeds. Other plants reproduce by spores, tubers, bulbs, buds, and grafts. The flowers of flowering plants contain the reproductive organs. Pollination is the joining of male and female gametes that is often facilitated by movement by wind or animals.

Fungi are eukaryotic, mostly multi-cellular organisms. All fungi are heterotrophs, obtaining nutrients from other organisms. More specifically, most fungi obtain nutrients by digesting and absorbing nutrients from dead organisms. Fungi secrete enzymes outside of their body to digest organic material and then absorb the nutrients through their cell walls.

Most fungi can reproduce asexually and sexually. Different types of fungi reproduce asexually by mitosis, budding, sporification, or fragmentation. Sexual reproduction of fungi is different from sexual reproduction of animals. The two mating types of fungi are plus and minus, not male and female. The fusion of hyphae, the specialized reproductive structure in fungi, between plus and minus types produces and scatters diverse spores.

Protists are eukaryotic, single-celled organisms. Most protists are heterotrophic, obtaining nutrients by ingesting small molecules and cells and digesting them in vacuoles. All protists reproduce asexually by either binary or multiple fission. Like bacteria, protists achieve genetic variation by exchange of DNA through conjugation.

Skill 8.3 Analyze factors (e.g., physiological, behavioral) that influence homeostasis within an organism.

Animal behavior is responsible for courtship leading to mating, communication between species, territoriality, and aggression between animals and dominance within a group. Behaviors may include body posture, mating calls, display of feathers or fur, coloration or bearing of teeth and claws.

Innate behaviors are inborn or instinctual. An environmental stimulus such as the length of day or temperature results in a behavior. Hibernation among some animals is an innate behavior, as is a change in color known as camouflage.

Learned behavior is modified behavior due to past experience.

Skill 8.4 Demonstrate an understanding of the human as a living organism with life functions comparable to those of other life forms.

Humans are living organisms that display the basic properties of life. Humans share functional characteristics with all living organisms, from simple bacteria to complex mammals. The basic functions of living organisms include reproduction, growth and development, metabolism, and homeostasis/response to the environment.

Reproduction – All living organisms reproduce their own kind. Life arises only from other life. Humans reproduce through sexual reproduction, requiring the interaction of a male and a female. Human sexual reproduction is nearly identical to reproduction in other mammals. In addition, while simpler organisms have different methods of reproduction, they all reproduce. For example, the major mechanism of bacterial reproduction is asexual binary fission in which the cell divides in half, producing two identical cells.

Growth and Development – Growth and development, as directed by DNA, produces an organism characteristic of its species. In humans and other higher-level mammals, growth and development is a very complex process. In humans, growth and development requires differentiation of cells into many different types to form the various organs, structures, and functional elements. While differentiation is unique to higher level organisms, all living organisms grow. For example, the simplest bacterial cell grows in size until it divides into two organisms. Human body cells undergo a similar process, growing in size until division is necessary.

Metabolism – Metabolism is the sum of all chemical reactions that occur in a living organism. Catabolism is the breaking down of complex molecules to release energy. Anabolism is the utilization of the energy from catabolism to build complex molecules. Cellular respiration, the basic mechanism of catabolism in humans, is common to many living organisms of varying levels of complexity.

Homeostasis/Response to the Environment – All living organisms respond and adapt to their environments. Homeostasis is the result of regulatory mechanisms that help maintain an organism's internal environment within tolerable limits. For example, in humans and mammals, constriction and dilation of blood vessels near the skin help maintain body temperature.

COMPETENCY 9.0 UNDERSTAND AND APPLY KNOWLEDGE OF HOW ORGANISMS INTERACT WITH EACH OTHER AND WITH THEIR ENVIRONMENT.

Skill 9.1 Identify living and nonliving components of the environment and how they interact with one another.

Succession is an orderly process of replacing a community that has been damaged or has begun where no life previously existed. Primary succession occurs where life never existed before, as in a flooded area or a new volcanic island. Secondary succession takes place in communities that were once flourishing but disturbed by some source, either man or nature, but not totally stripped. A climax community is a community that is established and flourishing.

Abiotic and biotic factors play a role in succession. **Biotic factors** are living things in an ecosystem: plants, animals, bacteria, fungi, etc. **Abiotic factors** are non-living aspects of an ecosystem: soil quality, rainfall, temperature, etc.

Abiotic factors affect succession by way of the species that colonize the area. Certain species will or will not survive depending on the weather, climate, or soil makeup. Biotic factors such as inhibition of one species due to another may occur. This may be due to some form of competition between the species.

Skill 9.2 Recognize the concepts of populations, communities, ecosystems, and ecoregions and the role of biodiversity in living systems.

A **population** is a group of individuals of one species that live in the same general area. Many factors can affect the population size and its growth rate. Population size can depend on the total amount of life a habitat can support. This is the carrying capacity of the environment. Once the habitat runs out of food, water, shelter, or space, the carrying capacity decreases, and then stabilizes.

Skill 9.3 Analyze factors (e.g., ecological, behavioral) that influence interrelationships among organisms.

Ecological and behavioral factors affect the interrelationships among organisms in many ways. Two important ecological factors are environmental conditions and resource availability. Important types of organismal behaviors include competitive, instinctive, territorial, and mating.

Environmental conditions, such as climate, influence organismal interrelationships by changing the dynamic of the ecosystem. Changes in climate such as moisture levels and temperature can alter the environment, changing the characteristics that are advantageous. For example, an increase in temperature will favor those organisms that can tolerate the temperature change. Thus, those organisms gain a competitive advantage. In addition, the availability of necessary resources influences interrelationships. For example, when necessary resources are scarce, interrelationships are more competitive than when resources are abundant.

Types of behavior that influence interrelationships:

Competitive – As previously mentioned, organisms compete for scarce resources. In addition, organisms compete with members of their own species for mates and territory. Many competitive behaviors involve rituals and dominance hierarchies. Rituals are symbolic activities that often settle disputes without undue harm. For example, dogs bare their teeth, erect their ears, and growl to intimidate competitors. A dominance hierarchy, or "pecking order", organizes groups of animals, simplifying interrelationships, conserving energy, and minimizing the potential for harm in a community.

Instinctive – Instinctive, or innate, behavior is common to all members of a given species and is genetically preprogrammed. Environmental differences do not affect instinctive behaviors. For example, baby birds of many types and species beg for food by raising their heads and opening their beaks.

Territorial – Many animals act aggressively to protect their territory from other animals. Animals protect territories for use in feeding, mating, and rearing of young.

Mating – Mating behaviors are very important interspecies interactions. The search for a mate with which to reproduce is an instinctive behavior. Mating interrelationships often involve ritualistic and territorial behaviors that are often competitive.

Skill 9.4   Develop a model or explanation that shows the relationships among organisms in the environment (e.g., food web, food chain, ecological pyramid).

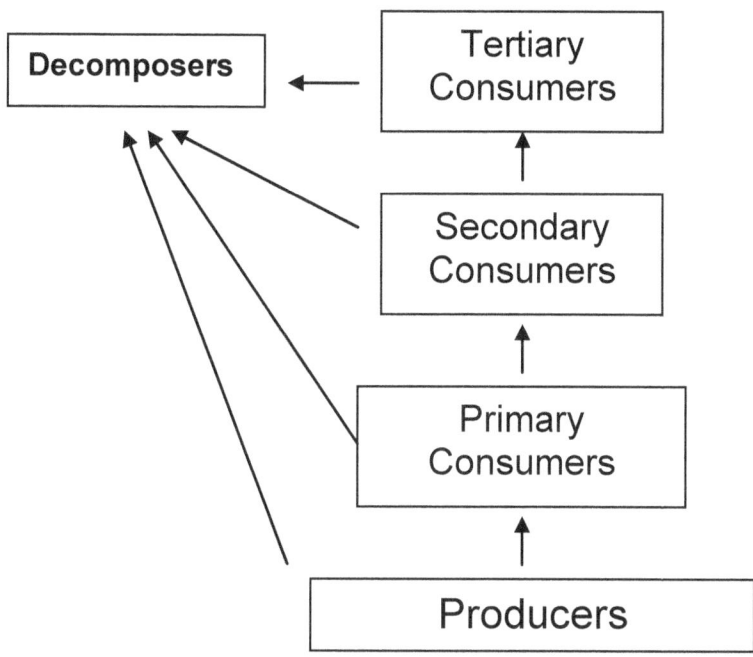

Skill 9.5   Recognize the dynamic nature of the environment, including how communities, ecosystems, and ecoregions change over time.

The environment is ever changing because of natural events and the actions of humans, animals, plants, and other organisms. Even the slightest changes in environmental conditions can greatly influence the function and balance of communities, ecosystems, and ecoregions. For example, subtle changes in salinity and temperature of ocean waters over time can greatly influence the range and population of certain species of fish. In addition, a slight increase in average atmospheric temperature can promote tree growth in a forest, but a corresponding increase in the viability of pathogenic bacteria can decrease the overall growth and productivity of the forest.

Another important concept in ecological change is succession. Ecological succession is the transition in the composition of species in an ecosystem, often after an ecological disturbance in the community. Primary succession begins in an environment virtually void of life, such as a volcanic island. Secondary succession occurs when a natural event disrupts an ecosystem, leaving the soil intact. An example of secondary succession is the reestablishment of a forest after destruction by a forest fire.

SCIENCE: CHEMISTRY

Factors that drive the process of succession include interspecies competition, environmental conditions, inhibition, and facilitation. In a developing ecosystem, species compete for scarce resources. The species that compete most successfully dominate. Environmental conditions, as previously discussed, influence species viability. Finally, the activities of certain species can inhibit or facilitate the growth and development of other species. Inhibition results from exploitative competition or interference competition. In facilitation, a species or group of species lays the foundation for the establishment of other, more advanced species. For example, the presence of a certain bacterial population can change the pH of the soil, allowing for the growth of different types of plants and trees.

Skill 9.6 Analyze interactions of humans with their environment.

The human population has been growing exponentially for centuries. People are living longer and healthier lives than ever before. Better health care and nutrition practices have helped in the survival of the population.

Human activity affects parts of the nutrient cycles by removing nutrients from one part of the biosphere and adding them to another. This results in nutrient depletion in one area and nutrient excess in another. This affects water systems, crops, wildlife, and humans.

Humans are responsible for the depletion of the ozone layer. This depletion is due to chemicals used for refrigeration and aerosols. The consequences of ozone depletion will be severe. Ozone protects the Earth from the majority of UV radiation. An increase of UV will promote skin cancer and unknown effects on wildlife and plants.

Humans have a tremendous impact on the world's natural resources. The world's natural water supplies are affected by human use. Waterways are major sources for recreation and freight transportation. Oil and wastes from boats and cargo ships pollute the aquatic environment. The aquatic plant and animal life is affected by this contamination.

Deforestation for urban development has resulted in the extinction or relocation of several species of plants and animals. Animals are forced to leave their forest homes or perish amongst the destruction. The number of plant and animal species that have become extinct due to deforestation is unknown. Scientists have only identified a fraction of the species on Earth. It is known that if the destruction of natural resources continues, there may be no plants or animals successfully reproducing in the wild.

Humans are continuously searching for new places to form communities. This encroachment on the environment leads to the destruction of wildlife communities. Conservationists focus on endangered species, but the primary focus should be on protecting the entire biome. If a biome becomes extinct, the wildlife dies or invades another biome.

Preservations established by the government aim at protecting small parts of biomes. While beneficial in the conservation of a few areas, the majority of the environment is still unprotected.

Skill 9.7 **Explain the functions and applications of the instruments and technologies used to study the life sciences at the organism and ecosystem level.**

Biologists use a variety of tools and technologies to perform tests, collect and display data, and analyze relationships at the organismal and ecosystem level. Examples of commonly used tools include computer-linked probes, computerized tracking devices, computer models and databases, and spreadsheets.

Biologists use computer-linked probes to measure various environmental factors including temperature, dissolved oxygen, pH, ionic concentration, and pressure. The advantage of computer-linked probes, as compared to more traditional observational tools, is that the probes automatically gather data and present it in an accessible format. This property of computer-linked probes eliminates the need for constant human observation and manipulation.

Biologists use computerized tracking devices to study the behavior of animals in an ecosystem. Biologists can implant computer chips on animals to track movement and migration, population changes, and general behavioral characteristics.

Computer models allow biologists to use data and information they collect in the field to make predictions and projections about the future of ecosystems and organisms. Because ecosystems are large and change very slowly, direct observation is not a suitable strategy for ecological studies. For example, while a scientist cannot reasonably expect to observe and gather data over an entire ecosystem, she can collect samples and use computer databases and models to make projections about the ecosystem as a whole.

Finally, biologists use spreadsheets to organize, analyze, and display data. For example, conservation ecologists use spreadsheets to model population growth and development, apply sampling techniques, and create statistical distributions to analyze relationships. Spreadsheet use simplifies data collection and manipulation and allows the presentation of data in a logical and understandable format.

TEACHER CERTIFICATION STUDY GUIDE

SUBAREA III.   **PHYSICAL SCIENCE**

COMPETENCY 10.0 UNDERSTAND AND APPLY KNOWLEDGE OF THE NATURE AND PROPERTIES OF ENERGY IN ITS VARIOUS FORMS.

"Energy is an abstract concept invented by physical scientists in the nineteenth century to describe quantitatively a wide variety of natural phenomena."
                                                                 David Rose, MIT

Skill 10.1   **Describe the characteristics of and relationships among thermal, acoustical, radiant, electrical, chemical, mechanical, and nuclear energies through conceptual questions.**

Abstract concept it might be, but energy is one of the most fundamental concepts in our world. We use it to move people and things from place to place, to heat and light our homes, to entertain us, to produce food and goods and to communicate with each other. It is not some sort of magical invisible fluid, poured, weighed or bottled. It is not a substance but rather the ability possessed by things.

Technically, **energy is the ability to do work or supply heat.** Work is the transfer of energy to move an object a certain distance. It is the motion against an opposing force. Lifting a chair into the air is work; the opposing force is gravity. Pushing a chair across the floor is work; the opposing force is friction.

Heat, on the other hand, is not a form of energy but a method of transferring energy.

This energy, according to the First Law of Thermodynamics, is conserved. That means energy is neither created nor destroyed in ordinary physical and chemical processes (non-nuclear). Energy is merely changed from one form to another. Energy in all of its forms must be conserved. In any system, $\Delta E = q + w$ (E = energy, q = heat and w = work).

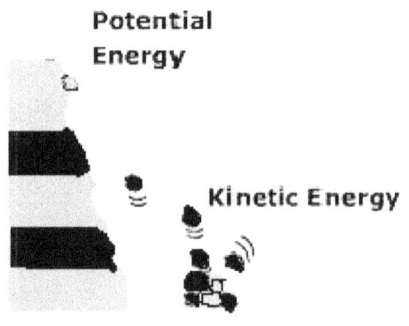

Potential Energy

Kinetic Energy

Energy exists in two basic forms, potential and kinetic. Kinetic energy is the energy of a moving object. Potential energy is the energy stored in matter due to position relative to other objects.

In any object, solid, liquid or gas, the atoms and molecules that make up the object are constantly moving (vibrational, translation and rotational motion) and colliding with each other. They are not stationary.

SCIENCE: CHEMISTRY   68

Due to this motion, the object's particles have varying amounts of kinetic energy. A fast moving atom can push a slower moving atom during a collision, so it has energy. All moving objects have energy and that energy depends on the object's mass and velocity. Kinetic energy is calculated: $K.E. = \frac{1}{2} mv^2$.

The temperature exhibited by an object is proportional to the average kinetic energy of the particles in the substance. Increase the temperature of a substance and its particles move faster so their average kinetic energies increase as well. But temperature is NOT an energy, it is not conserved.

The energy an object has due to its position or arrangement of its parts is called potential energy. Potential energy due to position is equal to the mass of the object times the gravitational pull on the object times the height of the object, or:

PE = mgh

Where PE = potential energy; m = mass of object; g = gravity; and h = height.

Heat is energy that is transferred between objects caused by differences in their temperatures. Heat passes spontaneously from an object of higher temperature to one of lower temperature. This transfer continues until both objects reach the same temperature. Both kinetic energy and potential energy can be transformed into heat energy. When you step on the brakes in your car, the kinetic energy of the car is changed to heat energy by friction between the brake and the wheels. Other transformations can occur from kinetic to potential as well. Since most of the energy in our world is in a form that is not easily used, man and mother nature has developed some clever ways of changing one form of energy into another form that may be more useful.

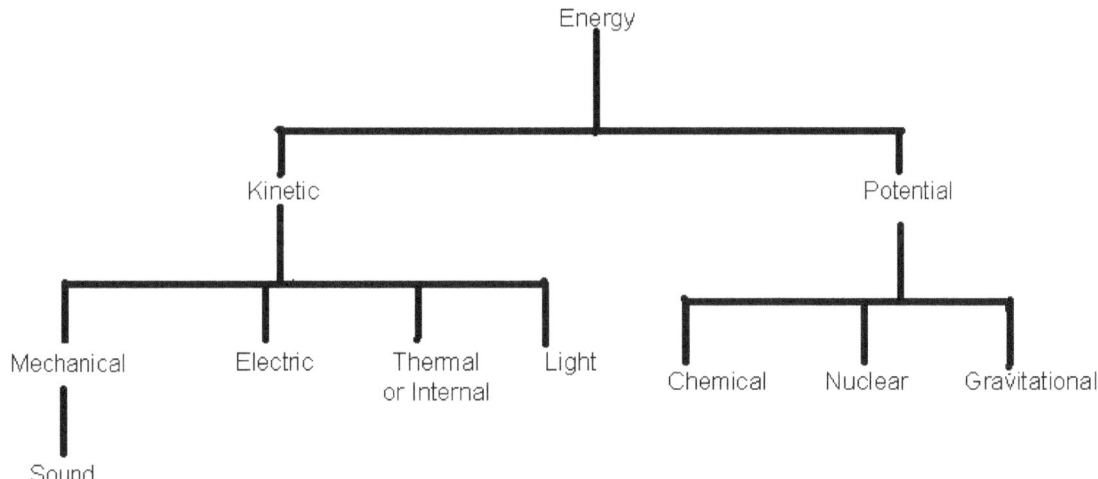

Gravitational Potential Energy:

When something is lifted or suspended in air, work is done on the object against the pull of gravity. This work is converted to a form of potential energy called gravitational potential energy.

Nuclear Potential Energy:

The nuclear energy trapped inside the atom is referred to as nuclear energy. When the atom is split, tremendous energy is released in the form of heat and light.

Chemical Potential Energy:

The energy generated from chemical reactions in which the chemical bonds of a substance are broken and rearranged to form new substances is called chemical potential energy.

Electrical Kinetic energy:

The flow of electrons along a circuit is called electrical energy. The movement of electrons creates an electric current which generates electricity

Mechanical Kinetic Energy:

Mechanical energy is the energy of motion doing work, like a pendulum moving back and forth in a grandfather clock.

Thermal Kinetic Energy:

Thermal Energy is defined as the energy that a substance has due to the chaotic motion of its molecules. Molecules are in constant motion, and always possess some amount of kinetic energy. It is also called Internal energy and is not the same as heat.

Light or Radiant Kinetic Energy:

Radiant energy comes from a light source, such as the sun. Energy released from the sun is in the form of photons. These tiny particles, invisible to the human eye, move in a way similar to a wave.

Energy transformations make it possible for us to use energy; do work. Here are some examples of how energy is transformed to do work:

1. Different types of stoves are used to transform the chemical energy of the fuel (gas, coal, wood, etc.) into heat.

2. Solar collectors can be used to transform solar energy into electrical energy.

3. Wind mills make use of the kinetic energy of the air molecules, transforming it into mechanical or electrical energy.

4. Hydroelectric plants transform the kinetic energy of falling water into electrical energy.

5. A flashlight converts chemical energy stored in batteries to light energy and heat. Most of the energy is converted to heat, only a small amount is actually changed into light energy.

Skill 10.2   Analyze the processes by which energy is exchanged or transformed through conceptual questions.

All energy transformations can be traced back to the sun -- the original source of energy for life on earth. The sun produces heat, light, and radiation through the process of fusion. The sun converts hydrogen to helium in a three-step process.

1. Two hydrogen atoms combine. This forms deuterium, also called heavy hydrogen.
2. Deuterium joins with another hydrogen atom. This forms a type of helium (helium-3).
3. Two helium-3 atoms collide, producing ordinary helium and two hydrogen atoms

Energy is released at every step. The energy comes in the form of tremendous heat, radiation that can kill us, and light that we need to survive. This energy forms in the core of the sun moves through several other layers to the photosphere and is emitted as light.

Once on earth, radiant energy (light) is transformed to the mechanical energy of wind and waves found in nature, through photosynthesis to the stored energy in plants, accumulated as chemical energy in deposits of coal, oil and gas.

Man uses mechanical, thermal and radiant energy to provide for his needs. Mechanical energy operates machines, thermal energy cooks food and heats homes while radiant energy provides light.

Plants capture the sunlight and through photosynthesis change it into chemical energy stored in carbohydrate (sugar) molecules in plant cells. The chlorophyll molecule found in plants captures light energy and uses it to build these carbohydrate molecules from the raw materials water, carbon dioxide and some minerals.

$$CO_2 (g) + H_2O (g) + chlorophyll + sunlight \rightarrow Oxygen (g) + sugar.$$

This process produces oxygen and glucose, $C_6H_{12}O_6$. The sugar (glucose) is stored in the plant.

A person eats the plant. The chemical energy stored in the plant is transferred to the person. Body processes like digestion, circulation and respiration are fueled by cells converting stored chemical energy into work and heat.

Inside muscle cells, the chemical energy is converted to mechanical energy and heat. The muscle twitches and the body jumps to life. Stored chemical energy has been converted into kinetic energy. Energy not used immediately by the cells is stored as potential energy in fat cells.

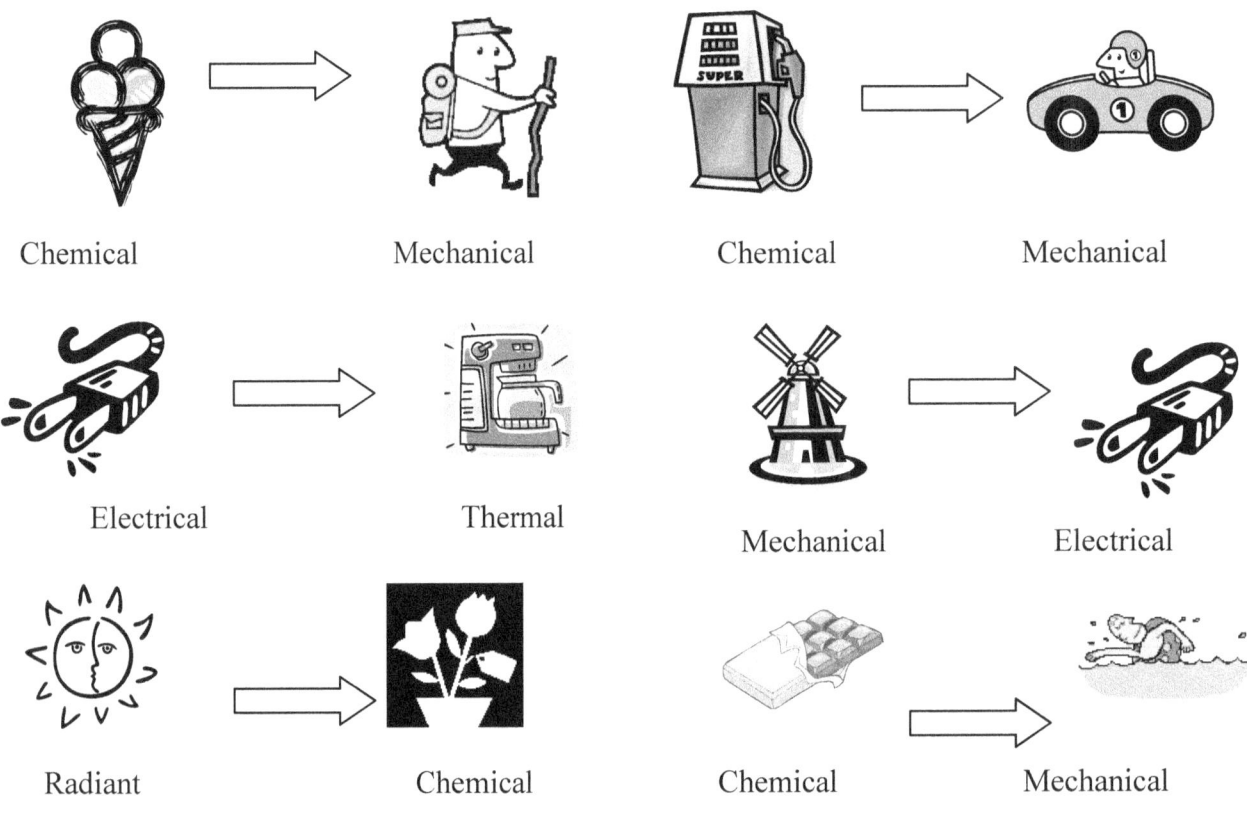

Skill 10.3 Apply the three laws of thermodynamics to explain energy transformations, including basic algebraic problem solving

The three laws of thermodynamics are as follows:

1. The total amount of energy in the universe is constant, energy cannot be created or destroyed, but can merely change form.

> Equation:
> $\Delta E = Q + W$
> Change in energy = (Heat energy entering or leaving) + (work done)

2. In energy transformations, entropy (disorder) increases and useful energy is lost (as heat).

> Equation:
> $\Delta S = \Delta Q/T$
> Change in entropy = (Heat transfer) / (Temperature)

3. As the temperature of a system approaches absolute zero, entropy (disorder) approaches a constant.

Sample Problems:
1. A car engine burns gasoline to power the car. An amount of gasoline containing 2000J of stored chemical energy produced 1500J of mechanical energy to power the engine. How much heat energy did the engine release?

Solution:
$\Delta E = Q + W$	the first law of thermodynamics
00J = Q + 1500J	apply the first law
Q (work) = 500J	

2. 18200J of heat leaks out of a hot oven. The temperature of the room is 25°C (298K). What is the increase in entropy resulting from this heat transfer?

Solution:
$\Delta S = \Delta Q/T$	the second law of thermodynamics
ΔS = 18200J / 298K	apply the second law
= 61.1 J/K	solve

Skill 10.4   Apply the principle of conservation as it applies to energy through conceptual questions and solving basic algebraic problems.

The law of conservation of energy states that energy is neither created nor destroyed. Thus, energy changes form when energy transactions occur in nature. Because the total energy in the universe is constant, energy continually transitions between forms. For example, an engine burns gasoline converting the chemical energy of the gasoline into mechanical energy, a plant converts radiant energy of the sun into chemical energy found in glucose, or a battery converts chemical energy into electrical energy.

COMPETENCY 11.0 UNDERSTAND AND APPLY KNOWLEDGE OF THE STRUCTURE AND PROPERTIES OF MATTER.

Skill 11.1 Describe the nuclear and atomic structure of matter, including the three basic parts of the atom.

Experimental evidence shows that the atom is mostly empty space. This empty space is called the electron cloud and it gives the atom its size. In the middle of the electron cloud is the nucleus that contains protons and neutrons. The nucleus gives the atom most of its mass. A proton has a mass of 1 atomic mass unit (amu) and a charge of +1 while a neutron has a similar mass, 1 amu, but no charge. An electron has a very small mass but compared to a proton or neutron it is negligible so it is considered to have no mass. It does, however, have a -1 charge.

Atoms of the same element always have the same number of protons, called the atomic number. However, elements can have isotopes. Isotopes are atoms of the same element but have differing numbers of neutrons have hence, differing atomic masses.

Isotopes are indicated using this symbol:

$^{1}_{1}H$ or $^{2}_{1}H$ or $^{3}_{1}H$ for example.

Skill 11.2 Analyze the properties of materials in relation to their chemical or physical structures (e.g., periodic table trends, relationships, and properties) and evaluate uses of the materials based on their properties.

The **periodic table of elements** is an arrangement of the elements in rows and columns so that it is easy to locate elements with similar properties. The elements of the modern periodic table are arranged in numerical order by atomic number.

The **periods** are the rows down the left side of the table. They are called first period, second period, etc. The columns of the periodic table are called **groups**, or **families.** Elements in a family have similar properties.

There are three types of elements that are grouped by color: metals, nonmetals, and metalloids.

Element Key
Atomic
Number

↓

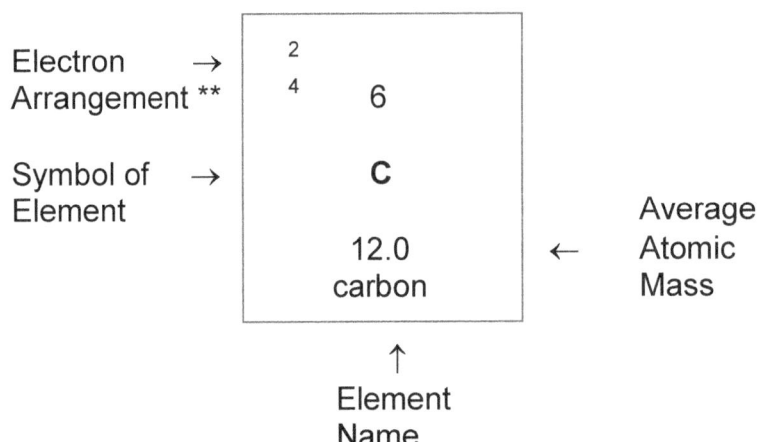

** Number of electrons on each level. Top number represents the innermost level.

The periodic table arranges metals into families with similar properties. The periodic table has its columns marked IA - VIIIA. These are the traditional group numbers. Arabic numbers 1 - 18 are also used, as suggested by the Union of Physicists and Chemists. The Arabic numerals will be used in this text.

Metals:

With the exception of hydrogen, all elements in Group 1 are **alkali metals**. These metals are shiny, softer, and less dense, and the most chemically active.

Group 2 metals are the **alkaline earth metals.** They are harder, denser, have higher melting points, and are chemically active.

The **transition elements** can be found by finding the periods (rows) from 4 to 7 under the groups (columns) 3 - 12. They are metals that do not show a range of properties as you move across the chart. They are hard and have high melting points. Compounds of these elements are colorful, such as silver, gold, and mercury.

Elements can be combined to make metallic objects. An **alloy** is a mixture of two or more elements having properties of metals. The elements do not have to be all metals. For instance, steel is made up of the metal iron and the non-metal carbon.

Nonmetals:

Nonmetals are not as easy to recognize as metals because they do not always share physical properties. However, in general the properties of nonmetals are the opposite of metals. They are not shiny, are brittle, and are not good conductors of heat and electricity.

Nonmetals are solids, gases, and one liquid (bromine).

Nonmetals have four to eight electrons in their outermost energy levels and tend to attract electrons to their outer energy levels. As a result, the outer levels usually are filled with eight electrons. This difference in the number of electrons is what caused the differences between metals and nonmetals. The outstanding chemical property of nonmetals is that react with metals.

The **halogens** can be found in Group 17. Halogens combine readily with metals to form salts. Table salt, fluoride toothpaste, and bleach all have an element from the halogen family.

The **Noble Gases** got their name from the fact that they did not react chemically with other elements, much like the nobility did not mix with the masses. These gases (found in Group 18) will only combine with other elements under very specific conditions. They are **inert** (inactive).

In recent years, scientists have found this to be only generally true, since chemists have been able to prepare compounds of krypton and xenon.

Metalloids:

Metalloids have properties in between metals and nonmetals. They can be found in Groups 13 - 16, but do not occupy the entire group. They are arranged in stair steps across the groups.

Physical Properties:
1. All are solids having the appearance of metals.
2. All are white or gray, but not shiny.
3. They will conduct electricity, but not as well as a metal.

Chemical Properties:
1. Have some characteristics of metals and nonmetals.
2. Properties do not follow patterns like metals and nonmetals. Each must be studied individually.

Boron is the first element in Group 13. It is a poor conductor of electricity at low temperatures. However, increase its temperature and it becomes a good conductor. By comparison, metals, which are good conductors, lose their ability as they are heated. It is because of this property that boron is so useful. Boron is a semiconductor. **Semiconductors** are used in electrical devices that have to function at temperatures too high for metals.

Silicon is the second element in Group 14. It is also a semiconductor and is found in great abundance in the earth's crust. Sand is made of a silicon compound, silicon dioxide. Silicon is also used in the manufacture of glass and cement.

Skill 11.3 Apply the principle of conservation as it applies to mass and charge through conceptual questions.

The principle of conservation states that certain measurable properties of an isolated system remain constant despite changes in the system. Two important principles of conservation are the conservation of mass and charge.

The principle of conservation of mass states that the total mass of a system is constant. Examples of conservation in mass in nature include the burning of wood, rusting of iron, and phase changes of matter. When wood burns, the total mass of the products, such as soot, ash, and gases, equals the mass of the wood and the oxygen that reacts with it. When iron reacts with oxygen, rust forms. The total mass of the iron-rust complex does not change. Finally, when matter changes phase, mass remains constant. Thus, when a glacier melts due to atmospheric warming, the mass of liquid water formed is equal to the mass of the glacier.

The principle of conservation of charge states that the total electrical charge of a closed system is constant. Thus, in chemical reactions and interactions of charged objects, the total charge does not change. Chemical reactions and the interaction of charged molecules are essential and common processes in living organisms and systems.

Skill 11.4 Analyze bonding and chemical, atomic, and nuclear reactions (including endothermic and exothermic reactions) in natural and man-made systems and apply basic stoichiometric principles.

Chemical reactions are the interactions of substances resulting in chemical change and change in energy. Chemical reactions involve changes in electron motion and the breaking and forming of chemical bonds. Reactants are the original substances that interact to form distinct products. Endothermic chemical reactions consume energy while exothermic chemical reactions release energy with product formation. Chemical reactions occur continually in nature and are also induced by man for many purposes.

Nuclear reactions, or **atomic reactions**, are reactions that change the composition, energy, or structure of atomic nuclei. Nuclear reactions change the number of protons and neutrons in the nucleus. The two main types of nuclear reactions are fission (splitting of nuclei) and fusion (joining of nuclei). Fusion reactions are exothermic, releasing heat energy. Fission reactions are endothermic, absorbing heat energy. Fission of large nuclei (e.g. uranium) releases energy because the products of fission undergo further fusion reactions. Fission and fusion reactions can occur naturally, but are most recognized as man-made events. Particle acceleration and bombardment with neutrons are two methods of inducing nuclear reactions.

Stoichiometry is the calculation of quantitative relationships between reactants and products in chemical reactions. Scientists use stoichiometry to balance chemical equations, make conversions between units of measurement (e.g. grams to moles), and determine the correct amount of reactants to use in chemical reactions.

Example:

The reaction of iron (Fe) and hydrochloric acid (HCl) produces H_2 and $FeCl_2$. Determine the amount of HCl required to react with 200g of Fe.

$Fe + HCl = H_2 + FeCl_2$

$Fe + 2HCl = H_2 + FeCl_2$ Balance equation (equal number of atoms on each side)

$$\frac{200 g\ Fe}{1} \cdot \frac{1\ mol\ Fe}{55.8 g\ Fe} \cdot \frac{2\ mol\ HCl}{1\ mol\ Fe} \cdot \frac{36.5 g\ HCl}{1\ mol\ HCl}$$

Perform stoichiometric calculations

= 262 g of HCl required to react completely with 200 g Fe   Solve

Skill 11.5 Apply kinetic theory to explain interactions of energy with matter, including conceptual questions on changes in state.

The kinetic theory states that matter consists of molecules, possessing kinetic energies, in continual random motion. The state of matter (solid, liquid, or gas) depends on the speed of the molecules and the amount of kinetic energy the molecules possess. The molecules of solid matter merely vibrate allowing strong intermolecular forces to hold the molecules in place. The molecules of liquid matter move freely and quickly throughout the body and the molecules of gaseous matter move randomly and at high speeds.

Matter changes state when energy is added or taken away. The addition of energy, usually in the form of heat, increases the speed and kinetic energy of the component molecules. Faster moving molecules more readily overcome the intermolecular attractions that maintain the form of solids and liquids. In conclusion, as the speed of molecules increases, matter changes state from solid to liquid to gas (melting and evaporation).

As matter loses heat energy to the environment, the speed of the component molecules decrease. Intermolecular forces have greater impact on slower moving molecules. Thus, as the speed of molecules decrease, matter changes from gas to liquid to solid (condensation and freezing).

Skill 11.6 Explain the functions and applications of the instruments and technologies used to study matter and energy.

Scientists utilize various instruments and technologies to study matter and energy. Commonly used instruments include spectrometers, basic measuring devices, thermometers, and calorimeters.

Spectroscopy is the study of absorption and emission of energy of different frequencies by molecules and atoms. The spectrometer is the instrument used in spectroscopy. Because different molecules and atoms have different spectroscopic properties, spectroscopy helps scientists determine the molecular composition of matter.

Basic devices, like scales and rulers, measure the physical properties of matter. Scientists often measure the size, volume, and mass of different forms of matter.

Thermometers and calorimeters measure the energy exchanged in chemical reactions. Temperature change during chemical reactions is indicative of the flow of energy into or out of a system of reactants and products.

COMPETENCY 12.0   UNDERSTAND AND APPLY
KNOWLEDGE OF   FORCES AND MOTION.

Skill 12.1   **Demonstrate an understanding of the concepts and interrelationships of position, time, velocity, and acceleration through conceptual questions, algebra-based kinematics, and graphical analysis.**

Position is relative. Your position in the center of the room is relative to the size of the room. A car's position on a track is relative to the determination of the track's start and end points. The velocity of an object can be defined as its speed in a particular direction. Both speed and direction are required to velocity. The symbol for velocity is v. It is the measurement of the rate of change of displacement from a fixed point. Acceleration (symbol: a) is defined as the rate of change (with respect to time) of velocity. Acceleration is measured in units of length/time², usually meters/second^2. To accelerate an object is to change its velocity, which is accomplished by altering either its speed or direction with respect to time. Acceleration has to do with changing how fast an object is moving. If an object is not changing its velocity, then the object is not accelerating. If an object is moving northward at a velocity of 10 m/s at 1 sec, and 20 m/s one second later (t= 2 sec), it is accelerating.

Skill 12.2   **Demonstrate an understanding of the concepts and interrelationships of force (including gravity and friction), inertia, work, power, energy, and momentum.**

Entropy is the measure of how much energy or heat is available for work. Work occurs only when heat is transferred from hot to cooler objects. Once this is done, no more work can be extracted. The energy is still being conserved, but is not available for work as long as the objects are the same temperature. Theory has it that, eventually, all things in the universe will reach the same temperature. If this happens, energy will no longer be usable.

Dynamics is the study of the relationship between motion and the forces affecting motion. **Force** causes motion. Mass and weight are not the same quantities. An object's **mass** gives it a reluctance to change its current state of motion. It is also the measure of an object's resistance to acceleration. The force that the earth's gravity exerts on an object with a specific mass is called the object's weight on earth. Weight is a force that is measured in Newtons. Weight (W) = mass times acceleration due to gravity (**W = mg**). To illustrate the difference between mass and weight, picture two rocks of equal mass on a balance scale. If the scale is balanced in one place, it will be balanced everywhere, regardless of the gravitational field. However, the weight of the stones would vary on a spring scale, depending upon the gravitational field. In other words, the stones would be balanced both on earth and on the moon. However, the weight of the stones would be greater on earth than on the moon.

SCIENCE: CHEMISTRY

Newton's laws of motion:

Newton's first law of motion is also called the law of inertia. It states that an object at rest will remain at rest and an object in motion will remain in motion at a constant velocity unless acted upon by an external force.

Newton's second law of motion states that if a net force acts on an object, it will cause the acceleration of the object. The relationship between force and motion is Force equals mass times acceleration. **(F = ma).**

Newton's third law states that for every action there is an equal and opposite reaction. Therefore, if an object exerts a force on another object, that second object exerts an equal and opposite force on the first.

Surfaces that touch each other have a certain resistance to motion. This resistance is **friction.**
1. The materials that make up the surfaces will determine the magnitude of the frictional force.
2. The frictional force is independent of the area of contact between the two surfaces.
3. The direction of the frictional force is opposite to the direction of motion.
4. The frictional force is proportional to the normal force between the two surfaces in contact.

Static friction describes the force of friction of two surfaces that are in contact but do not have any motion relative to each other, such as a block sitting on an inclined plane. **Kinetic friction** describes the force of friction of two surfaces in contact with each other when there is relative motion between the surfaces.

When an object moves in a circular path, a force must be directed toward the center of the circle in order to keep the motion going. This constraining force is called **centripetal force**. Gravity is the centripetal force that keeps a satellite circling the earth.

Push and pull –Pushing a volleyball or pulling a bowstring applies muscular force when the muscles expand and contract. Elastic force is when any object returns to its original shape (for example, when a bow is released).

Rubbing – Friction opposes the motion of one surface past another. Friction is common when slowing down a car or sledding down a hill.

Pull of gravity – is a force of attraction between two objects. Gravity questions can be raised not only on earth but also between planets and even black hole discussions.

Forces on objects at rest – The formula F= m/a is shorthand for force equals mass over acceleration. An object will not move unless the force is strong enough to move the mass. Also, there can be opposing forces holding the object in place. For instance, a boat may want to be forced by the currents to drift away but an equal and opposite force is a rope holding it to a dock.

Forces on a moving object - Overcoming inertia is the tendency of any object to oppose a change in motion. An object at rest tends to stay at rest. An object that is moving tends to keep moving.

Inertia and circular motion – The centripetal force is provided by the high banking of the curved road and by friction between the wheels and the road. This inward force that keeps an object moving in a circle is called centripetal force.

Simple machines include the following:

1. Inclined plane
2. Lever
3. Wheel and axle
4. Pulley

Compound machines are two or more simple machines working together. A wheelbarrow is an example of a complex machine. It uses a lever and a wheel and axle. Machines of all types ease workload by changing the size or direction of an applied force. The amount of effort saved when using simple or complex machines is called mechanical advantage or MA.

Work is done on an object when an applied force moves through a distance.

Power is the work done divided by the amount of time that it took to do it. (Power = Work / time)

Skill 12.3   Describe and predict the motions of bodies in one and two dimensions in inertial and accelerated frames of reference in a physical system, including projectile motion but excluding circular motion.

The science of describing the motion of bodies is known as **kinematics**. The motion of bodies is described using words, diagrams, numbers, graphs, and equations.

The following words are used to describe motion: vectors, scalars, distance, displacement, speed, velocity, and acceleration.

The two categories of mathematical quantities that are used to describe the motion of objects are scalars and vectors. **Scalars** are quantities that are fully described by magnitude alone. Examples of scalars are 5m and 20 degrees Celsius. **Vectors** are quantities that are fully described by magnitude and direction. Examples of vectors are 30m/sec, and 5 miles north.

Distance is a scalar quantity that refers to how much ground an object has covered while moving. **Displacement** is a vector quantity that refers to the object's change in position.

Example:

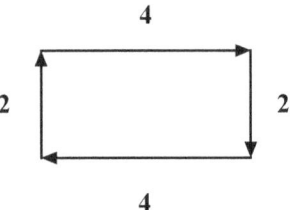

Jamie walked 2 miles north, 4 miles east, 2 miles south, and then 4 miles west. In terms of distance, she walked 12 miles. However, there is no displacement because the directions cancelled each other out, and she returned to her starting position.

Speed is a scalar quantity that refers to how fast an object is moving (ex. the car was traveling 60 mi./hr). **Velocity** is a vector quantity that refers to the rate at which an object changes its position. In other words, velocity is speed with direction (ex. the car was traveling 60 mi./hr east).

$$\text{Average speed} = \frac{\text{Distance traveled}}{\text{Time of travel}}$$

$$v = \frac{d}{t}$$

$$\text{Average velocity} = \frac{\Delta \text{position}}{\text{time}} = \frac{\text{displacement}}{\text{time}}$$

Instantaneous Speed - speed at any given instant in time.

Average Speed - average of all instantaneous speeds, found simply by a distance/time ratio.

Acceleration is a vector quantity defined as the rate at which an object changes its velocity.

$$a = \frac{\Delta velocity}{time} = \frac{v_f - v_i}{t}$$ where *f* represents the final velocity and *i* represents the initial velocity

Since acceleration is a vector quantity, it always has a direction associated with it. The direction of the acceleration vector depends on

- whether the object is speeding up or slowing down
- whether the object is moving in the positive or negative direction.

Newton's Three Laws of Motion:

First Law: An object at rest tends to stay at rest and an object in motion tends to stay in motion with the same speed and in the same direction unless acted upon by an unbalanced force, for example, when riding on a descending elevator that suddenly stops, blood rushes from your head to your feet. **Inertia** is the resistance an object has to a change in its state of motion.

Second Law: The acceleration of an object depends directly upon the net force acting upon the object, and inversely upon the mass of the object. As the net force increases, so will the object's acceleration. However, as the mass of the object increases, its acceleration will decrease.

$F_{net} = m * a$

Third Law: For every action, there is an equal and opposite reaction, for example, when a bird is flying, the motion of its wings pushes air downward; the air reacts by pushing the bird upward.

Projectile Motion

By definition, a **projectile** only has one force acting upon it – the force of gravity.

Gravity influences the vertical motion of the projectile, causing vertical acceleration. The horizontal motion of the projectile is the result of the tendency of any object in motion to remain in motion at constant velocity. (Remember, there are no horizontal forces acting upon the projectile. By definition, gravity is the only force acting upon the projectile.)

Projectiles travel with a parabolic trajectory due to the fact that the downward force of gravity accelerates them downward from their otherwise straight-line trajectory. Gravity affects the vertical motion, not the horizontal motion, of the projectile. Gravity causes a downward displacement from the position that the object would be in if there were no gravity.

SCIENCE: CHEMISTRY

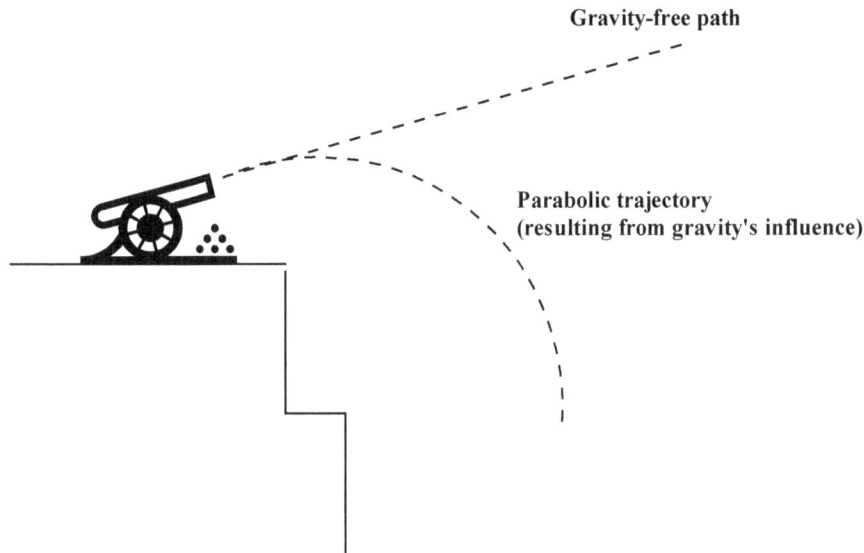

Skill 12.4   Analyze and predict motions and interactions of bodies involving forces within the context of conservation of energy and/or momentum through conceptual questions and algebra-based problem solving.

The Law of **Conservation of Energy** states that energy may neither be created nor destroyed. Therefore, the sum of all energies in the system is a constant.

Example:

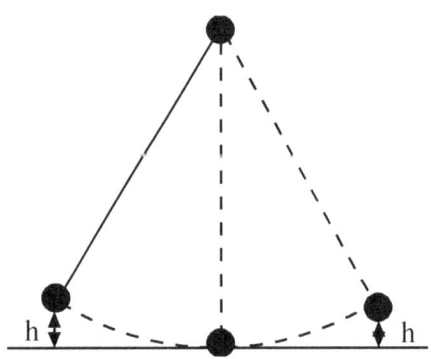

The formula to calculate the potential energy is PE = mgh.

The mass of the ball = 20kg
The height, h = 0.4m
The acceleration due to gravity, g = 9.8 m/s^2

PE = mgh
PE = 20(.4)(9.8)
PE = 78.4J (Joules, units of energy)

The position of the ball on the left is where the Potential Energy (PE) = 78.4J resides while the Kinetic Energy (KE) = 0. As the ball is approaching the center position, the PE is decreasing while the KE is increasing. At exactly halfway between the left and center positions, the PE = KE.

The center position of the ball is where the Kinetic Energy is at its maximum while the Potential Energy (PE) = 0. At this point, theoretically, the entire PE has transformed into KE. Now the KE = 78.4J while the PE = 0.

The right position of the ball is where the Potential Energy (PE) is once again at its maximum and the Kinetic Energy (KE) = 0.

We can now say that:

$$PE + KE = 0$$
$$PE = -KE$$

The sum of PE and KE is the **total mechanical energy:**

$$\text{Total Mechanical Energy} = PE + KE$$

The law of **momentum conservation** can be stated as follows: For a collision occurring between object 1 and object 2 in an isolated system, the total momentum of the two objects before the collision is equal to the total momentum of the two objects after the collision. That is, the momentum lost by object 1 is equal to the momentum gained by object 2.

Example:

A 90 kg soccer player moving west at 4 m/s collides with an 80 kg soccer player moving east at 5 m/s. After the collision, both players move east at 3 m/s. Draw a vector diagram in which the before and after collision momenta of each player is represented by a momentum vector.

BEFORE

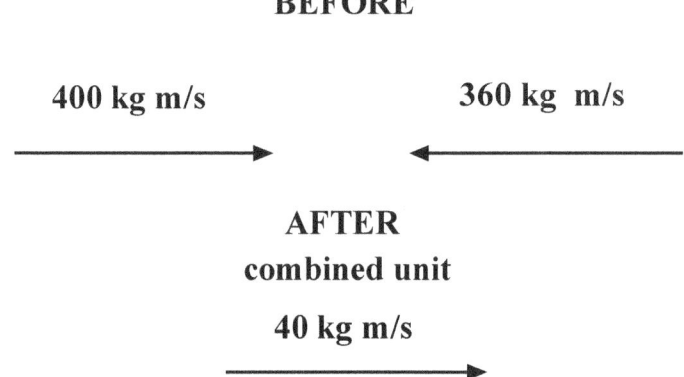

AFTER
combined unit

40 kg m/s

⟶

The combined momentum before the collision is +400 kg m/s + (- 360 kg m/s) or 40 kg m/s. According to the law of conservation of momentum, the combined momentum after a collision must be equal to the combined momentum before the collision.

Skill 12.5   Describe the effects of gravitational and nuclear forces in real-life situations through conceptual questions.

Gravitational and the two nuclear forces make up three of the four fundamental forces of nature, with electromagnetic force being the fourth.

Gravitational force is defined as the force of attraction between all masses in the universe. Every object exerts gravitational force on every other object. This force depends on the masses of the objects and the distance between them. The gravitational force between any two masses is given by Newton's law of universal gravitation, which states that the force is inversely proportional to the square of the distance between the masses. Near the surface of the Earth, the acceleration of an object due to gravity is independent of the mass of the object and therefore constant.

It is the gravitational attraction of the Earth that gives weight to objects with mass and causes them to fall to the ground when dropped. Gravitation is responsible for the existence of the objects in our solar system. Without it, the celestial bodies would not be held together. It keeps the Earth and all the other planets in orbit around the sun, keeps the moon in orbit around the Earth, and causes the formation of the tides.

Examples of mechanisms that utilize gravitation to some degree are intravenous drips and water towers where the height difference provides a pressure differential in the liquid. The gravitational potential energy of water is also used to generate hydroelectricity. Pendulum clocks depend upon gravity to regulate time.

There are two types of nuclear forces: strong and weak. The strong force is an interaction that binds protons and neutrons together in atomic nuclei. The strong force only acts on elementary particles directly, but is observed between hadrons (subatomic particles) as the nuclear force.

The weak force is an interaction between elementary particles involving neutrinos or antineutrinos. Its most familiar effects are beta decay and the associated radioactivity.

Skill 12.6   Explain the functions and applications of the instruments and technologies used to study force and motion in everyday life.

The **speedometer** in a car indicates how fast the car is going at any moment (instantaneous speed).

Tachometers measure the speed of rotation of a shaft or disk. In an automobile, this assists the driver in choosing gear settings with a manual transmission. Tachometers are also used in medicine to measure blood flow.

Gravity gradiometers are used in petroleum exploration to determine areas of higher or lower density in the earth's crust.

An **accelerometer** is a device for measuring acceleration. Accelerometers are used along with gyroscopes in inertial guidance systems for rocket programs. One of the most common uses for accelerometers is in airbag deployment systems in automobiles. The accelerometers are used to detect rapid deceleration of the vehicle to determine when a collision has occurred and the severity of the collision. Research is currently being done on the use of accelerometers to improve Global Positioning Systems (GPS). An accelerometer can infer position in places such as tunnels where the GPS cannot detect it. They are incorporated into Tablet PCs to align the screen based upon the direction in which the PC is being held and in many laptop computers to detect falling and protect the data on the hard drive. Accelerometers are incorporated into sports watches to indicate speed and distance (useful to runners).

A **gravimeter** is a device used to measure the local gravitational field. They are much more sensitive than accelerometers. Measurements of the surface gravity of the earth are part of geophysical analysis, which includes the study of earthquakes.

Weighing scales, such as spring scales, are sometimes used to measure force rather than mass or weight.

TEACHER CERTIFICATION STUDY GUIDE

COMPETENCY 13.0 UNDERSTAND AND APPLY KNOWLEDGE OF ELECTRICITY, MAGNETISM, AND WAVES.

Skill 13.1 Recognize the nature and properties of electricity and magnetism, including static charge, moving charge, basic RC circuits, fields, conductors, and insulators.

An **electric circuit** is a path along which electrons flow. A simple circuit can be created with a dry cell, wire, a bell, or a light bulb. When all are connected, the electrons flow from the negative terminal, through the wire to the device and back to the positive terminal of the dry cell. If there are no breaks in the circuit, the device will work. The circuit is closed. Any break in the flow will create an open circuit and cause the device to shut off.

The device (bell, bulb) is an example of a **load**. A load is a device that uses energy. Suppose that you also add a buzzer so that the bell rings when you press the buzzer button. The buzzer is acting as a **switch**. A switch is a device that opens or closes a circuit. Pressing the buzzer makes the connection complete and the bell rings. When the buzzer is not engaged, the circuit is open and the bell is silent.

A **series circuit** is one where the electrons have only one path along which they can move. When one load in a series circuit goes out, the circuit is open. An example of this is a set of Christmas tree lights that is missing a bulb. None of the bulbs will work.

A **parallel circuit** is one where the electrons have more than one path to move along. If a load goes out in a parallel circuit, the other load will still work because the electrons can still find a way to continue moving along the path.

When an electron goes through a load, it does work and therefore loses some of its energy. The measure of how much energy is lost is called the **potential difference**. The potential difference between two points is the work needed to move a charge from one point to another.

Potential difference is measured in a unit called the volt. **Voltage** is potential difference. The higher the voltage, the more energy the electrons have. This energy is measured by a device called a voltmeter. To use a voltmeter, place it in a circuit parallel with the load you are measuring.

Current is the number of electrons per second that flow past a point in a circuit. Current is measured with a device called an ammeter. To use an ammeter, put it in series with the load you are measuring.

SCIENCE: CHEMISTRY

As electrons flow through a wire, they lose potential energy. Some is changed into heat energy because of resistance. **Resistance** is the ability of the material to oppose the flow of electrons through it. All substances have some resistance, even if they are a good conductor such as copper. This resistance is measured in units called **ohms**. A thin wire will have more resistance than a thick one because it will have less room for electrons to travel. In a thicker wire, there will be more possible paths for the electrons to flow. Resistance also depends upon the length of the wire. The longer the wire, the more resistance it will have. Potential difference, resistance, and current form a relationship know as **Ohm's Law**. Current **(I)** is measured in amperes and is equal to potential difference **(V)** divided by resistance **(R)**.

$$I = V / R$$

If you have a wire with resistance of 5 ohms and a potential difference of 75 volts, you can calculate the current by

$$I = 75 \text{ volts} / 5 \text{ ohms}$$
$$I = 15 \text{ amperes}$$

A current of 10 or more amperes will cause a wire to get hot. 22 amperes is about the maximum for a house circuit. Anything above 25 amperes can start a fire.

Electrostatics is the study of stationary electric charges. A plastic rod that is rubbed with fur or a glass rod that is rubbed with silk will become electrically charged and will attract small pieces of paper. The charge on the plastic rod rubbed with fur is negative and the charge on glass rod rubbed with silk is positive.

Electrically charged objects share these characteristics:

1. Like charges repel one another.
2. Opposite charges attract each other.
3. Charge is conserved. A neutral object has no net change. If the plastic rod and fur are initially neutral, when the rod becomes charged by the fur a negative charge is transferred from the fur to the rod. The net negative charge on the rod is equal to the net positive charge on the fur.

SCIENCE: CHEMISTRY

Materials through which electric charges can easily flow are called **conductors**. Metals which are good conductors include silicon and boron. On the other hand, an **insulator** is a material through which electric charges do not move easily, if at all. Examples of insulators would be the nonmetal elements of the periodic table. A simple device used to indicate the existence of a positive or negative charge is called an **electroscope**. An electroscope is made up of a conducting knob and attached to it are very lightweight conducting leaves usually made of foil (gold or aluminum). When a charged object touches the knob, the leaves push away from each other because like charges repel. It is not possible to tell whether if the charge is positive or negative.

Charging by induction:

Touch the knob with a finger while a charged rod is nearby. The electrons will be repulsed and flow out of the electroscope through the hand. If the hand is removed while the charged rod remains close, the electroscope will retain the charge.

When an object is rubbed with a charged rod, the object will take on the same charge as the rod. However, charging by induction gives the object the opposite charge as that of the charged rod.

Grounding charge:

Charge can be removed from an object by connecting it to the earth through a conductor. The removal of static electricity by conduction is called **grounding**.

Skill 13.2 Recognize the nature and properties of mechanical and electromagnetic waves (e.g., frequency, source, medium, spectrum, wave-particle duality).

A mechanical wave can be defined as a disturbance that travels through a medium, moving energy from one place to another. This disturbance is also called an electrical force field. The wave is not capable of transporting energy without a medium, as in vacuum conditions. The medium is the material through which the disturbance is moving and can be thought of as a series of interacting particles. The example of a slinky wave is often used to illustrate the nature of a wave, where pressure exerted on the first coil moves through the remaining coils. A sound wave is also a mechanical wave. The frequency of a wave refers to how often the particles of the medium vibrate when a wave passes through the medium. Frequency is measured in units of cycles/second, waves/second, vibrations/second, or something/second. Another unit for frequency is the Hertz (abbreviated Hz) where 1 Hz is equivalent to 1 cycle/second. The period of a wave is the time required for a particle on a medium to make one complete vibrational cycle. Wave period is measured in units of time such as seconds, hours, days or years, and is NOT synonymous with frequency.

Electromagnetic waves are both electric and magnetic in nature and are capable of traveling through a vacuum. They do not require a medium in order to transport their energy. Light, microwaves, x-rays, and TV and radio transmissions are all kinds of electromagnetic waves. They are all a wavy disturbance that repeats itself over a distance called the wavelength. Electromagnetic waves come in varying sizes and properties, by which they are organized in the electromagnetic spectrum. The electromagnetic spectrum is measured in frequency (f) in hertz and wavelength (λ) in meters. The frequency times the wavelength of every electromagnetic wave equals the speed of light (3.0×10^9 meters/second).

Roughly, the range of wavelengths of the electromagnetic spectrum is:

	f	λ
Radio waves	$10^{5} - 10^{-1}$ hertz	$10^{3} - 10^{9}$ meters
Microwaves	$10^{-1} - 10^{-3}$ hertz	$10^{9} - 10^{11}$ meters
Infrared radiation	$10^{-3} - 10^{-6}$ hertz	$10^{11.2} - 10^{14.3}$ meters
Visible light	$10^{-6.2} - 10^{-6.9}$ hertz	$10^{14.3} - 10^{15}$ meters
Ultraviolet radiation	$10^{-7} - 10^{-9}$ hertz	$10^{15} - 10^{17.2}$ meters
X-Rays	$10^{-9} - 10^{-11}$ hertz	$10^{17.2} - 10^{19}$ meters
Gamma Rays	$10^{-11} - 10^{-15}$ hertz	$10^{19} - 10^{23.25}$ meters

Radio waves are used for transmitting data. Common examples are television, cell phones, and wireless computer networks. Microwaves are used to heat food and deliver Wi-Fi service. Infrared waves are utilized in night vision goggles. Visible light we are all familiar with as the human eye is most sensitive to this wavelength range. UV light causes sunburns and would be even more harmful if most of it were not captured in the Earth's ozone layer. X-rays aid us in the medical field and gamma rays are most useful in the field of astronomy.

Skill 13.3 Describe the effects and applications of electromagnetic forces in real-life situations, including electric power generation, circuit breakers, and brownouts.

Electricity can be used to change the chemical composition of a material. For instance, when electricity is passed through water, it breaks the water down into hydrogen gas and oxygen gas.

Circuit breakers in a home monitor the electric current. If there is an overload, the circuit breaker will create an open circuit, stopping the flow of electricity.

Computers can be made small enough to fit inside a plastic credit card by creating what is known as a solid state device. In this device, electrons flow through solid material such as silicon.

Resistors are used to regulate volume on a television or radio or through a dimmer switch for lights.

A bird can sit on an electrical wire without being electrocuted because the bird and the wire have about the same potential. However, if that same bird would touch two wires at the same time he would not have to worry about flying south next year.

When caught in an electrical storm, a car is a relatively safe place from lightening because of the resistance of the rubber tires. A metal building would not be safe unless there was a lightening rod that would attract the lightening and conduct it into the ground.

A brown-out occurs when there exists a condition of lower than normal power line voltage. This may be short term (minutes to hours) or long term (1/2 day or more). A power line voltage reduction of 8 - 12% is usually considered a Brown-out. Electric utilities may reduce line voltage to Brown-out levels in an effort to manage power generation and distribution. This is most likely to occur on very hot days, when most air conditioning and refrigeration equipment would be operating almost continuously. Even without purposeful intervention from the local utility company, extreme overloads (spikes) could tax the electrical system to the point where a permanent brown-out state could exist over much of the company's distribution network.

Skill 13.4 Analyze and predict the behavior of mechanical and electromagnetic waves under varying physical conditions, including basic optics, color, ray diagrams, and shadows.

The place where one medium ends and another begins is called a **boundary**, and the manner in which a wave behaves when it reaches that boundary is called **boundary behavior**. The following principles apply to boundary behavior in waves:

1) wave speed is always greater in the less dense medium
2) wavelength is always greater in the less dense medium
3) wave frequency is not changed by crossing a boundary
4) the reflected pulse becomes inverted when a wave in a less dense medium is heading towards a boundary with a more dense medium
5) the amplitude of the incident pulse is always greater than the amplitude of the reflected pulse.

For an example, we will use a rope whose left side is less dense, or thinner, than the right side of the rope.

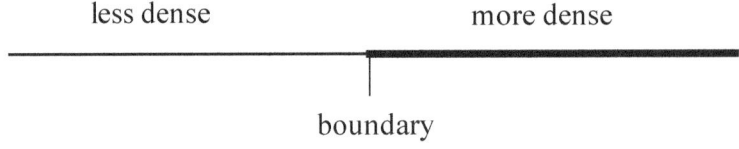

A pulse is introduced on the left end of the rope. This **incident pulse** travels right along the rope towards the boundary between the two thicknesses of rope. When the incident pulse reaches the boundary, two behaviors will occur:

1) Some of the energy will be reflected back to the left side of the boundary. This energy is known as the **reflected pulse**.
2) The rest of the energy will travel into the thicker end of the rope. This energy is referred to as the **transmitted pulse**.

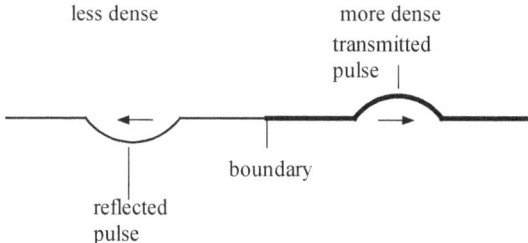

When the incident pulse travels from a denser medium to a less dense medium, the reflected pulse is not inverted.

Reflection occurs when waves bounce off a barrier. The **law of reflection** states that when a ray of light reflects off a surface, the angle of incidence is equal to the angle of reflection.

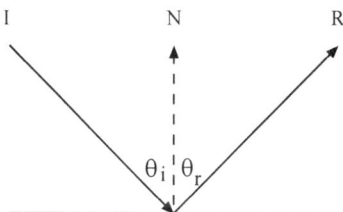

Line I represents the **incident ray**, the ray of light striking the surface. Line R is the **reflected ray**, the ray of light reflected off the surface. Line N is known as the **normal line**. It is a perpendicular line at the point of incidence that divides the angle between the incident ray and the reflected ray into two equal rays. The angle between the incident ray and the normal line is called the **angle of incidence**; the angle between the reflected ray and the normal line is called the **angle of reflection**.

Waves passing from one medium into another will undergo **refraction**, or bending. Accompanying this bending are a change in both speed and the wavelength of the waves.

In this example, light waves traveling through the air will pass through glass.

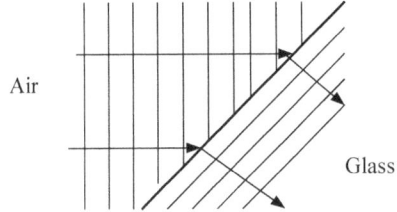

Refraction occurs only at the boundary. Once the wavefront passes across the boundary, it travels in a straight line.

Diffraction involves a change in direction of waves as they pass through an opening or around an obstacle in their path.

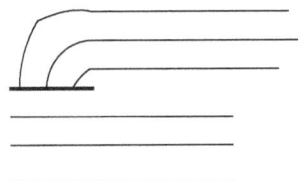

The amount of diffraction depends upon the wavelength. The amount of diffraction increases with increasing wavelength and decreases with decreasing wavelength. Sound and water waves exhibit this ability.
When we refer to light, we are usually talking about a type of electromagnetic wave that stimulates the retina of the eye, or visible light. Each individual wavelength within the spectrum of visible light represents a particular **color**. When a particular wavelength strikes the retina, we perceive that color. Visible light is sometimes referred to as ROYGBIV (red, orange, yellow, green, blue, indigo, violet). The visible light spectrum ranges from red (the longest wavelength) to violet (the shortest wavelength) with a range of wavelengths in between. If all the wavelengths strike your eye at the same time, you will see white. Conversely, when no wavelengths strike your eye, you perceive black.

A **shadow** results from the inability of light waves to diffract as sound and water waves can. An obstacle in the way of the light waves blocks the light waves, thereby creating a shadow.

TEACHER CERTIFICATION STUDY GUIDE

SUBAREA IV.   **EARTH SYSTEMS AND THE UNIVERSE**

COMPETENCY 14.0 UNDERSTAND AND APPLY KNOWLEDGE OF EARTH'S LAND, WATER, AND ATMOSPHERIC SYSTEMS AND THE HISTORY OF EARTH

Skill 14.1   **Identify the structure and composition of Earth's land, water, and atmospheric systems and how they affect weather, erosion, fresh water, and soil.**

Water is recycled throughout ecosystems. Just two percent of all the available water is fixed and held in ice or the bodies of organisms. Available water includes surface water (lakes, ocean, and rivers) and ground water (aquifers, wells). 96% of all available water is from ground water. Water is recycled through the processes of evaporation and precipitation. The water present now is the water that has been here since our atmosphere formed.

When water falls from the atmosphere it can have an erosive property. This can happen from impact alone but also from acid rain. Erosion is known for its destructive properties, but in an indirect way, it also builds by bringing materials to new locations. **Erosion** is the inclusion and transportation of surface materials by another moveable material, usually water, wind, or ice. The most important cause of erosion is running water. Streams, rivers, and tides are constantly at work removing weathered fragments of bedrock and carrying them away from their original location. A stream erodes bedrock by the grinding action of the sand, pebbles and other rock fragments. This grinding against each other is called abrasion. Streams also erode rocks by dissolving or absorbing their minerals. Limestone and marble are readily dissolved by streams.

The breaking down of rocks at or near to the earth's surface is known as **weathering**. Weathering breaks down these rocks into smaller and smaller pieces. There are two types of weathering: physical weathering and chemical weathering.

Physical weathering is the process by which rocks are broken down into smaller fragments without undergoing any change in chemical composition. Physical weathering is mainly caused by the freezing of water, the expansion of rock, and the activities of plants and animals.

Frost wedging is the cycle of daytime thawing and refreezing at night. This cycle causes large rock masses, especially the rocks exposed on mountain tops, to be broken into smaller pieces.

The peeling away of the outer layers from a rock is called exfoliation. Rounded mountain tops are called exfoliation domes and have been formed in this way.

SCIENCE: CHEMISTRY

Chemical weathering is the breaking down of rocks through changes in their chemical composition. An example would be the change of feldspar in granite to clay. Water, oxygen, and carbon dioxide are the main agents of chemical weathering. When water and carbon dioxide combine chemically, they produce a weak acid that breaks down rocks. In addition, acidic substances from factories and car exhausts dissolve in rain water forming **acid rain.** Acid rain forms predominantly from pollutant oxides in the air (usually nitrogen-based NO_x or sulfur-based SO_x), which become hydrated into their acids (nitric or sulfuric acid). When the rain falls into stone, the acids can react with metallic compounds and gradually wear the stone away.

Skill 14.2 Recognize the scope of geologic time and the continuing physical changes of Earth through time.

Geological time is divided into periods depending on the kind of life that existed at that time. These periods are grouped together into eras. The history of the Earth is calculated by studying the ages of the various layers of sedimentary rock.

Era	Period	Time	Characteristics
Cenozoic	Quaternary	1.6 million years ago to the present.	The Ice Age occurred, and human beings evolved.
	Tertiary	65-1.64 million years ago.	Mammals and birds evolved to replace the great reptiles and dinosaurs that had just become extinct. Forests gave way to grasslands, and the climate become cooler.
Mesozoic	Cretaceous	135-65 million years ago.	Reptiles and dinosaurs roamed the Earth. Most of the modern continents had split away from the large landmass, Pangaea, and many were flooded by shallow chalk seas.
	Jurassic Triassic	350-135 million years ago.	Reptiles were beginning to evolve. Pangaea started to break up. Deserts gave way to forests and swamps.
Paleozoic	Permian Carboniferous	355-250 million years ago.	Continents came together to form one big landmass, Pangaea. Forests (that formed today's coal) grew on deltas around the new mountains, and deserts formed.
	Devonian	410-355 million years ago.	Continents started moving toward each other. The first land animals, such as insects and amphibians, existed. Many fish swam in the seas.
	Silurian Ordovician	510-410 million years ago.	Sea life flourished, and the first fish evolved. The earliest land plants began to grow around shorelines and estuaries.
	Cambrian	570-510 million years ago.	No life on land, but all kinds of sea animals existed.
Precambrian	Proterozoic	Beginning of the Earth to 570 million years ago (seven-eighths of the Earth's history).	Some sort of life existed.
	Archaean		No life.

Skill 14.3 Evaluate scientific theories about Earth's origin and history and how these theories explain contemporary living systems

The dominant scientific theory about the origin of the Universe, and consequently the Earth, is the **Big Bang Theory**. According to this theory, an atom exploded about 10 to 20 billion years ago throwing matter in all directions. Although this theory has never been proven, and probably never will be, it is supported by the fact that distant galaxies in every direction are moving away from us at great speeds.

Earth, itself, is believed to have been created 4.5 billion years ago as a solidified cloud of gases and dust left over from the creation of the sun. As millions of years passed, radioactive decay released energy that melted some of Earth's components. Over time, the heavier components sank to the center of the Earth and accumulated into the core. As the Earth cooled, a crust formed with natural depressions. Water rising from the interior of the Earth filled these depressions and formed the oceans. Slowly, the Earth acquired the appearance it has today.

The **Heterotroph Hypothesis** supposes that life on Earth evolved from **heterotrophs**, the first cells. According to this hypothesis, life began on Earth about 3.5 billion years ago. Scientists have shown that the basic molecules of life formed from lightning, ultraviolet light, and radioactivity. Over time, these molecules became more complex and developed metabolic processes, thereby becoming heterotrophs. Heterotrophs could not produce their own food and fed off organic materials. However, they released carbon dioxide which allowed for the evolution of **autotrophs**, which could produce their own food through photosynthesis. The autotrophs and heterotrophs became the dominant life forms and evolved into the diverse forms of life we see today.

Proponents of **creationism** believe that the species we currently have were created as recounted in the book of Genesis in the Bible. This retelling asserts that God created all life about 6,000 years ago in one mass creation event. However, scientific evidence casts doubt on creationism.

Evolution

The most significant evidence to support the history of evolution is fossils, which have been used to construct a fossil record. Fossils give clues as to the structure of organisms and the times at which they existed. However, there are limitations to the study of fossils, which leave huge gaps in the fossil record.

Scientists also try to relate two organisms by comparing their internal and external structures. This is called **comparative anatomy**. Comparative anatomy categorizes anatomical structures as **homologous** (features in different species that point to a common ancestor), **analogous** (structures that have superficial similarities because of similar functions, but do not point to a common ancestor), and **vestigial** (structures that have no modern function, indicating that different species diverged and evolved). Through the study of **comparative embryology**, homologous structures that do not appear in mature organisms may be found between different species in their embryological development.

There have been two basic **theories of evolution: Lamarck's and Darwin's**. Lamarck's theory that proposed that an organism can change its structure through use or disuse and that acquired traits can be inherited has been disproved.

Darwin's theory of **natural selection** is the basis of all evolutionary theory. His theory has four basic points:

1. Each species produces more offspring than can survive.
2. The individual organisms that make up a larger population are born with certain variations.
3. The overabundance of offspring creates competition for survival among individual organisms (**survival of the fittest**).
4. Variations are passed down from parent to offspring.

Points 2 and 4 form the genetic basis for evolution.

New species develop from two types of evolution: divergent and convergent. **Divergent evolution**, also known as **speciation**, is the divergence of a new species from a previous form of that species. There are two main ways in which speciation may occur: **allopatric speciation** (resulting from geographical isolation so that species cannot interbreed) and **adaptive radiation** (creation of several new species from a single parent species). **Convergent evolution** is a process whereby different species develop similar traits from inhabiting similar environments, facing similar selection pressures, and/or use parts of their bodies for similar functions. This type of evolution is only superficial. It can never result in two species being able to interbreed.

Skill 14.4 **Recognize the interrelationships between living organisms and Earth's resources and evaluate the uses of Earth's resources.**

The region of the Earth and its atmosphere in which living things are found is known as the **biosphere**. The biosphere is made up of distinct areas called **ecosystems**, each of which has its own characteristic climate, soils, and communities of plants and animals.

The most important nonliving factors affecting an ecosystem are the chemical cycles, the water cycle, oxygen, sunlight, and the soil. The two basic chemical cycles are the carbon cycle and the nitrogen cycle. They involve the passage of these elements between the organisms and the environment.

In the **carbon cycle**, animals and plants use carbon dioxide from the air to produce glucose, which they use in respiration and other life processes. Animals consume plants, use what they can of the carbon matter and excrete the rest as waste. This waste decays into carbon dioxide. During respiration, plants and animals release carbon dioxide back into the air. The carbon used by plants and animals stays in their bodies until death, after which decay sends the organic compounds back into the Earth and carbon dioxide back into the air.

Nitrogen found in the atmosphere is generally unusable by living organisms. In the **nitrogen cycle,** nitrogen-fixing bacteria in the soil and/or the roots of legumes transform the inert nitrogen into compounds. Plants take these compounds, synthesize the twenty amino acids found in nature, and turn them into plant proteins. Animals can only synthesize eight of the amino acids. They eat the plants to produce protein from the plant's materials. Animals and plants give off nitrogen waste and death products in the form of ammonia. The ammonia will either be transformed into nitrites and nitrates by bacteria and reenter the cycle when they are taken up by plants, or be broken down by bacteria to produce inert nitrogen to be released back into the air.

Most of the Earth's water is found in the oceans and lakes. Through the **water cycle**, water evaporates into the atmosphere and condenses into clouds. Water then falls to the Earth in the form of precipitation, returning to the oceans and lakes on falling on land. Water on the land may return to the oceans and lakes as runoff or seep from the soil as groundwater.

The amount of **oxygen** available in a particular location may create competition. Oxygen is readily available to animals on land; but in order for it to be available to aquatic organisms, it must be dissolved in water.

Sunlight is also important to most organisms. Organisms on land compete for sunlight, but sunlight does not reach into the lowest depths of the ocean. Organisms in these regions must find another means of producing food.

The type of **soil** found in a particular ecosystem determines what species can live in that ecosystem.

The ecosystems of the Earth consist of: temperate forests, deserts, wetlands, tropical rain forests, oceans, grasslands, rivers and lakes, mountains, towns and cities, seashores, and polar and tundra lands.

COMPETENCY 15.0 UNDERSTAND AND APPLY KNOWLEDGE OF THE DYNAMIC NATURE OF EARTH

Skill 15.1 Analyze and explain large-scale dynamic forces, events, and processes that affect Earth's land, water, and atmospheric systems, including conceptual questions about plate tectonics, El Nino, drought, and climatic shifts.

El Niño refers to a sequence of changes in the ocean and atmospheric circulation across the Pacific Ocean. The water around the equator is unusually hot every two to seven years. Trade winds normally blowing east to west across the equatorial latitudes, piling warm water into the western Pacific. A huge mass of heavy thunderstorms usually forms in the area and produce vast currents of rising air that displace heat poleward. This helps create the strong mid-latitude jet streams. The world's climate patterns are disrupted by this change in location of the massive cluster of thunderstorms. The West coast of America experienced a wet winter. Sacramento, California recorded 103 days of rain.

Air masses moving toward or away from the Earth's surface are called air currents. Air moving parallel to Earth's surface is called **wind**. Weather conditions are generated by winds and air currents carrying large amounts of heat and moisture from one part of the atmosphere to another. Wind speeds are measured by instruments called anemometers.

The wind belts in each hemisphere consist of convection cells that encircle Earth like belts. There are three major wind belts on Earth (1) trade winds (2) prevailing westerlies, and (3) polar easterlies. Wind belt formation depends on the differences in air pressures that develop in the doldrums, the horse latitudes, and the polar regions. The Doldrums surround the equator. Within this belt heated air usually rises straight up into Earth's atmosphere. The Horse latitudes are regions of high barometric pressure with calm and light winds and the Polar regions contain cold dense air that sinks to the earth's surface

Winds caused by local temperature changes include sea breezes, and land breezes.

Sea breezes are caused by the unequal heating of the land and an adjacent, large body of water. Land heats up faster than water. The movement of cool ocean air toward the land is called a sea breeze. Sea breezes usually begin blowing about mid-morning; ending about sunset.

A breeze that blows from the land to the ocean or a large lake is called a **land breeze.**

Monsoons are huge wind systems that cover large geographic areas and that reverse direction seasonally. The monsoons of India and Asia are examples of these seasonal winds. They alternate wet and dry seasons. As denser cooler air over the ocean moves inland, a steady seasonal wind called a summer or wet monsoon is produced.

Cloud types:

Cirrus clouds - White and feathery high in sky

Cumulus – thick, white, fluffy

Stratus – layers of clouds cover most of the sky

Nimbus – heavy, dark clouds that represent thunderstorm clouds

Variation on the clouds mentioned above:

Cumulo-nimbus

Strato-nimbus

The air temperature at which water vapor begins to condense is called the **dew point.**

Relative humidity is the actual amount of water vapor in a certain volume of air compared to the maximum amount of water vapor this air could hold at a given temperature.

Skill 15.2 **Identify and explain Earth processes and cycles and cite examples in real-life situations, including conceptual questions on rock cycles, volcanism, and plate tectonics.**

Data obtained from many sources led scientists to develop the theory of plate tectonics. This theory is the most current model that explains not only the movement of the continents, but also the changes in the earth's crust caused by internal forces.

Plates are rigid blocks of earth's crust and upper mantle. These solid blocks make up the lithosphere. The earth's lithosphere is broken into nine large sections and several small ones. These moving slabs are called plates. The major plates are named after the continents they are "transporting."

The plates float on and move with a layer of hot, plastic-like rock in the upper mantle. Geologists believe that the heat currents circulating within the mantle cause this plastic zone of rock to slowly flow, carrying along the overlying crustal plates.

Movement of these crustal plates creates areas where the plates diverge as well as areas where the plates converge. A major area of divergence is located in the Mid-Atlantic. Currents of hot mantle rock rise and separate at this point of divergence creating new oceanic crust at the rate of 2 to 10 centimeters per year. Convergence is when the oceanic crust collides with either another oceanic plate or a continental plate. The oceanic crust sinks forming an enormous trench and generating volcanic activity. Convergence also includes continent to continent plate collisions. When two plates slide past one another a transform fault is created.

These movements produce many major features of the earth's surface, such as mountain ranges, volcanoes, and earthquake zones. Most of these features are located at plate boundaries, where the plates interact by spreading apart, pressing together, or sliding past each other. These movements are very slow, averaging only a few centimeters each year.

Boundaries form between spreading plates where the crust is forced apart in a process called rifting. Rifting generally occurs at mid-ocean ridges. Rifting can also take place within a continent, splitting the continent into smaller landmasses that drift away from each other, thereby forming an ocean basin between them. The Red Sea is a product of rifting. As the seafloor spreading takes place, new material is added to the inner edges of the separating plates. In this way the plates grow larger, and the ocean basin widens. This is the process that broke up the super continent Pangaea and created the Atlantic Ocean.

Boundaries between plates that are colliding are zones of intense crustal activity. When a plate of ocean crust collides with a plate of continental crust, the more dense oceanic plate slides under the lighter continental plate and plunges into the mantle. This process is called **subduction**, and the site where it takes place is called a subduction zone. A subduction zone is usually seen on the sea-floor as a deep depression called a trench.

The crustal movement that is identified by plates sliding sideways past each other produces a plate boundary characterized by major faults that are capable of unleashing powerful earth-quakes. The San Andreas Fault forms such a boundary between the Pacific Plate and the North American Plate.

Orogeny is the term given to natural mountain building.

A mountain is terrain that has been raised high above the surrounding landscape by volcanic action, or some form of tectonic plate collisions. The plate collisions could be intercontinental or ocean floor collisions with a continental crust (subduction). The physical composition of mountains would include igneous, metamorphic, or sedimentary rocks; some may have rock layers that are tilted or distorted by plate collision forces.

There are many different types of mountains. The physical attributes of a mountain range depends upon the angle at which plate movement thrust layers of rock to the surface. Many mountains (Adirondacks, Southern Rockies) were formed along high angle faults.

Folded mountains (Alps, Himalayas) are produced by the folding of rock layers during their formation. The Himalayas are the highest mountains in the world and contain Mount Everest, which rises almost 9 km above sea level. The Himalayas were formed when India collided with Asia. The movement that created this collision is still in process at the rate of a few centimeters per year.

Fault-block mountains (Utah, Arizona, and New Mexico) are created when plate movement produces tension forces instead of compression forces. The area under tension produces normal faults and rock along these faults is displaced upward.

Dome mountains are formed as magma tries to push up through the crust but fails to break the surface. Dome mountains resemble a huge blister on the earth's surface.

Upwarped mountains (Black Hills of South Dakota) are created in association with a broad arching of the crust. They can also be formed by rock thrust upward along high angle faults.

Faults are categorized on the basis of the relative movement between the blocks on both sides of the fault plane. The movement can be horizontal, vertical or oblique.

A dip-slip fault occurs when the movement of the plates is vertical and opposite. The displacement is in the direction of the inclination, or dip, of the fault. Dip-slip faults are classified as normal faults when the rock above the fault plane moves down relative to the rock below.

Reverse faults are created when the rock above the fault plane moves up relative to the rock below. Reverse faults having a very low angle to the horizontal are also referred to as thrust faults.

Faults in which the dominant displacement is horizontal movement along the trend or strike (length) of the fault are called **strike-slip faults**. When a large strike-slip fault is associated with plate boundaries it is called a **transform fault**. The San Andreas Fault in California is a well-known transform fault.

Faults that have both vertical and horizontal movement are called **oblique-slip faults.**

Volcanism is the term given to the movement of magma through the crust and its emergence as lava onto the earth's surface. Volcanic mountains are built up by successive deposits of volcanic materials.

An active volcano is one that is presently erupting or building to an eruption. A dormant volcano is one that is between eruptions but still shows signs of internal activity that might lead to an eruption in the future. An extinct volcano is said to be no longer capable of erupting. Most of the world's active volcanoes are found along the rim of the Pacific Ocean, which is also a major earthquake zone. This curving belt of active faults and volcanoes is often called the Ring of Fire. The world's best known volcanic mountains include: Mount Etna in Italy and Mount Kilimanjaro in Africa. The Hawaiian Islands are actually the tops of a chain of volcanic mountains that rise from the ocean floor.

There are three types of volcanic mountains: shield volcanoes, cinder cones, and composite volcanoes.

Shield Volcanoes are associated with quiet eruptions. Lava emerges from the vent or opening in the crater and flows freely out over the earth's surface until it cools and hardens into a layer of igneous rock. A repeated lava flow builds this type of volcano into the largest volcanic mountain. Mauna Loa found in Hawaii, is the largest volcano on earth.

Cinder Cone Volcanoes are associated with explosive eruptions as lava is hurled high into the air in a spray of droplets of various sizes. These droplets cool and harden into cinders and particles of ash before falling to the ground. The ash and cinder pile up around the vent to form a steep, cone-shaped hill called the cinder cone. Cinder cone volcanoes are relatively small but may form quite rapidly.

Composite Volcanoes are described as being built by both lava flows and layers of ash and cinders. Mount Fuji in Japan, Mount St. Helens in Washington, USA, and Mount Vesuvius in Italy are all famous composite volcanoes.

When lava cools, **igneous rock** is formed. This formation can occur either above ground or below ground.

Intrusive rock includes any igneous rock that was formed below the earth's surface. Batholiths are the largest structures of intrusive type rock and are composed of near granite materials; they are at the core of the Sierra Nevada Mountains.

Extrusive rock includes any igneous rock that was formed at the earth's surface.

Dikes are old lava tubes formed when magma entered a vertical fracture and hardened. Sometimes magma squeezes between two rock layers and hardens into a thin horizontal sheet called a **sill**. A **laccolith** is formed in much the same way as a sill, but the magma that creates a laccolith is very thick and does not flow easily. It pools and forces the overlying strata up, creating an obvious surface dome.

A **caldera** is normally formed by the collapse of the top of a volcano. This collapse can be caused by a massive explosion that destroys the cone and empties most, if not all, of the magma chamber below the volcano. The cone collapses into the empty magma chamber forming a caldera.

An inactive volcano may have magma solidified in its pipe. This structure, called a volcanic neck, is resistant to erosion and today may be the only visible evidence of the past presence of an active volcano.

Skill 15.3 **Analyze the transfer of energy within and among Earth's land, water, and atmospheric systems, including the idenrtification of energy sources of volcanoes, hurricanes, thunderstorms, and tornadoes.**

A **thunderstorm** is a brief, local storm produced by the rapid upward movement of warm, moist air within a cumulo-nimbus cloud. Thunderstorms always produce lightning and thunder, accompanied by strong wind gusts and heavy rain or hail.

A severe storm with swirling winds that may reach speeds of hundreds of km per hour is called a **tornado**. Such a storm is also referred to as a "twister". The sky is covered by large cumulo-nimbus clouds and violent thunderstorms; a funnel-shaped swirling cloud may extend downward from a cumulonimbus cloud and reach the ground. Tornadoes are narrow storms that leave a narrow path of destruction on the ground.

A swirling, funnel-shaped cloud that **extends** downward and touches a body of water is called a **waterspout.**

Hurricanes are storms that develop when warm, moist air carried by trade winds rotates around a low-pressure "eye". A large, rotating, low-pressure system accompanied by heavy precipitation and strong winds is called a tropical cyclone or is better known as a hurricane. In the Pacific region, a hurricane is called a typhoon.

Storms that occur only in the winter are known as blizzards or ice storms. A **blizzard** is a storm with strong winds, blowing snow and frigid temperatures. An **ice storm** consists of falling rain that freezes when it strikes the ground, covering everything with a layer of ice.

Skill 15.4 Explain the functions and applications of the instruments and technologies used to study the earth sciences, including seismographs, barometers, and satellite systems.

Satellites have improved our ability to communicate and transmit radio and television signals. Navigational abilities have been greatly improved through the use of satellite signals. Sonar uses sound waves to locate objects and is especially useful underwater. The sound waves bounce off the object and are used to assist in location. **Seismographs** record vibrations in the earth and allow us to measure earthquake activity. Common instruments for that forecasting weather include the **aneroid barometer** and the **mercury barometer,** which both measure air pressure. In the aneroid barometer, the air exerts varying pressures on a metal diaphragm that will then read air pressure. The mercury barometer operates when atmospheric pressure pushes on a pool of mercury in a glass tube. The higher the pressure, the higher up the tube mercury will rise.

Relative humidity is measured by two kinds of additional weather instruments, the psychrometer and the hair gygrometer.

TEACHER CERTIFICATION STUDY GUIDE

COMPETENCY 16.0 UNDERSTAND AND APPLY KNOWLEDGE OF OBJECTS IN THE UNIVERSE AND THEIR DYNAMIC INTERACTIONS.

Skill 16.1 Describe and explain the relative and apparent motions of the sun, the moon, stars, and planets in the sky.

Until the summer of 2006, there were nine recognized planets in our solar system: Mercury, Venus, Earth, Mars, Jupiter, Saturn, Uranus, Neptune, and Pluto. These nine planets are divided into two groups based on distance from the sun. The inner planets include: Mercury, Venus, Earth, and Mars. The outer planets include: Jupiter, Saturn, Uranus, Neptune and Pluto. Pluto's status as a planet is being reconsidered.

Mercury -- the closest planet to the sun. Its surface has craters and rocks. The atmosphere is composed of hydrogen, helium and sodium. Mercury was named after the Roman messenger god.

Venus -- has a slow rotation when compared to Earth. Venus and Uranus rotate in opposite directions from the other planets. This opposite rotation is called retrograde rotation. The surface of Venus is not visible due to the extensive cloud cover. The atmosphere is composed mostly of carbon dioxide. Sulfuric acid droplet in the dense cloud cover gives Venus a yellow appearance. Venus has a greater greenhouse effect than observed on Earth. The dense clouds Combined with carbon dioxide traps heat. Venus was named after the Roman goddess of love.

Earth -- considered a water planet with 70% of its surface covered with water. Gravity holds the masses of water in place. The different temperatures observed on earth allows for the different states of water to exist; solid, liquid or gas. The atmosphere is composed mainly of oxygen and nitrogen. Earth is the only planet that is known to support life.

Mars -- the surface of Mars contains numerous craters, active and extinct volcanoes, ridges and valleys with extremely deep fractures. Iron oxide found in the dusty soil makes the surface seem rust colored and the skies seem pink in color. The atmosphere is composed of carbon dioxide, nitrogen, argon, oxygen and water vapor. Mars has polar regions with ice caps composed of water. Mars has two satellites. Mars was named after the Roman war god.

Jupiter -- largest planet in the solar system. Jupiter has 16 moons. The atmosphere is composed of hydrogen, helium, methane and ammonia. There are white colored bands of clouds indicating rising gas and dark colored bands of clouds indicating descending gases, caused by heat resulting from the energy of Jupiter's core. Jupiter has a Great Red Spot that is thought to be a hurricane type cloud. Jupiter has a strong magnetic field.

SCIENCE: CHEMISTRY

Saturn -- the second largest planet in the solar system. Saturn has beautiful rings of ice and rock and dust particles circling it. Saturn's atmosphere is composed of hydrogen, helium, methane, and ammonia. Saturn has 20 plus satellites. Saturn was named after the Roman god of agriculture.

Uranus -- the second largest planet in the solar system with retrograde revolution. Uranus a gaseous planet and it has 10 dark rings and 15 satellites. Its atmosphere is composed of hydrogen, helium, and methane. Uranus was named after the Greek god of the heavens.

Neptune -- another gaseous planet with an atmosphere consisting of hydrogen, helium, and methane. Neptune has 3 rings and 2 satellites. Neptune was named after the Roman sea god that its atmosphere has the same color of the seas.

Pluto -- considered the smallest planet in the solar system. Pluto's atmosphere probably contains methane, ammonia, and frozen water. Pluto has 1 satellite. Pluto revolves around the sun every 250 years. Pluto was named after the Roman god of the underworld.

Skill 16.2   Recognize properties of objects (e.g., comets, asteroids) within the solar system and their dynamic interactions.

Astronomers believe that the rocky fragments that may have been the remains of the birth of the solar system that never formed into a planet. **Asteroids** are found in the region between Mars and Jupiter.

Comets are masses of frozen gases, cosmic dust, and small rocky particles. Astronomers think that most comets originate in a dense comet cloud beyond Pluto. Comet consists of a nucleus, a coma, and a tail. A comet's tail always points away from the sun. The most famous comet, **Halley's Comet,** is named after the person whom first discovered it in 240 B.C. It returns to the skies near earth every 75 to 76 years.

Meteoroids are composed of particles of rock and metal of various sizes. When a meteoroid travels through the earth's atmosphere, friction causes its surface to heat up and it begins to burn. The burning meteoroid falling through the earth's atmosphere is now called a **meteor** or also known as a "shooting star."

Meteorites are meteors that strike the earth's surface. A physical example of the impact of the meteorite on the earth's surface can be seen in Arizona, The Barringer Crater is a huge Meteor Crater. There many other such meteor craters found throughout the world.

Skill 16.3 Recognize the types, properties, and dynamics of objects external to the solar system (e.g., black holes, supernovas, galaxies).

Astronomers use groups or patterns of stars called **constellations** as reference points to locate other stars in the sky. Familiar constellations include: Ursa Major (also known as the big bear) and Ursa Minor (known as the little bear). Within the Ursa Major, the smaller constellation, The Big Dipper is found. Within the Ursa Minor, the smaller constellation, The Little Dipper is found.

Different constellations appear as the earth continues its revolution around the sun with the seasonable changes.

Magnitude stars are 21 of the brightest stars that can be seen from earth, these are the first stars noticed at night. In the Northern Hemisphere there are 15 commonly observed first magnitude stars.

A vast collection of stars is defined as **galaxies**. Galaxies are classified as irregular, elliptical, and spiral. An irregular galaxy has no real structured appearance; most are in their early stages of life. An elliptical galaxy is smooth ellipses, containing little dust and gas, but composed of millions or trillion stars. Spiral galaxies are disk-shaped and have extending arms that rotate around its dense center. Earth's galaxy is found in the Milky Way and it is a spiral galaxy.

A **pulsar** is defined as a variable radio source that emits signals in very short, regular bursts; believed to be a rotating neutron star.

A **quasar** is defined as an object that photographs like a star but has an extremely large redshift and a variable energy output; believed to be the active core of a very distant galaxy.

Black holes are defined as an object that has collapsed to such a degree that light can not escape from its surface; light is trapped by the intense gravitational field.

COMPETENCY 17.0 UNDERSTAND AND APPLY KNOWLEDGE OF THE ORIGINS OF AND CHANGES IN THE UNIVERSE.

Skill 17.1 Identify scientific theories dealing with the origin of the universe (e.g., big bang).

Two main theories to explain the origins of the universe include: (1) **The Big Bang Theory** and (2) **The Steady-State Theory.**

The Big Bang Theory has been widely accepted by many astronomers. It states that the universe originated from a magnificent explosion spreading mass, matter and energy into space. The galaxies formed from this material as it cooled during the next half-billion years.

The Steady-State Theory is the least accepted theory. It states that the universe is a continuously being renewed. Galaxies move outward and new galaxies replace the older galaxies. Astronomers have not found any evidence to prove this theory.

The future of the universe is hypothesized with the Oscillating Universe Hypothesis. It states that the universe will oscillate or expand and contract. Galaxies will move away from one another and will in time slow down and stop. Then a gradual moving toward each other will again activate the explosion or The Big Bang theory.

Skill 17.2 Analyze evidence relating to the origin and physical evolution of the universe (e.g., microwave background radiation, expansion).

Cosmic microwave background radiation (CMBR) is the oldest light we can see. It is a snapshot of how the universe looked in its early beginnings. First discovered in 1964, CMBR is composed of photons which we can see because of the atoms that formed when the universe cooled to 3000 K. Prior to that, after the Big Bang, the universe was so hot that the photons were scattered all over the universe, making the universe opaque. The atoms caused the photons to scatter less and the universe to become transparent to radiation. Since cooling to 3000K, the universe has continued to expand and cool.

COBE, launched in 1989, was the first mission to explore slight fluctuations in the background. WMAP, launched in 2001, took a clearer picture of the universe, providing evidence to support the Big Bang Theory and add details to the early conditions of the universe. Based upon this more recent data, scientists believe the universe is about 13.7 billion years old and that there was a period of rapid expansion right after the Big Bang. They have also learned that there were early variations in the density of matter resulting in the formation of the galaxies, the geometry of the universe is flat, and the universe will continue to expand forever.

Skill 17.3 **Compare the physical and chemical processes involved in the life cycles of objects within galaxies.**

Scientists believe that **stars** form when compression waves traveling through clouds of gas create knots of gas in the clouds. The force of gravity within these denser areas then attracts gas particles. As the knot grows, the force increases and attracts more gas particles, eventually forming a large sphere of compressed gas with internal temperatures reaching a few million degrees C. At these temperatures, the gases in the knot become so hot that nuclear fusion of hydrogen to form helium takes place, creating large amounts of nuclear energy and forming a new star. Pressure from the radiation of these new stars causes more knots to form in the gas cloud, initiating the process of creating more stars.

Scientists theorize that **planets** form from gas and dust surrounding young stars. As the density of the forming star increases, this gas and dust slowly condenses into a spinning disk. The denser areas of the disk develop a gravitational force which attracts more dust and gas as the disk orbits the star. Over millions of years, these dense areas consolidate and grow, forming planets. In the case of the Sun, the larger icy fragments surrounding it attracted more gas and dust forming the more massive planets such as Jupiter and Saturn. These larger planets developed gravitational forces great enough to attract hydrogen and helium atoms, turning them into gas giants. The smaller planets, such as Earth, could not attract these atoms and became mainly rocky.

It is believed that **black holes** form as stars evolve. As the nuclear fuels are used up in the core of a star, the pressure associated with the production of these fuels no longer exists to resist contraction of the core. Two new types of pressure, electron and neutron, arise. However, if the star is more than about five times as massive as the Sun, neither pressure will prevent the star from collapsing into a black hole.

When the universe was forming, most of the material became concentrated in the planets and moons. There were however many small, rocky objects called **planetesimals** that also formed from the gas and dust. These planetesimals include **comets** and **asteroids**. A large cloud of comets, known as the Oort cloud, exists beyond Pluto. A change in the gravitational pull of our galaxy may disturb the orbit of a comet causing it to fall toward the Sun. The ice in the comet turns into vapor, releasing dust from the body. Gas and dust then form the tail of the comet.

In the early life of the solar system, some of the planetesimals came together more toward the center of the solar system. The gravitational pull of Jupiter prevented these planetesimals from developing into full planets. They broke up into thousands of minor planets, known as asteroids.

It is believed that **black holes** form as stars evolve. As the nuclear fuels are used up in the core of a star, the pressure associated with the production of these fuels no longer exists to resist contraction of the core. Two new types of pressure, electron and neutron, arise. However, if the star is more than about five times as massive as the Sun, neither pressure will prevent the star from collapsing into a black hole.

When the universe was forming, most of the material became concentrated in the planets and moons. There were however many small, rocky objects called **planetesimals** that also formed from the gas and dust. These planetesimals include **comets** and **asteroids**. A large cloud of comets, known as the Oort cloud, exists beyond Pluto. A change in the gravitational pull of our galaxy may disturb the orbit of a comet causing it to fall toward the Sun. The ice in the comet turns into vapor, releasing dust from the body. Gas and dust then form the tail of the comet.

In the early life of the solar system, some of the planetesimals came together more toward the center of the solar system. The gravitational pull of Jupiter prevented these planetesimals from developing into full planets. They broke up into thousands of minor planets, known as asteroids.

Skill 17.4 Explain the functions and applications of the instruments, technologies, and tools used in the study of the space sciences, including the relative advantages and disadvantages of Earth-based versus space-based instruments and optical versus nonoptical instruments.

Types of telescopes used in the study of the space sciences include optical, radio, infrared, ultraviolet, x-ray, and gamma-ray. Optical telescopes work by collecting and magnifying visible light that is given off by stars or reflected from the surfaces of the planets. However, stars also give off other types of electromagnetic radiation, including radio waves, microwaves, infrared light, ultraviolet light, X rays, and gamma rays. Therefore, specific types of non-optical instruments have been developed to collect information about the universe through these other types of electromagnetic waves.

Many of the telescopes used by astronomers are earth-based, located in observatories around the world. However, only radio waves, visible light, and some infrared radiation can penetrate our atmosphere to reach the earth's surface. Therefore, scientists have launched telescopes into space, where the instruments can collect other types of electromagnetic waves. Space probes are also able to gather information from distant parts of the solar system. In addition to telescopes, scientists construct mathematical models and computer simulations to form a scientific account of events in the universe. These models and simulations are built using evidence from many sources, including the information gathered through telescopes and space probes.

TEACHER CERTIFICATION STUDY GUIDE

SUBAREA V. **MATTER, STRUCTURE, AND PRACTICAL KNOWLEDGE**

COMPETENCY 18.0 UNDERSTAND AND APPLY KNOWLEDGE OF BASIC SCIENTIFIC AND MATHEMATICAL SKILLS, SAFE LABORATORY PRACTICES, AND ISSUES OF PUBLIC CONCERN RELATED TO THE FIELD OF CHEMISTRY.

Skill 18.1 Apply appropriate mathematical skills (e.g., algebraic operations, graphing, statistics, scientific notation) and technology to collect, analyze, and report data and to solve problems in chemistry.

Collection of data, measurements, and their analysis plays an important role in understanding chemical concepts.

Units are a part of every measurement. Without the units, the numbers could mean many things. For example, the distance 10 could mean 10 cm or 10 m or 10 km. Dimensional analysis is a structured way to convert units. It involves a conversion factor that allows the units to be cancelled out when multiplied or divided. These are the steps to converting one dimension measurements.

1. Write the term to be converted, (both number and unit) 6.0 cm = ? km
2. Write the conversion formula(s) 100 cm = 0.00100 km
3. Make a fraction of the conversion formula, such that
   a. if the unit in step 1 is in the numerator, that same unit in step 3 must be in the denominator.
   b. if the unit in step 1 is in the denominator, that same unit in step 3 must be in the numerator.

   Since the numerator and denominator are equal, the fraction must equal 1.

$$\frac{0.00100 \text{ km}}{100 \text{ cm}} \quad \text{or} \quad \frac{100 \text{ cm}}{0.00100 \text{ km}}$$

4. Multiply the term in step 1 by the fraction in step 3. Since the fraction equals 1, you can multiply by it without changing the size of the term.
5. Cancel units: $6.0 \text{ cm} \times \dfrac{0.00100 \text{ km}}{100 \text{ cm}}$

6. Perform the indicated calculation, rounding the answer to the correct number of significant figures.

   0.000060 km or $6.0 \times 10^{-5} \text{ km}$

The process is nearly the same for two and three dimension conversions.

Example: How many cm^3 is $1\ m^3$?

Remember, 100 cm = 1 m and that $1\ m^3$ is really 1m x 1m x 1m. Substituting in the 100 cm for every meter the problem can be rewritten as 100 cm x 100 cm x 100 cm or $1m^3$ = 1 000 000 cm^3

$1\ m^3$ x 1 000 000 cm^3/$1m^3$ = 1 000 000 cm^3 or 1.0×10^6 cm.

Example: Convert 4.17 kg/m^2 to g/cm

First to convert from kg to g use 1000 g = 1.00 kg as the conversion factor.

4.17 kg/m^2 x 1000 g/1.00 kg = 4170g /m^2.

Then use 1.00 m = 100 cm to convert the denominator. Remember that m^2 is m x m and replacing m with 100 cm, the denominator becomes 100 cm x 100 cm. or 10 000 cm^2
The conversion factor for the denominator becomes $1.00 m^2$ = 10 000 cm^2

4170 g/m^2 x 1.00 m^2/10 000 cm^2 = 0.417 g/cm^2

The units are an important part of every measurement. The units and dimensional analysis will even help solve mathematical problems.

For example: The density of gold is 19.3 g/cm^3. How many grams of gold would be found in 55 cm^3?

Using dimensional analysis, some unit must cancel. The answer needs to be grams so the cm^3 needs to cancel out. Multiply or divide the units so that the cm^3 cancel. In this case

g/cm^3 x cm^3 = g so that is how to solve the problem.

19.3 g/cm^3 x 55 cm^3 = 1060 g of gold.

SCIENCE: CHEMISTRY

SI is an abbreviation of the French *Système International d'Unités* or the **International System of Units.** It is the most widely used system of units in the world and is the system used in science. The use of many SI units in the United States is increasing outside of science and technology. There are two types of SI units: **base units** and **derived units**. The base units are:

Quantity	Unit name	Symbol
Length	meter	m
Mass	kilogram	kg
Amount of substance	mole	mol
Time	second	s
Temperature	kelvin	K
Electric current	ampere	A
Luminous intensity	candela	cd

Amperes and candelas are rarely used in chemistry. The name "kilogram" occurs for the SI base unit of mass for historical reasons. Derived units are formed from the kilogram, but appropriate decimal prefixes are attached to the word "gram." Derived unitsmeasure a quantity that may be **expressed in terms of other units**. The derived units important for chemistry are:

Derived quantity	Unit name	Expression in terms of other units	Symbol
Area	square meter	m^2	
Volume	cubic meter	m^3	
	liter	$dm^3 = 10^{-3}\ m^3$	L or l
Mass	unified atomic mass unit	$(6.022 \times 10^{23})^{-1}$ g	u or Da
Time	minute	60 s	min
	hour	60 min=3600 s	h
	day	24 h=86400 s	d
Speed	meter per second	m/s	
Acceleration	meter per second squared	m/s^2	
Temperature*	degree Celsius	K	°C
Mass density	gram per liter	$g/L = 1\ kg/m^3$	
Amount-of-substance concentration (molarity†)	molar	mol/L	M
Molality‡	molal	mol/kg	m
Chemical reaction rate	molar per second†	M/s=mol/(L•s)	
Force	newton	$m \cdot kg/s^2$	N
Pressure	pascal	$N/m^2 = kg/(m \cdot s^2)$	Pa
	standard atmosphere§	101325 Pa	atm
Energy, Work, Heat	joule	$N \cdot m = m^3 \cdot Pa = m^2 \cdot kg/s^2$	J
	nutritional calorie§	4184 J	Cal
Heat (molar)	joule per mole	J/mol	
Heat capacity, entropy	joule per kelvin	J/K	
Heat capacity (molar), entropy (molar)	joule per mole kelvin	J/(mol•K)	
Specific heat	joule per kilogram kelvin	J/(kg•K)	
Power	watt	J/s	W
Electric charge	coulomb	s•A	C
Electric potential, electromotive force	volt	W/A	V
Viscosity	pascal second	Pa•s	
Surface tension	newton per meter	N/m	

*Temperature differences in kelvin are the same as those differences in degrees Celsius. To obtain degrees Celsius from Kelvin, subtract 273.15.
†Molarity is considered to be an obsolete unit by some physicists.
‡Molality, m, is often considered obsolete. Differentiate m and meters (m) by context.
§These are commonly used non-SI units.

Decimal multiples of SI units are formed by attaching a **prefix** directly before the unit and a symbol prefix directly before the unit symbol. SI prefixes range from 10^{-24} to 10^{24}. Only the prefixes you are likely to encounter in chemistry are shown below:

Factor	Prefix	Symbol	Factor	Prefix	Symbol
10^9	giga—	G	10^{-1}	deci—	d
10^6	mega—	M	10^{-2}	centi—	c
10^3	kilo—	k	10^{-3}	milli—	m
10^2	hecto—	h	10^{-6}	micro—	µ
10^1	deca—	da	10^{-9}	nano—	n
			10^{-12}	pico—	p

Example: 0.0000004355 meters is 4.355×10^{-7} m or 435.5×10^{-9} m. This length is also 435.5 nm or 435.5 nanometers.

Example: Find a unit to express the volume of a cubic crystal that is 0.2 mm on each side so that the number before the unit is between 1 and 1000.

Solution: Volume is length X width X height, so this volume is $(0.0002 \text{ m})^3$ or 8×10^{-12} m³. Conversions of volumes and areas using powers of units of length must take the power into account. Therefore:
$$1 \text{ m}^3 = 10^3 \text{ dm}^3 = 10^6 \text{ cm}^3 = 10^9 \text{ mm}^3 = 10^{18} \text{ µm}^3,$$
The length 0.0002 m is 2×10^2 µm, so the volume is also 8×10^6 µm³. This volume could also be expressed as 8×10^{-3} mm³, but none of these numbers are between 1 and 1000.

Expressing volume in liters is helpful in cases like these. There is no power on the unit of liters, therefore:
$$1 \text{ L} = 10^3 \text{ mL} = 10^6 \text{ µL} = 10^9 \text{ nL}.$$
Converting cubic meters to liters gives
$$8 \times 10^{-12} \text{ m}^3 \times \frac{10^3 \text{ L}}{1 \text{ m}^3} = 8 \times 10^{-9} \text{ L}.$$ The crystal's volume is 8 nanoliters (8 nL).

Example: Determine the ideal gas constant, R, in L•atm/(mol•K) from its SI value of 8.3144 J/(mol•K).

Solution: One joule is identical to one m³•Pa (see the table on the previous page).
$$8.3144 \frac{\text{m}^3 \cdot \text{Pa}}{\text{mol} \cdot \text{K}} \times \frac{1000 \text{ L}}{1 \text{ m}^3} \times \frac{1 \text{ atm}}{101325 \text{ Pa}} = 0.082057 \frac{\text{L} \cdot \text{atm}}{\text{mol} \cdot \text{K}}$$

A measurement is **precise** when individual measurements of the same quantity **agree with one another**. A measurement is **accurate** when they **agree with the true value** of the quantity being measured. An **accurate** measurement is **valid**. We get the right answer. A **precise** measurement is **reproducible**. We get a similar answer each time. These terms are related to **sources of error** in a measurement.

Precise measurements are near the **arithmetic mean** of the values. The arithmetic mean is the sum of the measurements divided by the number of measurements. The **mean** is commonly called the **average**. It is the **best estimate** of the quantity.

Random error results from **limitations in equipment or techniques**. A larger **random error decreases precision**. Remember that all measurements reported to proper number of significant digits contain an imprecise final digit to reflect random error.

Systematic error results from **imperfect equipment or technique**. A larger **systematic error decreases accuracy**. Instead of a random error with random fluctuations, there is a result that is too large or small.

Example: An environmental engineering company creates a solution of 5.00 ng/L of a toxin and distributes it to four toxicology labs to test their protocols. Each lab tests the material 5 times. Their results are charted as points on the number lines below. Interpret this data in terms of precision, accuracy, and type of error.

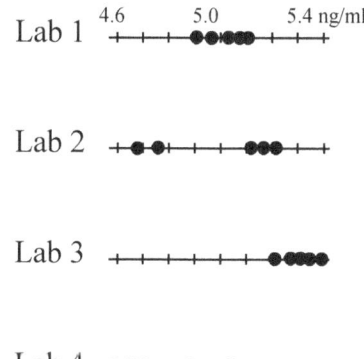

Solution: Results from lab 1 are both accurate and precise when compared to results from the other labs. Results from lab 2 are less precise than those from lab 1. Lab 2 seems to use a protocol that contains a greater random error. However, the mean result from lab 2 is still close to the known value. Lab 3 returned results that were about as precise as lab 1 but inaccurate compared to labs 1 and 2. Lab 3 most likely uses a protocol that yields a systematic error. The data from lab 4 is both imprecise and inaccurate. Systematic and random errors are larger than in lab 1.

Significant figures or **significant digits** are the digits indicating the **precision of a measurement**. There is uncertainty **only** in the last digit.

Example: You measure an object with a ruler marked in millimeters. The reading on the ruler is found to be about 2/3 of the way between 12 and 13 mm. What value should be recorded for its length?

Solution: Recording 13 mm does not give all the information that you found.

Recording $12\frac{2}{3}$ mm implies that an exact ratio was determined.

Recording 12.666 mm gives more information than you found. A value of 12.7 mm or 12.6 mm should be recorded because there is uncertainty only in the last digit.

There are five rules for determining the **number of significant digits** in a quantity.

1) All nonzero digits are significant and all zeros between nonzero digits are significant.
   Example: 4.521 kJ and 7002 u both have four significant figures.
2) Zeros to the left of the first nonzero digit are not significant.
   Example: 0.0002 m contains one significant figure.
3) Zeros to the right of the decimal point are significant figures.
   Example: 32.500 g contains five significant figures.
4) The situation for numbers ending in zeros that are not to the right of the decimal point can be unclear, so **this situation should be avoided** by using scientific notation or a different decimal prefix. Sometimes a decimal point is used as a placeholder to indicate the units-digit is significant. A word like "thousand" or "million" may be used in informal contexts to indicate the remaining digits are not significant.
   Example: 12000 Pa would be considered to have five significant digits by many scientists, but in the context, "The pressure rose from 11000 Pa to 12000 Pa," it almost certainly only has two. "12 thousand pascal" only has two significant figures, but 12000. Pa has five because of the decimal point. The value should be represented as 1.2×10^4 Pa (or 1.2000×10^4 Pa). The best alternative would be to use 12 kPa or 12.000 kPa.
5) Exact numbers have no uncertainty and contain an infinite number of significant figures. These relationships are **definitions**. They are not measurements.
   Example: There are exactly 1000 L in one cubic meter.

There are four rules for **roundingoff significant figures**.

1) If the leftmost digit to be removed is a four or less, then round down. The last remaining digit stays as it was. Example: Round 43.4 g to 2 significant figures. Answer: 43 g.
2) If the leftmost digit to be removed is a six or more, then round up. The last remaining digit increases by one. Example: Round 6.772 to 2 significant figures. Answer: 6.8 g.
3) If the leftmost digit to be removed is a five that is followed by nonzero digits, then round up. The last remaining digit increases by one. Example: Round 18.502 to 2 significant figures. Answer 19 g.
4) If the leftmost digit to be removed is a five followed by nothing or by only zeros, then force the last remaining digit to be even. If it is odd then round up by increasing it by one. If it is even (including zero) then it stays as it was. Examples: Round 18.50 g and 19.5 g to 2 significant figures. Answers: 18.50 g rounds off to 18 g and 19.5 g rounds off to 20 g.

There are three rules for **calculating with significant figures**.

1) For multiplication or division, the result has the same number of significant figures as the term with the least number of significant figures.
    Example: What is the volume of a compartment in the shape of a rectangular prism 1.2 cm long, 2.4 cm high and 0.9 cm deep?
    Solution: Volume=length x height x width.
    Volume $= 1.2 \text{ cm} \times 2.4 \text{ cm} \times 0.9 \text{ cm} = 2.592$ cm (as read on a calculator)
    Round to one digit because 0.9 cm has only one significant digit.
    Volume $= 3 \text{ cm}^3$

2) For addition or subtraction, the result has the same number of digits after the decimal point as the term with the least number of digits after the decimal point.
    Example: Volumes of 250.0 mL, 26 µL, and 4.73 mL are added to a flask. What is the total volume in the flask?
    Solution: Only identical units may be added to each other, so 26 µL is first converted to 0.026 mL.
    Volume $= 250.0 \text{ mL} + 0.026 \text{ mL} + 4.73 \text{ mL} = 254.756$ mL (calculator value)
    Round to one digit after the decimal because 250.0 mL has only one digit after the decimal. Volume $= 254.8$ mL.

3) For multi-step calculations, maintain all significant figures when using a calculator or computer and round off the final value to the appropriate number of significant figures after the calculation. When calculating by hand or when **writing down an intermediate value** in a multi-step calculation, maintain the first insignificant digit. In this text, insignificant digits in intermediate calculations are shown in italics except in the examples for the two rules above.

Experimentation is the method scientists, especially chemists, use to confirm ideas. In order for experiments to be worthwhile, their design is critical.

The design of chemical experiments must include every step to obtain the desired data. In other words, the design must be **complete** and it must include all required **controls**.

Complete design
Familiarity with individual experiments and equipment will help you evaluate if anything is missing from the design. For data requiring a difference between two values, the experiment **must determine both values**. For data utilizing the ideal gas law, the experiment **must determine three values of P, V, n, or T** in order to determine the fourth or one value and a ratio of the other two in order to determine the fourth.

Example: In a mercury manometer, the level of mercury in contact with a reaction vessel is 70.0 mm lower than the level exposed to the atmosphere. Use the following conversion factors:
$$760 \text{ mm Hg} = 1 \text{ atm} = 101.325 \text{ kPa}.$$
What additional information is required to determine the pressure in the vessel in kPa?

Solution: The barometric pressure is needed to determine vessel pressure from an open-ended manometer. A manometer reading is always a **difference** between two pressures. One standard atmosphere is 760 mm mercury, but on a given day at a given location, the actual ambient pressure may vary. If the barometric pressure on the day of the experiment is 104 kPa, the pressure of the vessel is:
$$104 \text{ kPa} + 70.0 \text{ mm Hg} \times \frac{101.325 \text{ kPa}}{760 \text{ mm Hg}} = 113 \text{ kPa}.$$

Controls
Experimental **controls** prevent factors other than those under study from impacting the outcome of the experiment. An **experimental sample** in a controlled experiment is the unknown to be compared against one or more **control samples**. These should be nearly identical to the experimental sample except for the one aspect whose effect is being tested.

A **negative control** is a control sample that is known to lack the effect. A **positive control** is known to contain the effect. Positive controls of varying strengths are often used to generate a **calibration curve** (also called a **standard curve**).

When determining the concentration of a component in a mixture, an **internal standard** is a known concentration of a different substance that is added to the experimental sample. An **external standard** is a known concentration of the substance of interest. External standards are more commonly used. They are not added to the experimental sample; they are analyzed separately.

Replicate samples decrease the impact of random error. A mean is taken of the results from replicate samples to obtain a best value. If one replicate is obviously inconsistent with the results from other samples, it may be discarded as an **outlier** and not counted as an observation when determining the mean. Discarding an outlier is equivalent to assuming the presence of a systematic error for that particular observation. In research, this must be done with great caution because some real-world behavior generates sporadically unusual results.

Example: A pure chemical in aqueous solution is known to absorb light at 615 nm. What controls would best be used with a spectrophotometer to determine the concentration of this chemical when it is present in a mixture with other solutes in an aqueous solution?

Solution: The other solutes may also absorb light at 615 nm. The best negative control would be an identical mixture with the chemical of interest entirely absent. Known concentrations of the chemical could then be added to the negative control to create positive controls (external standards) and develop a calibration curve of the spectrophotometer absorbance reading at 615 nm as a function of concentration. Replicate samples of each standard and of the unknown should be read.

Example: Ethanol is separated from a mixture of organic compounds by gas chromatography. The concentration of each component is proportional to its peak area. However, the chromatograph detector has a variable sensitivity from one run to the next. Is an internal standard required to determine the concentration of ethanol?

Solution: Yes. The variable detector sensitivity may only be accounted for by adding a known concentration of a chemical not found in the mixture as an internal standard to the experimental sample and control samples. The variable sensitivity of the detector will be accounted for by determining the ratio of the peak area for ethanol to the peak area of the added internal standard.

Experimental bias is when a researcher favors one particular outcome over another in an experimental setup. In order to avoid bias, it is imperative to set each experiment under exactly the same conditions, including a *control* experiment, an experiment with a known negative outcome. Additionally, in order to avoid experimental bias, a researcher must not "read" particular results into data.

An example of experimental bias can be seen in the classic example of the mouse in the maze experiment. In this example, a researcher is timing mice as they move through the maze towards a piece of cheese. The experiment relies on the mouse's ability to smell the cheese as it approaches. If one mouse chases a piece of cheddar cheese, while another chases Limburger, or so called "stinky" cheese, clearly the Limburger mouse has a huge advantage over the cheddar mouse. To remove the experimental bias from this experiment, the same cheese should be used in both tests.

Galileo studied the behavior of falling bodies in the 1590's. Almost a century later, Newton followed up on his work and established calculus and physics which governed mechanics for centuries. From that point on, science was on a new pathway. No longer would it merely be the philosophy of the ancient Greeks. It would be a qualitative and quantitative discourse.

Lavoisier made careful measurements in his conservation of mass experiments. Since then, data collection has become a central part of chemical investigations. Data collected, however, takes varied forms depending of the scientific field and complexity of the inquiry.

Data collected is initially organized into tables. Trends or patterns in data can be difficult to identify using tables of numbers. For example, here is a table of carbon dioxide concentrations taken over many years atop Mauna Loa Observatory in Hawaii.

Atmospheric CO_2 concentrations at Mauna Loa

Year	Jan.	Feb.	March	April	May	June	July	Aug.	Sept.	Oct.	Nov.	Dec.	Annual
1958	-99.99	-99.99	315.71	317.45	317.5	-99.99	315.86	314.93	313.19	-99.99	313.34	314.67	-99.99
1959	315.58	316.47	316.65	317.71	318.29	318.16	316.55	314.8	313.84	313.34	314.81	315.59	315.98
1960	316.43	316.97	317.58	319.03	320.03	319.59	318.18	315.91	314.16	313.83	315	316.19	316.91
1961	316.89	317.7	318.54	319.48	320.58	319.78	318.58	316.79	314.99	315.31	316.1	317.01	317.65
1962	317.94	318.56	319.69	320.58	321.01	320.61	319.61	317.4	316.26	315.42	316.69	317.69	318.45
1963	318.74	319.08	319.86	321.39	322.24	321.47	319.74	317.77	316.21	315.99	317.07	318.36	318.99
1964	319.57	-99.99	-99.99	-99.99	322.23	321.89	320.44	318.7	316.7	316.87	317.68	318.71	-99.99
1965	319.44	320.44	320.89	322.13	322.16	321.87	321.21	318.87	317.81	317.3	318.87	319.42	320.03
1966	320.62	321.59	322.39	323.7	324.07	323.75	322.4	320.37	318.64	318.1	319.79	321.03	321.37

Year	Jan	Feb	Mar	Apr	May	Jun	Jul	Aug	Sep	Oct	Nov	Dec
1967	322.33	322.5	323.04	324.42	325	324.09	322.55	320.92	319.26	319.39	320.72	321.96	322.18
1968	322.57	323.15	323.89	325.02	325.57	325.36	324.14	322.11	320.33	320.25	321.32	322.9	323.05
1969	324	324.42	325.64	326.66	327.38	326.7	325.89	323.67	322.38	321.78	322.85	324.12	324.62
1970	325.06	325.98	326.93	328.13	328.07	327.66	326.35	324.69	323.1	323.07	324.01	325.13	325.68
1971	326.17	326.68	327.18	327.78	328.92	328.57	327.37	325.43	323.36	323.56	324.8	326.01	326.32
1972	326.77	327.63	327.75	329.72	330.07	329.09	328.05	326.32	324.84	325.2	326.5	327.55	327.46
1973	328.54	329.56	330.3	331.5	332.48	332.07	330.87	329.31	327.51	327.18	328.16	328.64	329.68
1974	329.35	330.71	331.48	332.65	333.09	332.25	331.18	329.4	327.44	327.37	328.46	329.58	330.25
1975	330.4	331.41	332.04	333.31	333.96	333.59	331.91	330.06	328.56	328.34	329.49	330.76	331.15
1976	331.74	332.56	333.5	334.58	334.87	334.34	333.05	330.94	329.3	328.94	330.31	331.68	332.15
1977	332.92	333.42	334.7	336.07	336.74	336.27	334.93	332.75	331.58	331.16	332.4	333.85	333.9
1978	334.97	335.39	336.64	337.76	338.01	337.89	336.54	334.68	332.76	332.54	333.92	334.95	335.5
1979	336.23	336.76	337.96	338.89	339.47	339.29	337.73	336.09	333.91	333.86	335.29	336.73	336.85
1980	338.01	338.36	340.08	340.77	341.46	341.17	339.56	337.6	335.88	336.01	337.1	338.21	338.69
1981	339.23	340.47	341.38	342.51	342.91	342.25	340.49	338.43	336.69	336.85	338.36	339.61	339.93
1982	340.75	341.61	342.7	343.56	344.13	343.35	342.06	339.82	337.97	337.86	339.26	340.49	341.13
1983	341.37	342.52	343.1	344.94	345.75	345.32	343.99	342.39	339.86	339.99	341.16	342.99	342.78
1984	343.7	344.51	345.28	347.08	347.43	346.79	345.4	343.28	341.07	341.35	342.98	344.22	344.42
1985	344.97	346	347.43	348.35	348.93	348.25	346.56	344.69	343.09	342.8	344.24	345.56	345.9
1986	346.29	346.96	347.86	349.55	350.21	349.54	347.94	345.91	344.86	344.17	345.66	346.9	347.15
1987	348.02	348.47	349.42	350.99	351.84	351.25	349.52	348.1	346.44	346.36	347.81	348.96	348.93
1988	350.43	351.72	352.22	353.59	354.22	353.79	352.39	350.44	348.72	348.88	350.07	351.34	351.48
1989	352.76	353.07	353.68	355.42	355.67	355.13	353.9	351.67	349.8	349.99	351.3	352.53	352.91
1990	353.66	354.7	355.39	356.2	357.16	356.22	354.82	352.91	350.96	351.18	352.83	354.21	354.19
1991	354.72	355.75	357.16	358.6	359.34	358.24	356.17	354.03	352.16	352.21	353.75	354.99	355.59
1992	355.98	356.72	357.81	359.15	359.66	359.25	357.03	355	353.01	353.31	354.16	355.4	356.37
1993	356.7	357.16	358.38	359.46	360.28	359.6	357.57	355.52	353.7	353.98	355.33	356.8	357.04
1994	358.36	358.91	359.97	361.26	361.68	360.95	359.55	357.49	355.84	355.99	357.58	359.04	358.88
1995	359.96	361	361.64	363.45	363.79	363.26	361.9	359.46	358.06	357.75	359.56	360.7	360.88
1996	362.05	363.25	364.03	364.72	365.41	364.97	363.65	361.49	359.46	359.6	360.76	362.33	362.64
1997	363.18	364	364.57	366.35	366.79	365.62	364.47	362.51	360.19	360.77	362.43	364.28	363.76
1998	365.32	366.15	367.31	368.61	369.3	368.87	367.64	365.77	363.9	364.23	365.46	366.97	366.63
1999	368.15	368.86	369.58	371.12	370.97	370.33	369.25	366.91	364.6	365.09	366.63	367.96	368.29
2000	369.08	369.4	370.45	371.59	371.75	371.62	370.04	368.04	366.54	366.63	368.2	369.43	369.4
2001	370.17	371.39	372	372.75	373.88	373.17	371.48	369.42	367.83	367.96	369.55	371.1	370.89
2002	372.29	372.94	373.38	374.71	375.4	375.26	373.87	371.35	370.57	370.1	371.93	373.63	372.95

(Carbon Dioxide Information Analysis Center (CDIAC))

However, more often than not, the data is compiled into graphs. Graphs help scientists visualize and interpret the variation in data. Depending on the nature of the data, there are many types of graphs. Bar graphs, pie charts and line graphs are just a few methods used to pictorially represent numerical data.

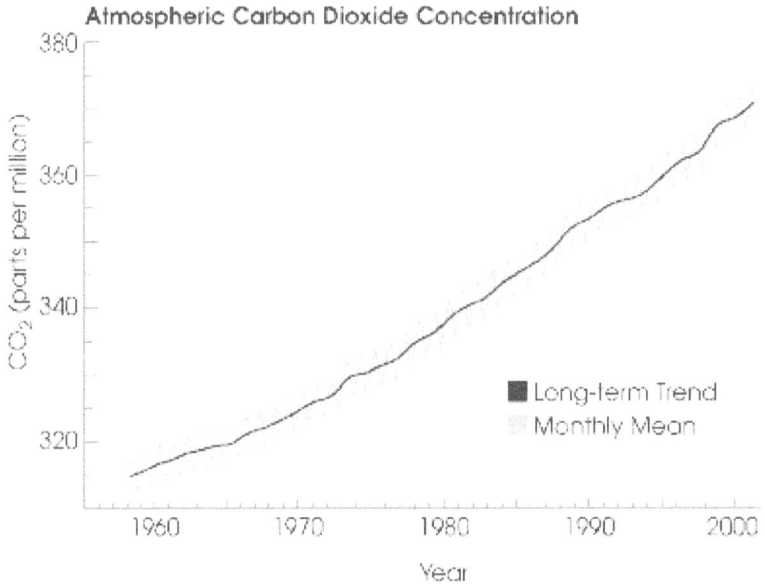

Atmospheric CO_2 measured at Mauna Loa. This is a famous graph called the Keeling Curve (courtesy NASA).

Interpretation of graphical data shows that on the x-axis is the variable of time in units of years and the y-axis represents the variable of CO_2 concentration in units of parts per million (ppm). The best fit line (solid dark line) shows the trend in CO_2 concentrations during the time period. The steady upward-sloping line indicates a trend of increasing CO_2 concentrations during the time period. However, the light blue line which indicates monthly mean CO_2 levels shows a periodic trend in CO_2 levels during the year. This periodic trend is accounted for by the changes in the seasons. In the spring and summer, deciduous trees and plants undergo increased increased photosynthesis and remove more CO_2 from the atmosphere in the Northern Hemisphere.

The interpretation of data and construction and interpretation of graphs are central practices in science. Graphs are effective visual tools which relay information quickly and reveal trends easily. While there are several different types of graphical displays, extracting information from them can be described in three basic steps.

1. Describe the graph: What does the title say? What is displayed on the x- and y-axis, including the units.
    - Determine the set-up of the graph.
    - Make sure the units used are understood.
      For example, g·cm^3 means g/cm^3
    - Notice symbols used and check for legend or explanation.

2. Describe the data: Identify the range of data. Are patterns reflected in the data?
3. Interpret the data: How do patterns seen in the graph relate to other things? What conclusions can be drawn from the patterns?

There are seven basic types of graphs.

Column Graphs

Column graphs, consist of patterned rectangles displayed along a baseline called the x-category or the horizontal axis. The height of the rectangle represents the amount of data. Column graphs best show:
• changes in data over time (short time series)
• comparisons of several items (relationship between two series)

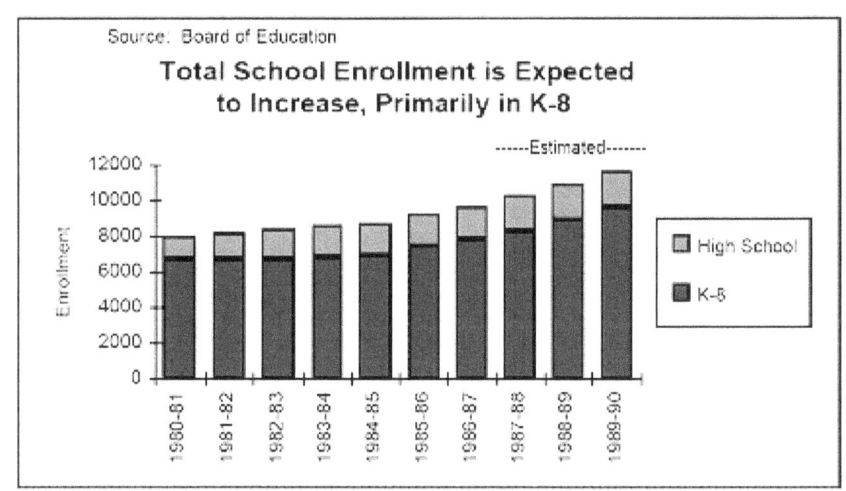

Bar Graphs

Column graphs in which the rectangles are arranged horizontally. The length of each rectangle represents its value. Bar graphs are sometimes referred to as histograms. Bar graphs best show:
- data series with no natural order.

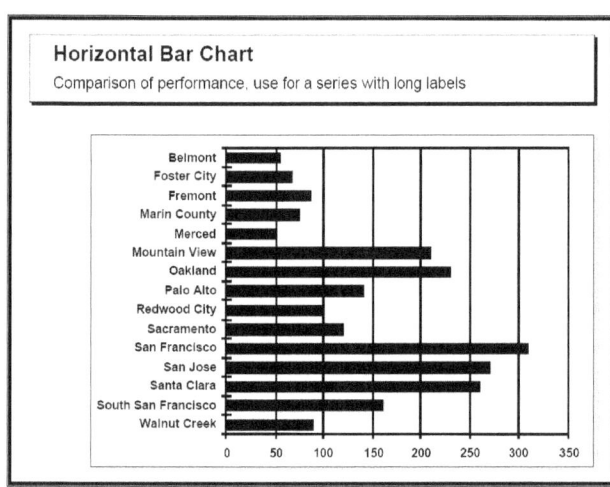

Bar graphs are good for looking at differences amongst similar things. If the data are a time series, a carefully chosen column graph is generally more appropriate but bar graphs can be used to vary a presentation when many column graphs of time series are used. One advantage of bar graphs is that there is greater horizontal space for variable descriptors because the vertical axis is the category axis.

Line Graphs

Line graphs show data points connected by lines; different series are given different line markings (for example, dashed or dotted) or different tick marks. Line graphs are useful when the data points are more important than the transitions between them. They best show:
- the comparison of long series
- a general trend is the message.

Line graphs are good for showing trends or changes over time.

Pie Charts

A pie chart is a circle with radii connecting the center to the edge. The area between two radii is called a slice. Data values are proportionate to the angle between the radii.
Pie charts best show:
- parts of a whole

Be careful of too many slices since they result in a cluttered graph. Six slices are as many as can be handled on one pie.

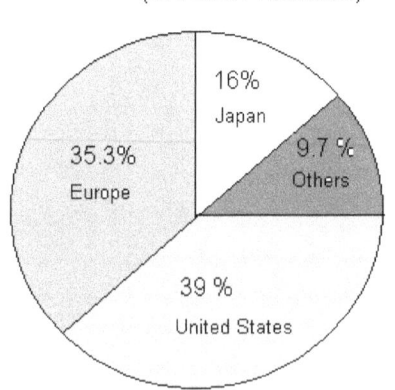

SCIENCE: CHEMISTRY 130

Area Graphs

Area charts show the relative contributions over time that each data series makes to a whole picture and are "stacked line graphs" in the sense that values are added to the variables below. Unlike line graphs, the space between lines is filled with shadings.

Area graphs are similar to line graphs with the added drama of shading

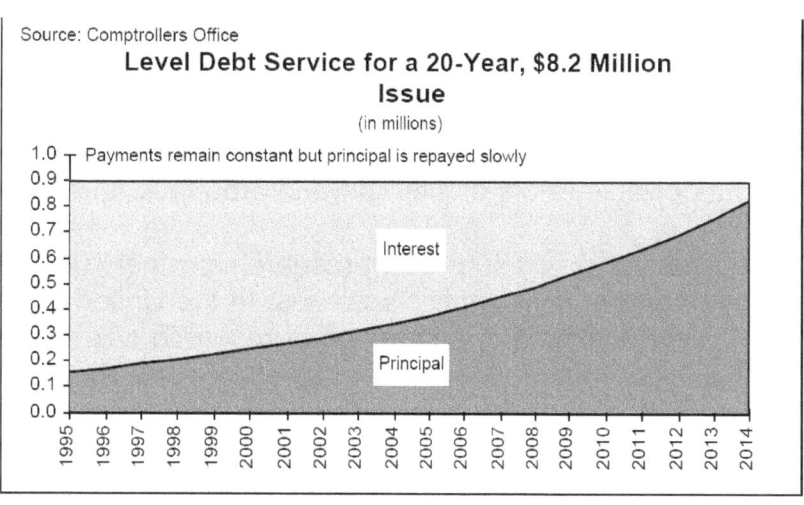

between lines to emphasize variation between whatever the lines represent. They differ from line graphs in that the shaded areas are "added" one on top of the next. Thus, the scale provides accurate measurements only for the lowest part of the graph. This can cause misinterpretation if not fully understood. If reasonable, consider putting the "flattest" graph on the bottom.

Scatter Graphs

A scatter plot is the simplest type of graph. It simply plots the data points against their values, without adding an connecting lines, bars or other stuff. The first variable is measured along the x-axis and the second along the y-axis. Because of this, scatter graphs do not have descriptors in the same sense as other graphs. Scatter graphs best show

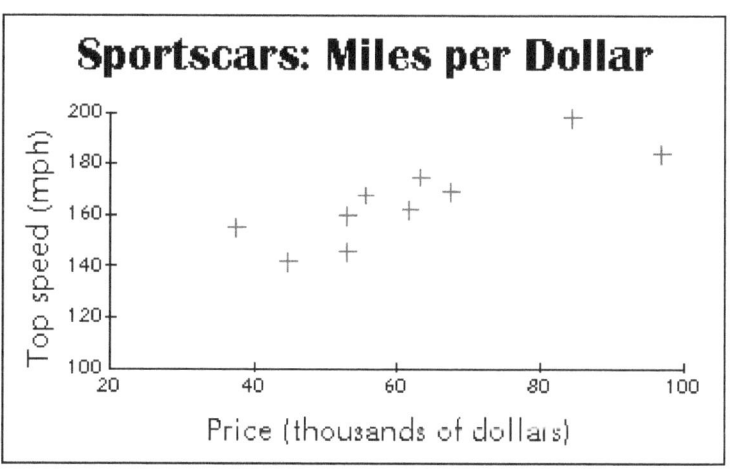

possible relationships between two variables. The purpose of the graph is to try to decide if some partial or indirect relationship—a correlation—exists.

When the results of repeated experiments are consistent and patterns become apparent, the next stage of the process is reporting the results, often by publishing a scientific paper. Hundreds of scientific societies throughout the world publish journals containing articles that report research. The published work is then permanently available to the scientific community. Other scientists are then free to examine the results, repeat the experiments, or take the research further by designing new experiments. Some may critique the oriiginal research, pointing out possible errors or alternative interpretations of the data.

A scientist may also present research to other scientists at meetings sponsoored by one of many scientific societies. In the United States, the American Chemical Society hosts many gatherings of research chemists. It is through presentations like these that the researcher has an opportunity to interact directly with others in the field.

As a result of publication and presentation of research, science is a group activity, providing many opportunities for correcting errors.

Skill 18.2   Select appropriate experimental procedures and equipment for the measurement and determination of chemical reactions and properties.

Equipment
The descriptions and diagrams in this skill are included to help you **identify** the techniques. They are **not meant as a guide to perform the techniques** in the lab.

Handling liquids
A **beaker** (below left)\ is a cylindrical cup with a notch at the top. They are often used for making solutions. An **Erlenmeyer** flask (below center) is a conical flask. A liquid in an Erlenmeyer flask will evaporate more slowly than when it is in a beaker and it is easier to swirl about. A **round-bottom flask** (below-right) is also called a Florence flask. It is designed for uniform heating, but it requires a stand to keep it upright.

A **test tube** has a rounded bottom and is designed to hold and to heat small volumes of liquid. A **Pasteur pipet** is a small glass tube with a long thin capillary tip and a latex suction bulb.

A **crucible** is a cup-shaped container made of porcelain or metal for holding chemical compounds when heating them to very high temperatures. A **watch glass** is a concave circular piece of glass that is usually used as surface to evaporate a liquid and observe precipitates or crystallization. A **Dewar flask** is a double walled vacuum flask with a metallic coating to provide good thermal insulation and short term storage of liquid nitrogen.

Fitting and cleaning glassware
If a thermometer or funnel must be threaded through a stopper or a piece of tubing and it won't fit, either **make the hole larger or use a smaller piece of glass**. Use soapy water or glycerol to **lubricate** the glass before inserting it. Hold the glass piece as close as possible to the stopper during insertion. It's also good practice to wrap a towel around the glass and the stopper during this time. **Never apply undue pressure**.

Glassware sometimes contains **tapered ground-glass joints** to allow direct glass-to-glass connections. A thin layer of joint **grease** must be applied when assembling an apparatus with ground-glass joints. Too much grease will contaminate the experiment, and too little will permit the components to be permanently locked together. Disassemble the glassware with a **twisting** motion immediately after the experiment is over.

Cleaning glassware becomes more difficult with time, so it should be cleaned soon after the experiment is completed. Wipe off any lubricant with paper towel moistened in a solvent like hexane before washing the glassware. Use a brush with lab soap and water. Acetone may be used to dissolve most organic residues. Spent solvents should be transferred to a waste container for proper disposal.

Heating
A **hot plate** (shown below) is used to heat Erlenmeyer flasks, beakers and other containers with a flat bottom. Hot plates often have a built-in **magnetic stirrer**. A **heating mantle** has a hemispherical cavity that is used to heat round-bottom flasks. A **Bunsen burner** is designed to burn natural gas. Burners are useful for heating high-boiling point liquids, water, or solutions of non-flammable materials. They are also used for bending glass tubing. Smooth boiling is achieved by adding **boiling stones** to a liquid.

Boiling and melting point determination

Boiling point is determined by heating the liquid along with a boiling stone in a clamped test tube with a clamped thermometer positioned just above the liquid surface and away from the tube walls. The constant highest-value temperature reading after boiling is achieved is the boiling point.

Melting point is determined by placing pulverized solid in a capillary tube and using a rubber band to fasten the capillary to a thermometer so the sample is at the level of the thermometer bulb. The thermometer and sample are inserted into a **Thiele tube** filled with mineral or silicon oil. The Thiele tube has a sidearm that is heated with a Bunsen burner to create a flow of hot oil. This flow maintains an even temperature during heating. The melting point is read when the sample turns into a liquid. Many **electric melting point devices** are also available that heat the sample more slowly to give more accurate results. These are also safer to use than a Thiele tube with a Bunsen burner.

Centrifugation

A **centrifuge** separates two immiscible phases by spinning the mixture (placed in a **centrifuge tube**) at high speeds. A **microfuge** or microcentrifuge is a small centrifuge. The weight of material placed in a centrifuge must be **balanced**, so if one sample is placed in a centrifuge, a tube with roughly an equal mass of water should be placed opposite the sample.

Filtration

The goal of **gravity filtration** is to remove solids from a liquid and obtain a liquid without solid particulates. Filter paper is folded, placed in a funnel on top of a flask, and wetted with the solvent to seal it to the funnel. Next the mixture is poured through, and the solid-free liquid is collected from the flask.

The goal of **vacuum filtration** is usually to remove liquids from a solid to obtain a solid that is dry. An **aspirator** or a **vacuum pump** is used to provide suction though a rubber tube to a **filter trap**. The trap is attached to a **filter flask** (show to the right) by a second rubber tube. The filter flask is an Erlenmeyer flask with a thick wall and a hose barb for the vacuum tube. Filter flasks are used to filter material using a **Büchner funnel** (shown to the right) or a smaller **Hirsch funnel** These porcelain or plastic funnels hold a circular piece of filter paper. A single-hole rubber stopper supports the funnel in the flask while maintaining suction.

Mixing

Heterogeneous reaction mixtures in flasks are often mixed by **swirling**. To use a magnetic stirrer, a bar magnet coated with Teflon called a flea or a **stir bar** is slid into the container, and the container is placed on the stirrer. The container should be moved and the stir speed adjusted for smooth mixing. Mechanical stirring paddles, agitators, vortexers, or rockers are also used for mixing.

Decanting
When a course solid has settled at the bottom of a flask of liquid, **decanting** the solution simply means pouring out the liquid and leaving the solid behind.

Extraction
Compounds in solution are often separated based on their **solubility differences**During **liquid-liquid extraction** (also called **solvent extraction**), a second solvent immiscible to the first is added to the solution in a **separatory funnel** (shown at right. Usually one solvent is nonpolar and the other is a polar solvent like water. The two solvents are immiscible and separate from each other after the mixture is shaken to allow solute exchange. One layer contains the compound of interest, and the other contains impurities to be discarded. The solutions in the two layers are separated from each other by draining liquid through the stopcock.

Titration
Titration is described in **Skill 22.5**

Distillation
Liquids in solution are often separated based on their **boiling point differences**. During simple **distillation**, the solution is placed in a round-bottom flask called the **distillation flask** or **still pot**, and boiling stones are added. The apparatus shown below is assembled (note that clamps and stands are not show), and the still pot is heated using a heating mantle. Hot vaporduring boiling escapes through the **distillation head**, enters the **condenser**and is cooled and condensed back to a liquid. The vapor loses its heat to water flowing through the outside of the condenser. The condensate or **distillate** falls into the **receiving flask**. The apparatus is open to the atmosphere through a vent above the receiving flask. The distillate will contain a higher concentration of material with the lower boiling point. The less volatile component will achieve a high concentration in the still pot. Head temperature is monitored during the process. Distillation may also be used to remove a solid from a pure liquid by boiling and condensing the liquid.

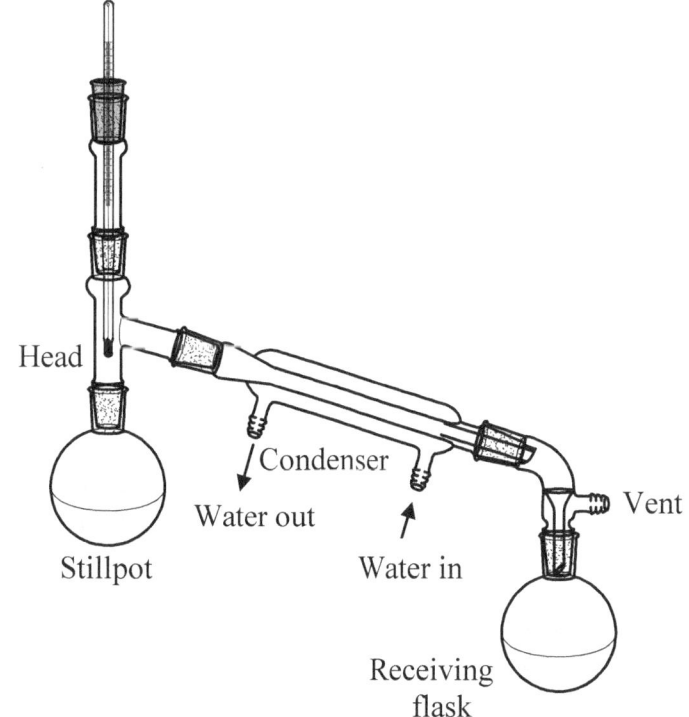

Skill 18.3 Recognize safety practices in the chemistry laboratory, including the characteristics and purposes of chemical hygiene plans.

The necessity of safety in a laboratory is obvious. The information below is meant as an aid to you. It is not an exhaustive list. It is your responsibility to obtain all pertinent safety regulations and information from your institution, state, and federal authorities where applicable. A chemical hygiene plan (CHP) is a written report or manual that summarizes all of the science department's safety regulations, proper laboratory procedures for handling hazardous chemicals, and training procedures. The goal in developing these rules and procedures should be to minimize the exposure of employees and students to hazardous chemicals. The CHP should include:

- General laboratory rules and procedures
- Personal protection equipment requirements
- Spill and accident procedures
- Chemical storage rules and procedures
- Safety equipment requirements and inspection procedures
- Employee safety training requirements
- Exposure and medical evaluation processes
- Emergency evacuation plan

Here is some information that will help with a chemical hygiene plan.

Chemical purchase, use, and disposal
- Inventory all chemicals on hand at least annually. Keep the list up-to-date as chemicals are consumed and replacement chemicals are received.
- If possible, limit the purchase of chemicals to quantities that will be consumed within one year and that are packaged in small containers suitable for direct use in the lab without transfer to other containers.
- Label all chemicals to be stored with date of receipt or preparation and have labels initialed by the person responsible.
- Generally, bottles of chemicals should not remain:
  - Unused on shelves in the lab for more than one week. Move these chemicals to the storeroom or main stockroom.
  - In the storeroom near the lab unused for more than one month. Move these chemicals to the main stockroom.
  - Check shelf life of chemicals. Properly dispose of any out dated chemicals.
- Ensure that the disposal procedures for waste chemicals conform to environmental protection requirements.
- Do not purchase or store large quantities of flammable liquids. Fire department officials can recommend the maximum quantities that may be kept on hand.
- Never open a chemical container until you understand the label and the relevant portions of the MSDS.

Chemical Storage Plan for Laboratories

- Chemicals should be stored according to hazard class (ex. flammables, oxidizers, health hazards/toxins, corrosives, etc.).
- Store chemicals away from direct sunlight or localized heat.
- All chemical containers should be properly labeled, dated upon receipt, and dated upon opening.
- Store hazardous chemicals below shoulder height of the shortest person working in the lab.
- Shelves should be painted or covered with chemical-resistant paint or chemical-resistant coating.
- Shelves should be secure and strong enough to hold chemicals being stored on them. Do not overload shelves.
- Personnel should be aware of the hazards associated with all hazardous materials.
- Separate solids from liquids.

Below are examples of chemical groups that can be used to categorize storage. Use these groups as examples when separating chemicals for compatibility. Please note: reactive chemicals must be more closely analyzed since they have a greater potential for violent reactions.

Acids

- Make sure that all acids are stored by compatibility (ex. separate inorganics from organics).
- Store concentrated acids on lower shelves in chemical-resistant trays or in a corrosives cabinet. This will temporarily contain spills or leaks and protect shelving from residue.
- Separate acids from incompatible materials such as bases, active metals (ex. sodium, magnesium, potassium) and from chemicals which can generate toxic gases when combined (ex. sodium cyanide and iron sulfide).

Bases

- Store bases away from acids.
- Store concentrated bases on lower shelves in chemical-resistant trays or in a corrosives cabinet. This will temporarily contain spills or leaks and protect shelving from residue.

SCIENCE: CHEMISTRY

Flammables

- Approved flammable storage cabinets should be used for flammable liquid storage.
- You may store 20 gallons of flammable liquids per 100 sq.ft. in a properly fire separated lab. The maximum allowable quantity for flammable liquid storage in any size lab is not to exceed 120 gallons.
- You may store up to 10 gallons of flammable liquids outside of approved flammable storage cabinets.
- An additional 25 gallons may be stored outside of an approved storage cabinet if it is stored in approved safety cans not to exceed 2 gallons in size.
- Use only explosion-proof or intrinsically safe refrigerators and freezers for storing flammable liquids.

Peroxide-Forming Chemicals

- Peroxide-forming chemicals should be stored in airtight containers in a dark, cool, and dry place.
- Unstable chemicals such as peroxide-formers must always be labeled with date received, date opened, and disposal/expiration date.
- Peroxide-forming chemicals should be properly disposed of before the date of expected peroxide formation (typically 6-12 months after opening).
- Suspicion of peroxide contamination should be immediately investigated. Contact Laboratory Safety for procedures.

Water-Reactive Chemicals

- Water reactive chemicals should be stored in a cool, dry place.
- Do not store water reactive chemicals under sinks or near water baths.
- Class D fire extinguishers for the specific water reactive chemical being stored should be made available.

Oxidizers

- Make sure that all oxidizers are stored by compatibility.
- Store oxidizers away from flammables, combustibles, and reducing agents.

Toxins

- Toxic compounds should be stored according to the nature of the chemical, with appropriate security employed when necessary.
- A "Poison Control Network" telephone number should be posted in the laboratory where toxins are stored. Color coded labeling systems that may be found in your lab:

Hazard	Color Code
Flammables	Red
Health Hazards/Toxins	Blue
Reactives/Oxidizers	Yellow
Contact Hazards	White
General Storage	Gray, Green, Orange

Please Note: Chemicals with labels that are colored and striped may react with other chemicals in the same hazard class. See MSDS for more information. Chemical containers which are not color coded should have hazard information on the label. Read the label carefully and store accordingly.

Schools are regulated by the Environmental Protection Agency, as well as state and local agencies when it comes to disposing of chemical waste. Check with your state science supervisor, local college or university environmental health and safety specialists and the Laboratory Safety Workshop for advice in the disposal of chemical waste. The American Chemical Society publishes an excellent guidebook, *Laboratory Waste Management, A Guidebook* (1994).

The following are merely guidelines for disposing of chemical waste.

You may dispose of hazardous waste as outlined below. It is the responsibility of the generator to ensure hazardous waste does not end up in ground water, soil or the atmosphere through improper disposal.

1. **Sanitary Sewer** - Some chemicals (acids or bases) may be neutralized and disposed to the sanitary sewer. This disposal option must be approved by the local waste water treatment authority prior to disposal. This may not be an option for some small communities that do not have sufficient treatment capacity at the waste water treatment plant for these types of wastes. Hazardous waste may NOT be disposed of in this manner. This includes heavy metals.

2. **Household Hazardous Waste Facility** - Waste chemicals may be disposed through a county household hazardous waste facility (HHW) or through a county contracted household hazardous waste disposal company. Not all counties have a program to accept waste from schools. Verify with your county HHW facility that they can handle your waste prior to making arrangements.

3. **Disposal Through a Contractor** - A contractor may be used for the disposal of the waste chemicals. Remember that you must keep documentation of your hazardous waste disposal for at least three years. This information must include a waste manifest, reclamation agreement or any written record which describes the waste and how much was disposed, where it was disposed and when it was disposed. Waste analysis records must also be kept when making a determination is necessary. **Any unknown chemicals should be considered hazardous!**

Safety

Disclaimer: The information presented below is intended as a starting point for identification purposes only and should not be regarded as a comprehensive guide for safety procedures in the laboratory. It is the responsibility of the readers of this book to consult with professional advisers about safety procedures in their laboratory.

The following list is a summary of the requirements for chemical laboratories contained in the above documents:

1) Dousing shower and eye-wash with a floor drain are required where students handle potentially dangerous materials.
2) Accessible fully-charged fire extinguishers of the appropriate type and fire blankets must be present if a fire hazard exists.
3) There must be a master control valve or switch accessible to and within 15 feet of the instructor's station for emergency cut-off of all gas cocks, compressed air valves, water, or electrical services accessible to students. Valves must completely shut-off with a one-quarter turn. This master control is in addition to the regular main gas supply cut-off, and the main supply cut-off must be shut down upon activation of the fire alarm system.
4) A high capacity emergency exhaust system with a source of positive ventilation must be installed, and signs providing instructions must be permanently installed at the emergency exhaust system fan switch.
5) Fume hoods must contain supply fans that automatically shut down when the emergency exhaust fan is turned on.
6) Rooms and/or cabinets for chemical storage must have limited student access and ventilation to the exterior of the building separate from the air-conditioning system. The rooms should be kept at moderate temperature, be well-illuminated, and contain doors lockable from the outside and operable at all times from the inside. Cabinet shelves must have a half-inch lip on the front and be constructed of non-corrosive material.
7) Appropriate caution signs must be placed at hazardous work and storage areas.

Therefore, all chemistry laboratories should be equipped with the following safety equipment. Both teachers and students should be familiar with the operation of this equipment.

Fire extinguisher: Fire extinguishers are rated for the type of fire it will extinguish. Chemical laboratories should have a combination ABC extinguisher along with a type D fire extinguisher. If a type D extinguisher is not available, a bucket of dry sand will do. Make sure you are trained to use the type of extinguisher available in your setting.

- **Class A** fires are ordinary materials like burning paper, lumber, cardboard, plastics etc.
- **Class B** fires involve flammable or combustible liquids such as gasoline, kerosene, and common organic solvents used in the laboratory.
- **Class C** fires involve energized electrical equipment, such as appliances, switches, panel boxes, power tools, hot plates and stirrers. Water is usually a dangerous extinguishing medium for class C fires because of the risk of electrical shock unless a specialized water mist extinguisher is used.
- **Class D** fires involve combustible metals, such as magnesium, titanium, potassium and sodium as well as pyrophoric organometallic reagents such as alkyllithiums, Grignards and diethylzinc. These materials burn at high temperatures and will react violently with water, air, and/or other chemicals. Handle with care!!
- **Class K** fires are kitchen fires. This class was added to the NFPA portable extinguishers Standard 10 in 1998. Kitchen extinguishers installed before June 30, 1998 are "grandfathered" into the standard.

Some fires may be a combination of these! Your fire extinguishers should have ABC ratings on them. These ratings are determined under ANSI/UL Standard 711 and look something like "3-A:40-B:C". Higher numbers mean more firefighting power. In this example, the extinguisher has a good firefighting capacity for Class A, B and C fires. NFPA has a brief description of UL 711 if you want to know more.

Eyewash:
In the event of an eye injury or chemical splash, use the eyewash immediately.

Help the injured person by holding their eyelids open while rinsing.

Rinse copiously and have the eyes checked by a physician afterwards.

Fire Blanket:

A fire blanket can be used to smother a fire. However, use caution when using a fire blanket on a clothing fire. Some fabrics are polymers that melt onto the skin. Stop, Drop and Roll is the best method for extinguishing clothing on fire.

Safety Shower:

Use a safety shower in the event of a chemical spill. Pull the overhead handle and remove clothing that may be contaminated with chemicals, to allow the skin to be rinsed.

Eye protection:
Everyone present must wear eye protection when anyone in the laboratory is performing any of the following activities:
1) Handling hazardous chemicals
2) Handling laboratory glassware
3) Using an open flame.

Safety glasses do not offer protection from splashing liquids. Safety glasses appear similar to ordinary glasses and may be used in an environment that only requires protection from **flying fragments**. Safety glasses with side-shields offer additional protection from **flying fragments approaching from the side**.

Safety goggles offer protection from both flying fragments and splashing liquids. **Only safety goggles** are suitable for eye protection where **hazardous chemicals** are used and handled. Safety goggles with no ventilation (type G) or with indirect ventilation (type H) are both acceptable. Goggles should be marked "Z87" to show they meet federal standards.

Skin protection:

Wear gloves made of a material known to resist penetration by the chemical being handled. Check gloves for holes and the absence of interior contamination. Wash hands and arms and clean under fingernails after working in a laboratory.

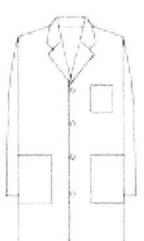

Wear a lab coat or apron. Wear footwear that completely covers the feet.

Ventillation:

Using a Fume Hood

A fume hood carries away vapors from reagents or reactions you may be working with. Using a fume hood correctly will reduce your personal exposure to potentially harmful fumes or vapors. When using a fume hood, keep the following in mind.

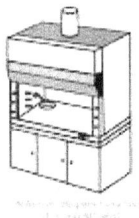

• Place equipment or reactions as far back in the hood as is practical. This will improve the efficiency of fume collection and removal.

• Turn on the light inside the hood using the switch on the outside panel, near the electrical outlets.

• The glass sash of the hood is a safety shield. The sash will fall automatically to the appropriate height for efficient operation and should not be raised above this level, except to move equipment in and out of the hood. Keep the sash between your body and the inside of the hood. If the height of the automatic stop is too high to protect your face and body, lower the sash below this point. Do not stick your head inside a hood or climb inside a hood.

• Wipe up all spills immediately. Clean the glass of your hood, if a splash occurs.

• When you are finished using a hood, lower the sash to the level marked by the sticker on the side.

Work habits
- Never work alone in a laboratory or storage area.
- Never eat, drink, smoke, apply cosmetics, chew gum or tobacco, or store food or beverages in a laboratory environment or storage area.
- Keep containers closed when they are not in use.
- Never pipet by mouth.
- Restrain loose clothing and long hair and remove dangling jewelry.
- Tape all Dewar flasks with fabric-based tape.
- Check all glassware before use. Discard if chips or star cracks are present.
- Never leave heat sources unattended.
- Do not store chemicals and/or apparatus on the lab bench or on the floor or aisles of the lab or storage room.
- Keep lab shelves organized.
- Never place a chemical, not even water, near the edges of a lab bench.
- Use a fume hood that is known to be in operating condition when working with toxic, flammable, and/or volatile substances.
- Never put your head inside a fume hood.
- Never store anything in a fume hood.
- Obtain, read, and be sure you understand the MSDS (see below) for each chemical that is to be used before allowing students to begin an experiment.
- Analyze new lab procedures and student-designed lab procedures in advance to identify any hazardous aspects. Minimize and/or eliminate these components before proceeding. Ask yourself these questions:
    - What are the hazards?
    - What are the worst possible things that could go wrong?
    - How will I deal with them?
    - What are the prudent practices, protective facilities and equipment necessary to minimize the risk of exposure to the hazards?
- Analyze close calls and accidents to eliminate their causes and prevent them from occurring again.
- Identify which chemicals may be disposed of in the drain by consulting the MSDS or the supplier. Clear one chemical down the drain by flushing with water before introducing the next chemical.
- Preplan for emergencies.
    - Keep the fire department informed of your chemical inventory and its location.
    - Consult with a local physician about toxins used in the lab and ensure that your area is prepared in advance to treat victims of toxic exposure.
    - Identify devices that should be shut off if possible in an emergency.
    - Inform your students of the designated escape route and alternate route.

Substitutions
- When feasible, substitute less hazardous chemicals for chemicals with greater hazards in experiments.
- Dilute substances when possible instead of using concentrated solutions.
- Use lesser quantities instead of greater quantities in experiments when possible.
- Use films, videotapes, computer displays, and other methods rather than experiments involving hazardous substances.

Label information

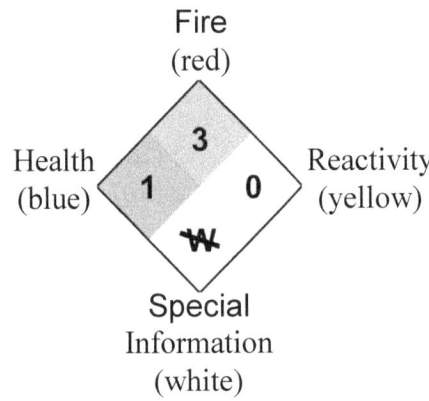

Chemical labels contain safety information in four parts:
1) There will be a signal word. From most to least potentially dangerous, this word will be "Danger!" "Warning!" or "Caution."
2) Statements of hazard (e.g., "Flammable", "May Cause Irritation") follow the signal word. Target organs may be specified.
3) Precautionary measures are listed such as "Keep away from ignition sources" or "Use only with adequate ventilation."
4) First aid information is usually included such as whether to induce vomiting and how to induce vomiting if the chemical is ingested.

Chemical hazard pictorial
Several different pictorials are used on labels to indicate the level of a chemical hazard. The most common is the **"fire diamond" NFPA (National Fire Prevention Association) pictorial** shown at left. A zero indicates a minimal hazard and a four indicates a severe risk. Special information includes if the chemical reacts with water, **OX** for an oxidizer, **COR ACID** for a corrosive acid, and **COR ALK** for a corrosive base. The "Health" hazard level is for **acute toxicity only**.

Pictorials are designed for **quick reference in emergency situations**, but they are also useful as minimal summaries of safety information for a chemical. They are not required on chemicals you purchase, so it's a good idea to add a label pictorial to every chemical you receive if one is not already present. **The entrance to areas where chemicals are stored should carry a fire diamond label** to represent the materials present.

Procedures for flammable materials: minimize fire risk The vapors of a flammable liquid **or solid** may travel across the room to an ignition source and cause a fire or explosion.
- Store in safety cans in an approved safety cabinet for flammable liquids.
- Minimize volumes and concentrations used in an experiment
- Minimize the time containers are open.
- Minimize ignition sources in the laboratory.
- Ensure that there is good air movement in the laboratory before the experiment.
- Make sure fire extinguishers are functional.
- Tell the students that the "Stop, Drop, and Roll" technique is best for a clothing fire outside the lab, but in the lab they should walk calmly to the safety shower and use it. Practice this procedure with students in drills.
- A fire blanket should not be used for clothing fires because clothes often contain polymers that melt onto the skin. Pressing these fabrics into the skin with a blanket increases burn damage.
- If a demonstration of an exploding gas or vapor is performed, it should be done behind a safety shield using glass vessels taped with fabric tape.

Procedures for corrosive materials: minimize risk of contact
Corrosive materials **destroy or permanently change living tissue** through chemical action. **Irritants** cause inflammation due to an immune response but not through chemical action. The effect is usually reversible but can be severe and long lasting. **Sensitizers** are irritants that cause no symptoms after the first exposure but may cause irritation during a later exposure.
- Always store corrosives below eye level.
- Only diluted corrosives should be used in pre-high school laboratories and their use at full-strength in high school should be limited.
- Dilute corrosive materials by **adding them to water**. Adding water to a concentrated acid or base can cause rapid boiling and splashing.
- Wear goggles and face shield when handling hazardous corrosives. The face, ears, and neck should be protected.
- Wear gloves known to be impervious to the chemical. Wear sleeve gauntlets and a lab apron made of impervious material if splashing is likely.
- Always wash your hands after handling corrosives.
- Splashes on skin should be flushed with flowing water for 15 minutes while a doctor is called.
- If someone splashes a corrosive material on their clothing have them remove all of their clothing in the safety shower.
- If someone splashes a corrosive in their eyes, immediately have them use the eyewash for 15 minutes, continuously moving their eyeballs to cleanse the optic nerve at the back of the eye. A doctor should be called.

Procedures for toxic materials: minimize exposure. Toxic effects are either **chronic** or **acute**. Chronic effects are seen after repeated exposures or after one long exposure. Acute effects occur within a few hours at most.
- Use the smallest amount needed at the lowest concentration for the shortest period of time possible. Weigh the risks against the educational benefits.
- Be aware of the five different routes of exposure
    1) Inhalation-the ability to smell a toxin is not a proper indication of unsafe exposure. Work in the fume hood when using toxins. Minimize dusts and mists by cleaning often, cleaning spills rapidly, and maintaining good ventilation in the lab.
    2) Absorption through intact skin-always wear impervious gloves if the MSDS indicates this route of exposure.
    3) Ingestion
    4) Absorption through other body orifices such as ear canal and eye socket.
    5) Injection by a cut from broken contaminated glassware or other sharp equipment.
- Be aware of the first symptoms of overexposure described by the MSDS. Often these are headache, nausea, and dizziness. Get to fresh air and do not return until the symptoms have passed. If the symptom returns when you come back into the lab, contact a physician and have the space tested.
- Be aware of whether vomiting should be induced in case of ingestion
- Be aware of the recommended procedure in case of unconsciousness.

Procedures for reactive materials: minimize incompatibility
Many chemicals are **self-reactive**. For example, they explode when dried out or when disturbed under certain conditions or they react with components of air. These materials generally **should not be allowed into the high school**. Other precautions must be taken to minimize reactions between **incompatible pairs**.
- Store fuels and oxidizers separately.
- Store reducing agents and oxidizing agents separately.
- Store acids and bases separately.
- Store chemicals that react with fire-fighting materials (i.e., water or carbon dioxide) under conditions that minimize the possibility of a reaction if a fire is being fought in the storage area.
- MSDSs list other incompatible pairs.
- Never store chemicals in alphabetical order by name.
- When incompatible pairs must be supplied to students, do so under direct supervision with very dilute solutions and/or small quantities.

Material Safety Data Sheet (MSDS) information Many chemicals have a mixture of toxic, corrosive, flammability, and reactivity risks. The **Material Safety Data Sheet** or **MSDS** for a chemical contains detailed safety information that is not presented on the label. This includes acute and chronic health effects, first aid and firefighting measures, what to do in case of a spill, and ecological and disposal considerations.

The MSDS will state whether the chemical is a known or suspected carcinogen, mutagen, or teratogen. A **carcinogen** is a compound that causes cancer (malignant tumors). A **mutagen** alters DNA with the potential effects of causing cancer or birth defects in unconceived children. A **teratogen** produces birth defects and acts during fetal development

There are many parts of an MSDS that are not written for the layperson. Their level of detail and technical content intimidate many people outside the fields of toxicology and industrial safety. According to the American Chemical Society (http://membership.acs.org/c/ccs/pubs/chemical_safety_manual.pdf), an MSDS places "an over-emphasis on the toxic characteristics of the subject chemical."

In a high school chemistry lab, the value of an MSDS is in the words and not in the numerical data it contains, but some knowledge of the numbers is useful for comparing the dangers of one chemical to another. Numerical results of animal toxicity studies are often presented in the form of **LD_{50} values**. These represent the **dose required to kill 50% of animals** tested.

Exposure limits may be presented in three ways:

1) PEL (Permissible Exposure Limit) or TLV-TWA (Threshold Limit Value-Time Weighted Average). This is the maximum permitted concentration of the airborne chemical in volume parts per million (ppm) for a **worker exposed 8 hours daily**.
2) TLV-STEL (Threshold Limit Value-Short Term Exposure Limit). This is the maximum concentration permitted for a 15-minute exposure period.
3) TLV-C (Threshold Limit Value-Ceiling). This is the concentration that should never be exceeded at any moment.

http://hazard.com/msds/index.php contains a large database of MSDSs. http://www.ilpi.com/msds/ref/demystify.html contains a useful "MSDS demystifier." Cut and paste an MSDS into the web page, and hypertext links will appear to a glossary of terms.

Facilities and equipment
- Use separate labeled containers for general trash, broken glass, for each type of hazardous chemical waste—ignitable, corrosive, reactive, and toxic.
- Keep the floor area around safety showers, eyewash fountains, and fire extinguishers clear of all obstructions.
- Never block escape routes.
- Never prop open a fire door.
- Provide safety guards for all moving belts and pulleys.
- Instruct everyone in the lab on the proper use of the safety showerand eyewashfountain (see Corrosive materials above). Most portable eyewash devices cannot maintain the required flow for 15 minutes. A permanent eyewash fountain is preferred.
- If contamination is suspected in the breathing air, arrange for sampling to take place.
- Regularly inspect fire blankets, if present, for rips and holes. Maintain a record of inspection.
- Regularly check safety showers and eyewash fountains for proper rate of flow. Maintain a record of inspection.
- Keep up-to-date emergency phone numbers posted next to the telephone.
- Place fire extinguishers near an escape route.
- Regularly maintain fire extinguishers and maintain a record of inspection. Arrange with the local fire department for training of teachers and administrators in the proper use of extinguishers.
- Regularly check fume hoods for proper airflow. Ensure that fume hood exhaust is not drawn back into the intake for general building ventilation.
- Secure compressed gas cylindersat all times and transport them only while secured on a hand truck.
- Restrict the use and handling of compressed gas to those who have received formal training.
- Install chemical storage shelves with lips. Never use stacked boxes for storage instead of shelves.
- Only use an explosion-proof refrigerator for chemical storage.
- Have appropriate equipment and materials available in advance for spill control and cleanup. Consult the MSDS for each chemical to determine what is required. Replace these materials when they become outdated.
- Provide an appropriate supply of first aid equipment and instruction on its proper use.

Additional comments: Teach safety to students
- Weigh the risks and benefits inherent in lab work, inform students of the hazards and precautions involved in their assignment, and involve students in discussions about safety before every assignment.
- If an incident happens, it can be used to improve lab safety via student participation. Ask the student involved. The student's own words about what occurred should be included in the report.
- Safety information supplied by the manufacturer on a chemical container should be seen by students who actually use the chemical. If you distribute chemicals into smaller containers to be used by students, copy the hazard and precautionary information from the original label onto the labels for the students' containers. Students interested in graphic design may be able to help you perform this task. Labels for many common chemicals may be found here: http://beta.ehs.cornell.edu/labels/cgi-bin/label_selection.pl
- Organize a student safety committee whose task is to conduct one safety inspection and present a report. A different committee may be organized each month or every other month.

Additional comments: General
- Every chemical is hazardous. The way it is used determines the probability of harm.
- Every person is individually and personally responsible for the safe use of chemicals.
- If an accident might happen, it will eventually happen. Proper precautions will ensure the consequences are minimized when it does occur.
- Every accident is predicted by one or more **close calls** where nobody is injured and no property is damaged but something out of the ordinary occurred. Examples might be a student briefly touching a hot surface and saying "Ouch!" with no injury, two students engaged in horseplay, or a student briefly removing safety goggles to read a meniscus level. **Eliminate the cause of a close call and you have stopped a future accident.**

Also see:
http://www.labsafety.org/40steps.htm,
http://www.flinnsci.com/Sections/Safety/safety.asp,

Skill 18.4 Evaluate the role of chemistry in daily life, including ways in which basic research and the development of new technology affect society.

The union of science, technology, and mathematics has shaped the world we live in today. Science describes the world. It attempts to explain how nature works; from our own bodies to the tiny particles making up the world, from the entire earth to the worlds beyond. Science lets us know in advance what will happen when a cell splits or when two chemicals react. Science is ever-changing. Throughout history, people have developed and validated many different ideas about the flow of the universe. Changing explanations as technology develops allows for new information to emerge.

Technology is the use of scientific knowledge to solve problems. For example, science studies the flow of electrons but technology takes the flow of electrons to create a supercomputer. Mathematics, in turn provides the language to allow this knowledge to be communicated. It creates models for science to use to explain natural phenomena.

The economy is dependent upon the existence of technology. The job market changes as new technologies develop. For example, with the advent of computer technologies, many trained workers are needed, moving our economy from the post-war production line economy to a knowledge-economy based on information technology. This economy is driven by start-ups and entrepreneurs looking for innovation but not radical breakthroughs. It relies on sources of capitol from venture capitalists, IPOs and investors. It is also forcing a new kind of research to occur. Industrial labs are being redefined or eliminated, creating a convergence between scientific disciplines and engineering, providing for new entrepreneur opportunities.

At the same time, advances in scientific knowledge and technology often present ethical dilemmas for society. Industrialization brought the consumption of great amounts of energy, for example. This in turned creates environmental problems, leads to wars, and a depletion of natural resources. Scientific knowledge tells us there is oil is shale that we have not accessed yet. Technology developments will allow us to reach the oil and power our economy. At the same time, new technologies will emerge providing for alternative power supplies like wind farms or soy fuels. New types of skills will be needed to support these new technologies and the job market; education and our society will shift in response.

Science and society are interconnected. Important discoveries in science influence society and have the potential to alter society. For example, the invention of the printing press caused a blurring of the classes and increased scientific endeavors all at the same time. The printing press made for cheap production of books so that common individuals, not just the wealthy, could access literary works. It made it easier to learn to read and write, increasing the education level of all classes. It also made it easier to dream of places, things, and worlds not yet discovered. Scientists could work from exactly the same book at the same time, allowing for fewer errors. The printing press also allowed for the scientific revolution to occur since scientists could communicate their research results with a larger community at faster rates. The printing press changed the way people thought and looked at their world.

At the same time, the needs of society drive the direction of scientific investigation. The fear that the world would be dominated by Hitler and a supply of powerful new weapons lead the United States to begin developing its own atomic bomb. The need to end World War II strengthened and hastened the need for the Manhattan Project to be successful. On August 6, 1945 the world changed forever. The creation of the atomic bomb changed the way society existed. It also changed the direction of science. Would we have discovered nuclear power, the television and computer, nuclear medicine and all of the millions of other discoveries that came from the work of the Manhattan Project scientists? Probably, but the pace and the development of such technologies might not have occurred so quickly.

The need for technology development drives science, and discoveries in science drive society. Arguably, the first personal computers were mass-marketed by IBM and Apple in the late 1970's. The IBM 5100 had 16K of memory, a five inch screen, and cost nearly $11,000 in 1975! A mere twenty-five years later, computers are everywhere and used for everything. They have gigabytes of memory and monitors larger than some televisions! Why did computers develop so quickly? This was because of the interconnection between science, technology, and society.

COMPETENCY 19.0 UNDERSTAND AND APPLY KNOWLEDGE OF PERIODIC RELATIONSHIPS AND THE NATURE OF MATTER.

Skill 19.1 Demonstrate knowledge of the chemical constitution of matter as elements, compounds, and mixtures.

The word "matter" describes everything that has physical existence, i.e. has mass and takes up space. However, the make up of matter allows it to be separated into categories. The two main classes of matter are **pure substance and mixture.** Each of these classes can also be divided into smaller categories such as element, compound, homogeneous mixture or heterogeneous mixture based on composition.

PURE SUBSTANCES: A pure substance is a form of matter with a definite composition and distinct properties. This type of matter can not be separated by ordinary processes like filtering, centrifuging, boiling or melting. Pure substances are divided into elements and compounds.

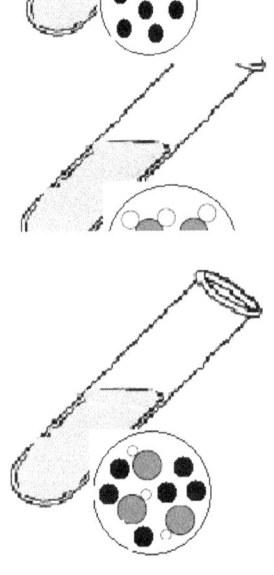

Elements: A single type of matter, called an atom, is present. Elements can not be broken down any farther by ordinary chemical processes. They are the smallest whole part of a substance that still represents that substance.

Compounds: Two or more elements chemically combined are present. A compound may be broken down into its elements by chemical processes such as heating or electric current. Compounds have a uniform composition regardless of the sample size or source of the sample.

MIXTURES: Two or more pure substances that are not chemically combined are present. Mixtures may be of any proportion and can be physically separated by processes like filtering, centrifuging, boiling or melting. Mixtures can be classified according to particle size.

Homogeneous Mixtures: Homogeneous mixtures have the same composition and properties throughout the mixture and are also known as solutions. They have a uniform color and distribution of solute and solvent particles throughout the mixture.

Heterogeneous Mixtures: Heterogeneous mixtures do not have a uniform distribution of particles throughout the mixture. The different components of the mixture can easily be identified and separated.

A **physical property** of matter is a property that can be determined without inducing a chemical change. All matter has mass and takes up space with an associated size. Matter experiencing gravity has a weight. Most matter we encounter exists in one of three phases. Some other examples of physical properties of matter include.

Melting point refers to the temperature at which a solid becomes a liquid. **Boiling point** refers to the temperature at which a liquid becomes a gas. Melting takes place when there is sufficient energy available to break the intermolecular forces that hold molecules together in a solid. Boiling occurs when there is enough energy available to break the intermolecular forces holding molecules together as a liquid.

Hardness describes how difficult it is to scratch or indent a substance. The hardest natural substance is diamond.

Density measures the mass of a unit volume of material. Units of g/cm^3 are commonly used. SI base units of kg/m^3 are also used. One g/cm^3 is equal to one thousand kg/m^3. Density (ρ) is calculated from mass (m) and volume (V) using the formula:

$$\rho = \frac{m}{V}.$$

The above expression is often manipulated to determine the mass of a substance if its volume and density are known ($m = \rho V$) or the volume of a substance if its mass and density are known ($V = m / \rho$).

Electrical conductivity measures a material's ability to conduct an electric current. The high conductivity of metals is due to the presence of metallic bonds. The high conductivity of electrolyte solutions is due to the presence of ions in solution.

Chemical characteristics or behavior are the ways substances interact with each other or the substance's ability to form different substances. Chemical properties are observable only during a chemical reaction.

Some common chemical properties are

Flammability: some substances have the property to react with oxygen under elevated temperature

Acidity: some substances have the property to produce hydrogen ions when in an aqueous solution.

Oxidation-reduction: some substances have the ability to gain or lose electrons. Some examples are tarnishing, rusting, patination.

Precipitation: some substances have the ability to combine with others, changing their solubility.

Skill 19.2 Distinguish between physical and chemical changes.

A **physical change** does not create a new substance. **Atoms are not rearranged into different compounds.** The material has the same chemical composition as it had before the change. Changes of state as described in the previous section are physical changes. Frozen water or gaseous water is still H_2O. Taking a piece of paper and tearing it up is a physical change. You simply have smaller pieces of paper.

Compare these two nails....They are still iron nails, made of iron atoms. The difference is that one is bent while the other is straight. This is a physical change.

A **chemical change** is a chemical reaction. It **converts one substance into another** because atoms are rearranged to form a different compound. Paper undergoes a chemical change when you burn it. You no longer have paper. A chemical change to a pure substance alters its properties.

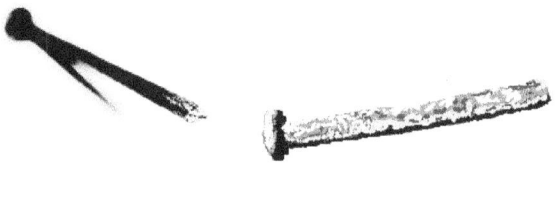

An iron nail rusts to form a rusty nail. The rusty nail, however, is not made up of the same iron atoms. It is now composed of iron (III) oxide molecules that form when the iron atoms combine with oxygen molecules during oxidation (rusting).

Skill 19.3 Demonstrate knowledge of basic techniques used to separate substances based on differences in properties.

A mixture consists of two or more substances that when put together retain their individual physical and chemical properties. That is, no new substances are formed. Differences in physical and chemical properties of the components of the mixture can be used to separate the mixture. For example, salt and pepper have different colors and can be separated by physically moving the white crystals away from the dark particles. Or salt dissolves in water while pepper does not and the two can be separated by adding water to the mixture. The salt will dissolve while the pepper will float on top of the water. Skim off the pepper and then evaporate the water. The salt and pepper are now separated.

SCIENCE: CHEMISTRY

Common methods for separating mixtures include filtration, chromatography, distillation and extraction. **Filtering** relies on one of the substances being soluble in the solvent, and the other being insoluble. The soluble substance ends up in the **filtrate** (the liquid that passes through the filter paper). The insoluble substance ends up in the filter paper as the **residue**.

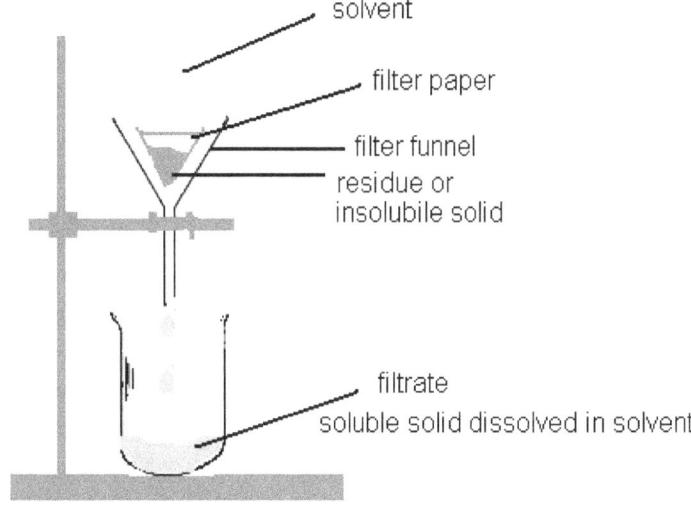

Distillation and **fractional distillation** rely on the fact that the liquids in the mixture are different. Each liquid has its own unique **boiling point**. As the temperature rises, it reaches the lowest boiling point liquid and so this liquid boils. The temperature remains at that temperature until all of the liquid has boiled away. The vapor passes

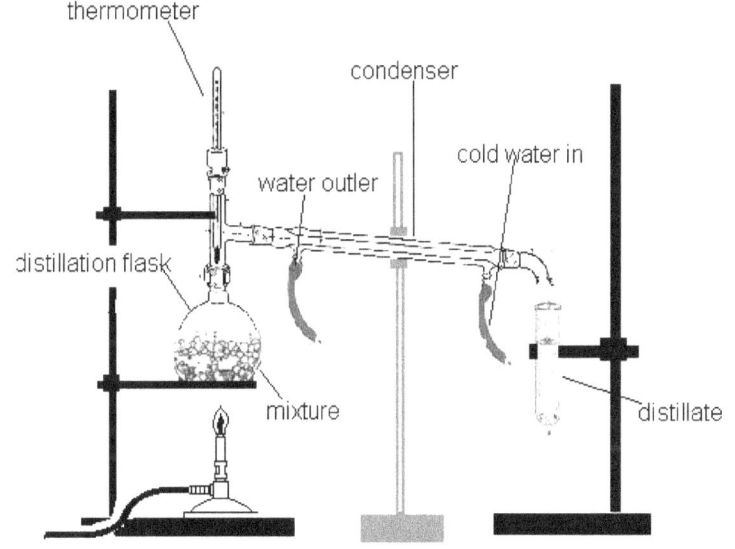

into a condenser and is cooled and so turns back into a liquid. The pure liquid is now in a different part of the apparatus and rolls down into a test tube. This liquid has been separated from the mixture.

Chromatography is a technique, which is used to separate mixtures based on differential migration. Differential migration uses differences in physical properties such as solubility, molecular size and polarity to separate the substance. The mixture is placed in a solution, which becomes the mobile phase. This solution then passes over a stationary phase. Different components of the mixture travel at different rates. After the separation, the time that component took to emerge from the instrument (or its location within the stationary phase) is found with a detector. These chromatographic separations have many different types of stationary phases including paper, silica on glass or plastic plates (thin-layer chromatography), volatile gases (gas chromatography) and liquids, (liquid chromatography including column and high-performance liquid chromatography or HPLC) as well as gels (electrophoresis).

The result is a **chromatogram** like the one shown below. The **identity of an unknown** peak is found by comparing its location on the chromatogram to standards. The **concentration** of a component is found from signal strength or peak area by comparison to calibration curves of known concentrations.

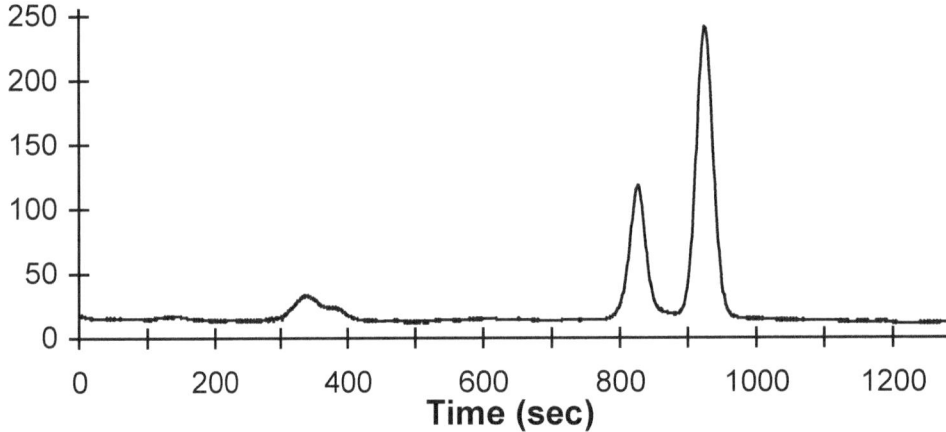

In **paper chromatography** and **thin layer chromatography (TLC)**, the sample rises up by capillary action through a solid phase.

In **gas chromatography (GC)**, the sample is vaporized and forced through a column filled with a packing material. GC is often used to separate and determine the concentration of **low molecular weight volatile organic** compounds.

In **liquid chromatography (LC)**, the sample is a liquid. It is either allowed to seep through an open column using the force of gravity or it is forced through a closed column under pressure. The variations of liquid chromatography depend on the identity of the packing material. For example, an ion-exchange liquid chromatograph contains a material with a charged surface. The mixture components with the opposite charge interact with this packing material and spend more time in the column. LC is often used to separate **large organic polymers** like proteins.

Each component in the mixture can be identified by its retention factor or retention time once it has been separated. Both retention factor, R_f, and retention time are quantitative indications of how far a particular compound travels in a particular solvent or how long the component is retained on the column before eluting with the mobile phase (for gas chromatography and liquid chromatography). By comparing the R_f of the components in the mixture to known values for substances, identification of the components in the mixture can be achieved.

R_f = distance the component color traveled from the point of application / distance the solvent front traveled from the point of application

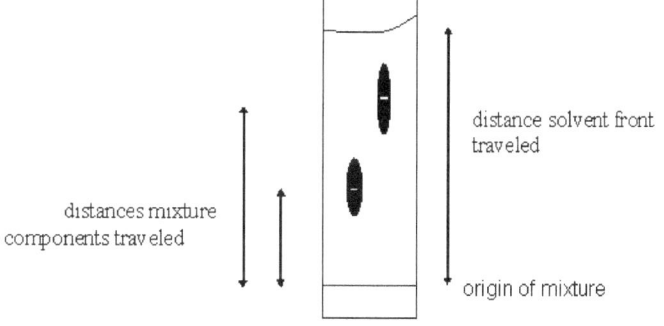

In an ideal chemical world, reactions would produce products in exactly the right amount and in exactly the right way; no product loss, no competing side reactions. But then things would be very simple for the chemist. In the real chemical world, things are not so simple for the chemist. Most chemical reactions produce product intermingled with by-products or impurities. **Extraction** is a method used to separate the desired product from impurities. This process is used in product purification and results from an unequal distribution of solute between two immiscible solvents. This process, then, makes use of differences is solubilities to separate components in what is called a work-up. The work-up is a planned sequence of extracting and washing.

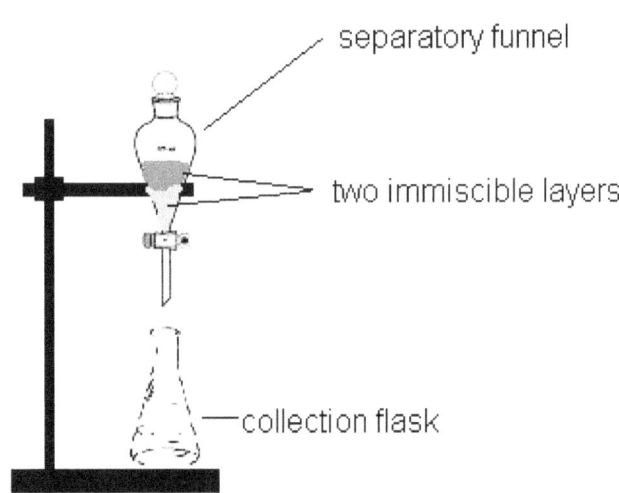

The planning involves determining the two solvents. One is usually water, the aqueous layer, while the other is an organic solvent, the organic layer. The important feature here is that the two solvents are immiscible and the mixture is the partition between the two solvents. The mixture is then separated as its components are attracted to the solvents differently. Most charged particles and inorganic salts will move towards the aqueous layer and dissolve in it, while the neutral organic molecules will move towards the organic layer

Skill 19.4   Analyze the periodic nature of the elements and the relationship between their electron configuration and the periodic table.

The first periodic table was developed in 1869 by Dmitri Mendeleev several decades before the nature of electron energy states in the atom was known. Mendeleev arranged the elements in order of increasing atomic mass into columns of similar physical and chemical properties. He then boldly predicted the existence and the properties of undiscovered elements to fill the gaps in his table. These interpolations were initially treated with skepticism until three of Mendeleev's theoretical elements were discovered and were found to have the properties he predicted. It is the correlation with properties—not with electron arrangements—that have placed the periodic table at the beginning of most chemistry texts.

The elements in a column are known as a group, and groups are numbered from 1 to 18. Older numbering styles used roman numerals and letters. **A row of the periodic table is known as a period**, and periods of the known elements are numbered from 1 to 7. The lanthanoids are all in period 6, and the actinoids are all in period 7.

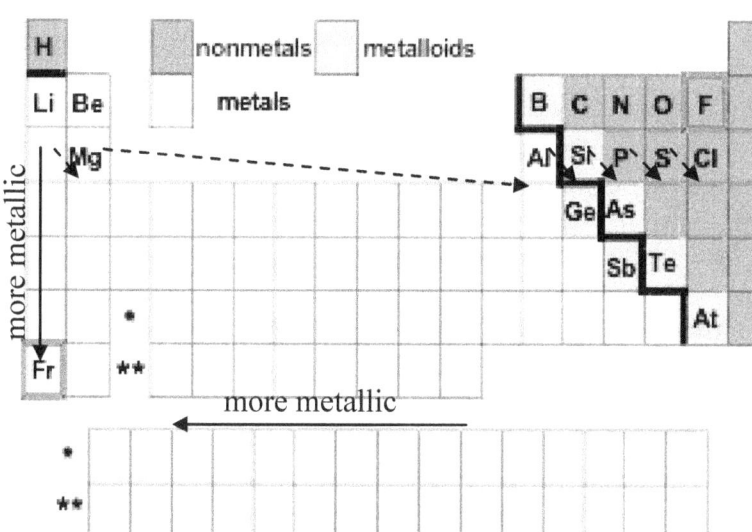

Metals, nonmetals, and atomic radius

Elements in the periodic table are divided into the two broad categories of **metals** and **nonmetals** with a jagged line separating the two as shown in the figure. Seven elements near the line dividing metals from nonmetals exhibit some properties of each and are called **metalloids** or **semimetals** These elements are boron, silicon, germanium, arsenic, antimony, tellurium and astatine.

The most metallic element is francium at the bottom left of the table. The most nonmetallic element is fluorine. The metallic character of elements within a group increases with period number. This means that **within a column, the more metallic elements are at the bottom**. The metallic character of elements within a period decreases with group number. This means that **within a row, the more metallic elements are on the left**. Among the main group atoms, **elements diagonal to each other** as indicated by the dashed arrows **have similar properties** because they have a similar metallic character. The noble gases are nonmetals, but they are an exception to the diagonal rule.

Physical properties relating to metallic character are summarized in the following table:

Element	Electrical/thermal conductivity	Malleable/ductile as solids?	Lustrous?	Melting point of oxides, hydrides, and halides
Metals	High	Yes	Yes	High
Metalloids	Intermediate. Altered by dopants (semiconductors)	No (brittle)	Varies	Varies (oxides). Low (hydrides, halides)
Nonmetals	Low (insulators)	No	No	Low

SCIENCE: CHEMISTRY

Malleable materials can **be beaten into sheets**. **Ductile** materials can **be pulled into wires**. **Lustrous** materials **have a shine**. Oxides, hydrides, and halides are compounds with O, H, and halogens respectively. Measures of intermolecular attractions other than melting point are also higher for metal oxides, hydrides, and halides than for the nonmetal compounds. A dopant is a small quantity of an intentionally added impurity. The controlled movement of electrons in doped silicon semiconductors carries digital information in computer circuitry.

The **size of an atom** is not an exact distance due to of the probabilistic nature of electron density, but we may compare radii among different atoms using some standard. As seen to the right, the sizes of neutral atoms increase with period number and decrease with group number. This trend is similar to the trend described above for metallic character. The smallest atom is helium.

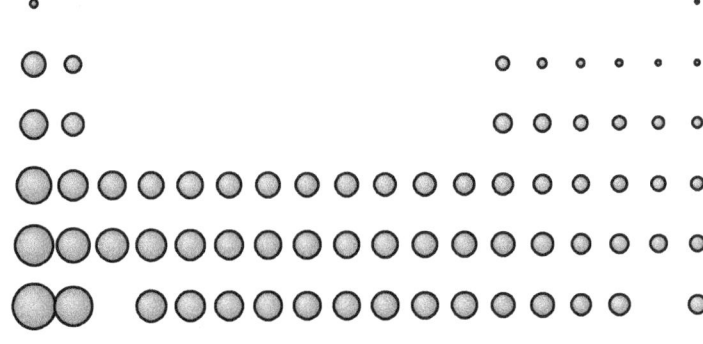

Group names, melting point, density, and properties of compounds

Groups 1, 2, 17, and 18 are often identified with a **group name**. These names are shown in the table to the right. Several elements are found as **diatomic molecules**: (H_2, N_2, O_2, and the halogens: F_2, Cl_2, Br_2, and I_2). Mnemonic devices to remember the diatomic elements are: "$Br_2I_2N_2Cl_2H_2O_2F_2$" (pronounced "Brinklehof" and "**H**ave **N**o **F**ear **O**f **I**ce **C**old **B**eer." These molecules are attracted to one another using **weak London dispersion forces**.

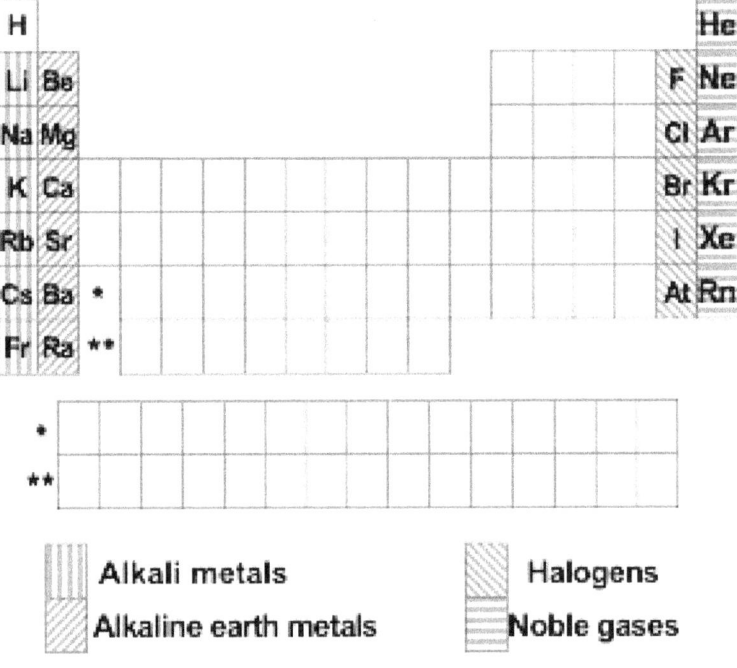

Note that **hydrogen** is not an alkali metal. Hydrogen is a colorless gas and is the most abundant element in the universe, but H_2 is very rare in the atmosphere because it is light enough to escape gravity and reach outer space. Hydrogen atoms form more compounds than any other element.

SCIENCE: CHEMISTRY

Alkali metals are shiny, soft, metallic solids. They have **low melting points and low densities** compared with other metals (see squares in figures on the following page) because they have a weaker metallic bond. Measures of intermolecular attractions including their **melting points decrease further down the periodic table due to weaker metallic bonds** as the size of atoms increases.

Alkaline earth metals (group 2 elements) are grey, metallic solids. They are harder, denser, and have a higher melting point than the alkali metals (see asterisks in figures on the following page), but values for these properties are still low compared to most of the transition metals. Measures of metallic bond strength like melting points for alkaline earths do not follow a simple trend down the periodic table.

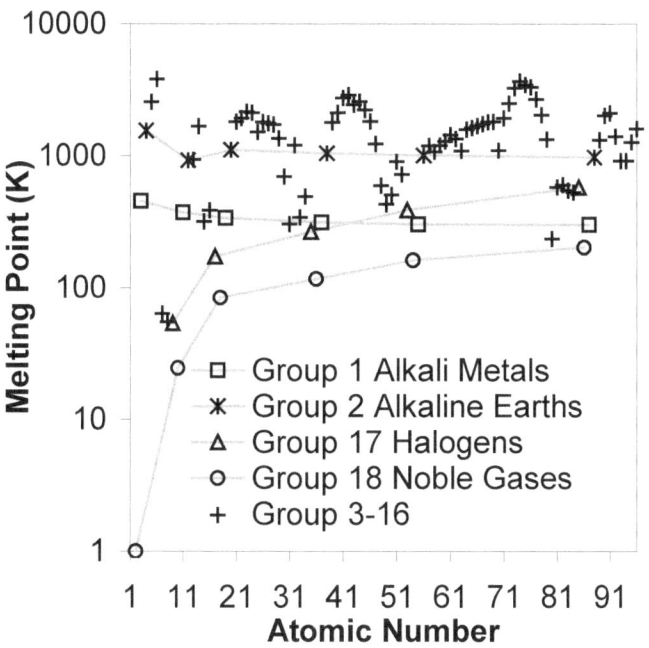

Halogens (group 17 elements) have an irritating odor. Unlike the metallic bonds between alkali metals, **London forces between halogen molecules increase in strength further down the periodic table**. Their melting points increase as shown by the triangles to the left. London forces make Br_2 a liquid and I_2 a solid at 25 °C. The lighter halogens are gases.

Noble gases (group 18 elements) have no color or odor and exist as **individual gas atoms** that experience London forces. These attractions also increase with period number as shown by the circles to the left.

The known **densities** of liquid and solid elements at room temperature are shown to the right. **Intermolecular forces contribute to density** by bringing nuclei closer to each other, so the periodicity is similar to trends for melting point.

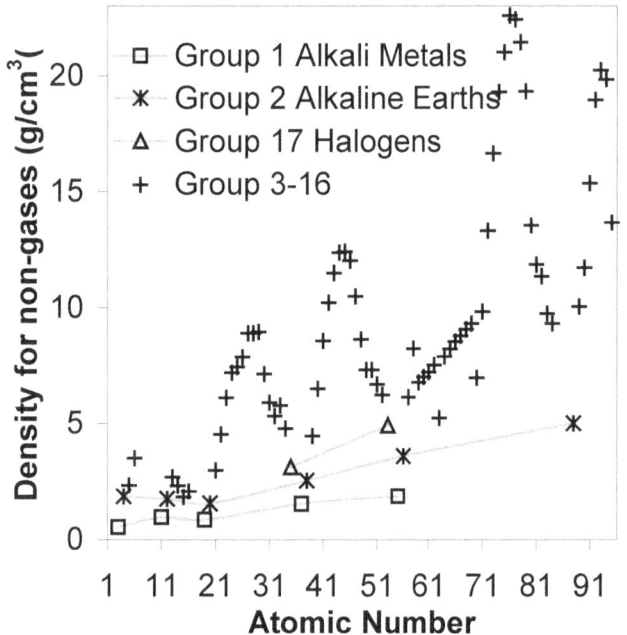

These group-to-group differences are superimposed on a general trend for **density** to **increase with period number** because heavier nuclei make the material denser.

Trends among properties of **compounds** may often be deduced from **trends among their atoms**, but caution must be used. For example, the densities of three potassium halides are:

2.0 g/cm^3 for KCl   2.7 g/cm^3 for KBr
3.1 g/cm^3 for KI.

We would expect this trend for increasing atomic mass within a group. We might also expect the density of KF to be less than 2.0 g/cm^3, but it is actually 2.5 g/cm^3 due to a change in crystal lattice structure.

Physics of electrons and stability of electron configurations

For an isolated atom, the **most stable system of valence electrons is a filled set of orbitals**. For the main group elements, this corresponds to group 18 (ns^2np^6 and $1s^2$ for helium), and, to a lesser extent, group 2 (ns^2). The next most stable state is a set of degenerate half-filled orbitals. These occur in group 15 (ns^2np^3)]. The least stable valence electron configuration is a single electron with no other electrons in similar orbitals. This occurs in group 1 (ns^1) and to a lesser extent in group 13 (ns^2np^1).

An atom's first **ionization energy** is the energy required to remove one electron by the reaction $M(g) \rightarrow M^+(g) + e^-$. Periodicity is in the opposite direction from the trend for atomic radius. The most metallic atoms have electrons further from the nucleus, and these are easier to remove. An atom's **electron affinity** is the energy released when one electron is added by the reaction $M(g) + e^- \rightarrow M^-(g)$. A large negative number for the exothermic reaction indicates a high electron affinity. Halogens have the highest electron affinities.

Trends in **ionization energy and electron affinity** within a period reflect the **stability of valence electron configurations**. A stable system requires more energy to change and releases less when changed. Note the peaks in stability for groups 2, 13, and 16 to the right.

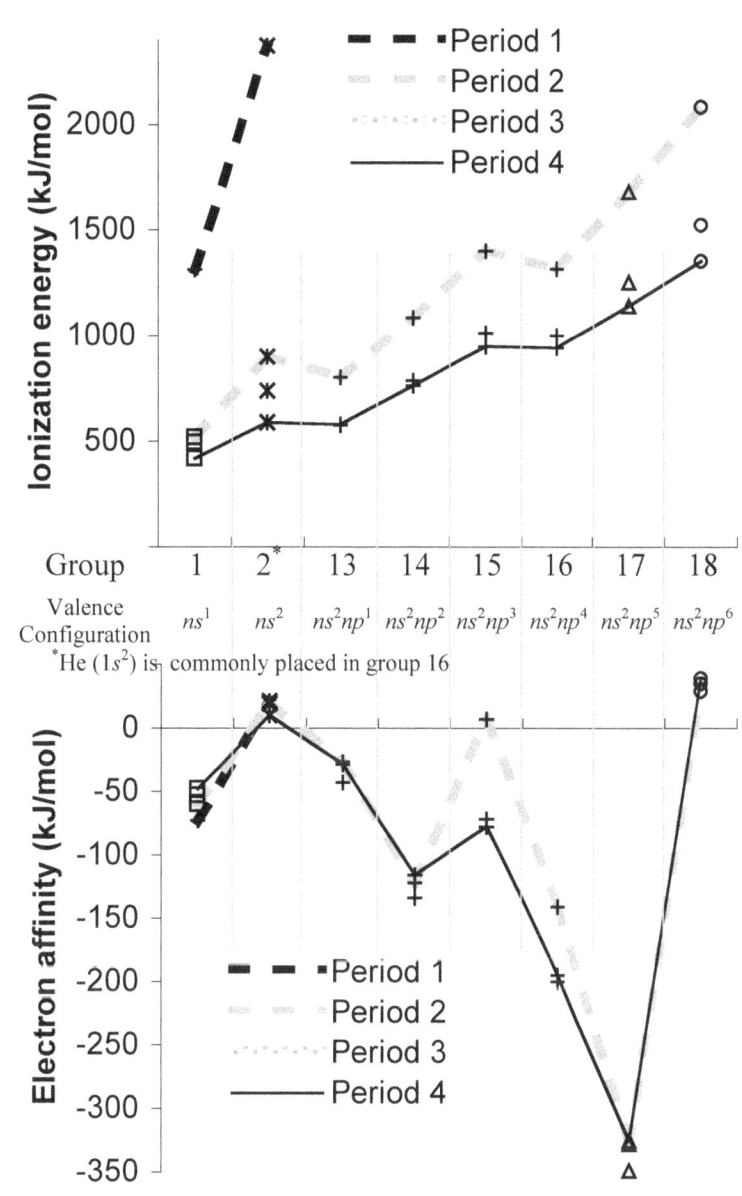

*He ($1s^2$) is commonly placed in group 16

Much of chemistry consists of atoms **bonding** to achieve stable valence electron configurations. **Nonmetals gain electrons or share electrons** to achieve these configurations and **metals lose electrons** to achieve them.

Qualitative group trends
When cut by a knife, the exposed surface of an **alkali metalor alkaline earth metal** quickly turns into an oxide. These elements **do not occur in nature as free metals**. Instead, they react with many other elements to form white or grey water-soluble salts. With some exceptions, the oxides of group 1 elements have the formula M_2O, their hydrides are MH, and their halides are MX (for example, NaCl). The oxides of group 2 elements have the formula MO, their hydrides are MH_2, and their halides are MX_2, for example, $CaCl_2$.

Halogens form a wide variety of oxides and also combine with other halogens. They combine with hydrogen to form HX gases, and these compounds are also commonly used as acids (hydrofluoric, hydrochloric, etc.) in aqueous solution. Halogens form salts with metals by gaining electrons to become X^- ions. Astatine is an exception to many of these properties because it is an artificial metalloid.

Noble gases are **nearly chemically inert**The heavier noble gases form a number of compounds with oxygen and fluorine such as KrF_2 and XeO_4

Electronegativity and reactivity series
Electronegativity measures the ability of an atom to attract electrons in a chemical bond. The most metallic elements have the lowest electronegativity. The most nonmetallic have the highest electronegativity.

In a reaction with a metal, the most reactive chemicals are the **most electronegative elements** or compounds containing those elements. In a reaction with a nonmetal, the most reactive chemicals are the **least electronegative elements** or compounds containing them. The reactivity of elements may be described by a **reactivity series**: an ordered list with chemicals that react strongly at one end and nonreactive chemicals at the other. The following reactivity series is for metals reacting with oxygen:

Metal	K	Na	Ca	Mg	Al	Zn	Fe	Pb	Cu	Hg	Ag	Au
Reaction with O_2	Burns violently	\multicolumn{6}{c}{Burns rapidly}				Oxidizes slowly			No reaction	

Copper, silver, and gold (group 11) are known as the **noble metals** or **coinage metals** because they rarely react.

Valence and oxidation numbers

The term **valence** is often used to describe the number of atoms that may react to form a compound with a given atom by sharing, removing, or losing **valence electrons**. A more useful term is **oxidation number**. The **oxidation number of an ion is its charge**. The oxidation number of an atom sharing its electrons is **the charge it would have if the bonding were ionic**. There are four rules for determining oxidation number:

1) The oxidation number of an element (i.e., a Cl atom in Cl_2) is zero because the electrons in the bond are shared equally.
2) In a compound, the more electronegative atoms are assigned negative oxidation numbers and the less electronegative atoms are assigned positive oxidation numbers equal to the number of shared electron-pair bonds. For example, hydrogen may only have an oxidation number of –1 when bonded to a less electronegative element or +1 when bonded to a more electronegative element. Oxygen almost always has an oxidation number of –2. Fluorine always has an oxidation number of –1 (except in F_2).
3) The oxidation numbers in a compound must add up to zero, and the sum of oxidation numbers in a polyatomic ion must equal the overall charge of the ion.
4) The charge on a polyatomic ion is equal to the sum of the oxidation numbers for the species present in the ion. For example, the sulfate ion, SO_4^{2-}, has a total charge of -2. This comes from adding the -2 oxidation number for 4 oxygen (total -8) and the +6 oxidation number for sulfur.

Example: What is the oxidation number of nitrogen in the nitrate ion, NO_3^-? Oxygen has the oxidation number of –2 (rule 2), and the sum of the oxidation numbers must be –1 (rule 3). The oxidation number for N may be found by solving for x in the equation $x + 3 \times (-2) = -1$. The oxidation number of N in NO_3^- is +5.

There is a **periodicity in oxidation numbers** as shown in the table below for examples of oxides with the maximum oxidation number. Remember that an element may occur in different compounds in several different oxidation states.

Group	1	2	13	14	15	16	17	18
Oxide with maximum oxidation number	Li_2O Na_2O	BeO MgO	B_2O_3 Al_2O_3	CO_2 SiO_2	N_2O_5 P_2O_5	SO_3	Cl_2O_7 Br_2O_7	XeO_4
Oxidation number	+1	+2	+3	+4	+5	+6	+7	+8

They are called "oxidation numbers" because oxygen was the element of choice for reacting with materials when modern chemistry began, and the result was Mendeleev arranging his first table to look similar to this one.

SCIENCE: CHEMISTRY

Acidity/alkalinity of oxides

Metal oxides form basic solutions in water because the ionic bonds break apart and the O^{2-} ion reacts to form hydroxide ions:

metal oxide $\rightarrow$ metal cation(aq) $+O^{2-}(aq)$ and $O^{2-}(aq) + H_2O(l) \rightarrow 2\ OH^-(aq)$

Ionic oxides containing a large cation with a low charge (Rb_2O, for example) are most soluble and form the strongest bases.

Covalent oxides form acidic solutions in water by reacting with water. For example:

$$SO_3(l) + H_2O(l) \rightarrow H_2SO_4(aq) \rightarrow H^+(aq) + HSO_4^-(aq)$$
$$Cl_2O_7(l) + H_2O(l) \rightarrow 2HClO_4(aq) \rightarrow 2H^+(aq) + 2ClO_4^-(aq)$$

Covalent oxides at high oxidation states and high electronegativities form the strongest acids. Acids and bases are discussed in **skill 4.13**. For this skill, note that the periodic trends for acid and base strength of the oxide of an element follows the same pattern we've seen before.

Summary

A summary of periodic trends is shown to the right. The properties tend to decrease or increase as shown depending on a given element's proximity to fluorine in the table.

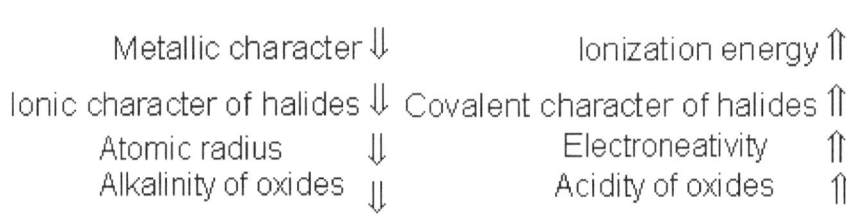

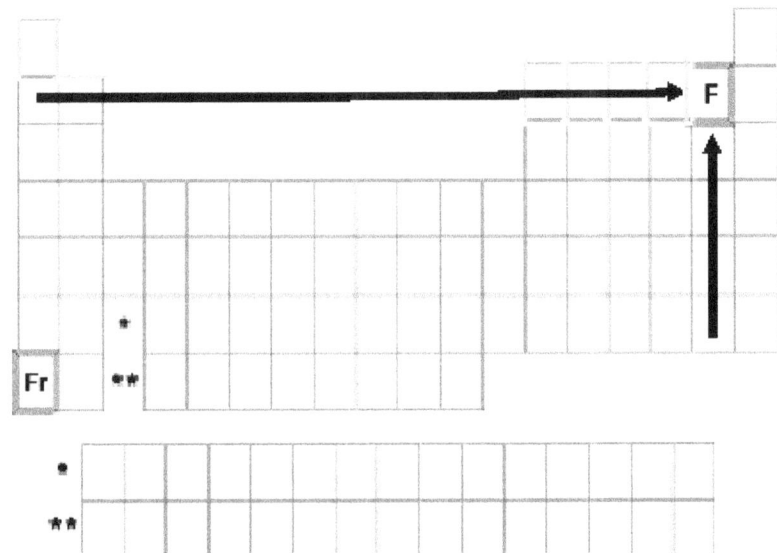

http://jcrystal.com/steffenweber/JAVA/jpt/jpt.html contains an applet of the periodic table and trends.

http://www.webelements.com is an on-line reference for information on the elements.

http://www.uky.edu/Projects/Chemcomics/ has comic book pages for each element.

An **electron configuration** is a **list of subshells** with superscripts representing the **number of electrons** in each subshell.

Electrons are found outside the nucleus in a fuzzy area called the electron cloud. We don't know exactly where the electron is but we do know the most probable place to find an electron with a certain energy. This is an orbital or an energy level.

When an electron is in its unexcited or ground state, there are seven energy levels. These seven energy levels match the seven periods (rows) of the Periodic Table. The valence, or outermost, electrons are found in the energy level that corresponds to the period number.

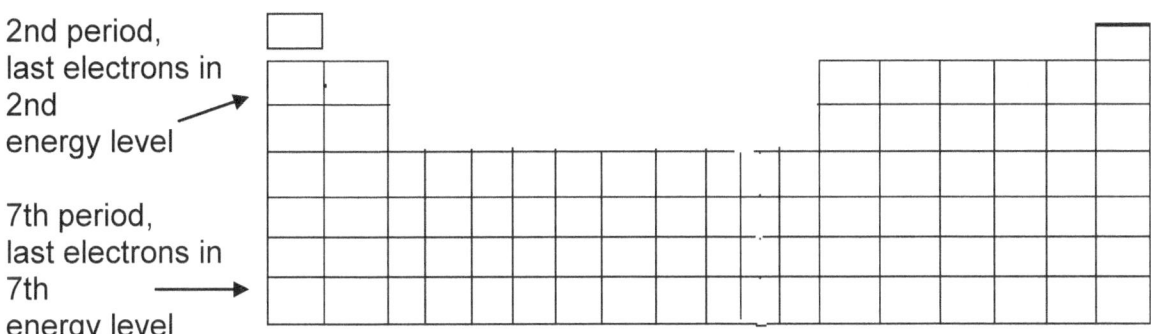

Each energy level varies in the number of electrons it can hold.

Within each energy level, the electrons are arranged into various sublevels called orbitals. The orbitals of the unexcited state atom include s, p, d, and f orbitals. The electrons fill these orbitals in a pre-determined pattern; filling the lowest energy orbitals first. "S" orbitals are the lowest energy so they fill with a maximum of two electrons first, followed by the "p" orbitals. There are three different "p" orbitals, each holding up to two electrons on each energy level. There are five different "d" orbitals followed by seven different "f" orbitals. Filling of the "d" and "f" orbitals are very complicated. The 3 d orbitals are of higher energy than the 4s but less energy than the 4 p so they fill between the 4 s and 4 p orbitals, completing the third energy level. The same holds true for the s, p, and d orbitals on the 4th, 5th and 6th energy levels. The 4f orbital has more energy than the 6s but less energy than the 6p or 5d orbitals so it fills between the 6s and the 5d orbitals. This pattern really does make sense.

Energy level	Maximum Number of Electrons
1	2
2	8
3	18
4	32
5	50, theoretical, not filled
6	72, theoretical, not filled
7	98, theoretical, not filled

According to the Pauli Exclusion Principle, and Hund's Rule for filling electron orbitals, each orbital of the same type must fill with two electrons, spinning in opposite directions, before a new type of orbital is occupied. However, before electrons can double up in an orbital, all orbitals on the same energy level of the same type must have one electron in it, all spinning in the same direction.

An electron of an atom can be identified using a shorthand notation called electron configuration. This gives the energy level, orbital type and number of electrons present.

For example, carbon has six electrons and they are located as follows:
    1st energy level, s orbital: 2 electrons,
    2nd energy level, 4 electrons; 2 in the s orbital and 2 in the p orbital.
For an electron configuration of: $1s^2, 2s^2, 2p^4$.

Chlorine has 17 electrons:
    1st energy level: 2 in the s orbital,
    2nd energy level: 2 in the s orbital, 6 in the p orbital
    3rd energy level: 2 in the s orbital, 5 in the p orbital.
For an electron configuration of: $1s^2, 2s^2, 2p^6, 3s^2, 3p^5$

Let's try a hard one: lead has 82 electrons.
   1st energy level: 2 in the s orbital,
   2nd energy level: 2 in the s orbital, 6 in the p orbital
   3rd energy level: 2 in the s orbital, 6 in the p orbital.

Then the 4s orbital fills with 2 electrons followed by the 3d orbital with 10 electrons then the 4p orbital with 6 electrons.
Now the 5s fills with 2 electrons, followed by the 4d orbital with 10 electrons, and then the 5p orbital with 6 electrons.
The sixth energy starts to fill next with 2 electrons in the 6s orbital, followed by 14 in the 4f and 10 electrons in the 5d and two electrons in the 6p orbital.
For an electron configuration of: $1s^2, 2s^2, 2p^6, 3s^2, 3p^6 4s^2 3d^{10} 4p^6 5s^2 4d^{10} 5p^6 6s^2 4f^{14} 5d^{10} 6p^2$

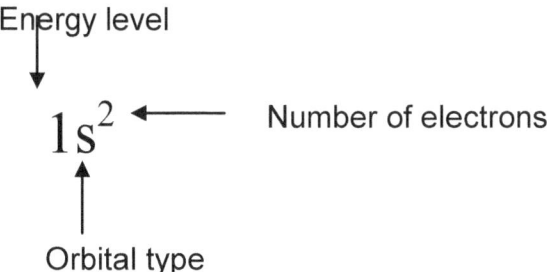

There is an electron configuration pattern that coincides with the Periodic Table. The last electrons in the electron cloud of all alkali and alkali earth metals are found in the "s" orbitals.

Element	Last electron to fill	Element	Last electron to fill
Li	$2s^1$	Be	$2s^2$
Na	$3s^1$	Mg	$3s^2$
K	$4s^1$	Ca	$4s^2$

Groups 13-18 have their last electrons in the "P" orbitals. Transition metals, groups 3-12, have their last electrons in the "d" orbitals. The lanthanide and actinide series have their last electrons in the "f" orbital.

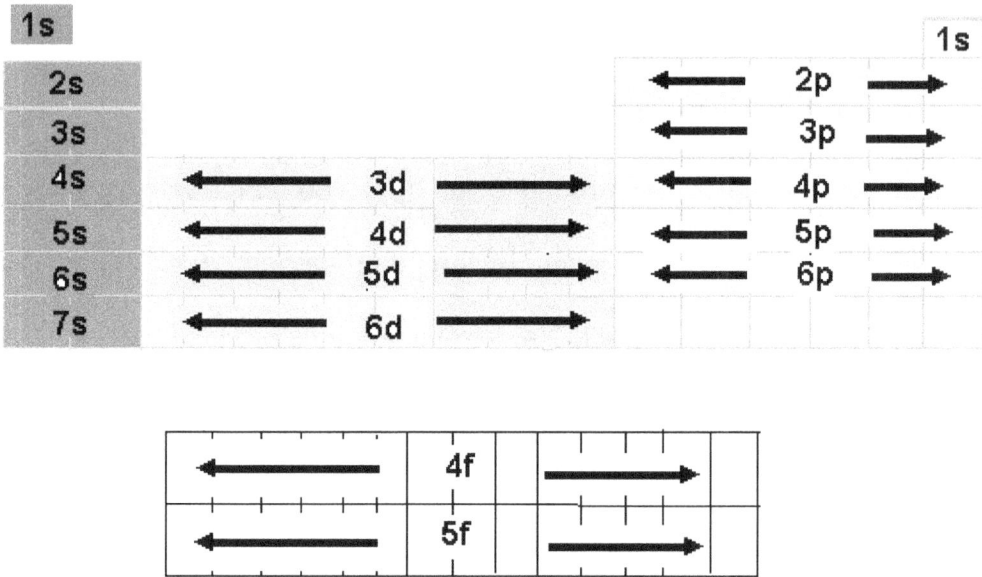

Skill 19.5 Connect the chemical and physical properties of elements to electron configuration.

Nonmetals gain electrons or share electrons to achieve stable configurations and **metals lose electrons** to achieve them.

Valence electrons are the electron involved in chemical reactions so let's take a look at the relationship between the valence electron configuration and chemical activity. Remember the octet rule, it seems logical that when there are less than four valence electrons, the atom would want to lose electrons to go back to the previous energy level that was full. And that when the outer energy level is more than half full (more than 4 valence electrons) that the atom would want to gain electrons to complete the valence energy level.

For example: aluminum has 13 electrons with a configuration of $1s^2, 2s^2, 2p^6, 3s^2, 3p^1$.

There are only three electrons in the 3rd energy level and the octet rule says there should be eight. Aluminum can try and find 5 more electrons to fill the 3 p orbital or lose the $3s^2$, and $3p^1$ electrons. It takes less energy to lose the three electrons (circled), when these electrons are lost an aluminum +3 ion forms with an electron configuration of $1s^2, 2s^2, 2p^6$ which has a complete octet in the outer shell.

Keeping this in mind, along with the electron configuration chart above, it seems that the families with valence configurations s^1, s^2 or s^2, p^1 would tend to lose electrons to form ionic compounds. Families with valence configurations s^2, p^2; s^2, p^3; s^2, p^4; s^2, p^5 would tend to gain electrons to form ionic compounds or share electrons to form molecular substances. The noble gas family with a s^2, p^6 configuration has a complete octet in its valence shell so this configuration tends to be unreactive. However, the heavier noble gases form a number of compounds with oxygen and fluorine such as KrF_2 and XeO_4. Don't forget that atoms with electrons in the "d" or "f" orbitals, have s^1 or s^2 as their valence configuration of electrons.

This information helps us to understand some other characteristics. For example, the elements in the alkali metal family, for example, are not found as free elements in nature. This is due to their high chemical activity. The one valence electron in the outermost energy level is high unstable, and it tends to be easily lost, forming many different ionic compounds in the process. The halogen family consists of molecules instead of free elements. The almost complete valence energy level is easily completed by two halogen atoms sharing electrons to form a covalent molecule.

In a reaction with a metal, the most reactive chemicals are the **most electronegative elements** or compounds containing those elements. In a reaction with a nonmetal, the most reactive chemicals are the **least electronegative elements** or compounds containing them. The reactivity of elements may be described by a **reactivity series**: an ordered list with chemicals that react strongly at one end and nonreactive chemicals at the other. The following reactivity series is for metals reacting with oxygen:

Metal	K	Na	Ca	Mg	Al	Zn	Fe	Pb	Cu	Hg	Ag	Au
Reaction with O_2	Burns violently		Burns rapidly						Oxidizes slowly		No reaction	

Skill 19.6   Demonstrate proficiency at naming compounds and writing formulas.

The IUPAC is the **International Union of Pure and Applied Chemistry**, an organization that formulates naming rules. **Organic compounds contain carbon**, and they have a separate system of nomenclature but some of the simplest molecules containing carbon also fall within the scope of inorganic chemistry.

Naming rules depend on whether the chemical is an ionic compound or a molecular compound containing only covalent bonds. There are special rules for naming acids. The rules below describe a group of traditional "semi-systematic" names accepted by IUPAC.

Ionic compounds: Cation

Ionic compounds are named with the **cation (positive ion) first**. Nearly all cations in inorganic chemistry are **monatomic**, meaning they just consist of one atom (like Ca^{2+}, the calcium ion.) This atom will be a **metal ion**. For common ionic compounds, the **alkali metals always have a 1+ charge** and the **alkali earth metals always have a 2+ charge.**

Many metals may form cations of more than one charge. In this case, a Roman numeral in parenthesis after the name of the element is used to indicate the ion's charge in a particular compound. This Roman numeral method is known as the **Stock system**. An older nomenclature used the suffix –*ous* for the lower charge and –*ic* for the higher charge and is still used occasionally.

Example: Fe^{2+} is the iron(II) ion and Fe^{3+} is the iron(III) ion.

The only common inorganic **polyatomic cation** is ammonium: NH_4^+.

Ionic compounds: Anion

The **anion** (negative ion) is named and written last. Monatomic anions are formed from nonmetallic elements and are named by **replacing the end of the element's name with the suffix –*ide*.**

Examples: Cl^- is the chloride ion, S^{2-} is the sulfide ion, and N^{3-} is the nitride ion.

These anions also end with –*ide*:

C_2^{2-}	N_3^-	O_2^{2-}	O_3^-	S_2^{2-}	CN^-	OH^-
carbide or acetylide	azide	peroxide	ozonide	disulfide	cyanide	hydroxide

Oxoanions (also called oxyanions) **contain one element in combination with oxygen.** Many common polyatomic anions are oxoanions that **end with the suffix –ate.** If an element has two possible oxoanions, the one with the element at a lower oxidation state **ends with –ite.** This anion will also usually have **less oxygen per atom.** See **Skill 27.1** for a discussion of oxidation numbers. Additional oxoanions are named with the prefix *hypo-* if they have a lower oxidation number than the *–ite* form and the prefix *per–* if they have a higher oxidation number than the *–ate* form.

Common examples:

				CO_3^{2-}	carbonate		
		SO_3^{2-}	sulfite	SO_4^{2-}	sulfate		
		PO_3^{3-}	phosphite	PO_4^{3-}	phosphate		
$N_2O_2^{2-}$	hyponitrite	NO_2^-	nitrite	NO_3^-	nitrate		
ClO^-	hypochlorite	ClO_2^-	chlorite	ClO_3^-	chlorate	ClO_4^-	perchlorate
BrO^-	hypobromite	BrO_2^-	bromite	BrO_3^-	bromate	BrO_4^-	perbromate
				MnO_4^{2-}	manganate	MnO_4^-	permanganate
				CrO_4^{2-}	chromate	CrO_8^{3-}	perchromate

Note that manganate/permanganate and chromate/perchromate are exceptions to the general rules because there are *–ate* ions but no *–ite* ions and because the charge changes.

Other polyatomic anions that end with *–ate* are:

$C_2O_4^{2-}$	$Cr_2O_7^{2-}$	SCN^-	HCO_2^-	$CH_3CO_2^-$
oxalate	dichromate	thiocyanate	formate	acetate

HCO_2^- and $CH_3CO_2^-$ are condensed **structural formulas** because they show how the atoms are linked together. Their molecular formulas would be CHO_2^- and $C_2H_3O_2^-$

If an H atom is added to a polyatomic anion with a negative charge greater than one, the word *hydrogen* or the prefix *bi-* are used for the resulting anion. If two H atoms are added, *dihydrogen* is used.

Examples: bicarbonate or hydrogen carbonate ion: HCO_3^-
dihydrogen phosphate ion: $H_2PO_4^-$

Ionic compounds: Hydrates

Water molecules often occupy positions within the lattice of an ionic crystal. These compounds are called **hydrates**, and the water molecules are known as **water of hydration**. The water of hydration is added after a centered dot in a formula. In a name, a number-prefix (listed below for molecular compounds) indicating the number of water molecules is followed by the root *–hydrate*.

Ionic compounds: Putting it all together

We now have the tools to name most common salts given a formula and to write a formula for them given a name. To determine a formula given a name, the number of anions and cations that are needed to achieve a neutral charge must be found.

Example: Determine the formula of cobalt(II) phosphite octahydrate.

Solution: For the cation, find the symbol for cobalt (Co) and recognize that it is present as Co^{2+} ions from the Roman numerals. For the anion, remember the phosphite ion is PO_3^{3-}. A neutral charge is achieved with 3 Co^{2+} ions for every 2 PO_3^{3-} ions. Add eight H_2O for water of hydration for the answer:
$$Co_3(PO_3)_2 \cdot 8H_2O.$$

Molecular compounds

Molecular compounds (compounds making up molecules with a neutral charge) are usually composed entirely of nonmetals and are named by placing the **less electronegative atom first**.

The suffix –ide is added to the second, more electronegative atom, and prefixes indicating numbers are added to one or both names if needed.

Prefix	mono-	di-	tri-	tetra-	penta-	hexa-	hepta-	octa-	nona-	deca-
Meaning	1	2	3	4	5	6	7	8	9	10

The final "o" or "a" may be left off these prefixes for oxides.

The electronegativity requirement is the reason the compound with two oxygen atoms and one nitrogen atom is called nitrogen dioxide, NO_2 and not dioxygen nitride O_2N. The hydride of sodium is NaH, sodium hydride, but the hydride of bromine is HBr, hydrogen bromide (or hydrobromic acid if it's in aqueous solution). Oxygen is only named first in compounds with fluorine such as oxygen difluoride, OF_2, and fluorine is never placed first because it is the most electronegative element.

Examples: N_2O_4, dinitrogen tetroxide (or tetraoxide)
Cl_2O_7, dichlorine heptoxide (or heptaoxide)
ClF_5 chlorine pentafluoride

Acids

There are special naming rules for acids that correspond with the **suffix of their corresponding anion** if hydrogen were removed from the acid. Anions ending with –*ide* correspond to acids with the prefix *hydro–* and the suffix –*ic*. Anions ending with –*ate* correspond to acids with no prefix that end with –*ic*. Oxoanions ending with –*ite* have associated acids with no prefix and the suffix –*ous*. The *hypo–* and *per–* prefixes are maintained. Some examples are shown in the following table:

anion	anion name	acid	acid name
Cl^-	chloride	$HCl(aq)$	hydrochloric acid
CN^-	cyanide	$HCN(aq)$	hydrocyanic acid
CO_3^{2-}	carbonate	$H_2CO_3(aq)$	carbonic acid
SO_3^{2-}	sulfite	$H_2SO_3(aq)$	sulfurous acid
SO_4^{2-}	sulfate	$H_2SO_4(aq)$	sulfuric acid
ClO^-	hypochlorite	$HClO(aq)$	hypochlorous acid
ClO_2^-	chlorite	$HClO_2(aq)$	chlorous acid
ClO_3^-	chlorate	$HClO_3(aq)$	chloric acid
ClO_4^-	perchlorate	$HClO_4(aq)$	perchloric acid

Example: What is the molecular formula of phosphorous acid?

Solution: If we remember that the –*ous* acid corresponds to the –*ite* anion, and that the –*ite* anion has one less oxygen than (or has an oxidation number 2 less than) the –*ate* form, we only need to remember that phosphate is PO_4^{3-}. Then we know that phosphite is PO_3^{3-} and phosphorous acid is H_3PO_3.

For additional resources, see:

http://chemistry.alanearhart.org/Tutorials/Nomen/nomen-part7.html has thousands of sample questions. Don't do them all in one sitting.

http://www.iupac.org/reports/provisional/abstract04/connelly_310804.html - IUPAC's latest report on inorganic nomenclature

Properly written and named formulas

Proper formulas will follow the rules of the previous skill. Here are some ways to identify improper formulas that are emphasized below by underlining them.

In all common names for **ionic compounds**, **number prefixes are not used** to describe the number of anions and cations.

Examples: $CaBr_2$ is calcium bromide, not calcium dibromide.
$Ba(OH)_2$ is barium hydroxide, not barium dihydroxide.
Cu_2SO_4 is copper(I) sulfate, not dicopper sulfate or copper(II) sulfate or

dicopper sulfur tetroxide.

All ionic compounds must have a **neutral charge in their formula** representations.

Example: MgBr is an improperly written formula because Mg ion always exists as 2+ and Br ion is always a 1– ion. $MgBr_2$, magnesium bromide, is correct.

Proper oxoanions and acids use the correct prefixes and suffixes.

Example: HNO_3 is nitric acid because NO_3^- is the nitrate ion.

In both ionic and molecular compounds, the **less electronegative element comes first**.

Example: CSi is an improperly written formula because Si is below C on the periodic table and therefore less electronegative. SiC, silicon carbide, is correct.

Organic compounds contain carbon, and have their own branch of chemistry because of the huge number of carbon compounds in nature, including nearly all the molecules in living things. The 1979 IUPAC organic nomenclature is used and taught most often today, and it is the nomenclature described here.

The simplest organic compounds are called **hydrocarbons** because they **contain only carbon and hydrogen.** Hydrocarbon molecules may be divided into the classes of **cyclic** and **open-chain** depending on whether they contain a ring of carbon atoms. Open-chain molecules may be divided into **branched** or **straight-chain** categories.

Hydrocarbons are also divided into classes called **aliphatic** and **aromatic**. Aromatic hydrocarbons are related to benzene and are always cyclic. Aliphatic hydrocarbons may be open-chain or cyclic. Aliphatic cyclic hydrocarbons are called **alicyclic**. Aliphatic hydrocarbons are one of three types: alkanes, alkenes, and alkynes.

Alkanes

Alkanes contain only single bonds. Alkanes have the maximum number of hydrogen atoms possible for their carbon backbone, so they are called **saturated**. Alkenes, alkynes, and aromatics are **unsaturated** because they have fewer hydrogens.

Straight-chain alkanes are also called **normal alkanes**. These are the simplest hydrocarbons. They consist of a linear chain of carbon atoms. The names of these molecules contain the suffix –ane and a **root based on the number of carbons in the chain** according to the table on the following page. The first four roots, *meth–*, *eth–*, *prop–*, and *but–* have historical origins in chemistry, and the remaining alkanes contain common Greek number prefixes. Alkanes have the general formula C_nH_{2n+2}.

A single molecule may be represented in multiple ways. Methane and ethane in the table are shown as three-dimensional structures with dashed wedge shapes attaching atoms behind the page and thick wedge shapes attaching atoms in front of the page.

Number of carbons	Name	Formula	Structure
1	Methane	CH_4	
2	Ethane	C_2H_6	
3	Propane	C_3H_8	
4	Butane	C_4H_{10}	
5	Pentane	C_5H_{12}	
6	Hexane	C_6H_{14}	
7	Heptane	C_7H_{16}	
8	Octane	C_8H_{18}	

Additional ways that pentane might be represented are

n-pentane (the *n* represents a *normal* alkane)
$CH_3CH_2CH_2CH_2CH_3$
$CH_3(CH_2)_3CH_3$

If one hydrogen is removed from an alkane, the residue is called an **alkyl** group. The *–ane* suffix is replaced by an *–yl–* infix when this residue is used as **functional group**. Functional groups are used to systematically build up the names of organic molecules.

Branched alkanes are named using a four-step process:

1) Find the longest continuous carbon chain. This is the parent hydrocarbon.
2) Number the atoms on this chain beginning at the end near the first branch point, so the lowest locant numbers are used. Number functional groups from the attachment point.
3) Determine the numbered locations and names of the substituted alkyl groups. Use *di–*, *tri–*, and similar prefixes for alkyl groups represented more than once. Separate numbers by commas and groups by dashes.
4) List the locations and names of alkyl groups in alphabetical order by their name (ignoring the *di–*, *tri–* prefixes) and end the name with the parent hydrocarbon.

Example—Name the following hydrocarbon:

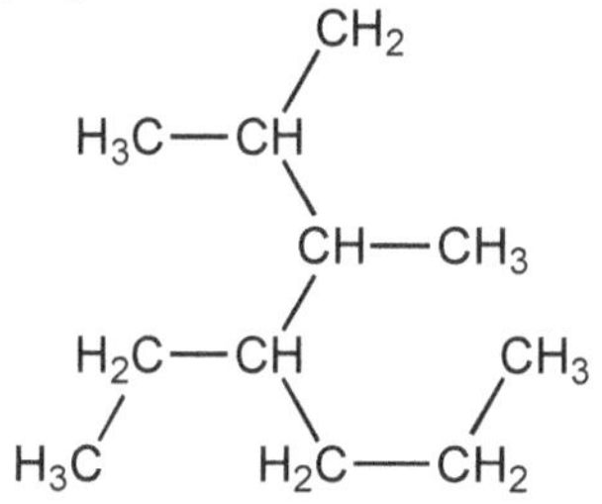

Solution—
1) The longest chain is seven carbons in length, as shown by the bold lines below. This molecule is a heptane.
2) The atoms are numbered from the end nearest the first branch as shown:

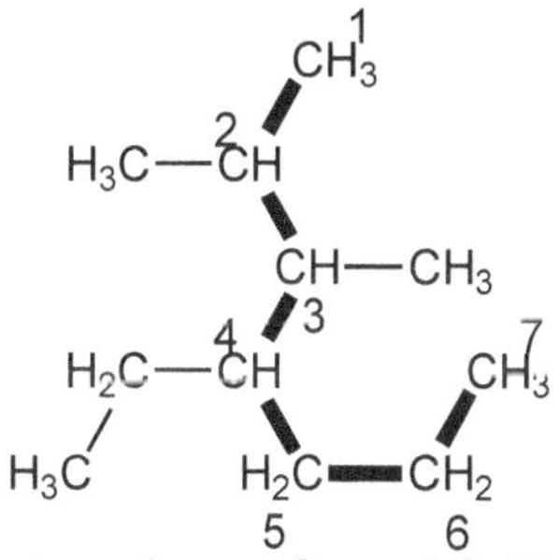

3) Methyl groups are located at carbons 2 and 3 (2,3-dimethyl), and an ethyl group is located at carbon 4.
4) "Ethyl" precedes "methyl" alphabetically. The hydrocarbon name is:
4-ethyl-2,3-dimethylheptane.

The following branched alkanes have IUPAC-accepted common names:

Structure	Systematic name	Common name
(H₃C)₂CH—CH₃	2-methylpropane	isobutane
H₃C—CH₂—CH(CH₃)—CH₃	2-methylbutane	isopentane
C(CH₃)₄	2,2-dimethylpropane	neopentane

The following alkyl groups have IUPAC-accepted common names. The systematic names assign a locant number of 1 to the attachment point:

Structure	Systematic name	Common name
(H₃C)₂CH—	1-methylethyl	isopropyl
(H₃C)₂CH—CH₂—	2-methylpropyl	isobutyl
H₃C—CH₂—CH(CH₃)—	1-methylpropyl	sec-butyl
(H₃C)₃C—	1,1-dimethylethyl	tert-butyl

Alkenes

Alkenes contain one or more double bonds. Alkenes are also called olefins. The suffix used in the naming of alkenes is –*ene*, and the number roots are those used for alkanes of the same length.

A number preceding the name shows the location of the double bond for alkenes of length four and above. Alkenes with one double bond have the general formula C_nH_{2n}. Multiple double bonds are named using –*diene*, –*triene*, etc. The suffix –*enyl*– is used for functional groups after a hydrogen is removed from an alkene. Ethene and propene have the common names **ethylene** and **propylene**. The ethenyl group has the common name **vinyl** and the 2-propenyl group has the common name **allyl**.

Examples:

$H_2C\!=\!CH_2$ is ethylene or ethene. $H_2C\!=\!CH\!-$ is a vinyl or ethenyl group.

$H_2C\!=\!CH\!-\!CH_3$ is propylene or propene. $H_2C\!=\!CH\!-\!CH_2\!-$ is an allyl or 2-propenyl group.

$H_3C\!-\!CH\!=\!CH\!-\!CH_2\!-\!CH_2\!-\!CH_3$ is 2-hexene.

$H_2C\!=\!C(CH_3)\!-\!CH\!=\!CH_2$ is 2-methyl-1,3-butadiene (common name: isoprene).

Cis-trans isomerism is often part of the complete name for an alkene. Note that isoprene contains two adjacent double bonds, so it is a **conjugated** molecule.

Alkynes and alkenynes

Alkynes contain one or more triple bonds. They are named in a similar way to alkenes. The suffix used for alkynes is *–yne*. Ethyne is often called **acetylene**. Alkynes with one triple bond have the general formula C_nH_{2n-2}. Multiple triple bonds are named using *–diyne*, *–triyne*, etc. The infix *–ynyl–* is used for functional groups composed of alkynes after the removal of a hydrogen atom.

Hydrocarbons with **both double and triple bonds are known as alkenynes** The locant number for the double bond precedes the name, and the locant for the triple bond follows the suffix *–en–* and precedes the suffix *–yne*.

Examples: HC≡CH is acetylene or ethyne.

HC≡C—CH₂—CH₃ is 1-butyne.

HC≡C—C≡C—CH₃ is 1,3-pentadiyne.

H₃C—C≡C—CH₂—CH₂—CH₂— is a 4-hexynyl group.

H₂C=CH—C≡CH is 1-buten-3-yne. This compound has the common name of vinylacetylene

Cycloalkanes, –enes, and –ynes

Alicyclic hydrocarbons use the prefix *cyclo*– before the number root for the molecule. The structures for these molecules are often written as if the molecule lay entirely within the plane of the paper even though in reality, these rings dip above and below a single plane. When there is more than one substitution on the ring, numbering begins with the first substitution listed in alphabetical order.

Examples: is cyclopropane

is methylcyclohexane.

is 1,3-cyclohexadiene.

is 1-ethyl-3-propylcyclobutane.

Cis-trans isomerism is often part of the complete name for a cycloalkane.

Aromatic hydrocarbons

Aromatic hydrocarbons are structurally related to benzene or made up of benzene molecules fused together. These molecules are called **arenes** to distinguish them from alkanes, alkenes, and alkynes. All atoms in arenes lie in the same plane. In other words, aromatic hydrocarbons are flat. Aromatic molecules have electrons in delocalized π orbitals that are free to migrate throughout the molecule.

Substitutions onto the benzene ring are named in alphabetical order using the lowest possible locant numbers. The prefix *phenyl*–may be used for C_6H_5- (benzene less a hydrogen) attached as a functional group to a larger hydrocarbon residue. Arenes in general form aryl functional groups. A phenyl group may be represented in a structure by the symbol Ø. The prefix *benzyl*–may used for $C_6H_5CH_2-$ (methylbenzene with a hydrogen removed from the methyl group) attached as a functional group.

Examples: (benzene structures) is benzene.

is 2-isopropyl-1,4-dimethylbenzene.

is 3-phenyloctane or (1-ethylhexyl)benzene.

The most often used common names for aromatic hydrocarbons are listed in the following table. Naphthalene is the simplest molecule formed by fused benzene rings.

Structure	Systematic name	Common name
(benzene ring with –CH₃)	methylbenzene	toluene
(benzene ring with two adjacent –CH₃ groups)	1,2-dimethylbenzene	ortho-xylene or o-xylene
(benzene ring with –CH₃ groups in 1,3 positions)	1,3-dimethylbenzene	meta-xylene or m-xylene
(benzene ring with –CH₃ groups in 1,4 positions)	1,4-dimethylbenzene	para-xylene or p-xylene
(benzene ring with –CH=CH₂)	ethenylbenzene	styrene
(two fused benzene rings)		naphthalene

COMPETENCY 20.0 UNDERSTAND AND APPLY KNOWLEDGE OF THE DEVELOPMENT AND CENTRAL CONCEPTS OF ATOMIC THEORY AND STRUCTURE, INCLUDING THE QUANTUM MECHANICAL MODEL.

Skill 20.1 Recognize the central concepts of atomic theory and atomic structure.

Atomic theory basically states that atoms are the basic, smallest building units of matter. Atoms themselves are made from **protons, neutrons, and electrons**. The nucleus of the atom is very small in relationship to the atom and much of the atom is actually empty space. The nucleus is the positively charged component of the atom and the neutron has a zero charge. Electrons circle the proton and carry a negative charge. If you break an atom into its smaller parts, you lose the property of the element.

Atoms differ depending upon the elemental form they make. The simplest atom is Hydrogen, which has one proton and one electron that are attracted to each other due to an electrical charge. The spinning force of the electron keeps the electron from crashing into the proton and keeps the electron always moving.

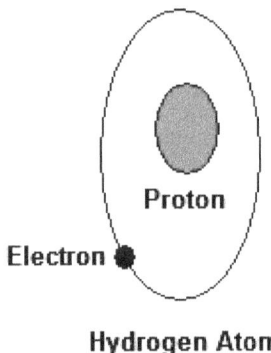

Hydrogen Atom

This is the hydrogen atom, abbreviated H. It has a single neutron and single rotating electron.

Skill 20.2 Demonstrate knowledge of the historical progression in the development of the theory of the atom, including the contributions of Dalton, Thomson, Rutherford, and Bohr.

Our current understanding of atomic structure and the nuclear atom took over two thousand of years and the work of many individuals, often thinking outside of the box.

The concept of the atom can be traced back to the ancient Greek philosophers but may have actually originated with the founder of Buddhism, Gutama who said " Death is actually the disaggreation of atoms" on his deathbed .

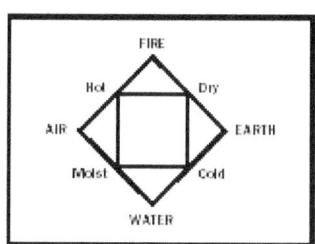

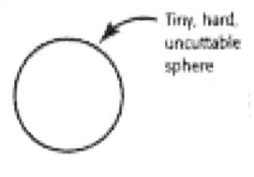

DEMOCRITUS'S MODEL

Atoms created quite a controversy in the Greek forum. Two opinions existed; those who believed that matter was continuous followed Aristotle and Plato and those who believed that matter was not continuous followed Leucippetius. Leucippitus believed that a fragment of matter existed that could not be divided and still retain properties of that matter. A student of Leucippetius, Democritus, named the smallest piece of matter atomos, Greek for indivisible.

"sweet or sour, hot or cold by convention, existing are only atoms and void"

Aristotle and Plato had reputations of being very wise and knowledgeable men. So most people believed them. Aristotle did not like the randomness of Democritus' ideas. He preferred a more ordered matter. Therefore, the idea of atoms and those who believed in their existence had to go underground.

Epicuious created a school and society for those who believed in atoms. Titus Leucritius wrote *de Rurum Natura* in 55 B.C. This poem described the nature of atoms. In the poem there is reference to some phrases of Parmenidis which bear a striking resemblance to what is now known as the law of mass conservation.

"the content of the universe was never before more or less condensed than it is today"
      de Rurum Natura

Dalton

The existence of fundamental units of matter called atoms of different types called elements was proposed by ancient philosophers without any evidence to support the belief. Modern atomic theory is credited to the work of **John Dalton** published in 1803-1807. Observations made by him and others about the composition, properties, and reactions of many compounds led him to develop the following postulates:

1) Each element is composed of small particles called atoms.
2) All atoms of a given element are identical in mass and other properties.
3) Atoms of different elements have different masses and differ in other properties.
4) Atoms of an element are not created, destroyed, or changed into a different type of atom by chemical reactions.
5) Compounds form when atoms of more than one element combine.
6) In a given compound, the relative number and kind of atoms are constant.

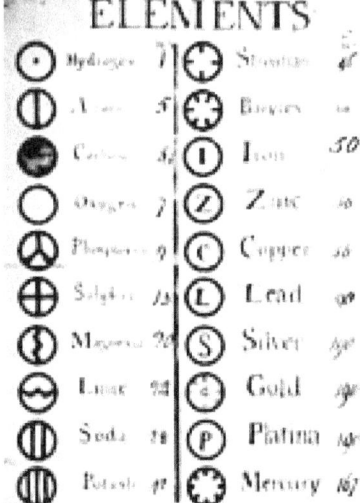

Dalton's table of atomic symbols and masses

Dalton determined and published the known relative masses of a number of different atoms. He also formulated the law of partial pressures (see **Skill 22.3**). Dalton's work focused on the ability of atoms to arrange themselves into molecules and to rearrange themselves via chemical reactions, but he did not investigate the composition of atoms themselves. **Dalton's model of the atom** was a tiny, indivisible, indestructible **particle** of a certain mass, size, and chemical behavior, but Dalton did not deny the possibility that atoms might have a substructure.

Prior to the late 1800s, atoms, following Dalton's ideas, were thought to be small, spherical and indivisible particles that made up matter. However, with the discovery of electricity and the investigations that followed, this view of the atom changed.

Thomson

Joseph John Thomson, often known as **J. J. Thomson**, was the first to examine this substructure. In the mid-1800s, scientists had studied a form of radiation called "cathode rays" or "electrons" that originated from the negative electrode (cathode) when electrical current was forced through an evacuated tube. Thomson determined in 1897 that **electrons have mass**, and because many different cathode materials release electrons, Thomson proposed that the **electron is a subatomic particle**. **Thomson's model of the atom** was a uniformly positive particle with electrons contained in the interior.

This has been called the "plum-pudding" model of the atom where the pudding represents the uniform sphere of positive electricity and the bits of plum represent electrons. For more on Thomson, see
http://www.aip.org/history/electron/jjhome.htm.

Planck

Max Planck determined in 1900 that **energy is transferred by radiation in exact multiples of a discrete unit of energy called a quantum**. Quanta of energy are extremely small, and may be found from the frequency of the radiation v, using the equation:

$$\Delta E = hv$$

where h is Planck's constant and hv is a quantum of energy.

Rutherford

Ernest Rutherford studied atomic structure in 1910-1911 by firing a beam of alpha particles at thin layers of gold leaf. According to Thomson's model, the path of an alpha particle should be deflected only slightly if it struck an atom, but Rutherford observed some alpha particles bouncing almost backwards, suggesting that **nearly all the mass of an atom is contained in a small positively charged nucleus**. **Rutherford's model of the atom** was an analogy to the sun and the planets A small positively charged nucleus is surrounded by circling electrons and mostly by empty space. Rutherford's experiment is explained in greater detail in this flash animation:
http://www.mhhe.com/physsci/chemistry/essentialchemistry/flash/ruther14.swf.

Bohr

Niels Bohr incorporated Planck's quantum concept into Rutherford's model of the atom in 1913 to explain the **discrete frequencies of radiation emitted and absorbed by atoms with one electron** (H, He^+, and Li^{2+}). This electron is attracted to the positive nucleus and is closest to the nucleus at the **ground state** of the atom. When the electron absorbs energy, it moves into an orbit further from the nucleus and the atom is said to be in an electronically **excited state**. If sufficient energy is absorbed, the electron separates from the nucleus entirely, and the atom is ionized:

$$H \rightarrow H^+ + e^-$$

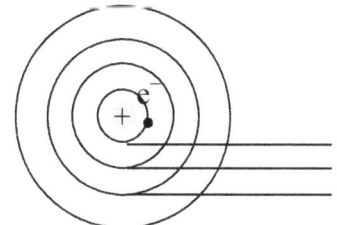

The energy required for ionization from the ground state is called the atom's **ionization energy**. The discrete frequencies of radiation emitted and absorbed by the atomcorrespond (using Planck's constant) to discrete energies and in turn to discrete distances from the nucleus. **Bohr's model of the atom** was a small positively charged nucleus surrounded mostly by empty space and by electrons orbiting at certain discrete distances ("shells") corresponding to discrete energy levels. Animations utilizing the Bohr model may be found at the following two URLs: http://artsci–ccwin.concordia.ca/facstaff/a–c/bird/c241/D1.html and http://www.mhhe.com/physsci/chemistry/essentialchemistry/flash/linesp16.swf.

Bohr's model of the atom didn't quite fit experimental observations for atoms other than hydrogen. He was, however, on the right track. DeBroglie was the first to suggest that possibly matter behaved like a wave. Until then, waves had wave properties of wavelength, frequency and amplitude while matter had matter properties like mass and volume. DeBroglie's suggestion was quite unique and interesting to scientists.

De Broglie
Depending on the experiment, radiation appears to have wave-like or particle-like traits. In 1923-1924, Louis de Broglie applied this **wave/particle duality to all matter with momentum**. The discrete distances from the nucleus described by Bohr corresponded to permissible distances where standing waves could exist. **De Broglie's model of the atom** described electrons as **matter waves in standing wave orbits** around the nucleus. The first three standing waves corresponding to the first three discrete distances are shown in the figure. De Broglie's model may be found here: http://artsci-ccwin.concordia.ca/facstaff/a-c/bird/c241/D1-part2.html.

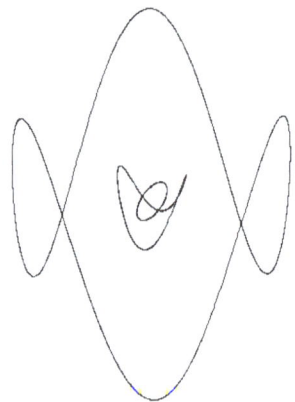

Heisenberg
The realization that both matter and radiation interact as waves led Werner Heisenberg to the conclusion in 1927 that the act of observation and measurement requires the interaction of one wave with another, resulting in an **inherent uncertainty** in the location and momentum of particles. This inability to measure phenomena at the subatomic level is known as the **Heisenberg uncertainty principle**, and it applies to the location and momentum of electrons in an atom. A discussion of the principle and Heisenberg's other contributions to quantum theory is located here: http://www.aip.org/history/heisenberg/.

Schrödinger

When Erwin Schrödinger studied the atom in 1925, he replaced the idea of precise orbits with regions in space called **orbitals** where electrons were likely to be found. **The Schrödinger equation** describes the **probability** that an electron will be in a given region of space, a quantity known as **electron density** or Ψ^2. The diagrams below are surfaces of constant Ψ^2 found by solving the Schrödinger equation for the hydrogen atom $1s$, $2p_z$ and $3d_0$ orbitals. Additional representations of solutions may be found here:
http://library.wolfram.com/webMathematica/Physics/Hydrogen.jsp.
Schrödinger's model of the atom is a mathematical formulation of quantum mechanics that describes the electron density of orbitals. It is the atomic model that has been in use from shortly after it was introduced up to the present.

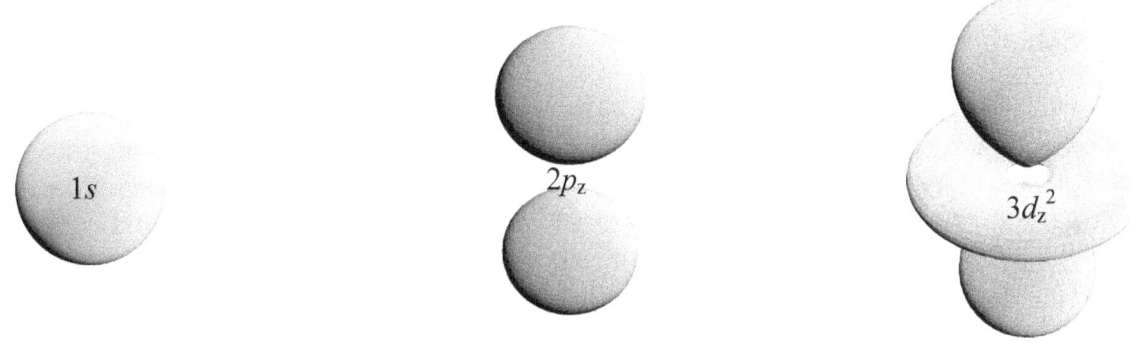

This model explains the movement of electrons to higher energy levels when exposed to energy. It also explains the movement of electrons to lower energy levels when the source of energy has disappeared. Accompanying this drop in energy level is the emission of electromagnetic radiation (light as one possibility).

Using Plank's equation, the frequency of that electromagnetic radiation, EMR, can be determined, radiation caused by the movement of matter.

The union of deBroglie's, Planck, Heisenberg, Schrodinger and Bohr's ideas lead to the development of the wave-mechanical view of the atom. The solution to Schrodinger's equation provides for 3 quantum numbers added to Pauli's idea that no two electrons could have the same solution set for Schrodinger's equation (known as Pauli exclusion principle), we have four quantum numbers that describe the most probable orbital for an electron of a given energy or the quantum mechanical model of the atom.

Skill 20.3 Describe the energy of an electron in an atom or ion in terms of the four quantum numbers.

Quantum numbers
The quantum-mechanical solutions from the Schrödinger Equation utilize three quantum numbers (n, l, and m_l) to describe an orbital and a fourth (m_s) to describe an electron in an orbital. This model is useful for understanding the frequencies of radiation emitted and absorbed by atoms and chemical properties of atoms.

The **principal quantum number n** may have positive integer values (1, 2, 3, …). n is a measure of the **distance** of an orbital from the nucleus, and orbitals with the same value of n are said to be in the same **shell**. This is analogous to the Bohr model of the atom. Each shell may contain up to $2n^2$ electrons.

The **azimuthal quantum number l** may have integer values from 0 to n-1. l describes the angular momentum of an orbital. This determines the orbital's **shape**. Orbitals with the same value of n and l are in the same **subshell**, and each subshell may contain up to ($4l$ + 2 electrons). Subshells are usually referred to by the principle quantum number followed by a letter corresponding to l as shown in the following table:

Azimuthal quantum number l	0	1	2	3	4
Subshell designation	s	p	d	f	g

The **magnetic quantum number m_l or m** may have integer values from $-l$ to l. m_l is a measure of how an individual orbital responds to an external magnetic field, and it often describes an orbital's **orientation**. A subscript—either the value of m_l or a function of the x-, y-, and z-axes—is used to designate a specific orbital. Each orbital may hold up to two electrons.

The **spin quantum number m_s or s** has one of two possible values: $-1/2$ or $+1/2$. m_s differentiates between the two possible electrons occupying an orbital. Electrons moving through a magnet behave as if they were tiny magnets themselves spinning on their axis in either a clockwise or counterclockwise direction. These two spins may be described as $m_s = -1/2$ and $+1/2$ or as down and up.

The **Pauli exclusion principle** states that **no two electrons in an atom may have the same set of four quantum numbers** and provides this forth quantum number, m_s.

The following table summarizes the relationship among n, l, and m_l through $n=3$:

n	l	Subshell	m_l	Orbitals in subshell	Maximum number of electrons in subshell
1	0	1s	0	1	2
2	0	2s	0	1	2
	1	2p	−1, 0, 1	3	6
3	0	3s	0	1	2
	1	3p	−1, 0, 1	3	6
	2	3d	−2, −1, 0, 1, 2	5	10

Subshell energy levels

In single-electron atoms (H, He^+, and Li^{2+}) above the ground state, subshells within a shell are all at the same energy level, and an orbital's energy level is only determined by n. However, in all other atoms, multiple electrons repel each other. Electrons in orbitals closer to the nucleus create a screening or **shielding effect** on electrons further away from the nucleus, preventing them from receiving the full attractive force of the nucleus. **In multi-electron atoms, both n and l determine the energy level of an orbital**. In the absence of a magnetic field, **orbitals in the same subshell with different m_l all have the same energy** and are said to be **degenerate orbitals**.

The following list orders subshells by increasing energy level:
$1s < 2s < 2p < 3s < 3p < 4s < 3d < 4p < 5s < 4d < 5p < 6s < 4f < 5d < 6p < 7s < 5f < ...$

This list may be constructed by arranging the subshells according to n and l and drawing diagonal arrows as shown below:

```
1s
2s  2p
3s  3p  3d
4s  4p  4d  4f
5s  5p  5d  5f  5g
6s  6p  6d  6f  6g
7s  7p  7d  7f  7g
8s  8p  8d  8f  8g
```

Skill 20.4 Demonstrate a qualitative knowledge of the role of probability in the description of an orbital's size and shape.

The initial Bohr model of electrons circling like planets in a solar system is not accurate. Since the development of Quantum Physics, it has been determined that electrons instead carry a certain probability of being in any given place at any given time. This results in a picture that looks more like an electron cloud around the proton core. This idea was borne out in experiments done from 1920-1950. The charge-cloud model, also known as the quantum-mechanical model, doesn't try to describe the pathway of each electron but instead describes the position of electrons in terms of probability. Using computers, we can calculate the particular points in space that carry the highest probability of an electron being there. What results is a three dimensional shape that looks like the following:

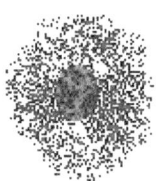

The above electron cloud describes the total of the various paths that electrons could be taking at very high speeds.

Electrons now reside in what's known as orbitals, rather than orbits (like a planet). An orbital is defined and named by three quantum numbers:
n=the shape or "subshell" of the orbital
l= the Azimuthal number which describes the angular momentum of the electron
y= the number of electrons in the orbital

For example, the orbital $1s^2$ (pronounced "one s two" means that the orbital is at its lowest energy level (n=1), has two electrons in it and an angular momentum of 0. All electrons at the same n-level are at the same distance from the nucleus. They are of same "shell". Electrons with the same n-level and l-level are of the same "sublevel".

In his studies, Heisenberg noted that it is impossible to find out both the position and momentum of an electron at the same time because, finding its position would change its momentum. This is known as the Heisenberg Uncertainty Principle and is the way scientists know that electrons don't follow a predictable path. In addition, any electron that is acted upon by a photon of light will change its momentum and position.

Nevertheless, electrons are found more likely in some areas of the atom than in other regions. In other words, there are places inside the atom, primarily the shells that have a higher probability of finding the electrons within those places. They can be defined by the principles of quantum physics and the quantum numbers. The higher the level of n, the larger the orbital is.

Skill 20.5   Analyze the properties of an atomic nucleus that affect its stability.

Some nuclei are unstable and emit particles and electromagnetic radiation. These emissions from the nucleus are known as **radioactivity**; the unstable isotopes are known as **radioisotopes**; and the nuclear reactions that spontaneously alter them are known as **radioactive decay**. Particles commonly involved in nuclear reactions are listed in the following table:

Particle	Neutron	Proton	Electron	Positron	Alpha particle	Beta particle	Gamma rays
Symbol	$^1_0 n$	$^1_1 p$ or $^1_1 H$	$^0_{-1} e$	$^0_1 e$	$^4_2 \alpha$ or $^4_2 He$	$^0_{-1} \beta$ or $^0_{-1} e$	$^0_0 \gamma$

The **half-life** of a reaction is the **time required to consume half the reactant**. The rate of radioactive decay for an isotope is usually expressed as a half-life. Solving these problems is straightforward if the given amount of time is an exact multiple of the half-life. For example, the half-life of ^{233}Pa is 27.0 days. This means that of 200 grams of ^{233}Pa will decay according to the following table:

Day	Number of half-lives	^{233}Pa remaining	^{233}Pa decayed since day 0
0	0	200 g	0 g
27.0	1	100 g	100 g
54.0	2	50.0 g	150.0 g
81.0	3	25.0 g	175.0 g
108.0	4	12.5 g	187.5 g

Regardless of whether the given amount of time is an exact multiple of the half-life, the following equation may be used:

$$A_{remaining} = A_{initially} \left(\frac{1}{2}\right)^{\frac{t}{t_{halflife}}}$$

where: $A_{remaining} \Rightarrow$ amount remaining

$A_{initially} \Rightarrow$ amount initially

$t \Rightarrow$ time

$t_{halflife} \Rightarrow$ half-life

Skill 20.6 Apply strategies for writing and balancing equations for nuclear reactions (e.g., fission, fusion, radioactivity and bombardment).

Nuclear equations are balanced by equating the sum of mass numbers on both sides of a reaction equation and the sum of atomic numbers on both sides of a reaction equation.

The electron is assigned an atomic number of –1 to account for the conversion during radioactive decay of a neutron to a proton and an emitted electron called a **beta particle**:

$$^{1}_{0}n \rightarrow {}^{1}_{1}p + {}^{0}_{-1}e.$$

Sulfur-35 is an isotope that decays by beta emission:

$$^{35}_{16}S \rightarrow {}^{35}_{17}Cl + {}^{0}_{-1}e.$$

In most cases nuclear reactions result in a **nuclear transmutation** from one element to another. Transmutation was originally connected to the mythical "philosopher's stone" of alchemy that could turn cheaper elements into gold. When Frederick Soddy and Ernest Rutherford first recognized that radioactive decay was changing one element into another, Soddy remembered saying, "Rutherford, this is transmutation!" Rutherford replied, "Soddy, don't call it transmutation. They'll have our heads off as alchemists."

Isotopes may also decay by **electron capture** from an orbital outside the nucleus:

$$^{196}_{79}Au + {}^{0}_{-1}e \rightarrow {}^{196}_{78}Pt.$$

A **positron** is a particle with the small mass of an electron but with a positive charge. A positron emission converts a proton into a neutron. Carbon-11 decays by positron emission:

$$^{11}_{6}C \rightarrow {}^{11}_{5}B + {}^{0}_{1}e.$$

Large isotopes often decay by **alpha particle** emission:

$$^{238}_{92}U \rightarrow {}^{234}_{90}Th + {}^{4}_{2}He.$$

Gamma rays are high-energy electromagnetic radiation, and gamma radiation is almost always emitted when other radioactive decay occurs. Gamma rays usually aren't written into equations because neither the mass number nor the atomic number is altered. One exception is the annihilation of an electron by a positron, an event that only produces gamma radiation:

$$^{0}_{-1}e + {}^{0}_{1}e \rightarrow 2{}^{0}_{0}\gamma.$$

Example: Balance the following nuclear transmutation:
$$^{14}_{6}C \rightarrow ^{14}_{7}N + \underline{}$$

Solution: The sum of the mass numbers on both the left and right side of the arrow must be the same:

Left side	Right side
14	14

They are the same so the particle emitted during decay has a mass of 0.

The sum of the charge must be the same on the left side and right side of the arrow.

Left side	Right side
6	7

The right side has one too many positive charges to balance 6 positive charges on the left side. Adding -1 to the right side will make it balance with 6 positive charges.

So the charge of the particle emitted during decay is -1.

That particle is an electron. $^{0}_{-1}e$ and should be placed in the equation to complete.

$$^{14}_{6}C \rightarrow ^{14}_{7}N + ^{0}_{-1}e$$

Example: Complete the following nuclear transmutation:

$$^{234}_{90}Th \rightarrow ^{0}_{-1}e + \underline{}$$

Solution: Again, the sum of the mass numbers on each side of the arrow must be the same as well as the sum of the charges on each side.

Left side	Right side
234	0

234 is needed on the right side to equal the left side.

Left side	Right side
90	-1

91 is needed on the right side to equal the left side so the particle that forms from the decay of this isotope is $^{234}_{91}Pa$ and should be inserted to complete the transmutation.

$$^{234}_{90}Th \rightarrow \, ^{0}_{-1}e + \, ^{234}_{91}Pa$$

Processes of nuclear fission and fusion

When two nuclei collide, they sometimes stick to each other and synthesize a new nucleus. This **nuclear fusion** was first demonstrated by the synthesis of oxygen from nitrogen and alpha particles:

$$^{14}_{7}N + \, ^{4}_{2}He \rightarrow \, ^{17}_{8}O + \, ^{1}_{1}H.$$

Fusion is also used to create new heavy elements, causing periodic tables to grow out of date every few years. In 2004, IUPAC approved the name roentgenium (in honor of Wilhelm Roentgen, the discoverer of X-rays) for the element first synthesized in 1994 by the following reaction:

$$^{209}_{83}Bi + \, ^{64}_{28}Ni \rightarrow \, ^{272}_{111}Rg + \, ^{1}_{0}n.$$

A heavy nucleus may also split apart into smaller nuclei by **nuclear fission**. **Nuclear power** currently provides 17% of the world's electricity. Heat is generated by **nuclear fission of uranium-235 or plutonium-239**. This heat is then converted to electricity by boiling water and forcing the steam through a turbine. Fission of ^{235}U and ^{239}Pu occurs when **a neutron strikes the nucleus and breaks it apart into smaller nuclei and additional neutrons**. One possible fission reaction is:

$$^1_0n + ^{235}_{92}U \rightarrow ^{141}_{56}Ba + ^{92}_{36}Kr + 3\,^1_0n$$

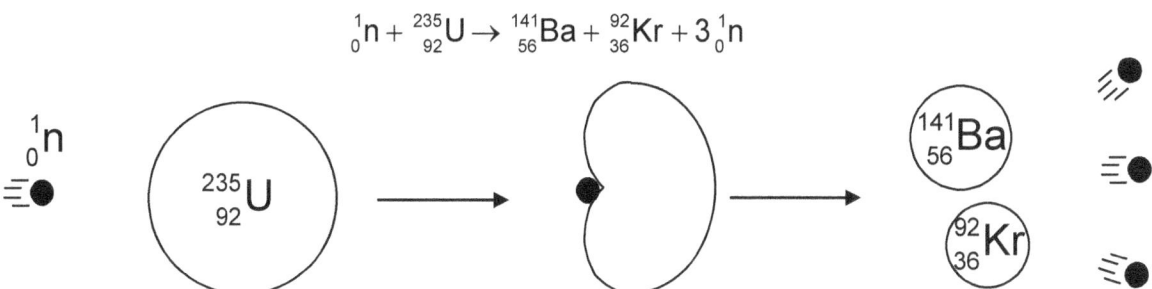

Gamma radiation, kinetic energy from the neutrons themselves, and the decay of the fission products (^{141}Ba and ^{92}Kr in the example above) all produce heat. The neutrons produced by the reaction strike other uranium atoms and produce more neutrons and more energy in a **chain reaction**. If enough neutrons are lost, the chain reaction stops and the process is called **subcritical**. If the mass of uranium is large enough so that one neutron on average from each fission event triggers another fission, the reaction is said to be **critical**.

If the mass is larger than this so that few neutrons escape, the reaction is called **supercritical**. The chain reaction then multiplies the number of fissions that occur and the violent explosion of an atomic bomb will take place if the process is not stopped. The concentration of **fissile material** in nuclear power plants is sufficient for a critical reaction to occur but too low for a supercritical reaction to take place.

The alpha decay of **Plutonium-238 is used as a heat source for localized power generation** in space probes and in heart pacemakers from the 1970s.

The most promising nuclear reaction for producing power by nuclear fusion is:

$$^2_1H + ^3_1H \rightarrow ^4_2He + ^1_0n$$

Hydrogen-2 is called **deuterium** and is often represented by the symbol D. Hydrogen-3 is known as **tritium** and is often represented by the symbol T. Nuclear reactions between very light atoms similar to the reaction above are the energy source behind the sun and the hydrogen bomb

COMPETENCY 21.0 UNDERSTAND AND APPLY KNOWLEDGE OF THE FORMATION OF BONDS AND THE GEOMETRY AND PROPERTIES OF THE RESULTING COMPOUNDS.

Skill 21.1 Analyze electron behavior in the formation of various types of bonds (e.g., ionic, covalent) and the polarity of compounds in terms of shape and electronegativity differences.

Chemical compounds form when two or more atoms join together. A stable compound occurs when the total energy of the combination of the atoms together is lower than the atoms separately. The combined state suggests an attractive force exists between the atoms. This attractive force is called a chemical bond.

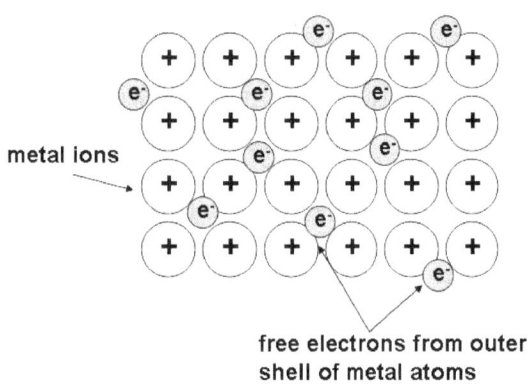

Metallic bonds occur when the bonding is between two metals. Metallic properties, such as low ionization energies, conductivity, and malleability, suggest that metals possess strong forces of attraction between atoms, but still have electrons that are able to move freely in all directions throughout the metal. This creates a "sea of electrons" model where electrons are quickly and easily transferred between metal atoms. In this model, the outer shell electrons are free to move. The metallic bond is the force of attraction that results from the moving electrons and the positive nuclei left behind. The strength of metal bonds usually results in regular structures and high melting and boiling points.

Ionic Bonds
An **ionic bond** describes the electrostatic forces that exist between **particles of opposite charge.** An ionic bond is the result of an atom(s) losing electrons to form a positive ion being attracted to an atom(s) that has gained electrons to form a negative ion.

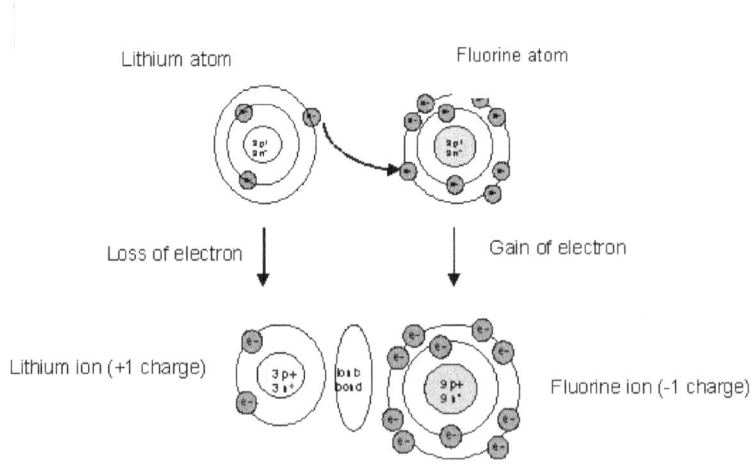

SCIENCE: CHEMISTRY

Due to low ionization energies, metals have a tendency to lose valence electrons relatively easily, whereas non-metals, which have high ionization energies and high electronegativites, gain electrons easily. This produces cations (positively charged) and anions (negatively charged). Coulomb's Law says that opposites attract, and so do the oppositely charged ions. This *electrostatic interaction* between the anion and the cation results in an ionic bond. Ionic bonds will only occur when a metal is bonding to a non-metal, and is the result of the periodic trends (ionization energy and electronegativity). Elements that form an ionic bond with each other have a large difference in their electronegativity. Anions and cations pack together into a crystal **lattice** as shown to the right for NaCl. Ionic compounds are also known as **salts**.

Single and multiple covalent bonds

A **covalent bond** forms when at least one pair of electrons is shared by two atoms. The shared electrons are found in the valence energy level and lead to a lower energy if they are shared in a way that creates a noble gas configuration (a full octet). Covalent, or molecular, bonds occur when a non-metal is bonding to a non-metal. This is due primarily to the fact that non-metals have high ionization energies and high electronegativities. Neither atom wants to give up electrons; both want to gain them. In order to satisfy both octets, the electrons can be shared between the two atoms.

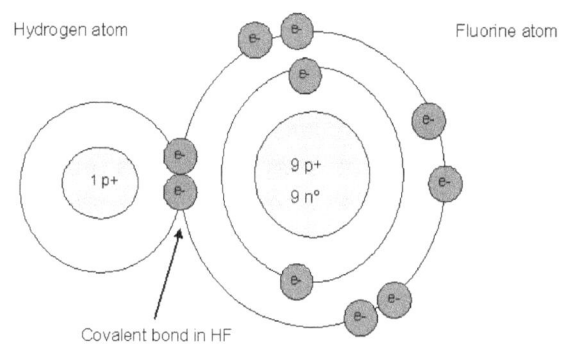

Sharing of electrons can be equal or unequal, resulting in a separation of charge (polar) or an even distribution of charge (non-polar). The polarity of a bond can be determined through an examination of the electronegativities of the atoms involved in the bond. The more electronegative atom will have a stronger attraction to the electrons, thus possessing the electrons more of the time. This results in a partial negative charge (δ^-) on the more electronegative atom and a partial positive charge (δ^+) on the less electronegative atom.

The simplest covalent bond is between the two single electrons of hydrogen atoms. Covalent bonds may be represented by an electron pair (a pair of dots) or a line as shown below. The shared pair of electrons provides each H atom with two electrons in its valence shell (the 1s orbital), so both have the stable electron configuration of helium.

H· + ·H → H:H
           H—H

Chlorine molecules have 7 electrons in their valence shell and share a pair of electrons so both have the stable electron configuration of argon.

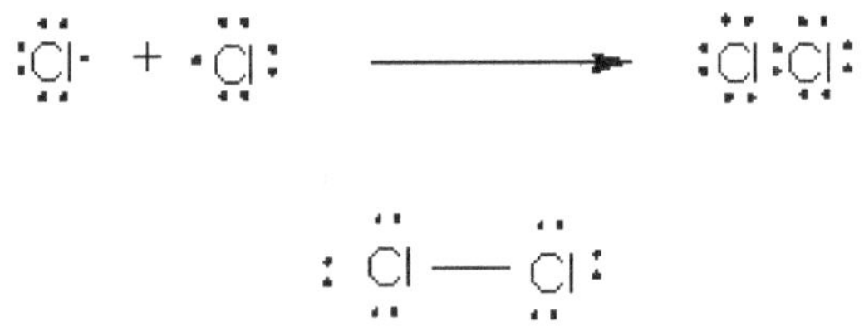

:Cl· + ·Cl: → :Cl:Cl:

:Cl—Cl:

In the previous two examples, a single pair of electrons was shared, and the resulting bond is referred to as a **single bond**. When two electron pairs are shared, two lines are drawn, representing a **double bond**, and three shared pairs of electrons represents a **triple bond** as shown below for CO_2 and N_2. The remaining electrons are in **unshared pairs**.

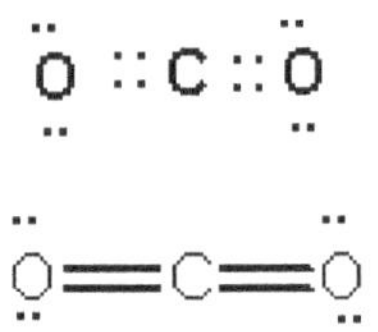

O::C::O

O=C=O

:N::N:

:N≡N:

Polar/nonpolar covalent bonds

Electron pairs shared between **two atoms of the same element are shared equally**. At the other extreme, **for ionic bonding there is no electron sharing** because the electron is transferred completely from one atom to the other. Most bonds fall somewhere between these two extremes, and the electrons are **shared unequally**. This will increase the probability that the shared electrons will be located on one of the two atoms, giving that atom a **partial negative charge** and the other atom a **partial positive charge** as shown below for gaseous HCl. Such bonds are referred to as **polar bonds**. A particle with a positive and a negative region is called a **dipole**. A lower-case delta (δ) is used to indicate partial charge or an arrow is draw from the partial positive to the partial negative atom.

$$\overset{\delta+\delta-}{H\!\!-\!\!Cl} \qquad \overset{\longrightarrow}{H\!\!-\!\!Cl}$$

Electronegativity is a measure of **the ability of an atom to attract electrons** in a chemical bond. Metallic elements have low electronegativities and nonmetallic elements have high electronegativities.

H							
2.2							
Li	Be		B	C	N	O	F
1.0	1.6		1.8	2.5	3.0	3.4	4.0
Na	Mg		Al	Si	P	S	Cl
0.9	1.3		1.6	1.9	2.2	2.6	3.2

Linus Pauling developed the concept of electronegativity and its relationship to different types of bonds in the 1930s.

A **large electronegativity difference** (greater than 1.7) results in an **ionic bond**. Any bond composed of two different atoms will be slightly polar, but for a **small electronegativity difference** (less than 0.4), the distribution of charge in the bond is so nearly equal that the result is called a **nonpolar covalent bond**. An **intermediate electronegativity difference** (from 0.4 to 1.7) results in a **polar covalent bond**. HCl is polar covalent because Cl has a very high electronegativity (it is near F in the periodic table) and H is a nonmetal (and so it will form a covalent bond with Cl), but H is near the dividing line between metals and nonmetals, so there is still a significant electronegativity difference between H and Cl. Using the numbers in the table above, the electronegativity for Cl is 3.2 and it is 2.2 for H. The difference of 3.2 – 2.2 = 1.0 places this bond in the middle of the range for polar covalent bonds.

Bond type is actually a continuum as shown in the following chart for common bonds. Note that the **C-H bond** is considered **nonpolar**.

Type of bonding	Electronegativity difference	Bond
		Fr^+-F^-
Very ionic		Na^+-F^-
	3.0	
⋮	⋮	⋮
Ionic		Na^+-Cl^-
	2.0	Na^+-Br^-
Mostly ionic		Na^+-I^-
Mostly polar covalent	1.5	$C^{\delta+}-F^{\delta-}$
		$H^{\delta+}-O^{\delta-}$
Polar covalent	1.0	$H^{\delta+}-Cl^{\delta-}$
		$C^{\delta+}=O^{\delta-}$
		$H^{\delta+}-N^{\delta-}$
		$C^{\delta+}-Cl^{\delta-}$
	0.5	$C^{\delta+}\equiv N^{\delta-}$
Mostly nonpolar covalent		C—H
Fully nonpolar covalent	0	$H_2, N_2, O_2,$ $F_2, Cl_2, Br_2, I_2,$ C—C, S—S

⇑ Increasing ionic character

A **polar molecule** has positive and negative regions as shown above for HCl. **Bond polarity is necessary but not sufficient for molecular polarity**. A molecule containing polar bonds will still be nonpolar if the most negative and most positive location occurs at the same point. In other words, **in a polar molecule, bond polarities must not cancel**.

To determine if a molecule is polar perform the following steps.

1) Draw the molecular structure.
2) Assign a polarity to each bond with an arrow (remember C-H is nonpolar). If none of the bonds are polar, the molecule is nonpolar.
3) Determine if the polarities cancel each other in space. If they do, the molecule is nonpolar. Otherwise the molecule is polar.

Examples: Which of the following are polar molecules: CO_2 CH_2Cl_2, CCl_4?

Solution: 1)

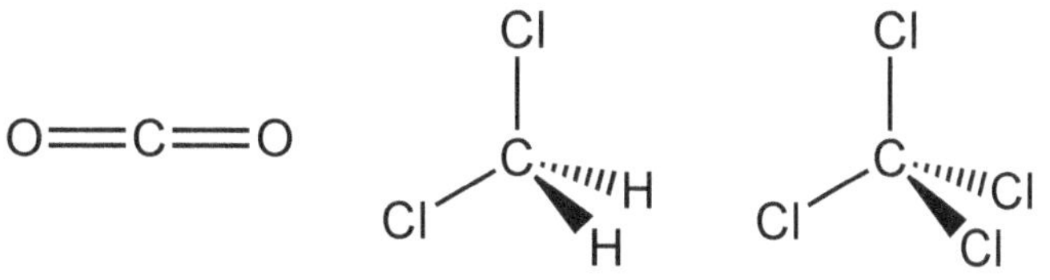

CO_2 CH_2Cl_2 CCl_4

2)

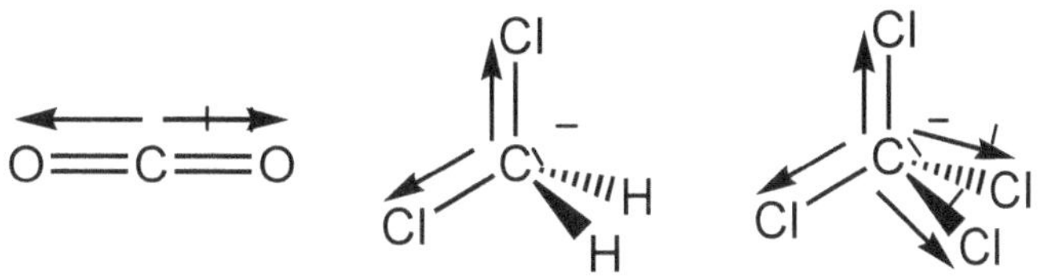

3)

charges cancel   net dipole   charges cancel

nonpolar   polar   nonpolar

The polarity of molecules is critical for determining a good solvent for a given solute. Additional practice on the topic of polar bonds and molecules is available at http://cowtownproductions.com/cowtown/genchem/09_17M.htm.

Skill 21.2 Apply the concepts of Lewis structures, valence-shell electron-pair repulsion, and hybridization to describe molecular geometry and bonding.

Lewis dot structures are a method for keeping track of each atom's valence electrons in a molecule. Drawing Lewis structures is a three-step process:

1) Add the number of valence shell electrons for each atom. If the compound is an anion, add the charge of the ion to the total electron count because anions have "extra" electrons. If the compound is a cation, subtract the charge of the ion.
2) Write the symbols for each atom showing how the atoms connect to each other.
3) Draw a single bond (one pair of electron dots or a line) between each pair of connected atoms. Place the remaining electrons around the atoms as unshared pairs. If every atom has an octet of electrons except H atoms with two electrons, the Lewis structure is complete. Shared electrons count towards both atoms. If there are too few electron pairs to do this, draw multiple bonds (two or three pairs of electron dots between the atoms) until an octet is around each atom (except H atoms with two). If there are two many electron pairs to complete the octets with single bonds then the octet rule Is broken for this compound.

Example: Draw the Lewis structure of HCN
Solution:
1) From their locations in the main group of the periodic table, we know that each atom contributes the following number of electrons: H—1, C—4, N—5. Because it is a neutral compound, the molecule will have a total of 10 valence electrons.
2) The atoms are connected with C at the center and will be drawn as: H C N.
Having H as the central atom is impossible because H has one valence electron and will always only have a single bond to one other atom. If N were the central atom then the formula would probably be written as HNC.

H : C̈ : N̈

3) Connecting the atoms with 10 electrons in single bonds gives
the structure to the right. H has two electrons to fill its valence subshells, but C and N only have six each. A triple bond between these atoms fulfills the octet rule for C and N and is the correct Lewis structure.

H : C:::N:

To select the most probable Lewis dot structure for a compound or molecule that follows the octet rule, review the structures and compare to the method for constructing Lewis dot structures from the previous page.

Example: Which of the electron-dot structures given below for nitrous oxide (laughing gas), N₂O, is/are acceptable?

I. :N::N:O:

II. :N: N::O:

III. :N:::N::O:

Solution: Both nitrogen and oxygen follow the octet rule so the Lewis structure should show each atom in the molecule with 8 electrons, either unshared or shared. Upon examination, only choice I provides each atom in the molecule with 8 electrons. Choice II has only 6 electrons around each of the nitrogen atoms and choice III has 10 electrons around the center nitrogen atom.

Molecular geometry is predicted using the valence-shell electron-pair repulsion or **VSEPR** model. VSEPR uses the fact that **electron pairs around the central atom of a molecule repel each other**. Imagine you are one of two pairs of electrons in bonds around a central atom (like a bonds in BeH₂ in the table below). You want to be as far away from the other electron pair as possible, so you will be on one side of the atom and the other pair will be on the other side. There is a straight line (or a 180° angle) between you to the other electron pair on the other side of the nucleus. In general, electron pairs lie at the **largest possible angles** from each other.

Electron pairs	Geometrical arrangement		Predicted bond angles	Example
2	:—X—:	Linear	180°	H—Be—H
3	(trigonal planar diagram)	Trigonal planar	120°	F—B(—F)—F
4	(tetrahedral diagram)	Tetrahedral	109.5°	CH₄ structure
5	(trigonal bipyramidal diagram)	Trigonal bipyramidal	120° and 90°	PF₅ structure
6	(octahedral diagram)	Octahedral	90°	SF₆ structure

X represents a generic central atom. Lone pair electrons on F are not shown in the example molecules.

Unshared Electron Pairs

The **shape of a molecule is given by the location of its atoms**. These are connected to central atoms by shared electrons, but unshared electrons also have an important impact on molecular shape. Unshared electrons may determine the angles between atoms. Molecular shapes in the following table take into account total and unshared electron pairs.

Electron pairs	Molecular shape				
	All shared pairs	1 unshared pair	2 unshared pairs	3 unshared pairs	4 unshared pairs
2	Linear				
3	Trigonal planar	Bent			
4	Tetrahedral	Trigonal pyramidal	Bent		
5	Trigonal bipyramidal	Seesaw or sawhorse	T-shaped	Linear	
6	Octahedral	Square pyramidal	Square planar	T-shaped	Linear

X represents a generic central atom bonded to atoms labeled A.

Altered Bond Angles

Unpaired electrons also have a less dramatic impact on molecular shape. Imagine you are an unshared electron pair around a molecule's central atom. The shared electron pairs are each attracted partially to the central atom and partially to the other atom in the bond, but you are different. You are attracted to the central atom, but there's nothing on your other side, so you are free to expand in that direction. That expansion means that you take up more room than the other electron pairs, and they are all squeezed a little closer together because of you. Multiple bonds have a similar effect because more space is required for more electrons. In general, **unshared electron pairs and multiple bonds decrease the angles between the remaining bonds**. A few examples are shown in the following tables.

Compound	CH_4	NH_3	H_2O
Unshared electrons	0	1	2
Shape	Tetrahedral	Trigonal pyramidal	Bent

Compound	BF_3	C_2H_4 (ethylene)
Multiple bonds	0	1
Shape	Trigonal planar	Trigonal planar

Summary

In order to use VSEPR to predict molecular geometry, perform the following steps:

1) Write out Lewis dot structures.
2) Use the Lewis structure to determine the number of unshared electron pairs and bonds around each central atom counting multiple bonds as one (for now).
3) The second table of this skill gives the arrangement of total and unshared electron pairs to account for electron repulsions around each central atom.
4) For multiple bonds or unshared electron pairs, decrease the angles slightly between the remaining bonds around the central atom.
5) Combine the results from the previous two steps to determine the shape of the entire molecule.

http://www.shef.ac.uk/chemistry/vsepr/ is a good site for explaining and visualizing molecular geometries using VSEPR.

http://cowtownproductions.com/cowtown/genchem/09_16T.htm provides some practice for determining molecular shape

Hybridized atomic orbitals
Electron shell structures are built up by considering different energy levels for different subshells to explain spectroscopic data about individual atoms. However, when Lewis dot structures are drawn or molecular geometries are determined (later in this skill), all valence electrons are treated identically to explain the bonding between atoms regardless of whether the electrons once belonged to the *s* or the *p* subshell of their atom. Reconciling these views of the individual and the bonded atom requires a theory known as hybridization.

Hybridization describes the pre-bonding **promotion of one or more electrons** from a lower energy subshell to a higher energy subshell followed by a **combination** of the orbitals into degenerate **hybrid orbitals**.

Example: A boron atom has the valence electron configuration $2s^2 2p^1$ as shown to the right. Before bonding to three other atoms, the capability to form three equivalent bonds is achieved by hybridization. First a 2s electron is promoted to an empty *p* orbital. Next the occupied orbitals combine into three hybrid $2sp^2$ orbitals. Now three electrons in degenerate orbitals are available to create covalent bonds with three atoms.

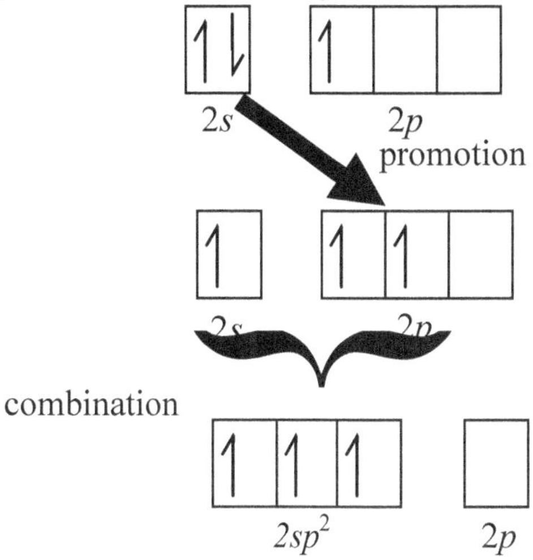

Hybridization occurs for atoms with a valence electron configuration of ns^2, ns^2np^1, or ns^2p^2. For period 2, this corresponds with Be, B, C, and N in the NH_3^+ ion.

An atom joined to its neighbor by **multiple covalent bonds** is prepared for bonding by hybridization with incomplete combination. Electrons that remain in *p* orbitals can contribute additional bonds between the same two atoms.

Example: An isolated carbon atom has the valence electron configuration $2s^2 2p^2$. Hybridization to four $2sp^3$ orbitals occurs before bonding to four atoms. Three hybrid sp^2 orbitals form if there is a double bond so the C atom is bonded to three atoms and one electron remains in the p orbital. Two hybrid sp orbitals occur if there is a triple bond or two double bonds. In this case, C is bonded to two atoms with two electrons remaining in p orbitals.

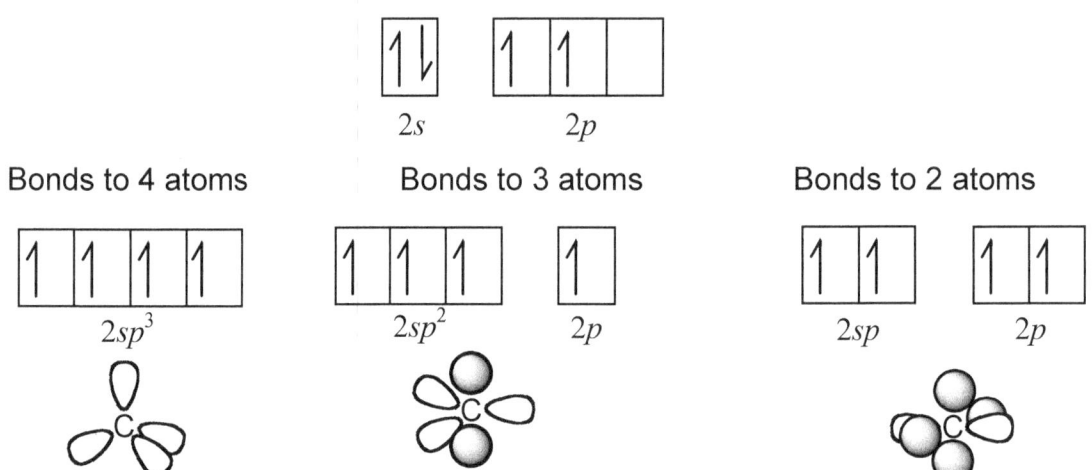

Note: p orbitals are shaded in the diagrams. These models are meant to illustrate the **locations** and **angles** of hybrid and p orbitals relative to the central atom. A mathematical solution would also show that each type of hybrid orbital (sp^3, sp^2, and sp) has a slightly different shape from the other two.

See http://www.mhhe.com/physsci/chemistry/essentialchemistry/flash/hybrv18.swf for a flash animation tutorial of hybridization.

Skill 21.3 Demonstrate knowledge of the general features and properties of compounds of metals, nonmetals, and transition elements and the materials derived from them.

The physical properties of substances usually result from the strength of the **intermolecular forces** at work between its molecules. The reactivity of substances is based on stability considerations that are often a result of high or low electronegativity. The reactivity of large molecules is often localized to the most polar regions or charged regions of the molecule.

The bonds in this skill are listed from strongest to weakest.

Covalent bonds in a network solid
A covalent network solid may be considered **one large molecule connected by covalent bonds**. These materials are **very hard, strong, and have a high melting point**. Diamond, C_n or C_∞, and quartz, $(SiO_2)_n$ or $(SiO_2)_\infty$, are two examples.

Ionic bonds
All common salts (compounds with **ionic bonds**) are solids at room temperature. **Salts are brittle, have a high melting point**, and do not conduct electricity because their ions are not free to move in the crystal lattice. Salts do conduct electricity in molten form. The formation of a salt is a highly exothermic reaction between a metal and a nonmetal.

Salts in solid form are generally stable compounds, but in molten form or in solution, their component ions often react to form a more stable salt.

Some salts decompose to form more stable salts, as in the decomposition of molten potassium chlorate to form potassium chloride and oxygen:
$$2KClO_3(l) \rightarrow 2KCl(s) + 3O_2(g).$$

Metallic bonds

The physical properties of metals are attributed to the **electron sea model of metallic bonds** shown on the right. Metals **conduct heat and electricity** because electrons are not associated with the bonding between two specific atoms and they are able to flow through the material. They are called **delocalized** electrons. Metals are **lustrous** because electrons at their surface reflect light at many different wavelengths. Metals are

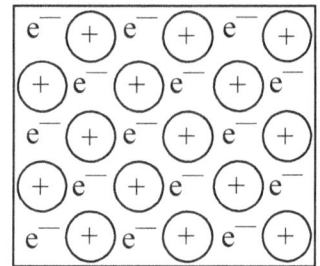

malleable and **ductile** because the electrons are able to rearrange their positions to maintain the integrity of the solid when the metallic lattice is deformed, acting like glue between the cations. The strengths of different metallic bonds can be related to the relative amounts and positions of electrons in this glue.

Alkali metals contain only one valence electron ("less glue"), and that electron is a considerable distance away from the nucleus ("weaker glue") because it is shielded from nuclear attraction by the noble gas configuration of the remaining electrons. The result is a weak metallic bond and a low melting point. Heavier alkali metals contain a valence electron even further from the nucleus, resulting in a very weak metallic bond and a lowering of the melting point. With two valence electrons and smaller atoms, alkaline earth metals have stronger metallic bonds than the alkali metals. This explains some of the periodic trends.

The metal with the weakest metallic bonds is mercury. Hg is a liquid at room temperature because Hg atoms hold on tightly to a stable valence configuration of full s, f, and d subshells. Fewer electrons are shared to create bonds than in other metals.

The reactivity of metals increases with lower electronegativity in reactions with nonmetals to form ionic bonds.

The following bonds are usually weaker, and are called intermolecular forces.

Ion-dipole interactions

Salts tend to dissolve in several polar solvents. An ion with a full charge in a polar solvent will **orient nearby solvent molecules** so that their opposite partial charges are pointing towards the ion. In aqueous solution, certain salts react to form solid **precipitates** if a combination of their ions is insoluble.

Hydrogen bonds
Hydrogen bonds are particularly **strong dipole-dipole interactions** that form between the H-atom of one molecule and an **F, O, or N** atom of an adjacent molecule. The partial positive charge on the hydrogen atom is attracted to the partial negative charge on the electron pair of the other atom. The hydrogen bond between two water molecules is shown as the dashed line below:

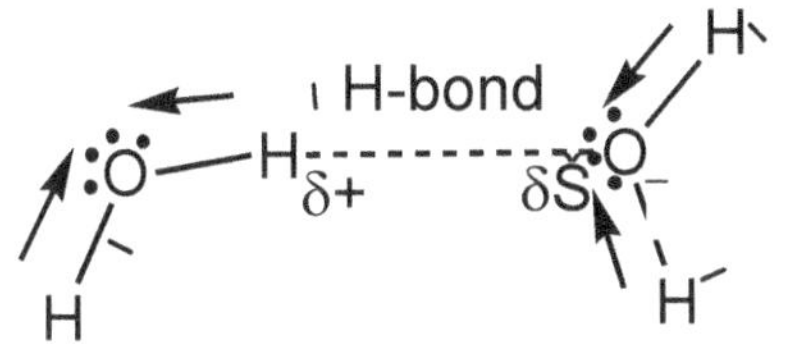

Dipole-dipole interactions The intermolecular forces between polar molecules are known as dipole-dipole interactions. The partial positive charge of one molecule is attracted to the partial negative charge of its neighbor.

Ion-induced dipole
When a nonpolar molecule (or a noble gas atom) encounters an ion, its **electron density is temporarily distorted** resulting in an **induced dipole** that will be attracted to the ion. Intermolecular attractions due to induced dipoles in a nonpolar molecule are known as **London forces or Van der Waals interactions**. These are very weak intermolecular forces.

For example, carbon tetrachloride, CCl_4, has polar bonds but is a nonpolar molecule due to the symmetry of those bonds. An aluminum cation will draw the unbonded electrons of the chlorine atom towards it, distorting the molecule (this distortion has been exaggerated in the figure) and creating an attractive force as shown by the dashed line below.

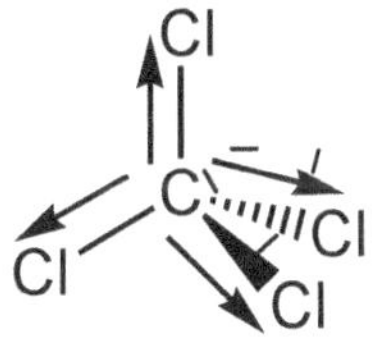

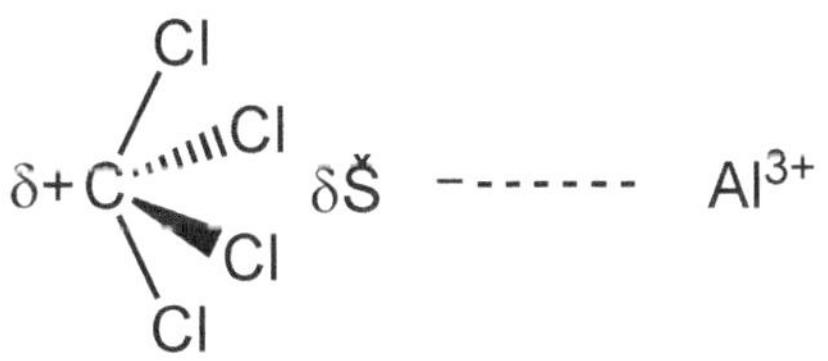

Dipole-induced dipole
The partial charge of **a permanent dipole may also induce a dipole in a nonpolar molecule** resulting in an attraction similar to—but weaker than—that created by an ion.

London dispersion force: induced dipole-induced dipole
The above two examples required a permanent charge to induce a dipole in a nonpolar molecule. A nonpolar molecule may also induce a temporary dipole on its identical neighbor in a pure substance. These forces occur because at any given moment, electrons are located within a certain region of the molecule, and **the instantaneous location of electrons will induce a temporary dipole** on neighboring molecules. For example, an isolated helium atom consists of a nucleus with a 2+ charge and two electrons in a spherical electron density cloud. An attraction of He atoms due to London dispersion forces (shown below by the dashed line) occurs because when the electrons happen to be distributed unevenly on one atom, a dipole is induced on its neighbor. This dipole is due to intermolecular repulsion of electrons and the attraction of electrons to neighboring nuclei.

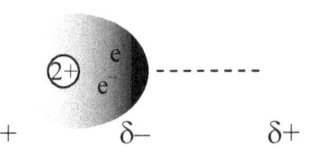 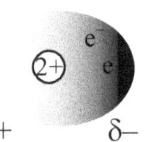

The strength of London dispersion forces **increases for larger molecules** because a larger electron cloud is more easily polarized. The strength of London dispersion forces also **increases for molecules with a larger surface area** because there is greater opportunity for electrons to influence neighboring molecules if there is more potential contact between the molecules. Paraffin in candles is an example of a solid held together by weak London forces between large molecules. These materials are soft.

Skill 21.4   Describe the hybridization of the central atom based on the geometry of coordination compounds.

Whenever two or more atoms are brought in proximity to one another to form molecules or compounds, their atomic orbitals must come sufficiently close to one another in order to interact. When covalent bonds are formed, the electrons in the orbitals of one atom interact with the atomic orbitals of the other atom, involving the sharing of electrons between the included atoms. In order to understand the basics of molecular geometry, one needs to consider the effect of the other orbitals interacting with the atom. One way to do this is to understand the "hybridization" of atomic orbitals.

The basic tenet of covalent bonding between atoms in molecules is called the valence bond theory. The basic idea is that covalent bonds are formed by the overlap of atomic orbitals of different atoms. The two electrons are involved in a paired spin that is shared by an atomic orbital of each of the two involved atoms. The more overlap you see, the stronger will be the covalent bond between the atoms. The atomic orbitals can be the same as the original orbitals of each atom; however, the bond can't happen if the original orbitals are maintained. The orbitals must come together into a new configuration, called reconfigured orbitals or "hybridized orbitals".

Using this approach to look at atomic orbitals, one receives little information about the energy levels going on within the molecules. It is more easily used when atoms surround the center of a single atom. The molecular geometry of the molecule is difficult to determine. This is solved by looking at Linus Pauling's demonstration that the wave components of the electrons in the orbitals of an atom could be added with their mathematical wave forms (By adding the amplitudes of their waves in 3D) so that mutual constructive and destructive interference will reveal a 3D configuration. This gives sets of equal Schroedinger wave functions that are essentially hybridized orbitals. Hybridization, for many molecule, gives us a completely new set of atomic orbitals that can overlap more effectively with the orbitals of the other atoms in a molecule. This results in a lower energy molecule with stronger bonds.

The following principles are derived from Linus Pauling's work:

- Orbitals that are empty, half full, or full don't hybridize with each other. Those that do must be half-full when talking about normal covalent bonding.
- Not all of the orbitals in any involved atom need to be used in the hybridization and can behave as they did before bonding took place.
- Full or empty orbitals are used in covalent bonding.
- The hybridized orbitals overlap with the normal or hybridized orbitals in the other atom or atoms.
- The number of orbitals made during hybridization is the same as the number of original orbitals used in hybridization.

By using the hybridization of atomic orbitals like these, you need only to look at the empty or half full orbitals on the primary atom. There are only limited types of hybridization possible in molecules as noted below:

sp Hybridization: This involves a hybrid of one s orbital and one p orbital on a central atom that gives rise to two sp orbitals. This leaves a molecule that is linear with orbitals that are 180 degrees apart.

sp^2 Hybridization: This hybridizes one s and 2 p orbitals around one primary atom. This gives three sp^2 orbitals. Each of the orbitals lies in a plane at 120 degrees apart.

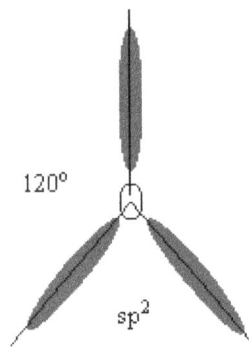

sp³ Hybridization: This involves one s orbital and all three p orbitals on a central atom and goes on to make four hybridized orbitals. The orbitals are identical, in a tetrahedral shape and are 109.5 degrees apart. It is found in molecules like NH3 and CH4, and is the way most carbon atoms combine with other atoms.

dsp² Hybridization: This involves atoms of the transitional metals and other elements which have d orbitals available. The hybridization involves one s, two p, and a d orbital on the central atom. This gives rise to square planes aligned 90 degrees apart.

dsp³ Hybridization: This works for atoms that have d orbitals that can be used to form various hybrid orbitals. This hybridization gives 5 orbitals, three of which are equatorial and two of which are axial. One of the p orbitals is perpendicular to the xy plane. It basically looks like two pyramids with their bases touching each other. It's called a trigonal bipyramid.

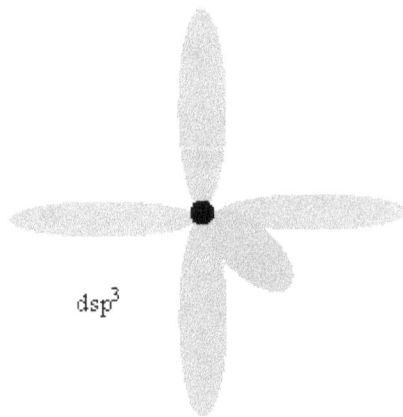

d²sp³ Hybridization: If an atom has more than two d orbitals available, it can use what it has in a form of hybridization. This hybridization gives six orbitals on a primary atom. All adjacent orbitals are 90 degrees apart and all non adjacent orbitals are 180 degrees apart. It has the geometric appearance of an octahedron.

The Jahn-Teller Effect

At times, the energy level is so high that the geometric shape of the molecule must distort itself to bring electrons out of the high energized state to a lower state. This is called the Jahn-Teller Effect and makes an unstable degenerate orbital more stable. Certain tetrahedral and octahedral geometric shapes are susceptible to this change in geometric shape.

COMPETENCY 22.0 UNDERSTAND AND APPLY KNOWLEDGE OF THE KINETIC MOLECULAR THEORY AND THE NATURE AND PROPERTIES OF MOLECULES IN THE GASEOUS, LIQUID, AND SOLID STATES.

Skill 22.1   Demonstrate knowledge of the basic principles of the kinetic molecular theory.

These relationships were found by experimental observation and may be explained by the kinetic molecular theory.

Gas **pressure** results from molecular collisions with container walls. The **number of molecules** striking an **area** on the walls and the **average kinetic energy** per molecule are the only factors that contribute to pressure. A higher **temperature** increases speed and kinetic energy. There are more collisions at higher temperatures, but the average distance between molecules does not change, and thus density does not change in a sealed container.

Kinetic molecular theory explains how the pressure and temperature influences behavior of gases by making a few assumptions, namely

1) The energies of intermolecular attractive and repulsive forces may be neglected.
2) The average kinetic energy of the molecules is proportional to absolute temperature.
3) Energy can be transferred between molecules during collisions and the collisions are elastic, so the average kinetic energy of the molecules doesn't change due to collisions.
4) The volume of all molecules in a gas is negligible compared to the total volume of the container.

Strictly speaking, molecules also contain some kinetic energy by rotating or experiencing other motions. The motion of a molecule from one place to another is called **translation**. Translational kinetic energy is the form that is transferred by collisions, and kinetic molecular theory ignores other forms of kinetic energy because they are not proportional to temperature.

The following table summarizes the application of kinetic molecular theory to an increase in container volume, number of molecules, and temperature:

Effect of an **increase** in one variable with other two constant	Impact on gas: − = decrease, 0 = no change, + = increase						
	Average distance between molecules	Density in a sealed container	Average speed of molecules	Average translational kinetic energy of molecules	Collisions with container walls per second	Collisions per unit area of wall per second	Pressure (P)
Volume of container (V)	+	−	0	0	−	−	−
Number of molecules	−	+	0	0	+	+	+
Temperature (T)	0	0	+	+	+	+	+

Additional details on the kinetic molecular theory may be found at http://hyperphysics.phy-astr.gsu.edu/hbase/kinetic/ktcon.html. An animation of gas particles colliding is located at http://comp.uark.edu/~jgeabana/mol_dyn/

Skill 22.2   Explain the properties of solids, liquids, and gases and changes of state in terms of the kinetic molecular theory and intermolecular forces.

Molecules have **kinetic energy (**they move around), and they also have **intermolecular attractive forces** (they stick to each other). The relationship between these two determines whether a collection of molecules will be a gas, liquid, or solid.

A **gas** has an indefinite shape and an indefinite volume. The kinetic model for a gas is a collection of widely separated molecules, each moving in a random and free fashion, with negligible attractive or repulsive forces between them. Gases will expand to occupy a larger container so there is more space between the molecules. Gases can also be compressed to fit into a small container so the molecules are less separated.

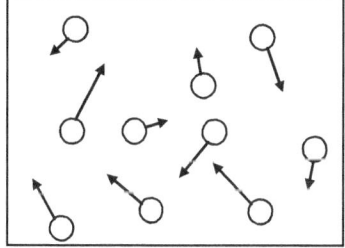

Diffusion occurs when one material spreads into or through another. Gases diffuse rapidly and move from one place to another.

A **liquid** assumes the shape of the portion of any container that it occupies and has a specific volume. The kinetic model for a liquid is a collection of molecules attracted to each other with sufficient strength to keep them close to each other but with insufficient strength to prevent them from moving around randomly. Liquids have a higher density and 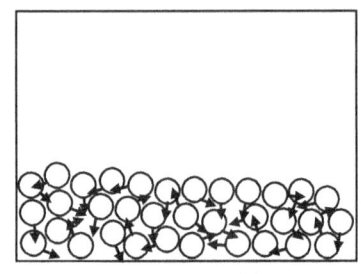 are much less compressible than gases because the molecules in a liquid are closer together. Diffusion occurs more slowly in liquids than in gases because the molecules in a liquid stick to each other and are not completely free to move.

A **solid** has a definite volume and definite shape. The kinetic model for a solid is a collection of molecules attracted to each other with sufficient strength to essentially lock them in place. Each molecule may vibrate, but it has an average position relative to its neighbors. If these positions form an ordered pattern, the solid is called **crystalline**. Otherwise, it is called **amorphous**. Solids have a high density and are almost incompressible because the molecules are close together. Diffusion occurs extremely slowly because the molecules almost never alter their position.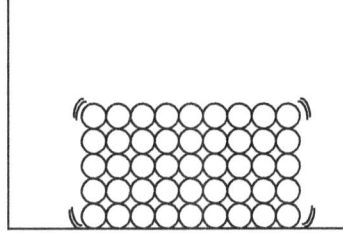

In a solid, the energy of intermolecular attractive forces is much stronger than the kinetic energy of the molecules, so kinetic energy and kinetic molecular theory are not very important. As temperature increases in a solid, the vibrations of individual molecules grow more intense and the molecules spread slightly further apart, decreasing the density of the solid.

In a liquid, the energy of intermolecular attractive forces is about as strong as the kinetic energy of the molecules and both play a role in the properties of liquids. Liquids will be discussed in detail in Skill 1.8.

In a gas, the energy of intermolecular forces is much weaker than the kinetic energy of the molecules. Kinetic molecular theory is usually applied for gases and is best applied by imagining ourselves shrinking down to become a molecule and picturing what happens when we bump into other molecules and into container walls.

Skill 22.3 Apply various laws related to the properties and behavior of ideal gases (e.g., combined gas laws, ideal gas law, Dalton's law of partial pressures, Graham's law of diffusion) to solve problems.

The kinetic molecular theory describes how an ideal gas behaves when conditions such as temperature, pressure, volume or quantity of gas are varied within a system. An **ideal gas** is an imaginary gas that obeys all of the assumptions of the kinetic molecular theory. While an ideal gas does not exist, most gases will behave like an ideal gas except when at very low temperatures or very high pressures. Under these conditions, gases vary from ideal behavior.

Charles's law states that the volume of a fixed amount of gas at constant pressure is directly proportional to absolute temperature, or:

$$V \propto T.$$

Or $V = kT$ where k is a constant. This gives a mathematical equation $\frac{V_1}{T_1} = \frac{V_2}{T_2}$.

Changes in temperature or volume can be found using Charles's law.

Problem: What is the new volume of gas if 0.50 L of gas at 25°C is allowed to heat up to 35°C at constant pressure?

Solution: This is a volume-temperature change so use Charles's law. Temperature must be on the Kelvin scale. K = °C + 273.

T_1 = 298K
V_1 = 0.50 L
T_2 = 308K
V_2 = ?

Use the equation: $\frac{V_1}{T_1} = \frac{V_2}{T_2}$ and rearrange for $V_2 = \frac{T_2 V_1}{T_1}$. Substitute and solve

V_2 = 0.52L.

Boyle's law states that the volume of a fixed amount of gas at constant temperature is inversely proportional to the gas pressure, or:

$$V \propto \frac{1}{P}.$$

Or $V = k/P$ where k is a constant. This gives a mathematical equation $P_1 V_1 = P_2 V_2$. Pressure-volume changes can be determined using Boyle's law.

SCIENCE: CHEMISTRY

Problem: A 1.5 L gas has a pressure of 0.56 atm. What will be the volume of the gas if the pressure doubles to 1.12 atm at constant temperature?

Solution: This is a pressure-volume relationship at constant temperature so usse Boyle's law.

P_1= 0.56 atm
V_1= 1.5 L
P_2= 1.12 atm
V_2=?

Use the equation $P_1V_1=P_2V_2$, rearrange to solve for $V_2 = \dfrac{P_1 V_1}{P_2}$.

Substitute and solve. V_2=0.75 L

Gay-Lussac's law states that the pressure of a fixed amount of gas in a fixed volume is proportional to absolute temperature, or:
$$P \propto T.$$
Or $P=kT$ where k is a constant. This gives a mathematical equation $\dfrac{P_1}{T_1} = \dfrac{P_2}{T_2}$.

Changes in temperature or pressure can be found using Gay-Lussac's law.

Problem: A 2.25 L container of gas at 25°C and 1.0 atm pressure is cooled to 15°C. How does the pressure change if the volume of gas remains constant?
Solution: This is a pressure-volume change so use Gay-Lussac's law.

P_1= 1.0 atm
T_1= 25 °C
T_2= 15 °C
Change the temperatures to the Kelvin scale. K=°C+ 273.
Use the equation $\dfrac{P_1}{T_1} = \dfrac{P_2}{T_2}$ to solve. Rearrange the equation to solve for P_2, substitute and solve.

$P_2 = \dfrac{P_1 T_2}{T_1}$ = 0.97 atm

The **combined gas law** uses the above laws to determine a proportionality expression that is used for a constant quantity of gas:

$$V \propto \frac{T}{P}.$$

The combined gas law is often expressed as an equality between identical amounts of an ideal gas at two different states ($n_1=n_2$):

$$\frac{P_1V_1}{T_1} = \frac{P_2V_2}{T_2}.$$

Problem: 1.5 L of a gas at STP is is allowed to expand to 2.0 L at a pressure of 2.5 atm. What is the temperature of the expanded gas?

Since pressure, temperature and volume are changing use the combined gas gas law to determine the new temperature of the gas.

P_1= 1.0 atm
T_1= 273K
V_1= 1.5 L
V_2= 2.0L
P_2= 2.5 atm
T_2=?

Using this equation, $\frac{P_1V_1}{T_1} = \frac{P_2V_2}{T_2}$, rearrange to solve for T_2.

$$T_2 = \frac{P_2V_2T_1}{P_1V_1}$$

Substitute and solve T_2=910 K or 637 °C

Avogadro's hypothesis states that equal volumes of different gases at the same temperature and pressure contain equal numbers of molecules.
Avogadro's law states that the volume of a gas at constant temperature and pressure is directly proportional to the quantity of gas, or:
   $V \propto n$ where n is the number of moles of gas.

Avogadro's law and the combined gas law yield $V \propto \frac{nT}{P}$. The proportionality constant R--the **ideal gas constant**--is used to express this proportionality as the **ideal gas law**:

$PV = nRT$.

The ideal gas law ($PV = nRT$) is useful because it contains all the information of Charles's, Avogadro's, Boyle's, and the combined gas laws in a single expression.

If pressure is given in atmospheres and volume is given in liters, a value for R of **0.08206 L-atm/(mol-K)** is used. If pressure is given in Pascal (newtons/m^2) and volume in cubic meters, then the SI value for R of **8.314 J/(mol-K)** may be used because a joule is defined as a Newton-meter. A value for R of **8.314 m^3-Pa/(mol-K)** is identical to the ideal gas constant using joules.

Many problems are given at "**standard temperature and pressure**" or "**STP**." Standard conditions are *exactly* **1 atm** (101.325 kPa) and **0 °C (273.15 K)**. At STP, one mole of an ideal gas has a volume of:

$$V = \frac{nRT}{P}$$

$$= \frac{(1 \text{ mole})\left(0.08206 \frac{\text{L-atm}}{\text{mol-K}}\right)(273 \text{ K})}{1 \text{ atm}} = 22.4 \text{ L}.$$

The value of 22.4 L is known as the **standard molar volume of any gas at STP**.

Solving gas law problems using these formulas is a straightforward process of algebraic manipulation. **Errors commonly arise from using improper units**, particularly for the ideal gas constant R. An absolute temperature scale must be used (never °C) and is usually reported using the Kelvin scale, but volume and pressure units often vary from problem to problem. Temperature in Kelvin is found from:

$$T \text{ (in K)} = T(\text{in °C}) + 273.15$$

Tutorials for gas laws may be found online at:
http://www.chemistrycoach.com/tutorials-6.htm. A flash animation tutorial for problems involving a piston may be found at
http://www.mhhe.com/physsci/chemistry/essentialchemistry/flash/gasesv6.swf.

Problem: What volume will 0.50 mole an ideal gas occupy at 20.0 °C and 1.5 atm?

Solution: Since the problem deals with moles of gas with temperature and pressure, use the ideal gas law to find volume.

$Pv = nRT$ $\qquad$ $V = nRT/P$

$P = 1.5$ atm $\qquad$ $= 0.50$ mol $(0.0821$ atm L/mol K$)$ 293 K/

$V = ?$ $\qquad\qquad$ 1.5 atm

$n = 0.50$ mol $\qquad$ $= 8.0$ L

$T = 20.0$ °C $= 293$ K

$R = 0.0821$ atm L/mol K

Problem: At STP, 0.250 L of an unknown gas has a mass of 0.491 g. Is the gas SO_2, NO_2, C_3H_8, or Ar? Support your answer.

Solution: Identify what is given and what is asked to determine.

Given: $T_1 = 273$K
$\qquad P_1 = 1.0$ atm
$\qquad V_1 = 0.250$ L
$\qquad$ Mass $= 0.419$ g

Determine: Identity of the gas. In order to do this, must find molar mass of the gas. $n = \dfrac{mass}{MM}$. Find the number of moles of gas present using PV=nRT and then determine the MM to compare to choices given in the problem.

Solve for $n = \dfrac{PV}{RT} = 0.011$ moles

$MM = \dfrac{mass}{n} = 38.1$ g/mol

Compare to MM of SO_2 (96 g/mol), NO_2 (46 g/mol), C_3H_8 (44 g/mol) and Ar (39.9 g/mol). It is closest to Ar, so the gas is probably Argon.

For mixtures of gases in a container, each gas exerts a **partial pressure** that it would have if it were present in the container alone. **Dalton's law** of partial pressures states that the total pressure of a gas mixture is simply the sum of these partial pressures:

$$P_{total} = P_1 + P_2 + P_3 + \ldots$$

Dalton's law may be applied to the ideal gas law:

$$P_{total}V = (P_1 + P_2 + P_3 + \ldots)V = (n_1 + n_2 + n_3 + \ldots)RT.$$

Effusion occurs when gas escapes through a tiny opening into a vacuum or into a region at lower pressure. **Graham's law** states that the rate of effusion (r) for a gas is inversely proportional to the square root of its molecular weight (M):

$$r \propto \frac{1}{\sqrt{M}}.$$

Graham's law may be used to compare the ratios of effusion rates and molecular weights for two different gases:

$$\frac{r_1}{r_2} = \sqrt{\frac{M_2}{M_1}}.$$

Graham's law uses the same two expressions above to describe the dependence of the **diffusion** rate on molecular weight.

Skill 22.4   Demonstrate an understanding of the differences between real and ideal gases.

The kinetic molecular theory describes how an ideal gas behaves when conditions such as temperature, pressure, volume or quantity of gas are varied within a system. An **ideal gas** is an imaginary gas that obeys all of the assumptions of the kinetic molecular theory. While an ideal gas does not exist, most gases will behave like an ideal gas except when at very low temperatures or very high pressures. Under these conditions, gases vary from ideal behavior.

Skill 22.5 Interpret phase diagrams and use them to explain the transitions between solids, liquids, and gases.

A **phase diagram** is a graphical way to summarize the conditions under which the different states of a substance are stable. The diagram is divided into three areas representing each state of the substance.
The curves separating each area represent the boundaries of phase changes Below is a typical phase diagram. It consists of three curves that divide the diagram into regions labeled "solid, liquid, and gas".

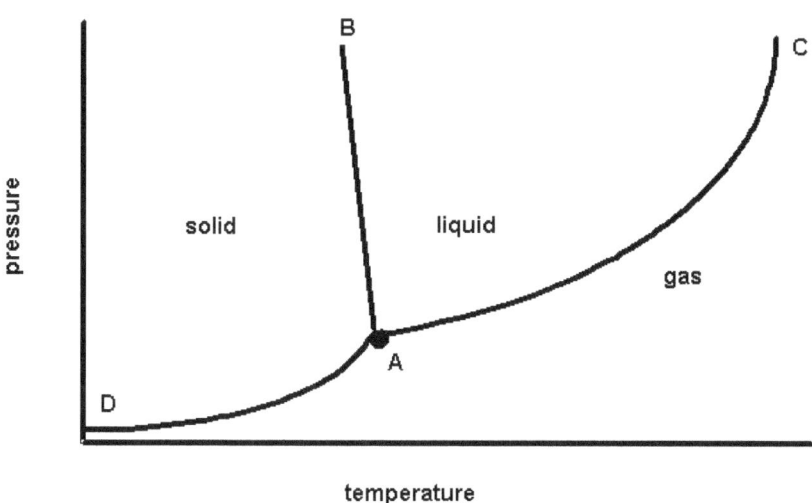

Curve **AB**, dividing the solid region from the liquid region, represents the conditions under which the solid and liquid are in equilibrium. Usually, the melting point is only slightly affected by pressure. For this reason, the melting point curve, AB, is nearly vertical

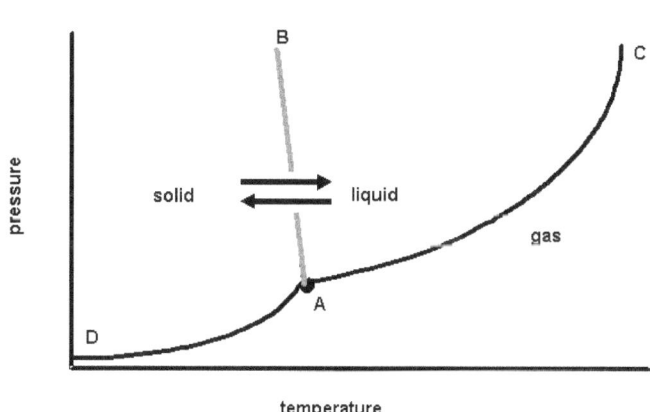

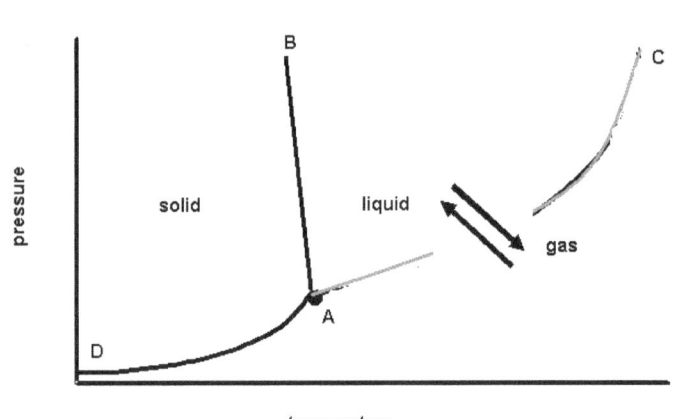

Curve **AC**, which divides the liquid region from the gaseous region, represents the boiling points of the liquid for various pressures.

Curve **AD**, which divides the solid region from the gaseous region, represents the vapor pressures of the solid at various temperatures

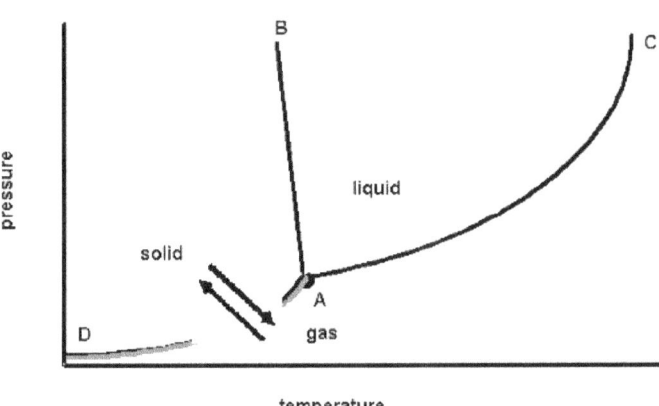

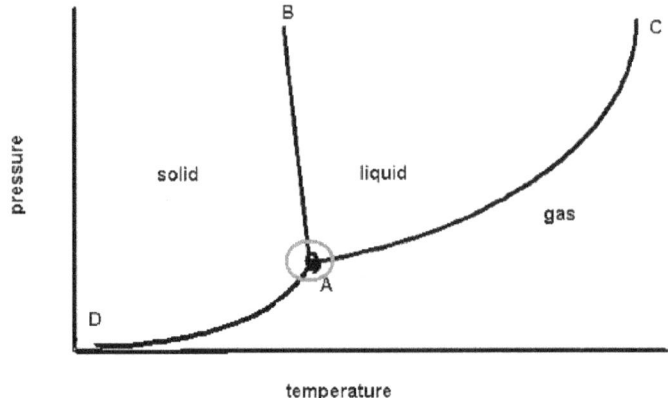

The curves intersect at **A**, the **triple point**, which is the temperature and pressure where three phases of a substance exist in equilibrium.

The temperature above which the liquid state of a substance no longer exists regardless of pressure is called the **critical temperature**.

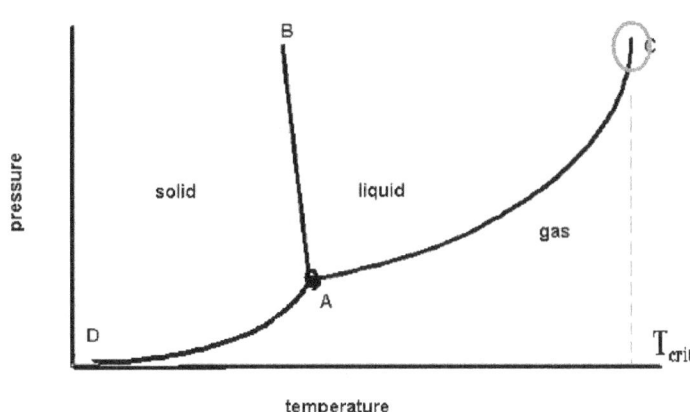

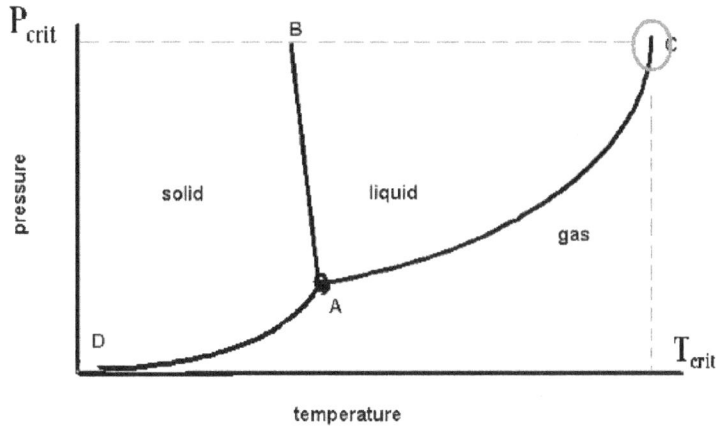

The vapor pressure at the critical temperature is called the **critical pressure**. Note that curve AC ends at the **critical point, C**.

The phase diagram for water (shown below) is unusual. The solid/liquid phase boundary slopes to the left with increasing pressure because the melting point of water decreases with increasing pressure. Note that the normal melting point of water is lower than its triple point. The diagram is not drawn to a uniform scale. Many anomalous properties of water are discussed here: http://www.lsbu.ac.uk/water/anmlies.html.

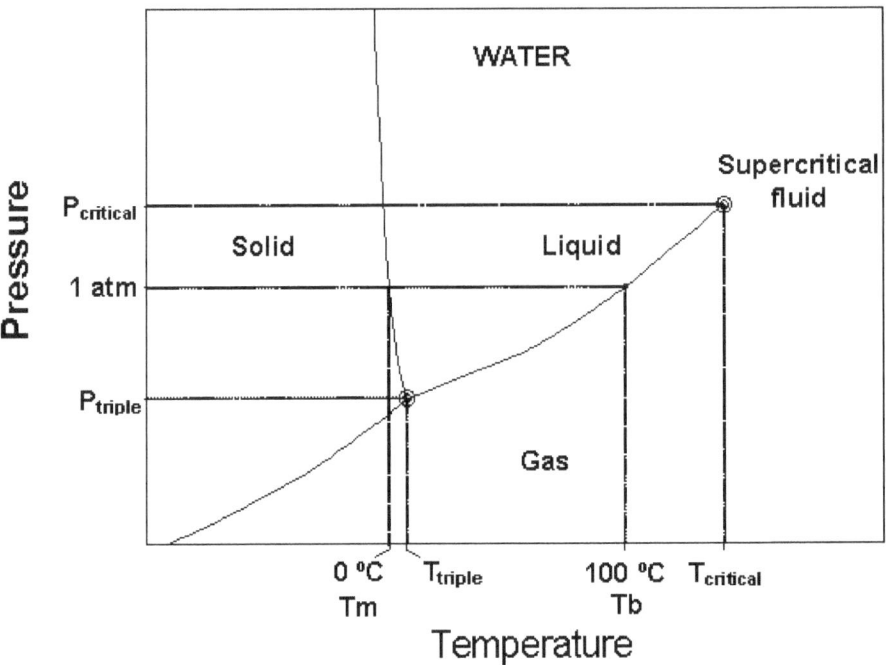

Normal melting point (T_m) and **normal boiling point** (T_b) are defined at 1 atm. Note that freezing point and melting point refer to an identical temperature approached from different directions, but they represent the same concept.

This is the phase diagram for carbon dioxide, CO_2. It shows the same features, only at different temperatures and pressures.

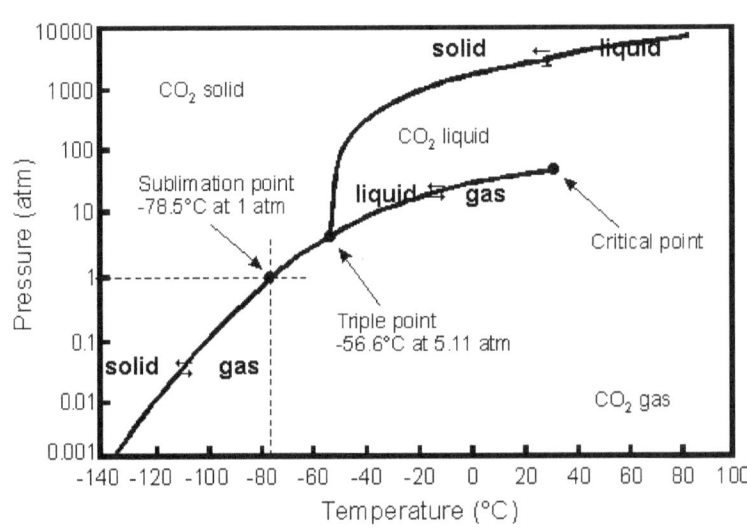

Skill 22.6 Classify unknown solids as molecular, metallic, ionic, and covalent network solids according to their physical and chemical properties.

The physical properties of substances usually result from the strength of the **intermolecular forces** at work between its molecules. The reactivity of substances is based on stability considerations that are often a result of high or low electronegativity. The reactivity of large molecules is often localized to the most polar regions or charged regions of the molecule.

The bonds in this skill are listed from strongest to weakest.

Covalent bonds in a network solid
A covalent network solid may be considered **one large molecule connected by covalent bonds**. These materials are **very hard, strong, and have a high melting point**. Diamond, C_n or C_∞, and quartz, $(SiO_2)_n$ or $(SiO_2)_\infty$, are two examples.

Ionic bonds
All common salts (compounds with **ionic bonds**) are solids at room temperature. **Salts are brittle, have a high melting point**, and do not conduct electricity because their ions are not free to move in the crystal lattice. Salts do conduct electricity in molten form. The formation of a salt is a highly exothermic reaction between a metal and a nonmetal.

Salts in solid form are generally stable compounds, but in molten form or in solution, their component ions often react to form a more stable salt.

Some salts decompose to form more stable salts, as in the decomposition of molten potassium chlorate to form potassium chloride and oxygen:
$$2KClO_3(l) \rightarrow 2KCl(s) + 3O_2(g).$$

Metallic bonds
The physical properties of metals are attributed to the **electron sea model of metallic bonds** shown on the right. Metals **conduct heat and electricity** because electrons are not associated with the bonding between two specific atoms and they are able to flow through the material. They are called **delocalized** electrons. Metals are **lustrous** because electrons at their surface reflect light at many different wavelengths. Metals are 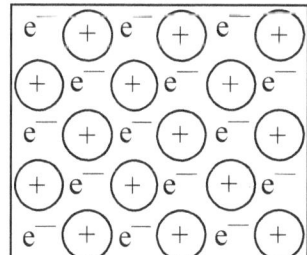 **malleable** and **ductile** because the electrons are able to rearrange their positions to maintain the integrity of the solid when the metallic lattice is deformed, acting like glue between the cations. The strengths of different metallic bonds can be related to the relative amounts and positions of electrons in this glue.

Alkali metals contain only one valence electron ("less glue"), and that electron is a considerable distance away from the nucleus ("weaker glue") because it is shielded from nuclear attraction by the noble gas configuration of the remaining electrons. The result is a weak metallic bond and a low melting point. Heavier alkali metals contain a valence electron even further from the nucleus, resulting in a very weak metallic bond and a lowering of the melting point. With two valence electrons and smaller atoms, alkaline earth metals have stronger metallic bonds than the alkali metals.

The metal with the weakest metallic bonds is mercury. Hg is a liquid at room temperature because Hg atoms hold on tightly to a stable valence configuration of full s, f, and d subshells. Fewer electrons are shared to create bonds than in other metals.

The reactivity of metals increases with lower electronegativity in reactions with nonmetals to form ionic bonds.

The following bonds are usually weaker, and are called intermolecular forces.

Ion-dipole interactions
Salts tend to dissolve in several polar solvents. An ion with a full charge in a polar solvent will **orient nearby solvent molecules** so that their opposite partial charges are pointing towards the ion. In aqueous solution, certain salts react to form solid **precipitates** if a combination of their ions is insoluble.

Hydrogen bonds
Hydrogen bonds are particularly **strong dipole-dipole interactions** that form between the H-atom of one molecule and an **F, O, or N** atom of an adjacent molecule. The partial positive charge on the hydrogen atom is attracted to the partial negative charge on the electron pair of the other atom. The hydrogen bond between two water molecules is shown as the dashed line below:

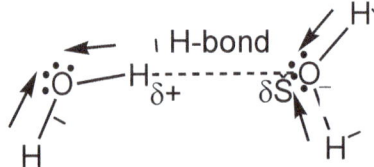

Dipole-dipole interactions
The intermolecular forces between polar molecules are known as dipole-dipole interactions. The partial positive charge of one molecule is attracted to the partial negative charge of its neighbor.

When a nonpolar molecule (or a noble gas atom) encounters an ion, its **electron density is temporarily distorted** resulting in an **induced dipole** that will be attracted to the ion. Intermolecular attractions due to induced dipoles in a nonpolar molecule are known as **London forces or Van der Waals interactions**. These are very weak intermolecular forces.

For example, carbon tetrachloride, CCl_4, has polar bonds but is a nonpolar molecule due to the symmetry of those bonds. An aluminum cation will draw the unbonded electrons of the chlorine atom towards it, distorting the molecule (this distortion has been exaggerated in the figure) and creating an attractive force as shown by the dashed line below.

Dipole-induced dipole
The partial charge of **a permanent dipole may also induce a dipole in a nonpolar molecule** resulting in an attraction similar to—but weaker than—that created by an ion.

London dispersion force: induced dipole-induced dipole
The above two examples required a permanent charge to induce a dipole in a nonpolar molecule. A nonpolar molecule may also induce a temporary dipole on its identical neighbor in a pure substance. These forces occur because at any given moment, electrons are located within a certain region of the molecule, and **the instantaneous location of electrons will induce a temporary dipole** on neighboring molecules. For example, an isolated heliumatom consists of a nucleus with a 2+ charge and two electrons in a spherical electron density cloud. An attraction of He atoms due to London dispersion forces (shown below by the dashed line) occurs because when the electrons happen to be distributed unevenly on one atom, a dipole is induced on its neighbor. This dipole is due to intermolecular repulsion of electrons and the attraction of electrons to neighboring nuclei.

The strength of London dispersion forces **increases for larger molecules** because a larger electron cloud is more easily polarized. The strength of London dispersion forces also **increases for molecules with a larger surface area** because there is greater opportunity for electrons to influence neighboring molecules if there is more potential contact between the molecules. Paraffin in candles is an example of a solid held together by weak London forces between large molecules. These materials are soft.

COMPETENCY 23.0 UNDERSTAND AND APPLY KNOWLEDGE OF THE INTERACTIONS OF PARTICLES IN SOLUTION AND THE PROPERTIES OF SOLUTIONS.

Skill 23.1 Describe the solution process, including the effects of temperature and pressure on the solubility of solids, liquids, and gases.

The solution process is dependent upon intermolecular forces
Solutions form when the intermolecular attractive forces between solute and solvent molecules are about as strong as those that exist in the solute alone or in the solvent alone. For example, NaCl dissolves in water because:

1) The water molecules interact with the Na^+ and Cl^- ions with sufficient strength to overcome the attraction between them in the crystalline form.

2) Na^+ and Cl^- ions interact with the water molecules with sufficient strength to overcome the attraction water molecules have for each other in the liquid.

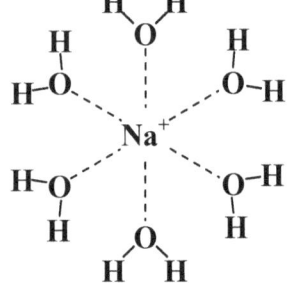

The intermolecular attraction between solute and solvent molecules is known as **solvation**. When the solvent is water, it is known as **hydration**. The figure to the left shows a hydrated Na^+ ion.

Polar and nonpolar solutes and solvents
A nonpolar liquid like heptane (C_7H_{16}) has intermolecular bonds with relatively weak London dispersion forces. Heptane is immiscible in water because the attraction that water molecules have for each other via hydrogen bonding is too strong.

Unlike Na^+ and Cl^- ions, heptane molecules cannot break these bonds. Because bonds of similar strength must be broken and formed for solvation to occur, nonpolar substances tend to be soluble in nonpolar solvents, while ionic and polar substances are soluble in polar solvents like water. Polar molecules are often called **hydrophilic** and non-polar molecules are called **hydrophobic** This observation is often stated as "**like dissolves like**." Network solids (e.g., diamond) are soluble in neither polar nor nonpolar solvents because the covalent bonds within the solid are too strong for these solvents to break.

Temperature and solubility: When attempting to dissolve a solid like NaCl into a liquid, the higher temperature facilitates the solubility of the ionic solution and more of the NaCl will enter into the solution. If the solution is highly saturated at a high temperature, the NaCl will fall out of solution and recrystallize as a solid as the solution cools.

Solids in Liquids

The formula for solutions is: C V = n, where C is the molar concentration in, V is the volume in liters of the liquid, and n is the number of moles of solute. Further, n = m/Fw, where m is the mass and Fw is the formula weight of the solute. Solving for the mass, m = C V Fw.

How do you make the solution of a solid in a liquid? First weigh the solid to get the mass. The concentration you want times the volume of solution times the formula weight of the solute will give you the mass of solute you need to weigh. Place the mass of solute in a volume measuring device such as a volumetric flask or a graduated cylinder. Use a small amount of water to dissolve the solute in the volumetric device. Add water to the volume desired and mix.

The act of dissolving a solid into a liquid is a process that happens on the surface of the particles of the solute. The smaller the particles (the larger the surface area) the faster the solute dissolves. 'Confectioner's sugar,' has smaller particles than regular 'table sugar.' Rock candy is just regular table sugar that has been crystallized in large lumps. When you put each crystal size of the chemically identical materials in your mouth, which one dissolves faster? The confectioner's sugar tastes sweetest because more of it has dissolved in the same short time. (You can only taste dissolved sugar.)

Expose the surface area of the solid to more solid and the solute will dissolve faster. Mixing helps dissolve the solid. You can try this with sugar. Take two glasses of water at the same temperature and add a spoonful of sugar to each. Mix one, but not the other. In which glass does the sugar dissolve more easily?

Most solid materials will dissolve faster with increased temperature. Since the increased temperature increases the motion of the molecules, you can think of this effect as being similar to mixing. You have seen this effect. Sugar dissolves more quickly in warm tea than iced tea. Table salt dissolves more quickly in hot water than in cold.

Electrolytes and precipitates

All NaCl is present in solution as ions. Compounds that are completely ionized in water are called **strong electrolytes** because these solutions easily conduct electricity. Most salts are strong electrolytes. Other compounds (including many acids and bases) may dissolve in water without completely ionizing. These are referred to as **weak electrolytes** and their state of ionization is at equilibrium with the larger molecule. Those compounds that dissolve with no ionization (e.g., glucose, $C_6H_{12}O_6$) are called **nonelectrolytes**.

Particles in solution are free to move about and collide with each other, vastly increasing the likelihood that a reaction will occur compared with particles in a solid phase. Aqueous solutions may react to produce an insoluble substance that will fall out of solution as a solid or gas **precipitate** in a **precipitation reaction**. Aqueous solution may also react to form **additional water** or a different chemical in aqueous solution.

Vapor pressure lowering, boiling point elevation, freezing point lowering

After a nonvolatile solute is added to a liquid solvent, only a fraction of the molecules at a liquid-gas interface are now volatile and capable of escaping into the gas phase. The vapor consists of essentially pure solvent that is able to condense freely. This imbalance drives equilibrium away from the vapor phase and into the liquid phase and **lowers the vapor pressure** by an amount proportional to the solute particles present.

It follows that from a lowered vapor pressure, a higher temperature is required for a vapor pressure equal to the external pressure over the liquid. Thus **the boiling point is raised** by an amount proportional to the solute particles present.

Solute particles in a liquid solvent are not normally soluble in the solid phase of that solvent. When solvent crystals freeze, they typically align themselves with each other at first and keep the solute out. This means that only a fraction of the molecules in the liquid at the liquid-solid interface are capable of freezing while the solid phase consists of essentially pure solvent that is able to melt freely. This imbalance drives equilibrium away from the solid phase and into the liquid phase and **lowers the freezing point** by an amount proportional to the solute particles present. Boiling point elevation and freezing point depression are both caused by a lower fraction of solvent molecules in the liquid phase than in the other phase.

Gases in Liquids

Gases in liquids are easily measured when you know the pressure, volume, and temperature of the gas. Seltzer water and ammonia water are two good examples of solutions of a gas in a liquid. Seltzer, which is carbonated water, consists of pressing the carbon dioxide gas into the water. The bubbles in beer or sparkling wines are also due to carbon dioxide, but the CO2 is a natural product of the fermentation process. Ammonia water, also called ammonium hydroxide solution, is made from ammonia (NH3) being pressed into water. It is used as a weak base and as a cleaning material.

Because the process is better done under pressure, it is often difficult to directly observe the actual dissolving process. The notable exception is the addition of dry ice, solid carbon dioxide, to water. As with a solid dissolving in a liquid, a gas dissolves in a liquid more easily with agitation or mixing. If you remove the carbonated beverage from its container, pressure is still necessary to keep the gas into solution. As the beverage sits for a few hours, the taste becomes what we describe as 'flat.' Almost all of the carbon dioxide has escaped from the liquid. The only CO2 remaining in the water will produce a partial pressure equal to the partial pressure of the gas in the atmosphere. Water carries dissolved oxygen from the partial pressure of the oxygen in the atmosphere.

As the combination of liquid and gas is NOT the lowest energy condition, an increase in temperature causes the separation. Lower temperature favors dissolving the gas into the liquid. Higher temperatures will cause the separation of the gas from the liquid.

Skill 23.2   Analyze the qualitative colligative properties of solutions, including the practical applications of these properties to technological problems.

A **colligative** property is a physical property of a solution that **depends on the number of solute particles present in solution** and usually not on the identity of the solutes involved. Colligative properties may be predicted by imagining ourselves shrinking down to the size of molecules in a solution and visualizing the impact of an increasing number of generic solute particles around us.

Vapor pressure lowering, boiling point elevation, freezing point lowering
After a nonvolatile solute is added to a liquid solvent, only a fraction of the molecules at a liquid-gas interface are now volatile and capable of escaping into the gas phase. The vapor consists of essentially pure solvent that is able to condense freely. This imbalance drives equilibrium away from the vapor phase and into the liquid phase and **lowers the vapor pressure** by an amount proportional to the solute particles present.

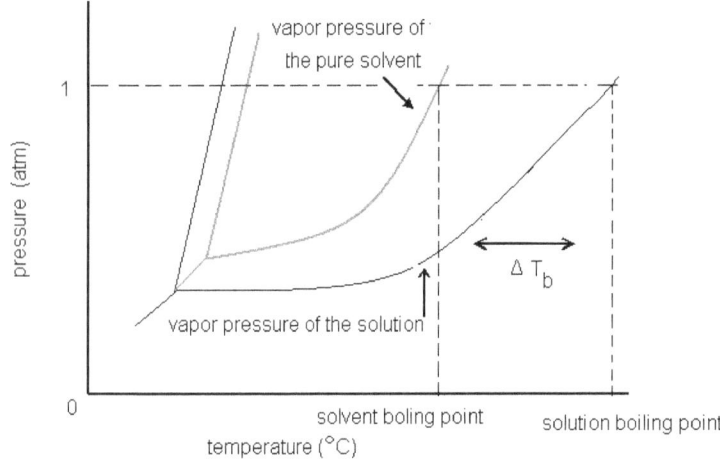

It follows from a lowered vapor pressure that a higher temperature is required for a vapor pressure equal to the external pressure over the liquid (see Skill 1.8). Thus **the boiling point is raised** by an amount proportional to the solute particles present.

Solute particles in a liquid solvent are not normally soluble in the solid phase of that solvent. When solvent crystals freeze, they typically align themselves with each other at first and keep the solute out. This means that only a fraction of the molecules in the liquid at the liquid-solid interface are capable of freezing while the solid phase consists of essentially pure solvent that is able to melt freely. This imbalance drives equilibrium away from the solid phase and into the liquid phase and **lowers the freezing point** by an amount proportional to the solute particles present.

Boiling point elevation and freezing point depression are both caused by a lower fraction of solvent molecules in the liquid phase than in the other phase. For pure water at 1 atm there is equilibrium at the normal boiling and freezing points:

At 100 °C, $H_2O(l) \underset{\text{condensation}}{\overset{\text{vaporization}}{\rightleftharpoons}} H_2O(g)$.

At 0 °C, $H_2O(l) \underset{\text{melting}}{\overset{\text{freezing}}{\rightleftharpoons}} H_2O(s)$.

For water with a high solute concentration, equilibrium is not present:

At 100 °C, less interfacial $H_2O(l) \underset{\text{condensation}}{\overset{\text{vaporization}}{\rightleftharpoons}} H_2O(g)$.

At 0 °C, less interfacial $H_2O(l) \underset{\text{melting}}{\overset{\text{freezing}}{\rightleftharpoons}} H_2O(s)$.

Osmotic pressure

A **semipermeable membrane** is a material that permits some particles to pass through it but not others. The diagram shows a membrane that permits solvent but not solute to pass through it. When a semipermeable membrane separates a dilute solution from a concentrated solution, the solvent flows from the dilute to the concentrated solution (i.e., from higher solvent to lower solvent concentration) in a process called **osmosis** until equilibrium is achieved.

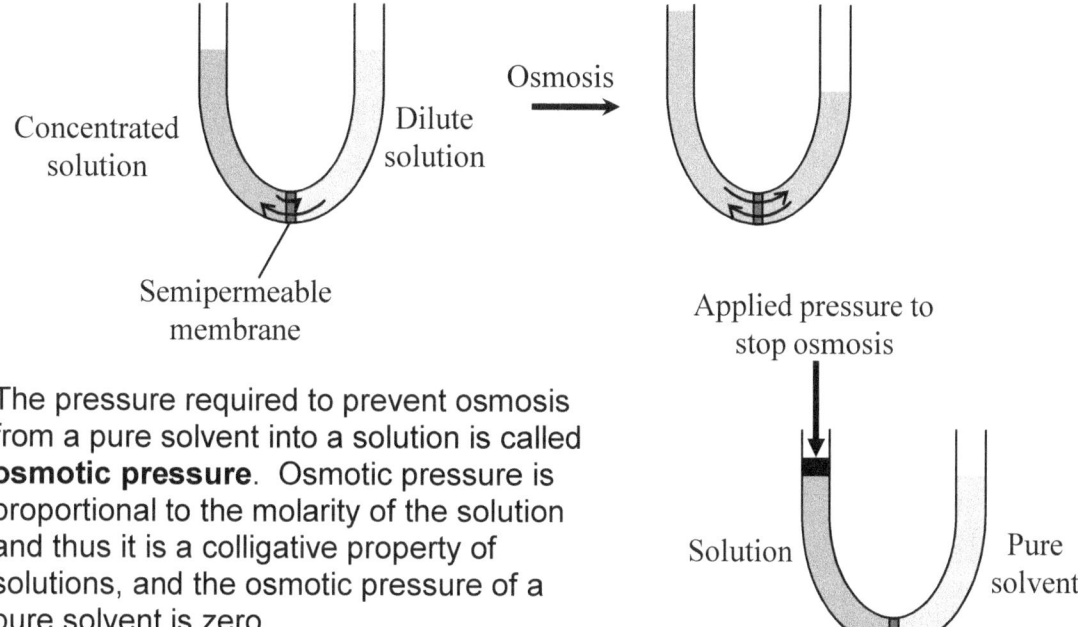

The pressure required to prevent osmosis from a pure solvent into a solution is called **osmotic pressure**. Osmotic pressure is proportional to the molarity of the solution and thus it is a colligative property of solutions, and the osmotic pressure of a pure solvent is zero.

A simulation of solutes and solvent molecules interacting and an animation of osmotic flow between two flexible compartments are located here: http://physioweb.med.uvm.edu/bodyfluids/osmosis.htm. A simulation of the osmotic pressure experiment above for NaCl, sucrose, and albumin (a protein) is found here:
http://arbl.cvmbs.colostate.edu/hbooks/cmb/cells/pmemb/hydrosim.html. Typical changes in a pressure/temperature phase diagram after adding a non-volatile solute are found here:
http://chemmovies.unl.edu/ChemAnime/SOLND/SOLND.html.

Quantitative colligative property problems typically involve a change related to a solute concentration by a direct proportionality.

Raoult's law states that the vapor pressure of a solution with nonvolatile solutes is the mole fraction of solvent multiplied by the pure solvent vapor pressure:

$$P^{vapor}_{solution} = P^{vapor}_{pure\ solvent} (\text{mole fraction})_{solvent}$$

Raoult's law is often used to describe the vapor pressure change from pure solvent using the solute concentration:

$$\Delta P^{vapor} = P^{vapor}_{solution} - P^{vapor}_{pure\ solvent} = P^{vapor}_{pure\ solvent}(\text{mole fraction})_{solvent} - P^{vapor}_{pure\ solvent}$$

$$= -P^{vapor}_{pure\ solvent}\left(1 - (\text{mole fraction})_{solvent}\right)$$

$$= -P^{vapor}_{pure\ solvent}(\text{mole fraction})_{solute}$$

Different concentration units are used for other colligative properties to express a **change from pure solvent**. The following table summarizes these expressions for nonelectrolytes:

Colligative property	Equation for property X $\Delta X = X_{solution} - X_{pure\ solvent}$	Proportionality constant
Vapor pressure lowering	$\Delta P^{vapor} = -P^{vapor}_{pure\ solvent}(\text{mole fraction})_{solute}$	Pure solvent vapor pressure
Boiling point elevation	$\Delta T_b = K_b (\text{molality})$	Solvent-dependant constant K_b
Freezing point lowering	$\Delta T_f = -K_f (\text{molality})$	Solvent-dependant constant K_f
Osmotic pressure	$P_{osmotic} = RT(\text{molarity})$	(Gas constant) □ (Temperature)

For solutions that contain electrolytes, the change from the pure solvent to solution is different from what is predicted by the above equations. Due to the dissolving process, these substances will dissociate to put many more ions in solution than their molal concentration would predict. And their numbers will change the colligative properties even more.

The van't Hoff factor is an important factor in the extent of the change in boiling point or freezing point of a solution after solute has been added. For substances that do not dissociate in water, such as sugar ($C_{12}H_{22}O_{11}$), has an *i* value of 1. Substances that dissociate in water to give two ion particles, such as salt (NaCl), have an *i* value of 2. This pattern continues for any number of particles into which a solute can dissociate.

The van 't Hoff factor is symbolized by the lower-case letter i. It is a unitless constant directly associated with the degree of dissociation of the solute in the solvent.

Substances which do not ionize in solution, like sugar, have i = 1.
Substances which ionize into two ions, like NaCl, have i = 2.
Substances which ionize into three ions, like $MgCl_2$, have i = 3.

What this implies is exactly what van 't Hoff observed as he was compiling and examining boiling point and freezing point data. At the time, he did not understand what i meant. His use of i was strictly to try and make the data fit together. He took a 1.0 molal aqueous solution of sugar, NaCl, and $MgCl_2$ and checked the boiling point temperature of each solution. He found that the NaCl had a boiling point elevation twice as high as that of the sugar and the $MgCl_2$ elevated the boiling point temperature three times higher than the sugar. Upon testing other substances, he found groups but he had no idea why until Svante Arrhenius' theory of electrolytic dissociation was published. The explanation seemed clear then. Many colligative property problems compare one solution to another and may be solved without the use of the above expressions. All that is required for these comparison problems is knowledge of what the colligative properties are, how they are altered, and which solution contains the greater concentration of dissolved particles.

Problem: One mole of each of the following compounds is added to water in separate flasks to make 1.0 L of solution.

> Potassium phosphate
> Silver chloride
> Sodium chloride
> Sugar (sucrose)

A. Which solution will provide the greatest change in the freezing point temperature?
B. Which solution will provide the least change in the boiling point temperature? Be sure to explain you choices.

Solution:
Analyze the choices for solubility and dissociation:

Potassium phosphate	soluble in water → 4 ions
Silver chloride	soluble in water → 2 ions
Sodium chloride	soluble in water → 2 ions
Sugar (sucrose)	soluble in water → 1 molecule (nonelectrolyte)

A. Of the choices, potassium phosphate forms the most ions so given the concentration of all of the choices is the same, K_3PO_4 will effect the boiling point temperature and the freezing point temperature the most. For every 1 mole of K_3PO_4 that dissolve, 4 moles of ions will be present in solution.

B. Sugar, a nonelectrolye, will have the least effect on the freezing point and boiling point temperatures due to the fact that it is a molecular substance and does not dissociate into ions. For every 1 mole of sugar in solution, only 1 mole of molecules will be present.

Changes to boiling point temperature and freezing point temperature may be determined by looking at the molal concentration of the solute in the pure substance.

Remember that a colligative property is one that depends only on the number of particles present, not their nature.

For boiling point temperature changes, $\Delta T_b = mk_b i$ where m is the molal concentration of the solute, K_b is a constant specific for each solvent and i is the number of particles or ions in solution. For water, $K_b = 0.52\ °C/m$

$\Delta T_f = mk_f i$ is the equation to use to determine changes in freezing point temperature. K_f is a constant specific for each solvent. For water, $K_f = -1.86\ °C/m$

Example: How much of an increase in boiling point temperature will 31.5 grams of potassium chloride make when added to 225 g of water?

Solution: KCl is an electrolyte so $i = 2$
Mass of water = 225 g = 0.225 kg
Mass KCl = 31.5 g, moles KCl = 0.423 mole
m = 0.423/0.225 kg = 1.88 m
$K_b = 0.52\ °C/m$
$\Delta T_b = mk_b i$
 = 1.88 m (0.56 °C/m) 2 = 1.96 °C

Example: How many grams of benzoic acid, $C_7H_6O_2$, a nonelectrolyte must be added to 178 g of water to increase the boiling point temperature 4°C?

Solution:
MM benzoic acid = 122 g/mol
Benzoic acid is a nonelectrolyte so i = 1,
Mass of water = 178 g = 0.178 kg
ΔT = 4 °C
K_b = 0.52 °C/m

$\Delta T_b = mk_b i$

m = $\Delta T_b / K_b i$ = 4/0.52 °C/m (1) = 7.69 m

7.69 m = moles benzoic acid/0.178 kg water = 1.37 mole benzoic acid

1.37 moles benzoic acid = grams benzoic acid / 122 g/mol = 167 g benzoic acid are needed.

Example: The custard used to make ice cream does not "freeze" until the temperature reaches –15 to –18 °C. With ice, it will only go down to 0 °C. In order to reach the lower temperature needed to freeze the custard, sodium chloride, NaCl, is added to the ice. How much salt is needed to freeze the ice cream?

Solution:

Each sodium chloride particle dissociates into a Na^+ ion and a Cl^- ion, making two solvated ions present for every one NaCl particle present. So, NaCl has an i value of 2.

The temperature change needed is -15°C and the K_f value for water is –1.86 °C/m.

Using the freezing point depression expression we can determine the *molality* of the salt-ice solution that will reach –15°C.

$\Delta T = K_f \, m \, i$ and rearranging it to solve for $m = \dfrac{\Delta T}{m \, i} = \dfrac{-15°C}{-1.86°C/m \, (2)} = 4.0 \, m$

Remember that $m = \dfrac{\text{\# moles solute}}{\text{kg solvent}}$ so the moles of NaCl can be determined if we know the kilograms of ice used. In this case, 1 bag of ice is about 2.3 kg. So the number of moles of NaCl needed would be:

\# moles solute = m (kg solute) = 4.0 *mol/kg* (2.3 kg) = 9.3 mol of NaCl.

Now, the mass of NaCl needed can be found by using the relationship between moles and molar mass: # mol = mass/ Molar Mass

In this case, mass = # mol (Molar Mass) = 9.3 mol (58.5 g/mol) or about 540 g of NaCl is needed for every bag of ice used.

The most common errors in solving all types of colligative property problems arise from considering some value other than **the number of particles in solution**. Remember that one mole of glucose(*aq*) forms one mole of hydrated particles, but one mole of NaCl(*aq*) forms two moles of hydrated particles, and one mole of $Al_2(SO_4)_3 (aq)$ forms five moles of them. We would expect a 0.5 M solution of glucose to have roughly the same colligative properties as a 0.25 M solution of sodium hydroxide and a 0.1 M solution of aluminum sulfate. Also remember that undissolved solids do not contribute anything to colligative properties.

Skill 23.3   Demonstrate knowledge of how to prepare solutions of specific concentrations, including molality, molarity, normality, mole fraction, and percent by weight.

The **molarity** (abbreviated M) of a solute in solution is defined as the number of moles of solute in a liter of solution.

$$\text{Molarity} = \frac{\text{moles solute}}{\text{volume of solution in liters}}$$

Molarity is the most frequently used concentration unit in chemical reactions because it reflects the number of solute moles available. By using Avogadro's number, the number of molecules in a flask--a difficult image to conceptualize in the lab--is expressed in terms of the volume of liquid in the flask—a straightforward image to visualize and actually manipulate.

Molarity is useful for dilutions because the moles of solute remain unchanged if more solvent is added to the solution:

$$(\text{Initial molarity})(\text{Initial volume}) = (\text{molarity after dilution})(\text{final volume})$$

or

$$M_{initial} V_{initial} = M_{final} V_{final}$$

Molality, m, compares the moles of solute present in the solution to the mass of the solvent in kilograms.

M = moles of solute / Kg of solvent

Problem: What is the molality of a solution composed of 2.55 g of acetone, $(CH_3)_2CO$ dissolved in 200g of water?

Solution: MM = 58.0 g/mol   mol acetone = 2.55 g × 1 mol/ 58 g = 0.0440 mol

m= mol solute/ kg solvent

0.0440 mol/ .200 kg water = 0.220 m

Mass percentage is frequently used to represent every component of a solution (possibly including the solvent) as a portion of the whole in terms of mass.

$$\text{Mass percentage of a component} = \frac{\text{mass of component in solution}}{\text{total mass of solution}} \times 100\%.$$

Parts per million (or ppm) in solution usually refers to a dilute component of a solution as a portion of the whole in terms of mass. A solute present in one part per million would amount to one gram in one million grams of solution. This is also one mg of solute in one kg of solution.

$$\text{Parts per million of a component} = \frac{\text{mass of solute}}{\text{total mass of solution}} \times 10^6$$

$$= \frac{\text{number of mg of solute}}{\text{number of kg of solution}}$$

Strictly speaking, the expression above is a **"ppm by mass."** Parts per million is also sometimes used for ratios of moles or volumes.

The **normality** (abbreviated N) of a solution is defined as the number of **equivalents** of a solute per liter of solution.

$$\text{Normality} = \frac{\text{equivalents solute}}{\text{volume of solution in liters}}$$

An equivalent is defined according to the type of reaction being examined, but the number of equivalents of solute is always a whole number multiple of the number of moles of solute, and so the normality of a solute is always a whole-number multiple of its molarity. An equivalent is defined so that one equivalent of one reagent will react with one equivalent of another reagent. For acid-base reactions (see competency 7), an equivalent of an acid is the quantity that supplies 1 mol of H^+ and an equivalent of a base is the quantity reacting with 1 mol of H^+.

For example, one mole of H_2SO_4 in an acid-base reaction supplies two moles of H+. The mass of one equivalent of H_2SO_4 is half of the mass of one mole of H_2SO_4, and its normality is twice its molarity. In a redox reaction (see competency 4.6), an equivalent is the quantity of substance that gains or loses 1 mol of electrons.

A **mole fraction** is used to represent a component in a solution as a portion of the entire number of moles present. If you were able to pick out a molecule at random from a solution, the mole fraction of a component represents the probability that the molecule you picked would be that particular component. Mole fractions for all components must sum to one, and mole fractions are just numbers with no units.

$$\text{Mole fraction of a component} = \frac{\text{moles of component}}{\text{total moles of all components}}$$

Skill 23.4 Select appropriate solvents for the dissolution or purification of solid compounds.

Polar and nonpolar solutes and solvents
A nonpolar liquid like heptane (C_7H_{16}) has intermolecular bonds with relatively weak London dispersion forces. Heptane is immiscible in water because the attraction that water molecules have for each other via hydrogen bonding is too strong. Unlike Na^+ and Cl^- ions, heptane molecules cannot break these bonds. Because bonds of similar strength must be broken and formed for solvation to occur, nonpolar substances tend to be soluble in nonpolar solvents, and ionic and polar substances are soluble in polar solvents like water. Polar molecules are often called **hydrophilic** and non-polar molecules are called **hydrophobic**. This observation is often stated as "**like dissolves like**." Network solids (e.g., diamond) are soluble in neither polar nor nonpolar solvents because the covalent bonds within the solid are too strong for these solvents to break.

Electrolytes
All NaCl is present in solution as ions. Compounds that are completely ionized in water are called **strong electrolytes** because these solutions easily conduct electricity. Most salts are strong electrolytes. Other compounds (including many acids and bases) may dissolve in water without completely ionizing. These are referred to as **weak electrolytes** and their state of ionization is at equilibrium with the larger molecule. Those compounds that dissolve with no ionization (e.g., glucose, $C_6H_{12}O_6$) are called **nonelectrolytes**.

SUBAREA VI.　　ISTOICHIOMETRY AND CHEMICAL REACTIONS

COMPETENCY 24.0　UNDERSTAND AND APPLY KNOWLEDGE OF THE CONCEPTS AND PRINCIPLES OF CHEMICAL EQUATIONS AND STOICHIOMETRY.

Skill 24.1　Classify types of chemical reactions and balance equations to describe chemical reactions.

There are chemical reactions occurring all around us everyday. Millions of them, in fact. So many different chemical reactions would be very difficult to understand. However, the millions of chemical reactions that take place each and everyday fall into only a few basic categories. Using these categories can help predict products of reactions that are unfamiliar or new.

Once we have an idea of the **reaction type**, we can make a good prediction about the products of chemical equations, and also balance the reactions. **General reaction types** are listed in the following table. Some reaction types have multiple names.

Reaction type	General equation	Example
Combination / Synthesis	$A + B \rightarrow C$	$2H_2 + O_2 \rightarrow 2H_2O$
Decomposition	$A \rightarrow B + C$	$2KClO_3 \rightarrow 2KCl + 3O_2$
Single substitution / Single displacement / Single replacement	$A + BC \rightarrow AB + B$	$Mg + 2HCl \rightarrow MgCl_2 + H_2$
Double substitution / Double displacement / Double replacement / Ion exchange / Metathesis	$AC + BD \rightarrow AD + BC$	$HCl + NaOH \rightarrow NaCl + H_2O$
Isomerization	$A \rightarrow A'$	cyclopropane (C_3H_6) $\rightarrow$ propene (C_3H_6)

Example: Determine the products of a reaction between Cl_2 and a solution of NaBr.

Solution: The first step is to write "$Cl_2 + NaBr(aq) \rightarrow ?$" Now examine the possible choices from the table. Decomposition and isomerization reactions require only one reactant. It also can't be a double substitution reaction because one of the reactants is an element. A synthesis reaction to form some NaBrCl compound would require very unusual valences! The most likely reaction is the remaining one: Cl replaces Br in aqueous solution with Na:

$Cl_2 + NaBr(aq) \rightarrow NaCl(aq) + Br_2$. After balancing, the equation is:
$Cl_2 + 2NaBr(aq) \rightarrow 2NaCl(aq) + Br_2$.

Chemical equations not only show the reactants and products, but they also must follow the Law of Conservation of Mass, which says that matter can not be created nor destroyed, merely rearranged in ordinary chemical reactions. Equations, then, must be **balanced**, to follow this law.

A properly written chemical equation must contain properly written formulas and must be **balanced**. Chemical equations are written to describe a certain number of moles of reactants becoming a certain number of moles of reaction products. The number of moles of each compound is indicated by its **stoichiometric coefficient**.

Example: In the reaction
$$2H_2(g) + O_2(g) \rightarrow 2H_2O(l),$$

hydrogen has a stoichiometric coefficient of two, oxygen has a coefficient of one, and water has a coefficient of two because 2 moles of hydrogen react with 1 mole of oxygen to form two moles of water.

In a balanced equation, the stoichiometric coefficients are chosen such that the equation contains an **equal number of each type of atom on each side**. In our example, there are four H atoms and two O atoms on both sides. Therefore, the equation is properly written.

Balancing equations is a four-step process.

1) Write an **unbalanced equation**. This requires writing the chemical formulas for the species involved in the reaction.
2) Determine the **number of each type of atom on each side** of the equation to find if the equation is balanced.
3) Assume that **the molecule with the most atoms** has a stoichiometric coefficient of one, and determine the other stoichiometric coefficients required to create the **same number of atoms on each side** of the equation.
4) Multiply all the stoichiometric coefficients by a whole number if necessary to eliminate fractional coefficients.

Example: Balance the chemical equation describing the combustion of methanol in oxygen to produce only carbon dioxide and water.

Solution:
1) The structural formula of methanol is CH_3OH, so its molecular formula is CH_4O. The formula for carbon dioxide is CO_2. Therefore the unbalanced equation is:
$$CH_4O + O_2 \rightarrow CO_2 + H_2O.$$

2) On the left there are 1C, 4H, and 3O. On the right, there are 1C, 2H, and 3O. It seems close to being balanced, but there's work to do.

3) Assuming that CH_4O has a stoichiometric coefficient of one means that the left side has 1C and 4H that also must be present on the right. Therefore the stoichiometric coefficient of CO_2 will be 1 to balance C and the stoichiometric coefficient of H_2O will be 2 to balance H. Now we have:
$$CH_4O + ?\,O_2 \rightarrow CO_2 + 2H_2O.$$

and only oxygen remains unbalanced. There are 4O on the right and one of these is accounted for by methanol leaving 3O to be accounted for by O_2. This gives a stoichiometric coefficient of 3/2 and a balanced equation:
$$CH_4O + \frac{3}{2}O_2 \rightarrow CO_2 + 2H_2O.$$

4) Whole-number coefficients are achieved by multiplying by two:
$$2CH_4O + 3O_2 \rightarrow 2CO_2 + 4H_2O.$$

SCIENCE: CHEMISTRY

Reactions among ions in aqueous solution may often be represented in three ways. When solutions of hydrochloric acid and sodium hydroxide are mixed, a reaction occurs and heat is produced. The **molecular equation** for this reaction is:

$$HCl(aq) + NaOH(aq) \rightarrow H_2O(l) + NaCl(aq).$$

It is called a molecular equation because the **complete chemical formulas** of reactants and products are shown. But in reality, both HCl and NaOH are strong electrolytes and exist in solution as ions. This is represented by a **complete ionic equation** that shows all the dissolved ions:

$$H^+(aq) + Cl^-(aq) + Na^+(aq) + OH^-(aq) \rightarrow H_2O(l) + Na^+(aq) + Cl^-(aq).$$

Because $Na^+(aq)$ and $Cl^-(aq)$ appear as both reactants and products, they play no role in the reaction. Ions that appear in identical chemical forms on both sides of an ionic equation are called **spectator ions** because they aren't part of the action. When spectator ions are removed from a complete ionic equation, the result is a **net ionic equation** that shows the actual changes that occur to the chemicals when these two solutions are mixed together:

$$H^+(aq) + OH^-(aq) \rightarrow H_2O(l)$$

An additional requirement for **redox** reactions is that the equation contains an **equal charge on each side**. Redox reactions may be divided into half-reactions which either gain or lose electrons.

Many **specific reaction types** also exist. Always determine the complete ionic equation for reactions in solution. This will help you determine the reaction type. The most common specific reaction types are summarized in the following table:

Reaction type	General equation	Example
Precipitation	Molecular: $AC(aq) + BD(aq) \rightarrow AD(s \text{ or } g) + BC(aq)$	Molecular: $NiCl_2(aq) + Na_2S(aq) \rightarrow NiS(s) + 2NaCl(aq)$
	Net ionic: $A^+(aq) + D^-(aq) \rightarrow AD(s \text{ or } g)$	Net ionic: $Ni^{2+}(aq) + S^{2-}(aq) \rightarrow NiS(s)$
Acid-base neutralization	Arrhenius: $H^+ + OH^- \rightarrow H_2O$	Arrhenius: $HNO_3 + NaOH \rightarrow NaNO_3 + H_2O$ $H^+ + OH^- \rightarrow H_2O$ (net ionic)
	Brønsted-Lowry: $HA + B \rightarrow HB + A$	Brønsted-Lowry: $HNO_3 + KCN \rightarrow HCN + KNO_3$ $H^+ + CN^- \rightarrow HCN$ (net ionic)
	Lewis: $A + {:}B \rightarrow A{:}B$	Lewis: $F_2B{-}F + {:}NH_3 \rightarrow F_3B{-}NH_3$
Redox	Full reaction: $A + B \rightarrow C + D$	$Ni + CuSO_4 \rightarrow NiSO_4 + Cu$ $Ni + Cu^{2+} \rightarrow Ni^{2+} + Cu$ (net ionic)
	Half reactions: $A \rightarrow C + e^-$ and $e^- + B \rightarrow D$	$Ni \rightarrow Ni^{2+} + 2e^-$ $2e^- + Cu^{2+} \rightarrow Cu$
Combustion	organic molecule $+ O_2 \rightarrow CO_2 + H_2O +$ heat	$2C_2H_6 + 7O_2 \rightarrow 4CO_2 + 6H_2O$

Whether precipitation occurs among a group of ions—and which compound will form the precipitate—may be determined by the solubility rules.

Ion	Solubility	Exception
All compounds containing alkali metals	All are soluble	
All compounds containing ammonium, NH_4^+	All are soluble	
All compounds containing nitrates, NO_3^-	All are soluble	
All compounds containing chlorates, ClO_3^- and perchlorates, ClO_4^-	All are soluble	
All compounds containing acetates, $C_2H_3O_2^-$	All are soluble	
Compounds containing Cl^-, Br^-, and I^-	Are soluble	Except halides of Ag^+, Hg_2^{2+}, and Pb^{2+}
Compounds containing F^-	Are soluble	Except fluorides of Mg^{2+}, Ca^{2+}, Sr^{2+}, Ba^{2+}, and Pb^2
Compounds containing sulfates, SO_4^{2-}	Are soluble	Except sulfates of Mg^{2+}, Ca^{2+}, Sr^{2+}, Ba^{2+}, and Pb^2
All compounds containing carbonates, CO_3^{2-}	Are insoluble	Except those containing alkali metals or NH_4^+
All compounds containing phosphates, PO_4^{3-}	Are insoluble	Except those containing alkali metals or NH_4^+
All compounds containing oxalates, $C_2O_4^{2-}$	Are insoluble	Except those containing alkali metals or NH_4^+
All compounds containing chromates, CrO_4^{2-}	Are insoluble	Except those containing alkali metals or NH_4^+
All compounds containing oxides, O^{2-}	Are insoluble	Except those containing alkali metals or NH_4^+
All compounds containing sulfides, S^{2-}	Are insoluble	Except those containing alkali metals or NH_4^+
All compounds containing sulfites, SO_3^{2-}	Are insoluble	Except those containing alkali metals or NH_4^+
All compounds containing silicates, SiO_4^{2-}	Are insoluble	Except those containing alkali metals or NH_4^+
All compounds containing hydroxides	Are insoluble	Except those containing alkali metals or NH_4^+, or Ba^{2+}

If protons are available for combination or substitution then it's likely they are being transferred from an acid to a base. An unshared electron pair on one of the reactants may form a bond in a Lewis acid-base reaction.

The possibility that oxidation numbers may change among the reactants indicates an electron transfer and a redox reaction. Combustion reactants consist of an organic molecule and oxygen.

Example: Determine the products and write a balanced equation for the reaction between sodium iodide and lead(II) nitrate in aqueous solution.

Solution: We know that sodium iodide is NaI and lead(II) nitrate is $Pb(NO_3)_2$.
The reactants of the complete ionic equation are:
$$Na^+(aq) + Pb^{2+}(aq) + I^-(aq) + NO_3^-(aq) \rightarrow ?$$

The solubility rules indicate that lead iodide is insoluble and will form as a precipitate. The unbalanced net ionic equation is then:
$$Pb^{2+}(aq) + I^-(aq) \rightarrow PbI_2(s)$$
and the unbalanced molecular equation is:
$$NaI(aq) + Pb(NO_3)_2(aq) \rightarrow PbI_2(s) + NaNO_3(aq).$$

Balancing yields:
$$2NaI(aq) + Pb(NO_3)_2(aq) \rightarrow PbI_2(s) + 2NaNO_3(aq).$$

Skill 24.2 Use mass and mole relationships in an equation to solve stoichiometric problems (including percent yield and limiting reactants).

The mole is the chemist's counting unit. Working with the mole should be second nature but lets review grams to mole calculations since they are very important in mass-mass stoichiometry and the balanced equations provides mole ratios not mass ratios.

Mass to moles:

1. First determine the molar mass of the substance by adding the masses for each element in the substance x number of atoms present:

Example: the molar mass of $CuSO_4$ is
Solution: 1 mole of Cu = 63.5 g + 1 mol of S = 32 g + 4 mol O = 4 x 16 or 48 g = 143.5 g/mol

2. Determine the number of moles present using the molar mass conversion 1 mol = molar mass of substance for example: 1 mol $CuSO_4$ = 143.5 g

Example: 315 g of $CuSO_4$ is how many moles of $CuSO_4$?

$$315 \text{ g} \times 1 \text{ mol}/ 143.5 \text{ g} = 2.20 \text{ mol } CuSO_4$$

Mole to grams conversions are just the reverse.

Solving these problems is a three-step process

1) Grams of the given compound are converted to moles.
2) Moles of the given compound are related to moles of a second compound by relating their stoichiometric coefficients from the balanced equation.
3) Moles of the second compound are converted to grams.

These steps are often combined in one series of multiplications, which may be described as **"grams to moles to moles to grams."**

Example: What mass of oxygen is required to consume 95.0 g of ethane in this reaction: $2C_2H_6 + 7O_2 \rightarrow 4CO_2 + 6H_2O$?

Solution:
$$95.0 \text{ g } C_2H_6 \times \underbrace{\frac{1 \text{ mol } C_2H_6}{30.1 \text{ g } C_2H_6}}_{\text{step 1}} \times \underbrace{\frac{7 \text{ mol } O_2}{2 \text{ mol } C_2H_6}}_{\text{step 2}} \times \underbrace{\frac{32.0 \text{ g } O_2}{1 \text{ mol } O_2}}_{\text{step 3}} = 359 \text{ g } O_2$$

The **limiting reagent** of a reaction is the **reactant that runs out first**. This reactant **determines the amount of product formed**, and any **other reactants remain unconverted** to product and are called **excess reagents**.

Example: Consider the reaction $3H_2 + N_2 \rightarrow 2NH_3$ and suppose that 3 mol H_2 and 3 mol N_2 are available for this reaction. What is the limiting reagent?
Solution: The equation tells us that 3 mol H_2 will react with one mol N_2 to produce 2 mol NH_3. This means that 2 mol N_2 will remain and H_2 is the limiting reagent because it runs out first.

The limiting reagent may be determined by **dividing the number of moles of each reactant by its stoichiometric coefficient**. This determines the moles of reactant if each reactant were limiting. The **lowest result** will indicate the actual limiting reagent. Remember to use moles and not grams for these calculations.

Example: 50.0 g Al and 400. g Br_2 react according the the following equation:

$$2Al + 3Br_2 \rightarrow 2AlBr_3$$

until the limiting reagent is completely consumed. Find the limiting reagent, the mass of $AlBr_3$ formed, and the excess reagent remaining after the limiting reagent is consumed.

Solution: First convert both reactants to moles:

$$50.0 \text{ g Al} \times \frac{1 \text{ mol Al}}{26.982 \text{ g Al}} = 1.853 \text{ mol Al} \quad \text{and} \quad 400. \text{ g Br}_2 \times \frac{1 \text{ mol Br}_2}{159.808 \text{ g Br}_2} = 2.503 \text{ mol Br}_2.$$

The final digits in the intermediate results above are italicized because they are insignificant. Dividing by stoichiometric coefficients gives:

$$1.853 \text{ mol Al} \times \frac{\text{mol reaction}}{2 \text{ mol Al}} = 0.9265 \text{ mol reaction if Al is limiting}$$

$$2.503 \text{ mol Br}_2 \times \frac{\text{mol reaction}}{3 \text{ mol Br}_2} = 0.8343 \text{ mol reaction if Br}_2 \text{ is limiting.}$$

Br_2 is the lower value and is limiting reagent.
The reaction is expected to produce:

$$2.503 \text{ mol Br}_2 \times \frac{2 \text{ mol AlBr}_3}{3 \text{ mol Br}_2} \times \frac{266.694 \text{ g AlBr}_3}{\text{mol AlBr}_3} = 445 \text{ g AlBr}_3.$$

The reaction is expected to consume:

$$2.503 \text{ mol Br}_2 \times \frac{2 \text{ mol Al}}{3 \text{ mol Br}_2} \times \frac{26.982 \text{ g Al}}{\text{mol Al}} = 45.0 \text{ g Al.}$$

50.0 g Al – 45.0 g Al = 5.0 g Al are expected to remain.

The **percent composition** of a substance is the **percentage by mass of each element**. Chemical composition is used to verify the purity of a compound in the lab. An impurity will make the actual composition vary from the expected one.

To determine percent composition for a chemical formula, do the following:

1) Write down the **number of atoms each element contributes** to the formula.
   For example in CO2 + NaCl, note that 2 oxygen atoms, one carbon atom and one sodium, and one chloride atom went into the equation.

2) Multiply these values by the molecular weight of the corresponding element to determine the **grams of each element in one mole** of the formula. This means you look at the periodic table to determine the molecular weight of a mole of each atom. Let's look at this equation:

$$Fe_2O_3(s) + 2Al(s) \rightarrow 2Fe(l) + Al_2O_3(s)$$

That is 2 iron and 3 oxygen and 2 aluminum moles with masses of:

Iron = 2 X 56 = 118 grams in 2 moles
Oxygen = 3 X 16 = 48 grams in 3 moles
Aluminum = 2 X 27 = 54 grams in 2 moles

This adds to a mass amount on the left side of the equation,

3) Add the values from step 2 to obtain the **formula mass**.

The total input of the equation is 220 grams of mass.

4) Divide each value from step 2 by the formula weight from step 3 and multiply by 100% to obtain the **percent composition**.

The percent yield being 100 % for the entire left side of the equation leaves a percent yield of Al_2O_3 is 54 grams plus 48 grams or 102 grams or a 46% yield of Al_2O_3.

Skill 24.3   **Use gas laws and solution concentrations to solve stoichiometric problems (including percent yield and limiting reactants).**

The Mole Concept

The **mole** concept is the key to both stoichiometry and gas laws. A mole is a definite amount of substance. Mole is a unit based on the number of identities (i.e. atoms, molecules, ions, or particles). A mole of anything has the same number of identities as the number of atoms in exactly 12 grams of carbon-12, the most abundant isotope of carbon.

The progress of reactions that produce or consume a gas may be described by measuring gas volume instead of mass. The best way to solve these problems is to use the ideal gas equation to interconvert volume and number of moles:

$$n = \frac{PV}{RT} \quad \text{and} \quad V = \frac{RT}{nP}.$$

If a volume is given, the steps are "**volume to moles to moles to grams**." If a mass is given, the steps will be "**grams to moles to moles to volume**."

Example: What volume of oxygen in liters is generated at 40 °C and 1 atm by the decomposition of 280 g of potassium chlorate in this reaction:
$$2KClO_3 \rightarrow 2KCl + 3O_2(g)?$$

Solution: We are given a mass and asked for a volume, so the steps in the solution will be "grams to moles to moles to volume."
"Grams to moles to moles...":

$$280 \text{ g KClO}_3 \times \frac{1 \text{ mol KClO}_3}{122.548 \text{ g KClO}_3} \times \frac{3 \text{ mol O}_2}{2 \text{ mol KClO}_3} = 3.427 \text{ mol O}_2.$$

"...to volume":

$$V = \frac{RT}{nP} = \frac{\left(0.08206 \frac{\text{L-atm}}{\text{mol-K}}\right)(273.15 + 40)\text{K}}{(3.427 \text{ mol O}_2)(1 \text{ atm})} = 7.50 \text{ L O}_2$$

The quantitative relationship of reactants and products is called **stoichiometry**. Stoichiometric problems require you to calculate the amounts of reactants required for certain amounts of products, or amounts of products produced from certain amounts of reactants. If, in a chemical reaction, one or more reactants or products are gases, gas laws must be considered for the calculation. Usually, the applications of the ideal gas law give results within 5% precision.

The Ideal Gas law

The volume (V) occupied by n moles of any gas has a pressure (P) at temperature (T) in Kelvin. The relationship for these variables,

$PV = nRT$,

where R is known as the gas constant (**.08205 L atm / (mol·K)**, is called the **ideal gas law** or **equation of state**.

Properties of the gaseous state predicted by the ideal gas law are within 5% for gases under ordinary conditions. In other words, given a set of conditions, we can predict or calculate the properties of a gas to be within 5% by applying the ideal gas law. Here we will review several important concepts that are helpful for solving Stoichiometry Problems Involving Gases.

Law of Partial Pressure

For gases, the partial pressure of a component is the same as if the component is by itself in the container. **The total pressure is the sum of all partial pressures of components**. This is Dalton's law of partial pressures.

In the following discussion, n_1, and P_1 represent number of moles and partial pressure of the component 1 respectively. A similar notation can be given to components 2, 3, 4, etc. When several components are present in a container, the total number of moles is the sum of number of moles of the components:

$$n_{total} = n_1 + n_2 + n_3 + \ldots + n_n$$

Since $n = (V/RT) P$, the number of moles of the first component is related to its partial pressure in the same formula,

$$n_i = (V/RT) P_i,$$

and

$$n_{total} = (V/RT) P_{total}.$$

Therefore,
$$P_{total} = P_1 + P_2 + P_3 + \ldots + P_n$$

Stoichiometry and Gas Laws

We can calculate the number of moles from certain volume, temperature and pressure of a HCl gas, for example. When n moles dissolved in V L solution, its concentration is n/V M.

Three examples are given to illustrate some calculations of stoichiometry involving gas laws. More are given in question form for you to practice.

Example 1

If 500 mL of HCl gas at 300 K and 100 kPa dissolve in 100 mL of pure water, what is the concentration? Data required: R value 8.314 kPa L / (K mol).

Solution:

$$n\_HCl = \frac{0.50 \text{ L} * 100 \text{ kPa}}{(8.314 \text{ kPa L/(K mol)}) * 300 \text{ K}}$$

$$= 0.02 \text{ mol}$$

Concentration of HCl, [HCl]

[HCl] = 0.02 mol / 0.1 L = 0.2 mol/L.

Discussion

Note that R = 0.08205 L atm /(K mol) will not be suitable in this case.

Example 2

If 500 mL of HCl gas at 300 K and 100 kPa dissolved in pure water requires 12.50 mL of the NaOH solution to neutralize in a titration experiment, what is the concentration of the NaOH solution?

Solution:
Solution in Example 1 showed n_{HCl} = 0.02 mol. From the titration experiment, we can conclude that there were 0.02 moles of NaOH in 12.50 mL. Thus,

[NaOH] = 0.02 mol / 0.0125 L = 1.60 mol/L

Discussion:
Think in terms of reaction,
  HCl + NaOH   = NaCl + H_2O <== Reaction
0.02 mol 0.02 mol   <== Quantities reacted

Note: that 0.02 mol of NaOH is in 0.0125 mL solution.

Example 3:

A 5.0-L air sample containing H_2S at STP is treated with a catalyst to promote the reaction,
  $H_2S + O_2 = H_2O + S(solid)$.
If 3.2 g of solid S was collected, calculate the volume percentage of H_2S in the original sample.

Solution:

$$3.2 \text{ g S} \cdot \frac{1 \text{ mol } H_2S}{32 \text{ g S}} = 0.10 \text{ mol } H_2S$$

V_H_2S = 0.10 mol * 22.4 L/mol
     = 2.24 L

Volume % = 2.25 L / 5.0 L
     = 0.45
     = 45 %

Discussion:

Data required: Atomic mass: H, 1; O, 16; S, 32. R = 0.08205 L atm /(K mol) is now suitable R values or molar volume at STP (22.4 L/mol)

The volume percentage is also the mole percentage yield, but not the weight percentage.

Skill 24.4 Demonstrate proficiency at converting between percent composition and the formulas of compounds (including both empirical and molecular formulas).

The **percent composition** of a substance is the **percentage by mass of each element**. Chemical composition is used to verify the purity of a compound in the lab. An impurity will make the actual composition vary from the expected one.

To determine percent composition from a formula, do the following:
5) Write down the **number of atoms each element contributes** to the formula.
6) Multiply these values by the molecular weight of the corresponding element to determine the **grams of each element in one mole** of the formula.
7) Add the values from step 2 to obtain the **formula mass**.
8) Divide each value from step 2 by the formula weight from step 3 and multiply by 100% to obtain the **percent composition**.

The first three steps are the same as those used to determine formula mass, but we use the intermediate results to obtain the composition.

Example: What is the chemical composition of ammonium carbonate $(NH_4)_2CO_3$?

Solution:
1) One $(NH_4)_2CO_3$ contains 2 N, 8 H, 1 C, and 3 O.

2) $$\frac{2 \text{ mol N}}{\text{mol }(NH_4)CO_3} \times \frac{14.0 \text{ g N}}{\text{mol N}} = 28.0 \text{ g N/mol }(NH_4)CO_3$$

$$8(1.0) = 8.0 \text{ g H/mol }(NH_4)CO_3$$
$$1(12.0) = 12.0 \text{ g C/mol }(NH_4)CO_3$$
$$3(16.0) = 48.0 \text{ g O/mol }(NH_4)CO_3$$

3) Sum is $\quad 96.0 \text{ g }(NH_4)CO_3/\text{mol }(NH_4)CO_3$

4) $\%N = \dfrac{28.0 \text{ g N/mol }(NH_4)_2CO_3}{96.0 \text{ g }(NH_4)_2CO_3/\text{mol }(NH_4)_2CO_3} = 0.292 \text{ g N/g }(NH_4)_2CO_3 \times 100\% = 29.2\%$

$\%H = \dfrac{8.0}{96.0} \times 100\% = 8.3\% \quad \%C = \dfrac{12.0}{96.0} \times 100\% = 12.5\% \quad \%O = \dfrac{48.0}{96.0} \times 100\% = 50.0\%$

If we know the chemical composition of a compound, we can calculate an **empirical formula** for it. An empirical formula is the **simplest formula** using the smallest set of integers to express the **ratio of atoms** present in a molecule.

To determine an empirical formula from a percent composition, do the following:
1) Change the "%" sign to grams for a basis of 100 g of the compound.
2) Determine the moles of each element in 100 g of the compound.
3) Divide the values from step 1 by the smallest value to obtain ratios.
4) Multiply by an integer if necessary to get a whole-number ratio.

Example: What is the empirical formula of a compound with a composition of 63.9% Cl, 32.5% C, and 3.6% H?

Solution:
1) We will use a basis of 100 g of the compound containing 63.9 g Cl, 32.5 g C, and 3.6 g H.

2) In 100 g, there are: $63.9 \text{ g Cl} \times \dfrac{\text{mol Cl}}{35.45 \text{ g Cl}} = 1.802 \text{ mol Cl}$

$32.5/12.01 = 2.706 \text{ mol C}$

$3.6/1.01 = 3.56 \text{ mol H}$

3) Dividing these values by the smallest yields:

$\dfrac{2.706 \text{ mol C}}{1.802 \text{ mol Cl}} = 1.502 \text{ mol C/mol Cl}$

$\dfrac{3.56 \text{ mol H}}{1.802 \text{ mol Cl}} = 1.97 \text{ mol H/mol Cl}$

Therefore, the elements are present in a ratio of C:H:Cl=1.50:2.0:1

4) Multiply the entire ratio by 2 because you cannot have a fraction of an atom. This corresponds to a ratio of 3:4:2 for an empirical formula of $C_3H_4Cl_2$.

The **molecular formula** describing the **actual number of atoms in the molecule** might also be $C_3H_4Cl_2$ or it might be $C_6H_8Cl_4$ or some other multiple that maintains a 3:4:2 ratio.

COMPETENCY 25.0 UNDERSTAND AND APPLY KNOWLEDGE OF THE CONCEPTS AND PRINCIPLES OF ACID-BASE CHEMISTRY.

Skill 25.1 Compare the Arrhenius, Brønsted-Lowry, and Lewis concepts of acids and bases.

It was recognized centuries ago that many substances could be divided into the two general categories. **Acids** have a sour taste (as in lemon juice), dissolve many metals, and turn litmus paper red. **Bases** have a bitter taste (as in soaps), feel slippery, and turn litmus paper blue. The chemical reaction between an acid and a base is called **neutralization**. The products of neutralization reactions are neither acids nor bases. Litmus paper is an example of an **acid-base indicator**, a substance that changes color when added to an acid to a base.

Arrhenius definition of acids and bases
Svante **Arrhenius** proposed in the 1880s that **acids form H^+ ions and bases form OH^- ions in water**. The net ionic reaction for neutralization between an Arrhenius acid and base always produces water as shown below for nitric acid and sodium hydroxide:

$$HNO_3(aq) + NaOH(aq) \rightarrow NaNO_3(aq) + H_2O(l)$$

$$H^+(aq) + NO_3^-(aq) + Na^+(aq) + OH^-(aq) \rightarrow NO_3^-(aq) + Na^+(aq) + H_2O(l) \text{ (complete ionic)}$$

$$H^+(aq) + OH^-(aq) \rightarrow H_2O(l) \text{ (net ionic)}$$

The $H^+(aq)$ ion
In acid-base systems, **"protonated water" or "$H^+(aq)$" are shorthand for a mixture of water ions**. For example, HCl reacting in water may be represented as a dissociation:

$$HCl(aq) \rightarrow H^+(aq) + Cl^-(aq)$$

The same reaction may be described as the transfer of a proton to water to form H_3O^+:

$$HCl(aq) + H_2O(l) \rightarrow Cl^-(aq) + H_3O^+(aq)$$

H_3O^+ is called a **hydronium ion**. Its Lewis structure is shown below to the left. In reality, the hydrogen bonds in water are so strong that H^+ ions exist in water as a mixture of species in a hydrogen bond network. Two of them are shown below at center and to the right. Hydrogen bonds are shown as dashed lines.

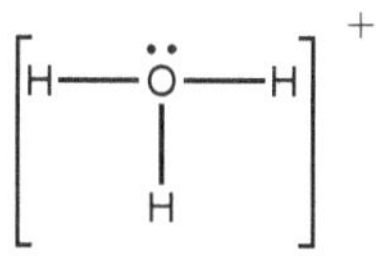

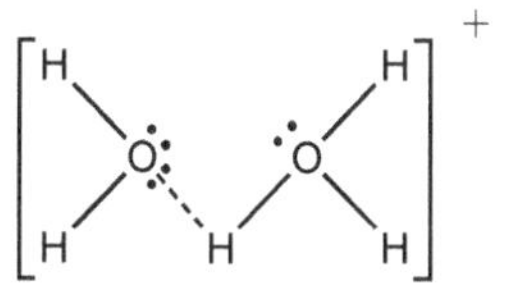

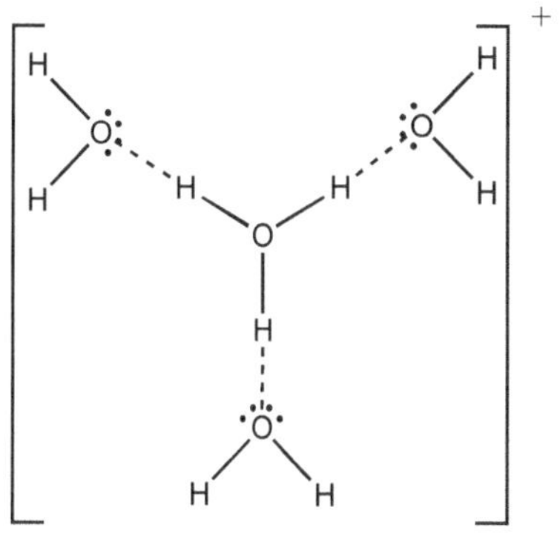

Brønsted-Lowry definition of acids and bases

In the 1920s, Johannes **Brønsted** and Thomas **Lowry** recognized that **acids can transfer a proton to bases** regardless of whether an OH^- ion accepts the proton. In an equilibrium reaction, the direction of proton transfer depends on whether the reaction is read left to right or right to left, so **Brønsted acids and bases exist in conjugate pairs with and without a proton**. Acids that are able to transfer more than one proton are called **polyprotic acids**.

Examples:
1) In the reaction:

$$HF(aq) + H_2O(l) \rightleftharpoons F^-(aq) + H_3O^+(aq),$$

HF transfers a proton to water. Therefore HF is the Brønsted acid and H_2O is the Brønsted base. But in the reverse direction, hydronium ions transfer a proton to fluoride ions. H_3O^+ is the conjugate acid of H_2O because it has an additional proton, and F^- is the conjugate base of HF because it lacks a proton.

2) In the reaction:

$$NH_3(aq) + H_2O(l) \rightleftharpoons NH_4^+(aq) + OH^-(aq),$$

water transfers a proton to ammonia. H_2O is the Brønsted acid and OH^- is its conjugate base. NH_3 is the Brønsted base and NH_4^+ is its conjugate acid.

3) In the reaction:

$$H_3PO_4 + HS^- \rightleftharpoons H_2PO_4^- + H_2S$$

$H_3PO_4/H_2PO_4^-$ is one conjugate acid-base pair and H_2S/HS^- is the other.

4) H_3PO_4 is a polyprotic acid. It may further dissociate to transfer more than one proton:

$$H_3PO_4 \rightleftharpoons H_2PO_4^- + H^+$$
$$H_2PO_4^- \rightleftharpoons HPO_4^{2-} + H^+$$
$$HPO_4^{2-} \rightleftharpoons PO_4^{3-} + H^+$$

Strong and weak acids and bases
Strong acids and bases are strong electrolytes, and weak acids and bases are weak electrolytes, so **strong acids and bases completely dissociate in water**, but weak acids and bases do not.

Example: $HCl(aq) + H_2O(l) \rightarrow H_3O^+(aq) + Cl^-(aq)$ goes to completion because HCl is a strong acid. The acids in the examples on the previous page were all weak.

The aqueous dissociation constants K_a and K_b quantify acid and base strength. Another way of looking at acid dissociation is that strong acids transfer protons more readily than H_3O^+ transfers protons, so they protonate water, the conjugate base of H_3O^+. In general, **if two acid/base conjugate pairs are present, the stronger acid will transfer a proton to the conjugate base of the weaker acid**.

Acid and base **strength is not related to safety**. Weak acids like HF may be extremely corrosive and dangerous.

The most **common strong acids and bases** are listed in the following table:

Strong acid		Strong base	
HCl	Hydrochloric acid	LiOH	Lithium hydroxide
HBr	Hydrobromic acid	NaOH	Sodium hydroxide
HI	Hydroiodic acid	KOH	Potassium hydroxide
HNO_3	Nitric acid	$Ca(OH)_2$	Calcium hydroxide
H_2SO_4	Sulfuric acid	$Sr(OH)_2$	Strontium hydroxide
$HClO_4$	Perchloric acid	$Ba(OH)_2$	Barium hydroxide

A flash animation tutorial demonstrating the difference between strong and weak acids is located at
http://www.mhhe.com/physsci/chemistry/essentialchemistry/flash/acid13.swf.

Trends in acid and base strength

The strongest acid in a polyprotic series is always **the acid with the most protons** (e.g. H_2SO_4 is a stronger acid than HSO_4^-). The strongest acid in a series with the same central atom is always **the acid with the central atom at the highest oxidation number** (e.g. $HClO_4 > HClO_3 > HClO_2 > HClO$ in terms of acid strength). The strongest acid in a series with different central atoms at the same oxidation number is usually **the acid with the central atom at the highest electronegativity** (e.g. the K_a of $HClO > HBrO > HIO$).

Lewis definition of acids and bases

The transfer of a proton from a Brønsted acid to a Brønsted base requires that the base accept the proton. When Lewis diagrams are used to draw the proton donation of Brønsted acid-base reactions, it is always clear that the base must contain an unshared electron pair to form a bond with the proton. For example, ammonia contains an unshared electron pair in the following reaction:

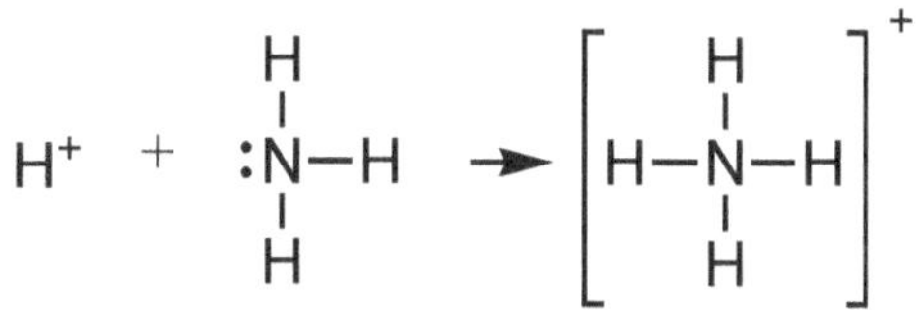

$$H^+ + :NH_3 \rightarrow [NH_4]^+$$

In the 1920s, Gilbert N. **Lewis** proposed that **bases donate unshared electron pairs to acids**, regardless of whether the donation is made to a proton or to another atom. Boron trifluoride is an example of a Lewis acid that is not a Brønsted acid because it is a chemical that accepts an electron pair without involving an H^+ ion:

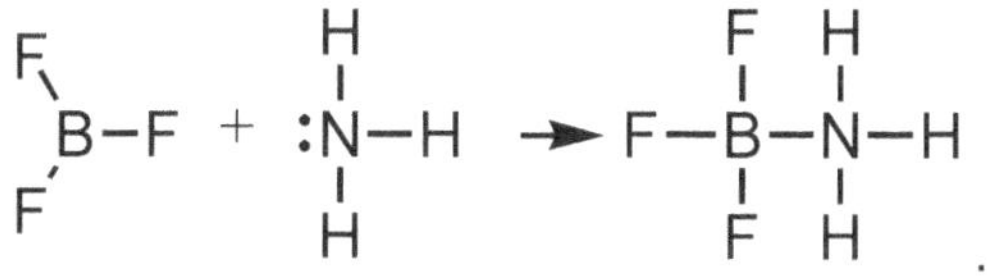

$$BF_3 + :NH_3 \rightarrow F_3B-NH_3$$

The Lewis theory of acids and bases is more general than Brønsted-Lowry theory, but Brønsted-Lowry's definition is used more frequently. The terms "acid" and "base" most often refer to Brønsted acids and bases, and the term "Lewis acid" is usually reserved for chemicals like BF_3 that are not also Brønsted acids.

Summary of definitions

A Lewis base transfers an electron pair to a Lewis acid. A Brønsted acid transfers a proton to a Brønsted base. These exist in conjugate pairs at equilibrium. In an Arrhenius base, the proton acceptor (electron pair donor) is OH^-. All Arrhenius acids/bases are Brønsted acids/bases and all Brønsted acids/bases are Lewis acids/bases. Each definition contains a subset of the one that comes after it.

Skill 25.2   Recognize the relationship between acid and base strength, pH, and molecular structure.

K_a and K_b are particular types of equilibrium constants that give us an idea of the relative strengths of acids and bases, respectively. **The acid-dissociation constant, K_a, is the equilibrium constant for the ionization of a weak acid to a hydrogen ion and its conjugate base.** Likewise, **the base-dissociation constant, K_b, is the equilibrium constant for the addition of a proton to a weak base by water to form its conjugate acid and an OH⁻ ion.**

If we examine the reaction for a generic acid, HA, it is clear that these constants are derived just like other equilibrium constants:

$$HA(aq) \rightarrow H^+(aq) + A^-(aq) \qquad K_a = \frac{[H^+][A^-]}{[HA]}$$

Note that polyprotic acids have unique values for each dissociation: K_{a1}, K_{a2}, etc. K_b is simply the analogous constant in reactions involving bases.

Because K_a and K_b values vary over many orders of magnitude, it is common practice to **take the log of the value and present pK_a and pK_b values** (that is, pK_a= -log$_{10}K_a$). We can then reckon that **smaller pK_a values indicate stronger acids**, since this indicates a greater extent of dissociation. Analogously, **a larger pK_b indicates a stronger base**.

The concentration of H⁺(*aq*) ions is often expressed in terms of pH. **The pH of a solution is the negative base-10 logarithm of the hydrogen-ion molarity.**

$$pH = -\log[H^+] = \log\left(\frac{1}{[H^+]}\right).$$

A ten-fold increase in [H⁺] decreases the pH by one unit. [H⁺] may be found from pH using the expression:

$$[H^+] = 10^{-pH}.$$

The concentration of H⁺ ions has been shown as $[H^+] = 10^{-7}$ M for pure water with $[H^+] = [OH^-]$. Thus **the pH of a neutral solution is 7**. In an **acidic solution**, $[H^+] > 10^{-7}$ M and **pH < 7**. In a basic solution, $[H^+] < 10^{-7}$ M and **pH > 7**.

The negative base-10 log is a convenient way of representing other small numbers used in chemistry by placing the letter "p" before the symbol. Values of K_a are often represented as pK_a, with $pK_a = -\log K_a$. The concentration of OH^- (aq) ions may also be expressed in terms of pOH, with $pOH = -\log[OH^-]$.

The ion-product constant of water, $K_w = [H^+][OH^-] = 1.0 \times 10^{-14}$ at 25 °C. The value of K_w can used to determine the relationship between pH and pOH by taking the negative log of the expression:
$$-\log K_w = -\log[H^+] - \log[OH^-] = -\log(10^{-14}).$$
Therefore: $pH + pOH = 14$.

Example: An aqueous solution has an H^+ ion concentration of 4.0×10^{-9}. Is the solution acidic or basic? What is the pH of the solution? What is the pOH?

Solution: The solution is basic because $[H^+] < 10^{-7}$ M.
$$pH = -\log[H^+] = -\log 4 \times 10^{-9}$$
$$= 8.4.$$
$pH + pOH = 14$. Therefore $pOH = 14 - pH = 14 - 8.4 = 5.6$.

Skill 25.3 Explain the characteristics of buffered solutions in terms of chemical equilibrium of weak acids.

A **buffer solution** is a solution that **resists a change in pH** after addition of small amounts of an acid or a base. Buffer solutions require the presence of an acid to neutralize an added base and also the presence of a base to neutralize an added acid. These two components present in the buffer also must not neutralize each other! A **conjugate acid-base pair is present in buffers** to fulfill these requirements.

Buffers are prepared by mixing together **a weak acid or base and a salt of the acid or base** that provides the conjugate.

Consider the buffer solution prepared by mixing together acetic acid—$HC_2H_3O_2$—and sodium acetate—$C_2H_3O_2^-$ containing Na^+ as a spectator ion. The equilibrium reaction for this acid/conjugate base pair is:
$$HC_2H_3O_2 \rightleftharpoons C_2H_3O_2^- + H^+.$$

If H^+ ions from a strong acid are added to this buffer solution, Le Chatelier's principle predicts that the reaction will shift to the left and much of this H^+ will be consumed to create more $HC_2H_3O_2$ from $C_2H_3O_2^-$. If a strong base that consumes H^+ is added to this buffer solution, Le Chatelier's principle predicts that the reaction will shift to the right and much of the consumed H^+ will be replaced by the dissociation of $HC_2H_3O_2$. The net effect is that **buffer solutions prevent large changes in pH that occur when an acid or base is added to pure water** or to an unbuffered solution.

The amount of acid or base that a buffer solution can neutralize before dramatic pH changes begins to occur is called its **buffering capacity**. Blood and seawater both contain several conjugate acid-base pairs to buffer the solution's pH and decrease the impact of acids and bases on living things.

An excellent flash animation with audio to explain the action of buffering solutions is found at
http://www.mhhe.com/physsci/chemistry/essentialchemistry/flash/buffer12.swf.

Skill 25.4   Demonstrate an understanding of how to prepare a standardized solution or a buffer of a specified pH, given the Ka of various acids and a standardized NaOH solution.

Buffers are usually composed of weak acids and their salts, or weak bases and their salts. An appropriate acid or base/ salt combination will buffer a solution only when it is at sufficient concentration and has a pK_a close to the desired pH of the solution. Thus, a buffered solution can be created as follows:

1. Select a compound with a pK_a close the desired pH.
2. Determine what the buffer concentration must be; typical concentrations are between 1mM and 200 mM.
3. Using the pK_a, calculate the number of moles of acid/salt or base/salt that must be present at the desired pH.
4. Covert moles to grams and weigh out the components
    a. If both salt and acid (or base) are available, use the appropriate amount of each.
    b. If only the acid is available, add the entire needed compound in acid form and then use enough base (NaOH) to convert the proper portion to salt.
5. Dissolve all components in slightly less water than is needed to reach the final volume.
6. Check the pH and adjust if necessary. Add water to reach the final volume.

Skill 25.5 Design and analyze the results of an acid-base titration (which may include selecting an appropriate indicator or interpreting a titration curve).

Standard titration

In a typical acid-base **titration, an acid-base indicator** (such as *phenolphthalein*) or a **pH meter** is used to monitor the course of a **neutralization reaction**. The usual goal of titration is to **determine an unknown concentration** of an acid (or base) by neutralizing it with a known concentration of base (or acid).

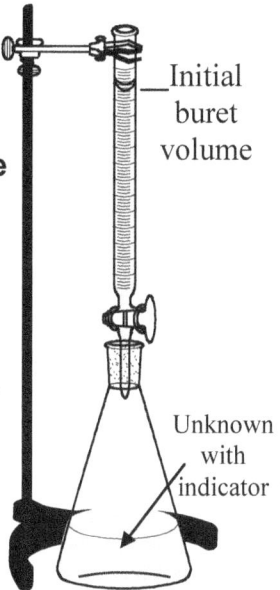

The reagent of known concentration is usually used as the **titrant**. The titrant is poured into a **buret** (also spelled *burette*) until it is nearly full, and an initial buret reading is taken. Buret numbering is close to zero when nearly full. A known volume of the solution of unknown concentration is added to a flask and placed under the buret. The indicator is added or the pH meter probe is inserted. The initial state of a titration experiment is shown to the right above.

The buret stopcock is opened and titrant is slowly added until the solution permanently changes color or the pH rapidly changes. This is the titration **endpoint**, and a final buret reading is made. The final state of a titration experiment is shown to the right below. The endpoint occurs when the number of **acid and base equivalents in the flask are identical**:
$N_{acid} = N_{base}$. Therefore, $C_{acid}V_{acid} = C_{base}V_{base}$.
The endpoint is also known as the titration **equivalence point**.

Titration data typically consist of:
$V_{inital} \Rightarrow$ Initial buret volume $V_{final} \Rightarrow$ Final buret volume
$C_{known} \Rightarrow$ Concentration of known solution
$V_{unknown} \Rightarrow$ Volume of unknown solution.

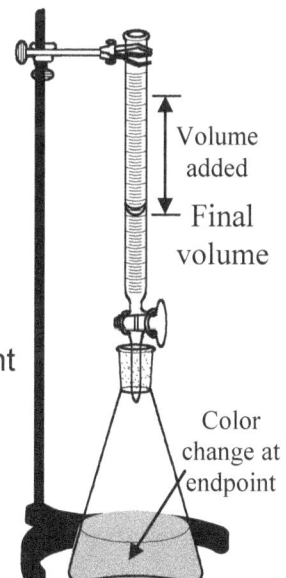

To determine the unknown concentration, first find the volume of titrant at the known concentration added: $V_{known} = V_{final} - V_{initial}$.

At the equivalence point, $N_{unknown} = N_{known}$.

Therefore, $C_{unknown} = \dfrac{C_{known}V_{known}}{V_{unknown}} = \dfrac{C_{known}\left(V_{final} - V_{initial}\right)}{V_{unknown}}$.

Units of molarity may be used for concentration in the above expressions **unless a mole of either solution yields more than one acid or base equivalent.** In that case, concentration must be expressed using **normality**.

Example: A 20.0 mL sample of an HCl solution is titrated with 0.200 M NaOH. The initial buret volume is 1.8 mL and the final buret volume at the titration endpoint is 29.1 mL. What is the molarity of the HCl sample?

Solution: Two solution methods will be used. The first method is better for those who are good at unit manipulations and less skilled at memorizing formulas. HCl contains one acid equivalent and NaOH contains one base equivalent, so we may use molarity in all our calculations.

1) Calculate the moles of the known substance added to the flask:

$$0.200 \frac{\text{mol}}{\text{L}} \times \frac{1 \text{ L}}{1000 \text{ mL}} \times (29.1 \text{ mL} - 1.8 \text{ mL}) = 0.00546 \text{ mol NaOH}.$$

At the endpoint, this base will neutralize 0.00546 mol HCl. Therefore, this amount of HCl must have been present in the sample before the titration.

$$\frac{0.00546 \text{ mol HCl}}{0.0200 \text{ L}} = 0.273 \text{ M HCl}.$$

2) Utilize the formula: $C_{unknown} = \dfrac{C_{known}(V_{final} - V_{initial})}{V_{unknown}}$.

$$C_{HCl} = \frac{C_{NaOH}(V_{final} - V_{initial})}{V_{HCl}} = \frac{0.200 \text{ M }(29.1 \text{ mL} - 1.8 \text{ mL})}{20.0 \text{ mL}} = 0.273 \text{ M HCl}.$$

Titrating with the unknown
In a common variation of standard titration, the unknown is added to the buret as a titrant and the reagent of known concentration is placed in the flask. The chemistry involved is the same as in the standard case, and the mathematics is also identical except for the identity of the two volumes. For this variation, V_{known} will be the volume added to the flask before titration begins and $V_{unknown} = V_{final} - V_{initial}$. Therefore:

$$C_{unknown} = \frac{C_{known} V_{known}}{V_{unknown}} = \frac{C_{known} V_{known}}{V_{final} - V_{initial}}.$$

Example: 30.0 mL of a 0.150 M HNO₃ solution is titrated with Ca(OH)₂. The initial buret volume is 0.6 mL and the final buret volume at the equivalent point is 22.2 mL. What is the molarity of Ca(OH)₂ used for the titration?

Solution: The same two solution methods will be used as in the previous example. 1 mol Ca(OH)₂ contains 2 base equivalents because it reacts with 2 moles of H⁺ via the reaction
$Ca(OH)_2 + 2HNO_3 \rightarrow Ca(NO_3)_2 + 2H_2O$. Therefore, normality must be used in the formula for solution method 2.

1) First calculate the moles of the substance in the flask:

$$0.150 \frac{mol}{L} \times 0.0300 \text{ L} = 0.00450 \text{ mol HNO}_3.$$

This acid must be titrated with 0.00450 base equivalents for neutralization to occur at the end point. We calculate moles Ca(OH)₂ used in the titration from stoichiometry:

$$0.00450 \text{ base equivalents} \times \frac{1 \text{ mol Ca(OH)}_2}{2 \text{ base equivalents}} = 0.00225 \text{ mol Ca(OH)}_2.$$

The molarity of Ca(OH)₂ is found from the volume used in the titration:

$$\frac{0.00225 \text{ mol Ca(OH)}_3}{0.0222 \text{ L} - 0.0006 \text{ L}} = 0.104 \text{ M Ca(OH)}_3.$$

2) Utilize the formula: $C_{unknown} = \frac{C_{known} V_{known}}{V_{final} - V_{initial}}$ using units of normality.

For HNO₃, molarity=normality because 1 mol contains 1 acid equivalent.

$$C_{Ca(OH)_2} = \frac{C_{HNO_3} V_{HNO_3}}{V_{final} - V_{initial}} = \frac{\left(0.150 \text{ M} \times \frac{1 \text{ N}}{1 \text{ M}}\right)(30.0 \text{ mL})}{22.2 \text{ mL} - 0.6 \text{ mL}} = 0.208 \text{ N Ca(OH)}_2.$$

This value is converted to molarity. For Ca(OH)₂, normality is twice molarity because 1 mol contains 2 base equivalents.

$$0.208 \text{ N Ca(OH)}_2 \times \frac{1 \text{ M Ca(OH)}_2}{2 \text{ N Ca(OH)}_2} = 0.104 \text{ M Ca(OH)}_2.$$

Interpreting titration curves

A **titration curve** is a plot of a solution's **pH charted against the volume of an added acid or base**. Titration curves are obtained if a pH meter is used to monitor the titration instead of an indicator. At the equivalence point, the titration curve is nearly vertical. This is the point where the most rapid change in pH occurs. In addition to determining the equivalence point, the **shape of titration curves** may be interpreted to determine **acid/base strength and the presence of a polyprotic acid.**

The pH at the equivalence point of a titration is the **pH of the salt solution obtained when the amount of acid is equal to amount of base**. For a strong acid and a strong base, the equivalence point occurs at the neutral pH of 7. For example, an equimolar solution of HCl and NaOH will contain NaCl(aq) at its equivalence point.

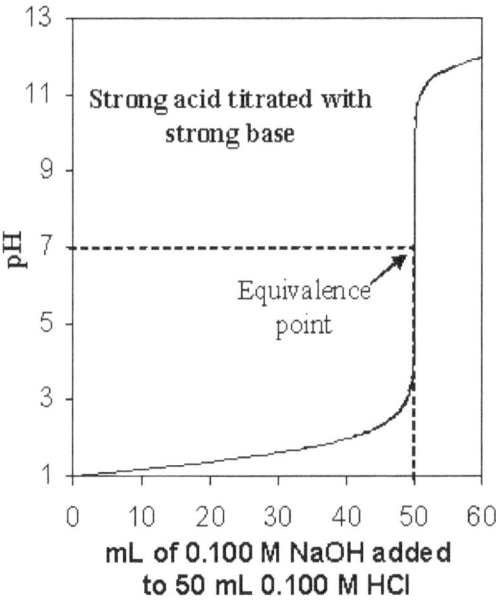
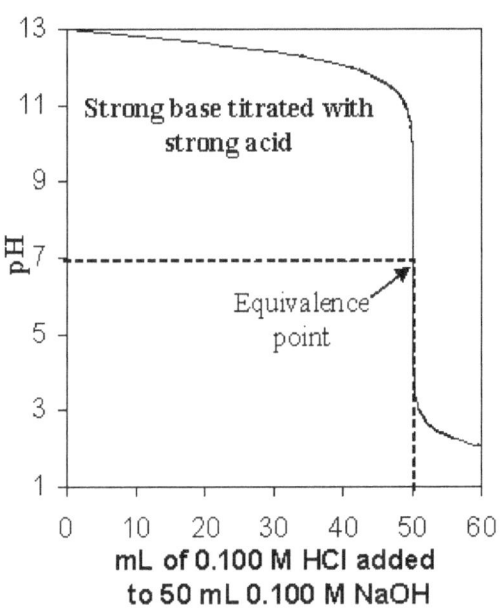

The salt solution at **the equivalence point of a titration involving a weak acid or base will not be at neutral pH**. For example, an equimolar solution of NaOH and hypochlorous acid HClO at the equivalence point of a titration will be a base because it is indistinguishable from a solution of sodium hypochlorite. A pure solution of NaClO(aq) will be a base because the ClO$^-$ ion is the conjugate base of HClO, and it consumes H$^+$(aq) in the reaction: $ClO^- + H^+ \rightleftharpoons HClO$.

In a similar fashion, an equimolar solution of HCl and NH$_3$ will be an acid because a solution of NH$_4$Cl(aq) is an acid. It generates H$^+$(aq) in the reaction: $NH_4^+ \rightleftharpoons NH_3 + H^+$.

Contrast the following **titration curves for a weak acid or base** with those for a strong acid and strong base on the preceding page:

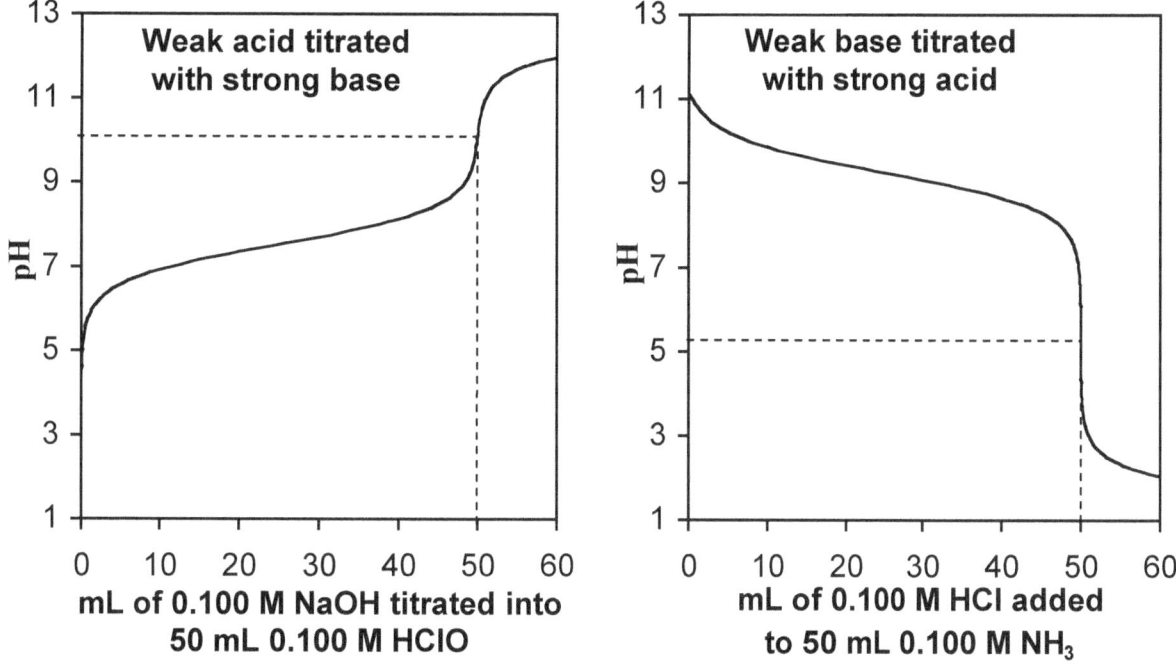

Titration of a polyprotic acid results in **multiple equivalence points** and a curve with more "bumps" as shown below for sulfurous acid and the carbonate ion

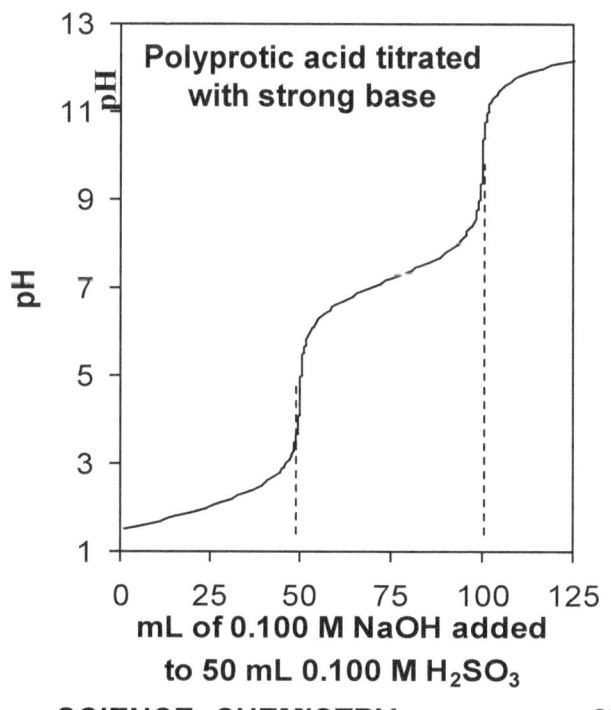

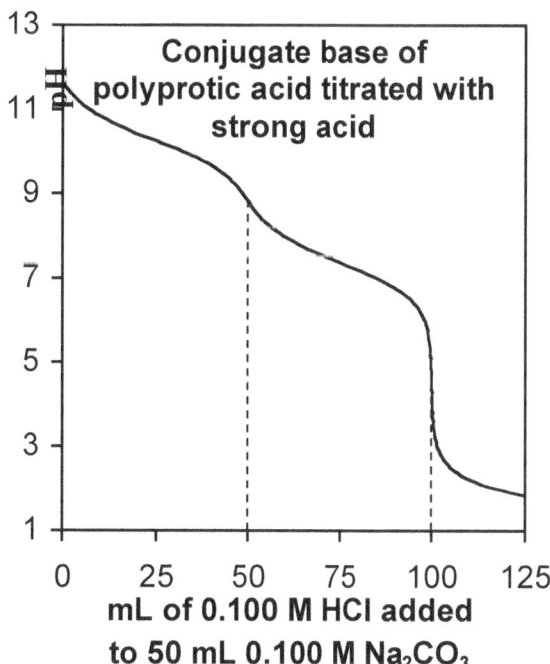

TEACHER CERTIFICATION STUDY GUIDE

COMPETENCY 26.0   **UNDERSTAND AND APPLY KNOWLEDGE OF THERMODYNAMICS AND THEIR APPLICATIONS TO CHEMICAL SYSTEMS.**

Skill 26.1   **Recognize the relationships among enthalpy, entropy, Gibbs free energy, and the equilibrium constant.**

Enthalpy, ΔH, is the internal energy of the molecules within a system.

Entropy, ΔS, may be thought of as **the disorder in a system** or as a measure of the **number of states a system may occupy**. Changes due to entropy occur in one direction with no driving force. For example, a small volume of gas released into a large container will expand to fill it, but the gas in a large container never spontaneously collects itself into a small volume. This occurs because a large volume of gas has more disorder and has more places for gas molecules to be. This change occurs because **processes increase in entropy** when given the opportunity to do so.

Gibbs Free Energy, ΔG, is the free energy within the system that is, energy available to do work. It is determined by ΔG= ΔH-T ΔS. When ΔG = 0 the system is at equilibrium. If ΔG >0 the reaction is nonspontaneous. When ΔG < 0, the reaction is spontaneous.

Spontaneity
A reaction with a negative ΔH and a positive ΔS causes a decrease in energy and an increase in entropy. **These reactions will always occur spontaneously.** A reaction with a positive ΔH and a negative ΔS causes an increase in energy and a decrease in entropy. These reactions never occur to an appreciable extent because the reverse reaction takes place spontaneously.

Whether reactions with the remaining two possible combinations (ΔH and ΔS both positive or both negative) occur depends on the temperature. If ΔH–TΔS (known as the **Gibbs Free Energy**) is negative, the reaction will take place. If it is positive, the reaction will not occur to an appreciable extent. If ΔH–TΔS=0 exactly, then at equilibrium there will be 50% reactants and 50% products.

This chart will help identify four possible scenarios for the values of ΔH, ΔS and ΔG to predict spontaneity of the reaction.

ΔH	ΔS	ΔG
-	+	-, spontaneous
-	-	-, spontaneous
+	+	- if |TΔS|< |ΔH|, spontaneous
+	-	- if TΔS > ΔH

SCIENCE: CHEMISTRY

A spontaneous reaction is called *exergonic*. A non-spontaneous reaction is known as *endergonic*. These terms are used much less often than *exothermic* and *endothermic*.

Skill 26.2 Evaluate the thermodynamic feasibility of various reactions and calculate energy changes during chemical reactions.

Energy is the **driving force for change**. Energy has units of joules (J). Temperature remains constant during phase changes, so the **speed** of molecules and their **translational kinetic energy do not change** during a change in phase.

The **internal energy** of a material is the **sum of the total kinetic energy** of its molecules and the **potential energy** of interactions between those molecules. Total kinetic energy includes the contributions from translational motion and other components of motion such as rotation. The potential energy includes **energy stored in the form of resisting intermolecular attractions** between molecules.

The **enthalpy** (*H*) of a material is the **sum of its internal energy and the mechanical work** it can do by driving a piston. We usually don't deal with mechanical work in high school chemistry, so the differences between internal energy and enthalpy are not important. The key concept is that a change in the **enthalpy** of a substance is the total **energy** change caused by **adding/removing heat** at constant pressure.

When a material is heated and experiences a phase change, **thermal energy is used to break the intermolecular bonds** holding the material together. Similarly, bonds are formed with the release of thermal energy when a material changes its phase during cooling. Therefore, **the energy of a material increases during a phase change that requires heat and decreases during a phase change that releases heat**. For example, the energy of H_2O increases when ice melts and decreases when water freezes.

Hess's law states that energy changes are state functions. The amount of energy depends only on the states of the reactants and the state of the products, but not on the intermediate steps. Energy (enthalpy) changes in chemical reactions are the same, regardless whether the reactions occur in one or several steps. The total energy change in a chemical reaction is the sum of the energy changes in its many steps leading to the overall reaction.

A **standard** thermodynamic value occurs with all components at 25 °C and 100 kPa. This *thermodynamic standard state* is slightly different from the *standard temperature and pressure* (STP) often used for gas law problems (0 °C and 1 atm=101.325 kPa). Standard properties of common chemicals are listed in tables.

The **heat of formation, ΔH_f**, of a chemical is the heat required (positive) or emitted (negative) when elements react to form the chemical. It is also called the enthalpy of formation. The **standard heat of formation** ΔH_f is the heat of formation with all reactants and products at 25 °C and 100 kPa.

Elements in their **most stable form** are assigned a value of $\Delta H_f° = 0$ kJ/mol. Different forms of an element in the same phase of matter are known as **allotropes**.

Example: The heat of formation for carbon as a gas is:

$\Delta H_f°$ for $C(g) = 718.4 \frac{kJ}{mol}$. Carbon in the solid phase exists in three

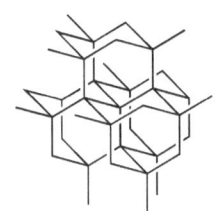

allotropes. A C_{60} *buckyball* (one face is shown to the left), contains C atoms linked with aromatic bonds and arranged in the shape of a soccer ball. C_{60} was discovered in 1985. *Diamond* (below left) contains single C–C bonds in a three dimensional network. The most stable form at 25 °C is *graphite* (below right). Graphite is composed of C atoms with aromatic bonds in sheets.

$\Delta H_f°$ for C_{60} (*buckminsterfullerene or buckyball*) $= 38.0 \frac{kJ}{mol}$

$\Delta H_f°$ for C_{∞} (*diamond*) $= 1.88 \frac{kJ}{mol}$

$\Delta H_f°$ for C_{∞} (*graphite*) $= 0 \frac{kJ}{mol}$.

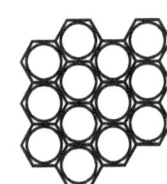

Heat of combustion ΔH_c (also called enthalpy of combustion) is the heat of reaction when a chemical **burns in O_2** to form completely oxidized products such as **CO_2 and H_2O**. It is also the heat of reaction for **nutritional molecules that are metabolized** in the body. The standard heat of combustion $\Delta H_c°$ takes place at 25 °C and 100 kPa. **Combustion is always exothermic**, so the negative sign for values of ΔH_c is often omitted. If a combustion reaction is used in Hess's Law, the value must be negative.

Example: Determine the standard heat of formation $\Delta H_f°$ for ethylene:\
$2C(graphite) + 2H_2(g) \rightarrow C_2H_4(g)$.

    Use the heat of combustion for ethylene:

$$\Delta H_c° = 1411.2 \frac{kJ}{mol\ C_2H_4} \quad \text{for} \quad C_2H_4(g) + 3O_2(g) \rightarrow 2CO_2(g) + 2H_2O(l)$$

and the following two heats of formation for CO_2 and H_2O:

$$\Delta H_f° = -393.5 \frac{kJ}{mol\ C} \quad \text{for} \quad C(graphite) + O_2(g) \rightarrow CO_2(g)$$

$$\Delta H_f° = -285.9 \frac{kJ}{mol\ H_2} \quad \text{for} \quad H_2(g) + \frac{1}{2}O_2(g) \rightarrow H_2O(l).$$

Solution: Use Hess's Law after rearranging the given reactions so they cancel to yield the reaction of interest. Combustion is exothermic, so ΔH for this reaction is negative. We are interested in C_2H_4 as a product, so we take the opposite (endothermic) reaction. The given ΔH are multiplied by stoichiometric coefficients to give the reaction of interest as the sum of the three:

$$2CO_2(g) + 2H_2O(l) \rightarrow C_2H_4(g) + 3O_2(g) \quad \Delta H = 1411.2 \frac{kJ}{mol\ reaction}$$

$$2C(graphite) + 2O_2(g) \rightarrow 2CO_2(g) \quad \Delta H = -787.0 \frac{kJ}{mol\ reaction}$$

$$2H_2(g) + O_2(g) \rightarrow 2H_2O(l) \quad \Delta H = -571.8 \frac{kJ}{mol\ reaction}$$

$$2C(graphite) + 2H_2(g) \rightarrow C_2H_4(g) \quad \Delta H_f° = 52.4 \frac{kJ}{mol}$$

For example, in the diagram below, we look at the oxidation of carbon into CO and CO_2. The direct oxidation of carbon (graphite) into CO_2 yields an enthalpy of -393 kJ/mol. When carbon is oxidized into CO and then CO is oxidized to CO_2, the enthalpies are -110 and -283 kJ/mol respectively. The sum of enthalpy in the two steps is exactly -393 kJ/mol, same as the one-step reaction.

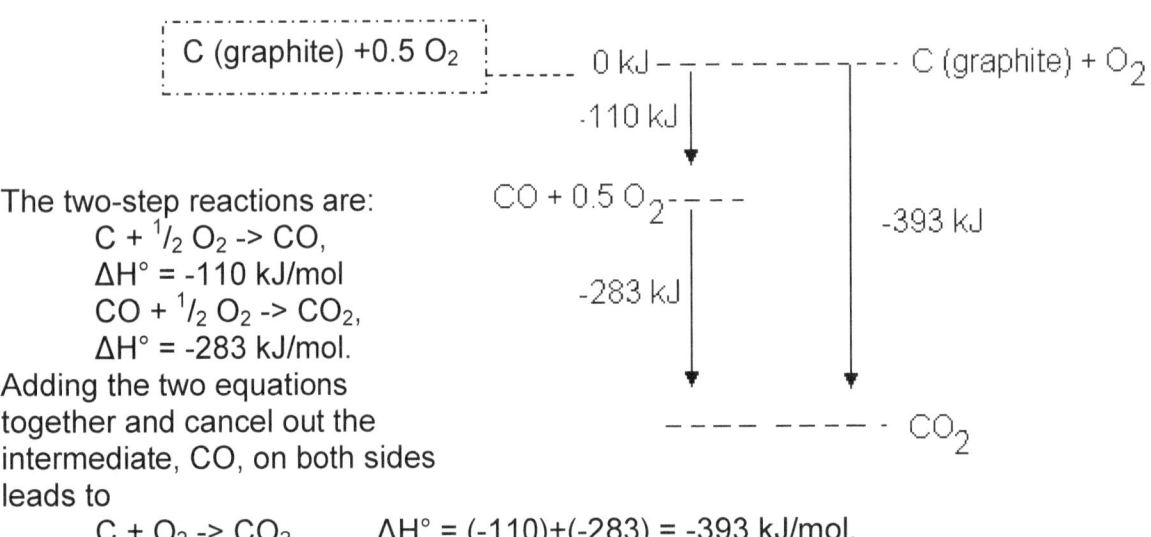

The two-step reactions are:
  $C + \frac{1}{2} O_2 \rightarrow CO$, $\Delta H° = -110$ kJ/mol
  $CO + \frac{1}{2} O_2 \rightarrow CO_2$, $\Delta H° = -283$ kJ/mol.
Adding the two equations together and cancel out the intermediate, CO, on both sides leads to
  $C + O_2 \rightarrow CO_2$, $\Delta H° = (-110)+(-283) = -393$ kJ/mol.

Application of Hess's law enables us to calculate ΔH, $\Delta H°$, and ΔH_f for chemical reactions that impossible to measure, providing that we have all the data of related reactions.

For example:

The enthalpy of combustion for H_2, C(graphite) and CH_4 are -285.8, -393.5, and -890.4 kJ/mol respectively. Calculate the standard enthalpy of formation ΔH_f for CH_4.

Using the equations and their ΔH values
(1) $H_2(g) + 0.5\ O_2(g) \rightarrow H_2O(l)$ ΔH = -285.8 kJ/mol
(2) C(graphite) + $O_2(g) \rightarrow CO_2(g)$ ΔH = -393.5 kJ/mol
(3) $CH_4(g) + 2O_2(g) \rightarrow CO_2(g) + 2H_2O(l)$ ΔH = -890.4 kJ/mol

Find: C + $2H_2 \rightarrow CH_4$

2 ($H_2(g) + 0.5\ O_2(g) \rightarrow H_2O(l)$) ΔH = -285.8 kJ/mol)

or $2H_2(g) + O_2(g) \rightarrow 2H_2O(l)$ ΔH = -571.6 kJ

+   C(graphite) + $O_2(g) \rightarrow CO_2(g)$ ΔH = -393.5 kJ

+ $CO_2(g) + 2H_2O(l) \rightarrow CH_4(g) + 2O_2(g)$ ΔH = +890.4 kJ

C(graphite) + $2H_2(g) \rightarrow CH_4(g)$ ΔH = -74.7 kJ

From these data, we can construct an energy level diagram for these chemical combinations as follows:

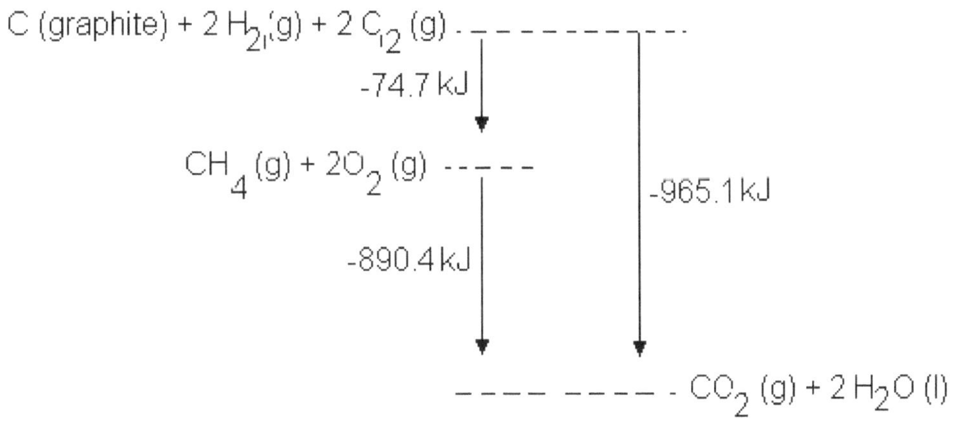

Chemical energy is an important source of energy. It is the energy stored in substances by virtue of the arrangement of atoms within the substance. When atoms are rearranged during chemical reactions, energy is either released or consumed. It is the energy released from chemical reactions that fuel our economy and power our bodies. Most of the electricity produced comes from chemical energy released by the burning of petroleum, coal and natural gas. ATP is the molecule used by our body to carry chemical energy form cell to cell.

The energy found in molecules is found in the bonds between the atoms in the molecule. To break these bonds requires energy. Once broken apart, the atoms, ions or molecules rearrange themselves to form new substances, making new bonds. Making new bonds releases energy.

If during a chemical reaction, more energy is needed to break the reactant bonds than released when product bonds form, the reaction is endothermic and heat is absorbed from the environment becomes colder.

On the other hand, if more energy is released due to product bonds forming than is needed to break reactant bonds the energy is exothermic and the excess energy is released to the environment as heat. The temperature of the environment goes up.

The total energy absorbed or released in the reaction can be determined by using bond energies. The total energy change of the reaction is equal to the total energy of all of the bonds of the products minus the total energy of all of the bonds of the reactants.

For example, propane, C_3H_8, is a common fuel used in heating homes and backyard grills. When burned, excess energy from the combustion reaction is released and used to cook our food, for example.

$$C_3H_8 \text{ (g)} + 5\, O_2 \text{ (g)} \rightarrow 3\, CO_2 \text{ (g)} + 4\, H_2O\text{(l)}$$

The total energy of the products is from the bonds found in the carbon dioxide molecules and the water molecules.

$$3\ O=C=O\ +\ 4\ H\text{-}O\text{-}H$$

or 6 C=O bonds and 8 H-O bonds.

A table of bond energies gives the following information:

C=O   743 kJ/mol
H-O   463 kJ/mol

So for these molecules there would be: (6 x 743 kJ) + 8 x 463 kJ) =8162 kJ of energy released when these molecules form.

The reactants are these:

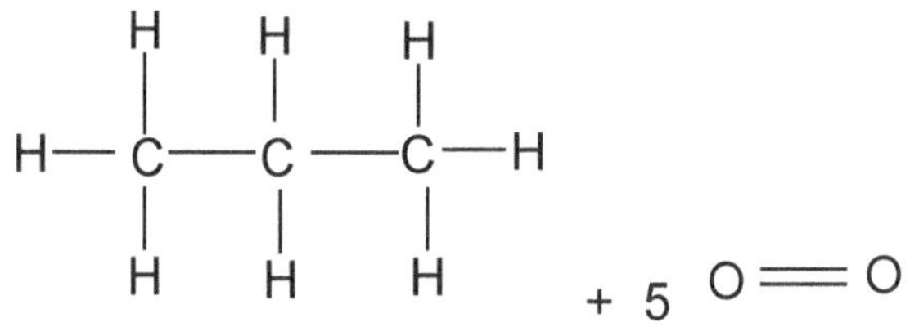

$$\text{H}_3\text{C}-\text{CH}_2-\text{CH}_3 + 5\ \text{O}=\text{O}$$

or

2 C-C bonds
8 C-H bonds and
5 O=O bonds

These bonds require the following energy to break:

C-C   348 kJ/ mol
C-H   412 kJ/mol
O=O 498 kJ.mol

The total energy required for the reactants would be
(2 x 348 kJ) + (8 x 412 kJ) +(5 x 498 kJ) = 6482 kJ of energy.

The total energy change that occurs during the combustion of propane is then:

8162 kJ – 6482 kJ = 680 kJ of energy is released for every mole of propane that burns in excess oxygen.

Skill 26.3 Analyze the thermodynamics and kinetic dynamics that move a reversible reaction to a position of chemical equilibrium.

Several factors are important in the progress of a reaction. The most basic first step in any reaction is that the **reactants must collide with one another**. However, only a fraction of the collisions between the reactants allow the reaction to begin. This is because **the molecules must collide in the proper orientation and with sufficiently high energy**. This **activation energy E_a is the minimum energy needed to overcome the barrier to the formation of products**. That is, it is the minimum energy needed for the reaction to occur. The activation energy, E_a, is the difference between the energy of reactants and the energy of the activated complex, which is an intermediate form. The energy change during the reaction, ΔE, is the difference between the energy of the products and the energy of the reactants. If the energy of the products is lower than that of the reactants, the reaction will be exothermic. If reactants are lower than products, the reaction will be endothermic. Thus, **energy must be added to allow an endothermic reaction to progress towards equilibrium**. However, high activation energies can be overcome with the use of a catalyst. A **catalyst decreases E_a and so increases the rate of both the forward and reverse reactions by lowering the activation energy for the reaction**. Note that a catalyst does not change the position of equilibrium, but merely reduces the energy requirements of a reaction.

If we return to the question of collisions between molecules, it becomes apparent that **kinetic energy** will have a bearing on the likelihood of these collisions. **Molecules that are moving around quickly will be more likely to collide and the higher number of collisions also increases the chance that the molecules will meet in the correct orientation**. Additionally, if the molecules generally have higher energy, it will be more likely for them to obtain the E_a required for the reaction to proceed. Therefore, **anything that increases the probability of these collisions and the energy of the molecules will speed the reaction's obtainment of equilibrium**. Thus it is clear that **temperature, pressure, and concentration must have an effect** on systems in equilibrium. Their effect is generalized in LeChatelier's Principle.

Skill 26.4 Apply Le Chatelier's principle to analyze reversible reactions.

A system at equilibrium is in a state of balance because forward and reverse processes are taking place at equal rates. If equilibrium is disturbed by changing concentration, pressure, or temperature, the state of balance is upset for a period of time before the equilibrium shifts to achieve a new state of balance. **Le Chatelier's principle states that equilibrium will shift to partially offset the impact of an altered condition**.

Change in reactant and product concentrations

If a chemical reaction is at equilibrium, Le Chatelier's principle predicts that **adding a substance**—either a reactant or a product—will shift the reaction so **a new equilibrium is established by consuming some of the added substance**. Removing a substance will cause the reaction to move in the direction that forms more of that substance.

Example: The reaction $CO + 2H_2 \rightleftharpoons CH_3OH$ is used to synthesize methanol. Equilibrium is established, and then additional CO is added to the reaction vessel. Predict the impact on each reaction component after CO is added.

Solution: Le Chatelier's principle states that the reaction will shift to partially offset the impact of the added CO. Therefore, CO concentration will decrease, and the reaction will "shift to the right." H_2 concentration will also decrease and CH_3OH concentration will increase.

Change in pressure for gases

If a chemical reaction is at equilibrium in the gas phase, Le Chatelier's principle predicts that **an increase in pressure** will shift the reaction so **a new equilibrium is established by decreasing the number of gas moles present**. A decrease in the number of moles partially offsets this rise in pressure. Decreasing pressure will cause the reaction to move in the direction that forms more moles of gas. These changes in pressure might result from altering the volume of the reaction vessel at constant temperature.

Example: The reaction $N_2 + 3H_2 \rightleftharpoons 2NH_3$ is used to synthesize ammonia. Equilibrium is established. Next the reaction vessel is expanded at constant temperature. Predict the impact on each reaction component after this expansion occurs.

Solution: The expansion will result in a decrease in pressure. Le Chatelier's principle states that the reaction will shift to partially offset this decrease by increasing the number of moles present. There are 4 moles on the left side of the equation and 2 moles on the right, so the reaction will shift to the left. N_2 and H_2 concentration will increase. NH_3 concentration will decrease.

Change in temperature

Le Chatelier's principle predicts that **when heat is added** at constant pressure to a system at equilibrium, **the reaction will shift in the direction that absorbs heat** until a new equilibrium is established. For an endothermic process, the reaction will shift to the right towards product formation. For an exothermic process, the reaction will shift to the left towards reactant formation. If you understand the application of Le Chatelier's principle to concentration changes then writing "heat" on the appropriate side of the equation will help you understand its application to changes in temperature.

Example: $N_2 + 3H_2 \rightleftharpoons 2NH_3$ is an exothermic reaction. First equilibrium is established and then the temperature is decreased. Predict the impact of the lower temperature on each reaction component.

Solution: Since the reaction is exothermic, we may write it as:
$N_2 + 3H_2 \rightleftharpoons 2NH_3 + Heat$. For the purpose of finding the impact of temperature on equilibrium processes, we may consider heat as if it were a reaction component. Le Chatelier's principle states that after a temperature decrease, the reaction will shift to partially offset the impact of a loss of heat. Therefore more heat will be produced, and the reaction will shift to the right. N_2 and H_2 concentration will decrease. NH_3 concentration will increase.

A flash animation with audio that demonstrates Le Chatelier's principle is at http://www.mhhe.com/physsci/chemistry/essentialchemistry/flash/lechv17.swf.

COMPETENCY 27.0 UNDERSTAND AND APPLY KNOWLEDGE OF ELECTROCHEMISTRY.

Skill 27.1 Demonstrate an understanding of oxidation/reduction reactions and their relationship to standard reduction potentials.

Redox is shorthand for *reduction* and *oxidation*. **Reduction** is the **gain of an electron** by a molecule, atom, or ion. **Oxidation** is the **loss of an electron** by a molecule, atom, or ion. These two processes always occur together. Electrons lost by one substance are gained by another. In a redox process, the **oxidation numbers** of atoms are altered. Reduction decreases the oxidation number of an atom. Oxidation increases the oxidation number.

The easiest redox processes to identify are those involving monatomic ions with altered charges. For example, the reaction
$$Zn(s) + Cu^{2+}(aq) \rightarrow Zn^{2+}(aq) + Cu(s)$$
is a redox process because electrons are transferred from Zn to Cu.

However, many redox reactions involve the transfer of electrons from one molecular compound to another. In these cases, **oxidation numbers must be determined** as follows:

Oxidation numbers, sometimes called oxidation states, are signed numbers assigned to atoms in molecules and ions. They allow us to keep track of the electrons associated with each atom. Oxidation numbers are frequently used to write chemical formulas, to help us predict properties of compounds, and to help balance equations in which electrons are transferred. Knowledge of the oxidative state of an atom gives us an idea about its positive or negative character. In themselves, oxidation numbers have no physical meaning; they are used to simplify tasks that are more difficult to accomplish without them.

The Rules:

1. Free elements are assigned an oxidation state of 0.

e.g. Al, Na, Fe, H_2, O_2, N_2, Cl_2 etc have zero oxidation states.

2. The oxidation state for any simple one-atom ion is equal to its charge.

e.g. the oxidation state of Na^+ is +1, Be^{2+}, +2, and of F^-, -1.

3. The alkali metals (Li, Na, K, Rb, Cs and Fr) in compounds are always assigned an oxidation state of +1.

e.g. in LiOH (Li, +1), in Na_2SO_4 (Na, +1).

4. Fluorine in compounds is always assigned an oxidation state of -1.

    e.g. in HF_2^-, BF_2^-.

5. The alkaline earth metals (Be, Mg, Ca, Sr, Ba, and Ra) and also Zn and Cd in compounds are always assigned an oxidation state of +2. Similarly, Al & Ga are always +3.

    e.g. in $CaSO_4$ (Ca, +2), $AlCl_3$ (Al, +3).

6. Hydrogen in compounds is assigned an oxidation state of +1. Exception - Hydrides, e.g. LiH (H=-1).

    e.g. in H_2SO_4 (H, +1).

7. Oxygen in compounds is assigned an oxidation state of -2. Exception - Peroxide, e.g. H_2O_2 (O = -1).

    e.g. in H_3PO_4 (O, -2).

8. The sum of the oxidation states of all the atoms in a species must be equal to net charge on the species.

    e.g. Net Charge of $HClO_4$ = 0, i.e. [+1(H)+7(Cl)-2*4(O)] = 0

Net Charge of CrO_4^{2-} = -2,

To solve Cr's oxidation state: x - 4*2(O) = -2, x = +6, so the oxidation state of Cr is +6.

For example, the reaction

$$H_2 + F_2 \rightarrow 2HF$$

is a redox process because the oxidation numbers of atoms are altered. The oxidation numbers of elements are always zero, and oxidation numbers in a compound are never zero. Fluorine is the more electronegative element, so in HF it has an oxidation number of –1 and hydrogen has an oxidation number of +1. This is a redox process where electrons are transferred from H_2 to F_2 to create HF.

In the reaction

$$HCl + NaOH \rightarrow NaCl + H_2O,$$

the H-atoms on both sides of the reaction have an oxidation number of +1, the atom of Cl has an oxidation number of –1, the Na-atom has an oxidation number of +1, and the atom of O has an oxidation number of –2. **This is not a redox process because oxidation numbers remain unchanged** by the reaction.

When electrons are being transferred, there is a flow of electrons from the anode to the cathode. This flow of electrons is electricity. When electrons are flowing spontaneously, the cell potential is positive. This cell potential is calculated from the standard reduction potentials of each half reaction occurring in the electrochemical cell.

A **standard cell potential,** E°_{cell}, is the voltage generated by an electrochemical cell at **100 kPa and 25 °C** when all components of the reaction are pure materials or solutes at a **concentration of 1 M**. Older textbooks may use 1 atm instead of 100 kPa. Standard solute concentrations may differ from 1 M for solutions that behave in a non-ideal way, but this difference is beyond the scope of general high school chemistry.

Standard cell potentials are calculated from the **sum of the two half-reaction potentials** for the reduction and oxidation reactions occurring in the cell:

$$E^\circ_{cell} = E^\circ_{red}(\text{cathode}) + E^\circ_{ox}(\text{anode})$$

All half-reaction potentials are relative to the reduction of H^+ to form H_2. This potential is assigned a value of zero:

$$\text{For } 2H^+(aq \text{ at } 1\text{ M}) + 2e^- \to H_2(g \text{ at } 100\text{ kPa}), \quad E^\circ_{red} = 0\text{ V}.$$

The standard potential of an oxidation half-reaction E°_{ox} **is equal in magnitude but has the opposite sign to the potential of the reverse reduction reaction**. Standard half-cell potentials are **tabulated as reduction potentials**. These are sometimes referred to as **standard electrode potentials** E°. Therefore,

$$E^\circ_{cell} = E^\circ(\text{cathode}) - E^\circ(\text{anode}).$$

Example: Given E°=0.34 V for $Cu^{2+}(aq)+2e^- \to Cu(s)$ and
E°= –0.76 V for $Zn^{2+}(aq)+2e^- \to Zn(s)$, what is the standard cell potential of the $Zn(s) + Cu^{2+}(aq) \to Zn^{2+}(aq) + Cu(s)$ system ?

Solution:
$$E^\circ_{cell} = E^\circ(\text{cathode}) - E^\circ(\text{anode})$$
$$= E^\circ\left(Cu^{2+}(aq) + 2e^- \to Cu(s)\right) - E^\circ\left(Zn^{2+}(aq) + 2e^- \to Zn(s)\right)$$
$$= 0.34\text{ V} - (-0.76\text{ V}) = 1.10\text{ V}.$$

Spontaneity

When the value of E° is positive, the reaction is spontaneous. If the E° value is negative, an outside energy source is necessary for the reaction to occur. In the above example, the E° is a positive 1.10 V, therefore this reaction is spontaneous.

Skill 27.2 Demonstrate an understanding of electrolysis reactions.

Electrolytic cells use electricity to force nonspontaneous redox reactions to occur while **electrochemical cells generate electricity** by permitting spontaneous redox reactions to occur. The two types of cells have some components in common.

Both systems contain two **electrodes**. An electrode is a piece of conducting metal that is used to make contact with a nonmetallic material. One electrode is an **anode**. An **oxidation reaction occurs at the anode**, so electrons are removed from a substance there. The other electrode is a **cathode**. A **reduction reaction occurs at the cathode**, so electrons are added to a substance there. Electrons flow from anode to cathode outside either device.

Electrolytic systems
Electrolysis is a chemical process **driven by a battery** or another source of electromotive force. This source pulls electrons out of the chemical process at the anode and forces electrons in the cathode. The result is a **negatively charged cathode and a positively charged anode**.

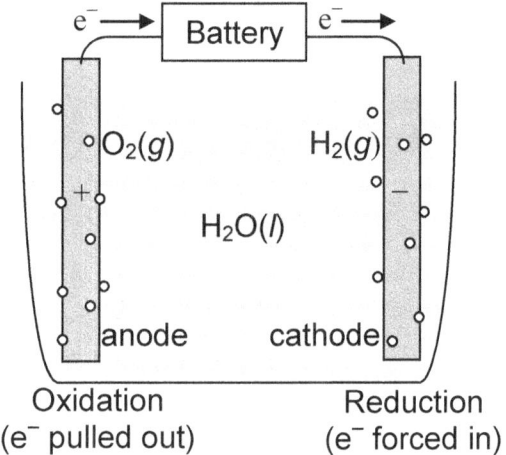

Electrolysis of pure water forms O_2 bubbles at the anode by the oxidation half-reaction:
$$2H_2O(l) \rightarrow 4H^+(aq) + O_2(g) + 4e^-$$
and forms H_2 bubbles at the cathode by the reduction half-reaction:
$$2H_2O(l) + 2e^- \rightarrow H_2(g) + 2OH^-(aq).$$
The net redox reaction is:
$$2H_2O(l) \rightarrow 2H_2(g) + O_2(g).$$

Neither electrode took part in the reaction described above. An electrode that is only used to contact the reaction and deliver or remove electrons is called an **inert electrode**. An electrode that takes part in the reaction is called an **active electrode**.

Electroplating is the process of **depositing dissolved metal cations** in a smooth even coat onto an object used as an active electrode. Electroplating is used to protect metal surfaces or for decoration. For example, to electroplate a copper surface with nickel, a nickel rod is used for the anode and the copper object is used for the cathode. $NiCl_2(aq)$ or another substance with free nickel ions is used in the electrolytic cell. $Ni(s) \rightarrow Ni^{2+}(aq) + 2e^-$ occurs at the anode and $Ni^{2+}(aq) + 2e^- \xrightarrow{\text{onto Cu}} Ni(s)$ occurs at the cathode.

Skill 27.3   Balance redox reactions.

An **oxidizing agent** (also called an oxidant or oxidizer) has the ability to oxidize other substances by removing electrons from them. The **oxidizing agent is reduced** in the process. A **reducing agent** (also called a reductive agent, reductant or reducer) is a substance that has the ability to reduce other substances by transferring electrons to them. The **reducing agent is oxidized** in the process.

Redox reactions may always be written as **two half-reactions**, a **reduction half-reaction** with **electrons as a reactant** and an **oxidation half-reaction** with **electrons as a product**.

For example, the redox reactions considered in the previous skill:
$$Zn(s) + Cu^{2+}(aq) \rightarrow Zn^{2+}(aq) + Cu(s) \quad \text{and} \quad H_2 + F_2 \rightarrow 2HF$$
may be written in terms of the half-reactions:
$$2e^- + Cu^{2+}(aq) \rightarrow Cu(s) \qquad 2e^- + F_2 \rightarrow 2F^-$$
$$Zn(s) \rightarrow Zn^{2+}(aq) + 2e^-. \quad \text{and} \quad H_2 \rightarrow 2H^+ + 2e^-.$$
An additional (non-redox) reaction, $2F^- + 2H^+ \rightarrow 2HF$, achieves the final products for the second reaction.

Determining whether a chemical equation is balanced requires an additional step for redox reactions because there must be a **charge balance.** For example, the equation:
$$Sn^{2+} + Fe^{3+} \rightarrow Sn^{4+} + Fe^{2+}$$
contains one Sn and one Fe on each side but it is not balanced because the sum of charges on the left side of the equation is +5 and the sum on the right side is +6. One electron is gained in the reduction half-reaction ($Fe^{3+} + e^- \rightarrow Fe^{2+}$), but two are lost in the oxidation half-reaction ($Sn^{2+} \rightarrow Sn^{4+} + 2e^-$).

The equation:
$$Sn^{2+} + 2Fe^{3+} \rightarrow Sn^{4+} + 2Fe^{2+}$$
is properly balanced because both sides contain the same sum of charges (+8) and electrons cancel from the half-reactions:
$$2Fe^{3+} + 2e^- \rightarrow 2Fe^{2+}$$
$$Sn^{2+} \rightarrow Sn^{4+} + 2e^-.$$

Oxidation Number Method:

Redox reactions must be balanced to observe the Law of Conservation of Mass. This process is a little more complicated than balancing other reactions because the number of electrons lost must equal the number of electrons gained. Balancing redox reactions, then, conserves not only mass but also charge or electrons. It can be accomplished by slightly varying our balancing process.

$$Cr_2O_3(s) + Al(s) \longrightarrow Cr(s) + Al_2O_3(s)$$

Assign oxidation numbers to identify which atoms are losing and gaining electrons.

$$Cr_2O_3(s) + Al(s) \longrightarrow Cr(s) + Al_2O_3(s)$$
$$\;\;3+\;\;2-\;\;\;\;\;0\;\;\;\;\;\;\;\;\;\;\;0\;\;\;\;\;\;\;3+\;\;2-$$

Identify those atoms gaining and losing electrons:

$Cr^{3+} \longrightarrow Cr^0$ gained 3 electrons : reduction

$Al^0 \longrightarrow Al^{3+}$ lost 3 electrons: oxidation

Balance the atoms and electrons:

$$Cr_2O_3(s) \longrightarrow 2Cr(s) + 6\text{ electrons}$$
$$2Al(s) + 6\text{ electrons} \longrightarrow Al_2O_3(s)$$

Balance the half reactions by adding missing elements. Ignore elements whose oxidation number does not change. Add H_2O for oxygen and H^+ for hydrogen.

$$Cr_2O_3(s) \longrightarrow 2Cr(s) + 6\text{ electrons} + \mathbf{3\;H_2O}$$

Need 3 oxygen atoms on product side. This requires $6H^+$ on the reactant side.

$$Cr_2O_3(s) + \mathbf{6\;H^+} \longrightarrow 2Cr(s) + 6\text{ electrons} + \mathbf{3\;H_2O}$$

AND

$$2Al(s) + 6\text{ electrons} + 3\;H_2O \longrightarrow Al_2O_3(s) + 6\;H^+$$

Need 3 oxygen atoms on reactant side. This requires $6H^+$ on the product side.

Put the two half reactions together and add the species. Cancel out the species that occur in both the reactants and products.

$Cr_2O_3(s) + 6\;H^+ + 2Al(s) + 6\text{ electrons} + 3\;H_2O \longrightarrow 2Cr(s) + 6\text{ electrons} + 3\;H_2O + Al_2O_3(s) + 6\;H^+$

The balanced equation is:

$$Cr_2O_3(s) + 2Al(s) \longrightarrow 2Cr(s) + Al_2O_3(s)$$

Try another: $AgNO_3 + Cu \longrightarrow CuNO_3 + Ag$

Assign oxidation numbers to identify which atoms are losing and gaining electrons.

$$AgNO_3 + Cu \longrightarrow Cu(NO_3)_2 + Ag$$
$$1+ \; 5+ \; 2- \quad 0 \qquad 2+ \; 5+ \; 2- \quad 0$$

Identify those atoms gaining and losing electrons:

$$Ag^{1+} + 1\,e^- \longrightarrow Ag^0 \quad \text{1 electron gained: reduction}$$
$$Cu^0 \longrightarrow Cu^{2+} + 2\,e^- \quad \text{2 electrons lost: oxidation}$$

Balance the atoms and electrons:

$$AgNO_3 + 1\,e^- \longrightarrow Ag^0$$
$$Cu^0 \longrightarrow Cu(NO_3)_2 + 2\,e^-$$
$$Cu^0 \longrightarrow Cu^{2+} + 2\,e^-$$

Balance the electrons:

$$AgNO_3 + 1\,e^- \longrightarrow Ag^0$$
$$Cu^0 \longrightarrow Cu(NO_3)_2 + 2\,e^-$$

1 electron gained and 2 electrons lost. Needs to be equal so 2 electrons need to be gained.

$$2\,[Ag + 1\,e^- \longrightarrow Ag^0] = \mathbf{2\,AgNO_3 + 2\,e^- \longrightarrow 2\,Ag^{0+}}$$

Reduction: $2\,AgNO_3 + 2\,e^- \longrightarrow 2\,Ag^{0+}$

Oxidation: $Cu^0 \longrightarrow Cu(NO_3)_2 + 2\,e^-$

Balance the half reactions by adding missing elements. Ignore elements whose oxidation number does not change. Add H_2O for oxygen and H^+ for hydrogen

$$2\,AgNO_3 + 2\,e^- \longrightarrow 2\,Ag^{0+} \; \mathbf{+ \; 2\,NO_3}$$
$$\mathbf{2NO_3} + \; Cu^0 \longrightarrow Cu(NO_3)_2 + 2\,e^-$$

Put the two half reactions together and add the species. Cancel out the species that occur in both the reactants and products.

Reduction: $2\,AgNO_3 + 2\,e^- \longrightarrow 2\,Ag^{0+} + 2\,NO_3$

Oxidation: $2NO_3 + Cu^0 \longrightarrow Cu(NO_3)_2 + 2\,e^-$

The balanced reaction is:

$2\,AgNO_3 + Cu \longrightarrow Cu(NO_3)_2 + 2\,Ag$

Try this one: $Ag_2S + HNO_3 \longrightarrow AgNO_3 + NO + S + H_2O$

Assign oxidation numbers:

$$Ag_2S + HNO_3 \longrightarrow AgNO_3 + NO + S + H_2O$$
$$\text{1+ 2-} \quad \text{1+ 5+ 2-} \quad \text{1+ 5+ 2-} \quad \text{2+ 2-} \quad 0 \quad \text{1+ 2-}$$

Identify those atoms gaining and losing electrons:

oxidation: $S^{2-} \longrightarrow S^0 + 2e^-$

reduction: $N^{5+} + 3e^- \longrightarrow N^{2+}$

3. Balance the atoms:

Oxidation: $2NO_3 + Ag_2S \longrightarrow S + 2e^- + 2AgNO_3$

Reduction: $3H^+ + HNO_3 + 3e^- \longrightarrow NO + 2H_2O$

Balance electrons lost and gained:

    2 electrons lost and 3 electron gained. Need to be equal so find multiple: 6

Oxidation: $3[\ 2NO_3 + Ag_2S \longrightarrow S + 2e^- + 2AgNO_3]$

$6NO_3 + 3Ag_2S \longrightarrow 3S + 6e^- + 6AgNO_3$

Reduction: $2[\ 3H^+ + HNO_3 + 3e^- \longrightarrow NO + 2H_2O]$

$6H^+ + 2HNO_3 + 6e^- \longrightarrow 2NO + 4H_2O$

5. Put the two half reactions together and add the species. Cancel out the species that occur in both the reactants and products.

$6NO_3 + 3Ag_2S + 6H^+ + 2HNO_3 + 6e^- \longrightarrow 3S + 6e^- + 6AgNO_3 + 2NO + 4H_2O$

The balanced equation is:

$$3 Ag_2S + 8 HNO_3 \longrightarrow 6 AgNO_3 + 2 NO + 3 S + 4 H_2O$$

To balance a redox reaction which occurs in basic solution is a very similar to balancing a redox reaction which occurs in acidic conditions. First, balance the reaction as you would for an acidic solution and then adjust for the basic solution. Here is an example using the half-reaction method:

Solid chromium(III) hydroxide, $Cr(OH)_3$, reacts with aqueous chlorate ions, ClO_3^-, in basic conditions to form chromate ions, CrO_4^{2-}, and chloride ions, Cl^-.

$$Cr(OH)_3(s) + ClO_3^-(aq) \rightarrow CrO_4^{2-}(aq) + Cl^-(aq) \quad \text{(basic)}$$

1. Write the half-reactions:

    $$Cr(OH)_3(s) \rightarrow CrO_4^{2-}(aq) \text{ and}$$
    $$ClO_3^-(aq) \rightarrow Cl^-(aq)$$

2. Balance the atoms in each half-reaction. Use H_2O to add oxygen atoms and H^+ to add hydrogen atoms.

    $$H_2O(l) + Cr(OH)_3(s) \rightarrow CrO_4^{2-}(aq) + 5 H^+(aq)$$

    $$6H^+(aq) + ClO_3^-(aq) \rightarrow Cl^-(aq) + 3 H_2O(l)$$

3. Balance the charges of both half-reactions by adding electrons.

$H_2O\ (l) + Cr(OH)_3(s) \rightarrow CrO_4^{2-}(aq) + 5\ H^+\ (aq)$

has a charge of +3 on the right and 0 on the left. Adding 3 electrons to the right side will give that side a 0 charge as well.

$H_2O\ (l) + Cr(OH)_3(s) \rightarrow CrO_4^{2-}(aq) + 5\ H^+\ (aq) + 3e^-$

$6H^+\ (aq) + ClO_3^-(aq) \rightarrow Cl^-(aq) + 3\ H_2O\ (l)$

has a charge of -1 on the right side and a +5 on the left. Six electrons need to be added to the left side to equal the -1 charge on the right side.

$6\ e^- + 6H^+\ (aq) + ClO_3^-(aq) \rightarrow Cl^-(aq) + 3\ H_2O\ (l)$

4. The number of electrons lost must equal the number of electrons gained so multiply each half-reactions by a number that will give equal numbers of electrons lost and gained.

$H_2O\ (l) + Cr(OH)_3(s) \rightarrow CrO_4^{2-}(aq) + 5\ H^+\ (aq) + 3e^-$
$6\ e^- + 6H^+\ (aq) + ClO_3^-(aq) \rightarrow Cl^-(aq) + 3\ H_2O\ (l)$

The first half reaction needs to be multiplied by 2 to equal the 6 electrons gained in the second half-reaction.

$2[H_2O\ (l) + Cr(OH)_3(s) \rightarrow CrO_4^{2-}(aq) + 5\ H^+\ (aq) + 3e^-] =$
$2H_2O\ (l) + 2\ Cr(OH)_3(s) \rightarrow 2\ CrO_4^{2-}(aq) + 10\ H^+\ (aq) + 6e^-$

5. Add the two half-reactions together; canceling out species that appear on both sides of the reaction.

$2H_2O + 2\ Cr(OH)_3(s) + 6e^- + 6H^+\ (aq) + ClO_3^-(aq) \rightarrow 2\ CrO_4^{2-}(aq) + 10\ H^+\ (aq) + 6e^- + Cl^-(aq) + 3H_2O$

$\downarrow \qquad\qquad\qquad\qquad \downarrow$

$4\ H^+\ (aq) \qquad\qquad 1\ H_2O\ (l)$

6. Since the reaction occurs in basic solution and there are 4 H⁺ ions on the right side, 4 OH⁻ need to be added to both sides. Combine the H⁺ and OH⁻ where appropriate to make water molecules.

$$4\ OH^-(aq) + 2\ Cr(OH)_3(s) + ClO_3^-(aq) \rightarrow 2\ CrO_4^{2-}(aq) + 4\ H^+(aq) + Cl^-(aq) + 1H_2O(l) + 4\ OH^-(aq)$$

$$4\ H_2O\ (l)$$

7. Write final balanced equation:

$$4\ OH^-(aq) + 2\ Cr(OH)_3(s) + ClO_3^-(aq) \rightarrow 2\ CrO_4^{2-}(aq) + Cl^-(aq) + 5\ H_2O\ (l)$$

57 videos of redox experiments are presented here:
http://chemmovies.unl.edu/chemistry/redoxlp/redox000.html.

Skill 27.4 Demonstrate knowledge of devising and building electrochemical cells.

An **electrochemical cell** separates the half-reactions of a redox process into two compartments or half-cells. Electrochemical cells are also called *galvanic cells* or *voltaic cells*.

A **battery** consists of one or more electrochemical cells connected together. Electron transfer from the oxidation to the reduction reaction may only take place through an external circuit.

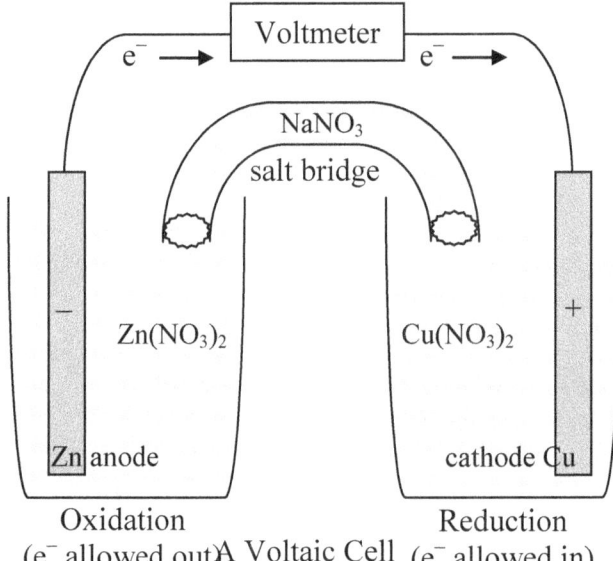

A Voltaic Cell

Oxidation (e⁻ allowed out)   Reduction (e⁻ allowed in)

Electrochemical systems provide a **source of electromotive force**.
This force is also called or *voltage* or *cell potential* and is measured in **volts**. Electrons are allowed to leave the chemical process at the anode and permitted to enter at the cathode. The result is a **negatively charged anode and a positively charged cathode**.

Electrical neutrality is maintained in the half-cells by **ions migrating** through a **salt bridge**. A salt bridge in the simplest cells is an inverted U-tube filled with a non-reacting electrolyte and plugged at both ends with a material like cotton or glass wool that permits ion migration but prevents the electrolyte from falling out.

The spontaneous redox reaction $Zn(s) + Cu^{2+}(aq) \rightarrow Zn^{2+}(aq) + Cu(s)$ generates a voltage in the cell above. The oxidation half-reaction $Zn(s) \rightarrow Zn^{2+}(aq) + 2e^-$ occurs at the anode. Electrons are allowed to flow through a voltmeter before they are consumed by the reduction half-reaction $Cu^{2+}(aq) + 2e^- \rightarrow Cu(s)$ at the cathode. Zinc dissolves away from the anode into solution, and copper from the solution builds up onto the cathode.

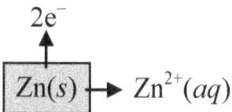

To maintain electrical neutrality in both compartments, positive ions (Zn^{2+} and Na^+) migrate through the salt bridge from the anode half-cell to the cathode half-cell and negative ions (NO_3^-) migrate in the opposite direction.

An animation of the cell described above is located at http://www.mhhe.com/physsci/chemistry/essentialchemistry/flash/galvan5.swf. A summary of anode and cathode properties for both cell types is contained in the table below.

		Electrolytic cell	Electrochemical cell
Anode	Half-reaction	Oxidation	Oxidation
	Electron flow	Pulled out	Allowed out
	Electrode polarity	+	−
Cathode	Half-reaction	Reduction	Reduction
	Electron flow	Forced in	Allowed in
	Electrode polarity	−	+

The reducing and oxidizing agents in a standard electrochemical cell are depleted with time. In a **rechargeable battery** (e.g., lead storage batteries in cars) the direction of the spontaneous redox reaction is reversed and **reactants are regenerated** when electrical energy is added into the system. A **fuel cell** has the same components as a standard electrochemical cell except that **reactants are continuously supplied**.

COMPETENCY 28.0 UNDERSTAND AND APPLY KNOWLEDGE OF THE MECHANISMS OF CHEMICAL REACTIONS AND THE THEORY AND PRACTICAL APPLICATIONS OF REACTION RATES.

Skill 28.1 Recognize the basics of collision and transition-state theories and the significance of the Arrhenius equation.

The Arrhenius equation is a formula that **relates temperature to the rate constant of a chemical reaction**. Developed in 1884 by JH van't Hoff and physically verified by Svante Arrhenius, this important equation is both simple and accurate for many reactions. It is:

$$k = Ae^{\frac{-E_a}{RT}}$$

where
k = the reaction rate constant
E_a = activation energy
T = absolute temperature
R = the gas constant
A = the frequency factor (a constant specific to a given reaction)

The implication of this equation is that **the rate of a reaction can be increased by increasing the temperature or by decreasing the activation energy** (as is done by a catalyst).

The Arrhenius equation is also very important in experimental chemical kinetics. To see why, we must take the natural log of the equation:

$$\ln(k) = \frac{-E_a}{R}\frac{1}{T} + \ln(A)$$

This means that a plot of ln(k) versus 1/T will yield a straight line and its slope and intercept allow the calculation of E_a and A. This **allows chemists to determine the activation energy of any chemical reaction** that obeys the Arrhenius equation.

In order for one species to be converted to another during a chemical reaction, the reactants must collide. The collisions between the reactants determine how fast the reaction takes place. However, during a chemical reaction, only a fraction of the collisions between the appropriate reactant molecules convert them into product molecules. This occurs for two reasons:

1) Not all collisions occur with a **sufficiently high energy** for the reaction to occur.
2) Not all collisions **orient the molecules properly** for the reaction to occur.

The **activation energy**, E_a, of a reaction is the **minimum energy to overcome the barrier to the formation of products**. This is the minimum energy needed for the reaction to occur.

At the scale of individual molecules, a reaction typically involves a very small period of time when old bonds are broken and new bonds are formed. During this time, the molecules involved are in a **transition state** between reactants and products. A threshold of maximum energy is crossed when the arrangement of molecules is in an unfavorable intermediate between reactants and products known as the **activated complex**. Formulas and diagrams of activated complexes are often written within brackets to indicate they are transition states that are present for extremely small periods of time.

The activation energy, E_a, is the difference between the energy of reactants and the energy of the activated complex. The energy change during the reaction, ΔE, is the difference between the energy of the products and the energy of the reactants. The activation energy of the reverse reaction is $E_a - \Delta E$. These energy levels are represented in an **energy diagram** such as the one shown below for $NO_2 + CO \rightleftharpoons NO + CO_2$. This is an exothermic reaction because products are lower in energy than reactants.

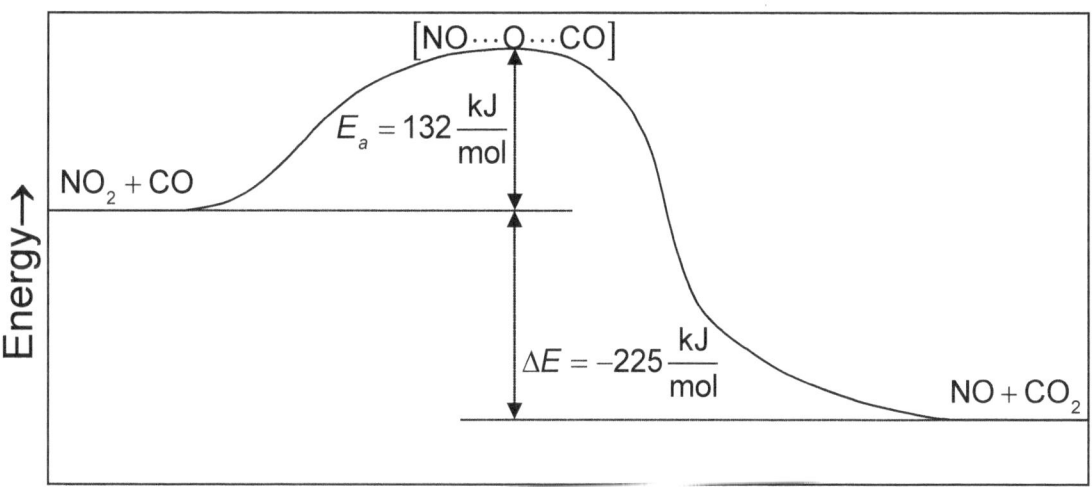

Reaction pathway→

An energy diagram is a conceptual tool, so there is some variability in how its axes are labeled. The y-axis of the diagram is usually labeled energy (E), but it is sometimes labeled "enthalpy (H)" or (rarely) "free energy (G)." There is an even greater variability in how the x-axis is labeled. The terms "reaction pathway," "reaction coordinate," "course of reaction," or "reaction progress" may be used on the x-axis, or the x-axis may remain without a label.

The energy diagrams of an endothermic and exothermic reaction (See **Skill 2.1**) are compared below.

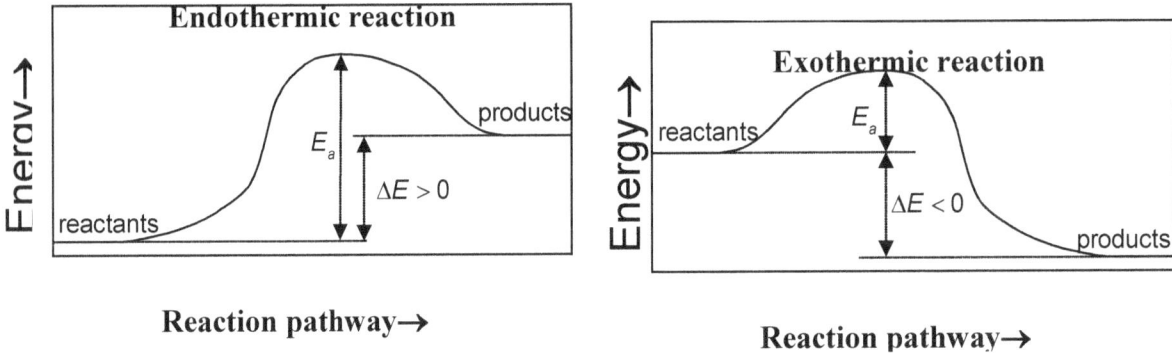

Skill 28.2 Explain how various factors (e.g., temperature, catalysts) influence reaction rates.

The rate of most simple reactions **increases with temperature** because a **greater fraction of molecules have the kinetic energy** required to overcome the reaction's activation energy. The chart below shows the effect of temperature on the distribution of kinetic energies in a sample of molecules. These curves are called **Maxwell-Boltzmann distributions**. The shaded areas represent the fraction of molecules containing sufficient kinetic energy for a reaction to occur. This area is larger at a higher temperature; so more molecules are above the activation energy and more molecules react per second.

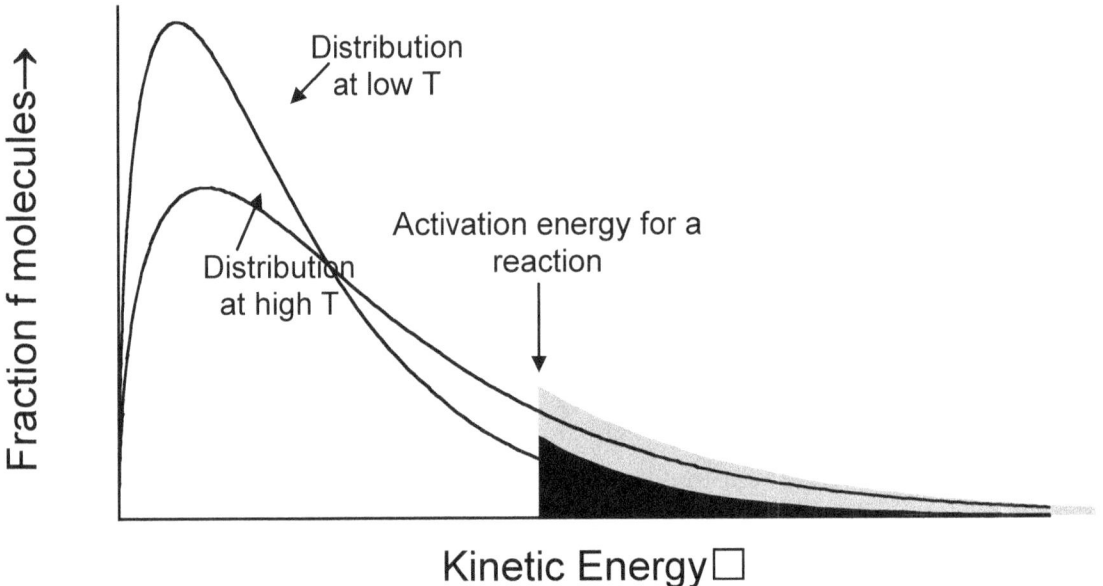

http://www.mhhe.com/physsci/chemistry/essentialchemistry/flash/activa2.swf provides an animated audio tutorial on energy diagrams.

Kinetic molecular theory may be applied to reaction rates in addition to physical constants like pressure. **Reaction rates increase with reactant concentration** because more reactant molecules are present and more are likely to collide with one another in a certain volume at higher concentrations. The nature of these relationships determines the rate law for the reaction. For ideal gases, the concentration of a reactant is its molar density, and this varies with pressure and temperature as discussed in.

Kinetic molecular theory also predicts that **reaction rate constants (values for k) increase with temperature** because of two reasons:
1) More reactant molecules will collide with each other per second.
2) These collisions will each occur at a higher energy that is more likely to overcome the activation energy of the reaction.

A **catalyst** is a material that increases the rate of a chemical reactionwithout changing itself permanently in the process. Catalysts provide an alternate reaction mechanism for the reaction to proceed in the forward and in the reverse direction. Therefore, **catalysts have no impact on the chemical equilibrium** of a reaction. They will not make a less favorable reaction more favorable.

Catalysts reduce the activation energy of a reaction. This is the amount of energy needed for the reaction to begin. Molecules with such low energies that they would have taken a long time to react will react more rapidly if a catalyst is present.

The impact of a catalyst may also be represented on an energy diagram. **A catalyst increases the rate of both the forward and reverse reactions by lowering the activation energy** for the reaction. Catalysts provide a different activated complex for the reaction at a lower energy state.

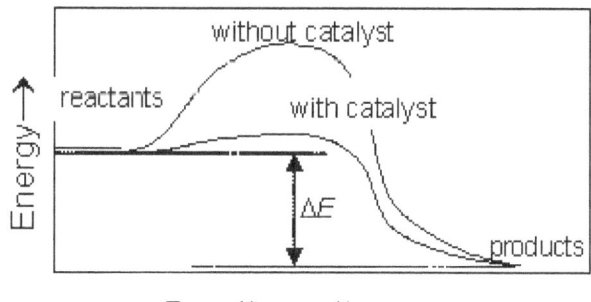

There are two types of catalysts: **Homogeneous catalysts** are in the same physical phase as the reactants. Biological catalysts are called **enzymes**, and most are homogeneous catalysts. A typical homogenous catalytic reaction mechanism involves an initial reaction with one reactant followed by a reaction with a second reactant and release of the catalyst:

$$A + C \rightarrow AC$$
$$B + AC \rightarrow AB + C$$
$$\text{Net reaction: } A + B \xrightarrow{\text{catalyst C}} AB$$

Heterogeneous catalysts are present in a different physical state from the reactants. A typical heterogeneous catalytic reaction involves a solid surface onto which molecules in a fluid phase temporarily attach themselves in such a way to favor a rapid reaction. Catalytic converters in cars utilize heterogeneous catalysis to break down harmful chemicals in exhaust.

Skill 28.3   Analyze experimental data involving reaction rates, concentration, and/or time to determine kinetic parameters (e.g., reaction order, rate constants, activation energy).

Obtaining reaction rates from concentration data
The rate of any process is measured by its change per unit time. The speed of a car is measured by its change in position with time using units of miles per hour. The speed of a chemical reaction is usually measured by a change in the concentration of a reactant or product with time using units of **molarity per second** (M/s). The molarity of a chemical is represented in mathematical equations using brackets.

The **average reaction rate** is the change in concentration either reactant or product per unit time during a time interval:

$$\text{Average reaction rate} = \frac{\text{Change in concentration}}{\text{Change in time}}$$

Reaction rates are positive quantities. Product concentrations increase and reactant concentrations decrease with time, so a different formula is required depending on the identity of the component of interest:

$$\text{Average reaction rate} = \frac{[\text{product}]_{final} - [\text{product}]_{initial}}{\text{time}_{final} - \text{time}_{initial}}$$

$$= \frac{[\text{reactant}]_{initial} - [\text{reactant}]_{final}}{\text{time}_{final} - \text{time}_{initial}}$$

The **reaction rate** at a given time refers to the **instantaneous reaction rate**. This is found from the absolute value of the **slope of a curve of concentration vs. time**. An estimate of the reaction rate at time *t* may be found from the average reaction rate over a small time interval surrounding *t*. For those familiar with calculus notation, the following equations define reaction rate, but calculus is not needed for this skill:

Reaction rate at time $t = \dfrac{d[\text{product}]}{dt} = -\dfrac{d[\text{reactant}]}{dt}$.

Example: The following concentration data describes the decomposition of N_2O_5 according to the reaction $2N_2O_5 \rightarrow 4NO_2 + O_2$:

Time (sec)	[N₂O₅] (M)
0	0.0200
1000	0.0120
2000	0.0074
3000	0.0046
4000	0.0029
5000	0.0018
7500	0.0006
10000	0.0002

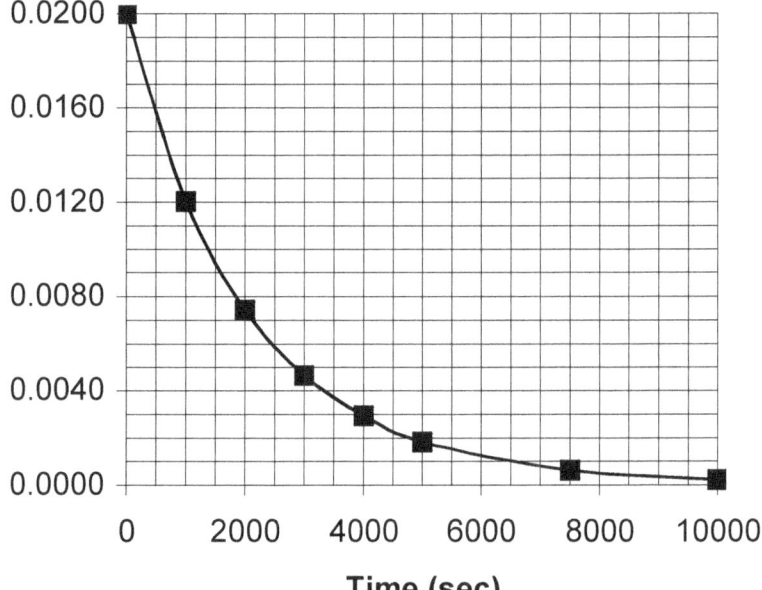

Determine the average reaction rate from 1000 to 5000 seconds and the instantaneous reaction rate at 0 and at 4000 seconds.

Solution: Average reaction rate from 0 to 7500 seconds is found from:

$$\dfrac{[\text{reactant}]_{\text{initial}} - [\text{reactant}]_{\text{final}}}{\text{time}_{\text{final}} - \text{time}_{\text{initial}}} = \dfrac{0.0120\ M - 0.0018\ M}{5000\ \text{sec} - 1000\ \text{sec}} = 2.55 \times 10^{-6}\ \dfrac{M}{s}.$$

Instantaneous reaction rates are found by drawing lines tangent to the curve, finding the slopes of these lines, and forcing these slopes to be positive values.

At 0 seconds:
$$\text{rate} = \text{slope} = \frac{0.0200 \text{ M}}{2000 \text{ s}}$$
$$= 1.00 \times 10^{-5} \frac{M}{s}.$$

At 4000 seconds:
$$\text{rate} = \text{slope} = \frac{0.0090 \text{ M}}{6000 \text{ s}}$$
$$= 1.5 \times 10^{-6} \frac{M}{s}.$$

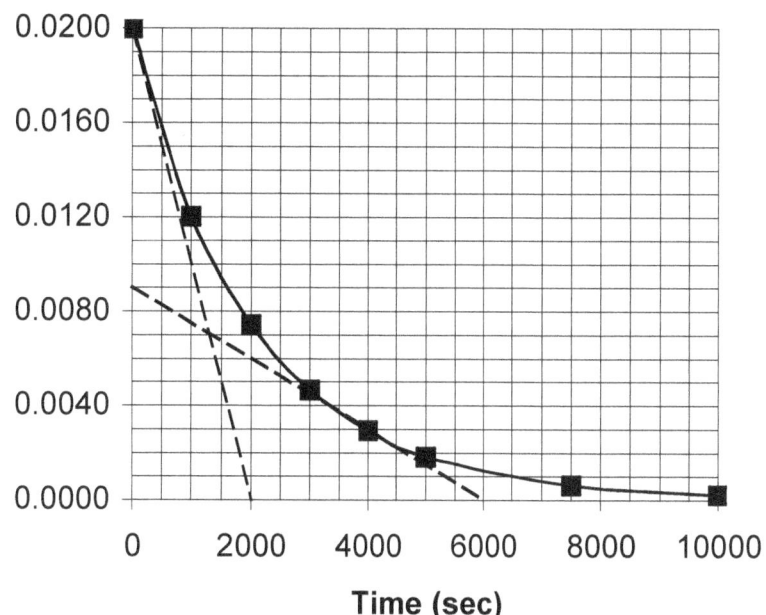

Time (sec)

Deriving rate laws from reaction rates

A **rate law** is an **equation relating a reaction rate to concentration**. The rate laws for most reactions discussed in high-school level chemistry are of the form:

Rate = $k[\text{reactant 1}]^a [\text{reactant 2}]^b \ldots$

In the above general equation, k is called the **rate constant**. a and b are called **reaction orders**. Most reactions considered in introductory chemistry have a reaction order of zero, one, or two. The sum of all reaction orders for a reaction is called the **overall reaction order**. Rate laws cannot be predicted from the stoichiometry of a reaction. They must be determined by experiment or derived from knowledge of reaction mechanism.

If a reaction is zero order for a reactant, the concentration of that reactant has no impact on rate as long as some reactant is present. If a reaction is first order for a reactant, the reaction rate is proportional to the reactant's concentration. For a reaction that is second order with respect to a reactant, doubling that reactant's concentration increases reaction rate by a factor of four. Rate laws are determined by finding the appropriate reaction order describing **the impact of reactant concentration on reaction rate**.

Reaction rates typically have units of M/s (moles/liter-sec) and concentrations have units of M (moles/liter). For units to cancel properly in the expression above, the units found on the rate constant k must vary with overall reaction order as shown in the following table. The value of k may be determined by finding the slope of a plot charting a function of concentration against time. These functions may be memorized or computed using calculus.

Overall reaction order	Units of rate constant k	Method to determine k for rate laws with one reactant
0	M/sec	−(slope) of a chart of [reactant] vs. t
1	sec^{-1}	−(slope) of a chart of ln[reactant] vs. t
2	$M^{-1}\text{sec}^{-1}$	slope of a chart of 1/[reactant] vs. t

As an alternative to using the rate constant k, the course of **first order reactions** may be expressed in terms of a **half-life**, $t_{halflife}$. The half-life of a reaction is the time required for reactant concentration to reach half of its initial value. First order rate constants and half-lives are inversely proportional:

$$t_{halflife} = \frac{\ln 2}{k_{first\ order}} = \frac{0.693}{k_{first\ order}}$$

Example: Derive a rate law for the reaction $2N_2O_5 \rightarrow 4NO_2 + O_2$ using data from the previous example.

Solution: Three methods will be used to solve this problem.

1) In the previous example, we found the following two **instantaneous reaction rates**:

Time (sec)	$[N_2O_5]$ (M)	Reaction rate (M/sec)
0	0.0200	1.00×10^{-5}
4000	0.0029	1.5×10^{-6}

A decrease in reactant concentration to 0.0029/0.0200=14.5% of its initial value led to a nearly proportional decrease in reaction rate to 15% of its initial value. In other words, reaction rate remains proportional to reactant concentration. The reaction is first order:

$$\text{Rate} = k[N_2O_5].$$

We may estimate a value for the rate constant by dividing reaction rates by the concentration:

$$k_{\text{first order}} = \frac{\text{Rate}}{[N_2O_5]}.$$

Time (sec)	$[N_2O_5]$ (M)	Reaction rate (M/sec)	k (sec^{-1})
0	0.0200	1.00×10^{-5}	5.00×10^{-4}
4000	0.0029	1.5×10^{-6}	5.2×10^{-4}

2) We could estimate this rate constant by finding **average reaction rates** in each small time interval and assuming this rate occurs halfway between the two concentrations:

Time (sec)	$[N_2O_5]$ (M)	Average rate (M/sec)	Halfway $[N_2O_5]$ (M)	k (sec^{-1})
0	0.0200			
1000	0.0120	8.00×10^{-6}	0.0160	5.00×10^{-4}
2000	0.0074	4.6×10^{-6}	0.0097	4.7×10^{-4}
3000	0.0046	2.8×10^{-6}	0.0060	4.7×10^{-4}
4000	0.0029	1.7×10^{-6}	0.0038	4.5×10^{-4}
5000	0.0018	1.1×10^{-6}	0.0024	4.7×10^{-4}
7500	0.0006	4.8×10^{-7}	0.0012	4.0×10^{-4}
10000	0.0002	2×10^{-7}	0.0004	4×10^{-4}

3) If **concentration data** are given then no rate data needs to be found to determine a rate constant. For a first order reaction, chart the natural logarithm of concentration against time and find the slope.

Time (sec)	$[N_2O_5]$ (M)	$\ln[N_2O_5]$
0	0.0200	-3.91
1000	0.0120	-4.41
2000	0.0074	-4.90
3000	0.0046	-5.37
4000	0.0029	-5.83
5000	0.0018	-6.30
7500	0.0006	-7.39
10000	0.0002	-8.46

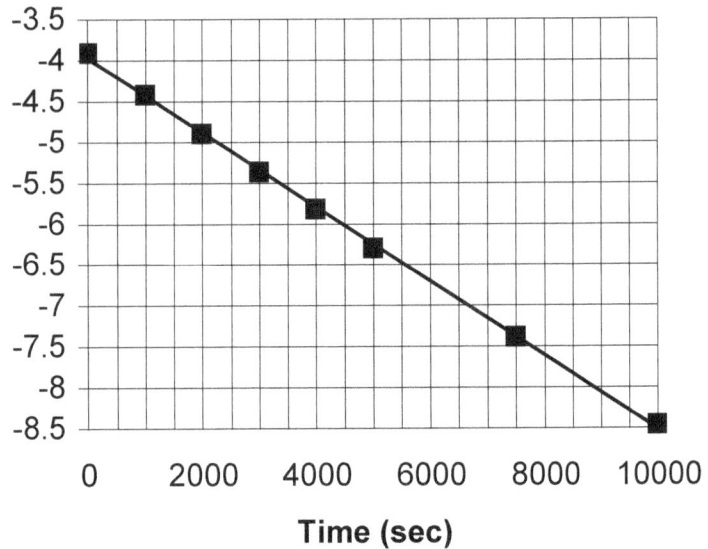

The slope may be determined from a best-fit method or it may be estimated from $\frac{-8.46-(-3.91)}{10000} = -5 \times 10^{-4}$.

The rate law describing this reaction is:

$$\text{Rate} = \left(5 \times 10^{-4} \frac{M}{\text{sec}}\right)[N_2O_5]$$

Sample problem:
Given the following data for a reaction at 25°C.
$$2I^- \text{ (aq)} + S_2O_8^{2-} \text{ (aq)} \rightarrow I_2 \text{ (aq)} + 2\ SO_4^{2-} \text{ (aq)}$$

Experiment	[I⁻] (mol/L)	[S₂O₈] (mol/L)	Initial Rate (mol/L·s)
1	0.080	0.040	12.5 x 10⁻⁶
2	0.040	0.040	6.25 x 10⁻⁶
3	0.080	0.020	6.25 x 10⁻⁶
4	0.032	0.040	5.00 x 10⁻⁶
5	0.060	0.030	7.00 x 10⁻⁶

a. What is the rate law?
b. What is the order of the reaction with respect to I^-, S_2O_8 and overall?
c. What is the value of the rate law constant?

Skill 28.4   Demonstrate an understanding of the relationship of rate laws to reaction mechanisms.

Derive rate laws from simple reaction mechanisms
A **reaction mechanism** is a series of **elementary reactions** that explain how a reaction occurs. These elementary reactions are also called elementary processes or elementary steps. **A reaction mechanism cannot be determined from reaction stoichiometry.** Stoichiometry indicates the number of molecules of reactants and products in an **overall reaction**. Elementary steps represent a **single event.** This might be a collision between two molecules or a single rearrangement of electrons within a molecule.

The simplest reaction mechanisms consist of a single elementary reaction. The number of molecules required determines the rate laws for these processes. For a **unimolecular process:**
$A \rightarrow$ products
the number of molecules of A that decompose in a given time will be proportional to the number of molecules of A present. Therefore unimolecular processes are first order:

$\text{Rate} = k[A]$.

For **bimolecular processes**, the rate law will be second order.

For $A+A \rightarrow$ products, Rate=$k[A]^2$

For $A+B \rightarrow$ products, Rate=$k[A][B]$.

Most reaction mechanisms are multi-step processes involving **reaction intermediates**. Intermediates are chemicals that are formed during one elementary step and consumed during another, but they are not overall reactants or products. In many cases one elementary reaction in particular is the slowest and determines the overall reaction rate. This slowest reaction in the series is called the **rate-limiting step** or rate determining step.

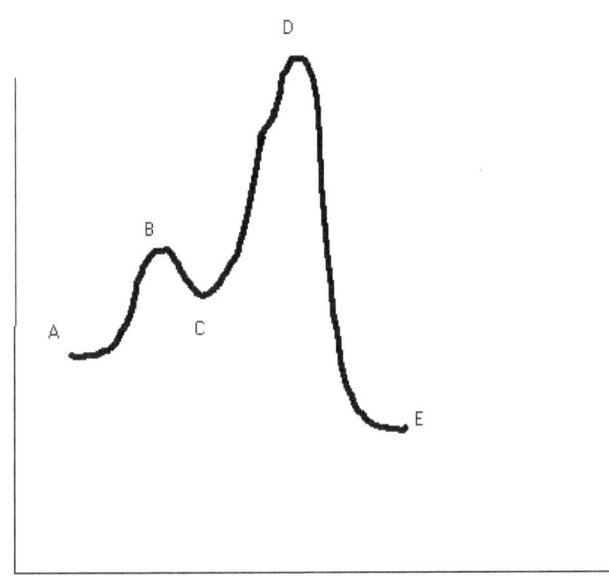

This energy diagram represents a two-step process for the reaction A→E. A is the energy of the reactants while B represents the activation energy for the reaction A→C. C is an intermediate, which when formed is immediately converted into E in the reaction C→E with an activation energy represented by D. Since the reaction C→E has a greater activation energy, it is the slow step, hence the rate determining step.

Example: The reaction $NO_2(g) + CO(g) \rightarrow NO(g) + CO_2(g)$ is composed of the following elementary reactions in the gas phase:

$NO_2 + NO_2 \rightarrow NO + NO_3$

$NO_3 + CO \rightarrow NO_2 + CO_2$.

The first elementary reaction is very slow compared to the second. Determine the rate law for the overall reaction if NO_2 and CO are both present in sufficient quantity for the reaction to occur. Also name all reaction intermediates.

Solution: The first step will be rate limiting because it is slower. In other words, almost as soon as NO_3 is available, it reacts with CO, so the rate-limiting step is the formation of NO_3. The first step is bimolecular. Therefore, the rate law for the entire reaction is: Rate=$k[NO_2]^2$.

NO_3 is formed during the first step and consumed during the second. NO_3 is the only reaction intermediate because it is neither a reactant nor a product of the overall reaction.

COMPETENCY 29.0 UNDERSTAND AND APPLY KNOWLEDGE OF MAJOR ASPECTS OF ORGANIC CHEMISTRY.

Skill 29.1 Identify the functional group classification and nomenclature of organic compounds and the general characteristics and reactions of each group.

Many organic molecules contain functional groups that are groups of atoms of a particular arrangement that gives the entire molecule certain characteristics. Function groups are named according to the composition of the group. The carboxyl group is the arrangement of -COOH atoms to make a molecule exhibit acidic properties.

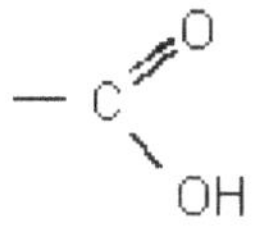

Some functional groups are polar and can ionize. For example, the hydrogen atom in the –COOH group can be removed (providing H^+ ions in solution). When this occurs, the oxygen retains both the electrons it shared with the hydrogen and will give the molecule a negative charge.

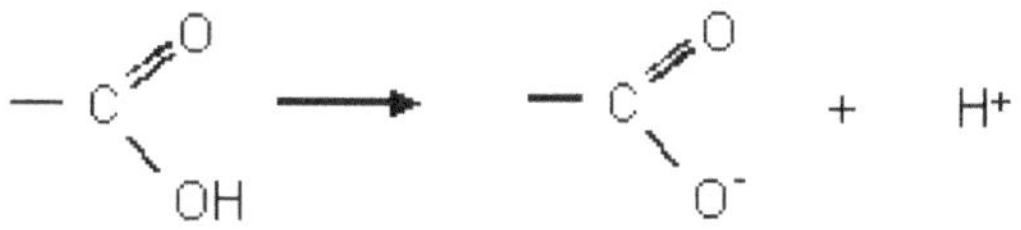

If polar or ionizing functional groups are attached to hydrophobic molecules, the molecule may become hydrophilic due to the functional group. Some ionizing functional groups are: -COOH, -OH, -CO, and $-NH_2$.

Some common functional groups include:

Hydroxyl group:

The hydroxyl group, -OH, is the functional group identifying alcohols. The hydroxyl group makes the molecule polar which increase the solubility of the compound.

Carbonyl group:

The carbonyl group is a -C=O attached to either a carbon chain or a hydrogen atom. It is found in aldehydes and ketones. If the carbon is bonded to a hydrogen, the molecule is an aldehyde.

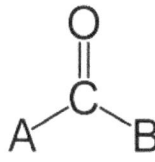

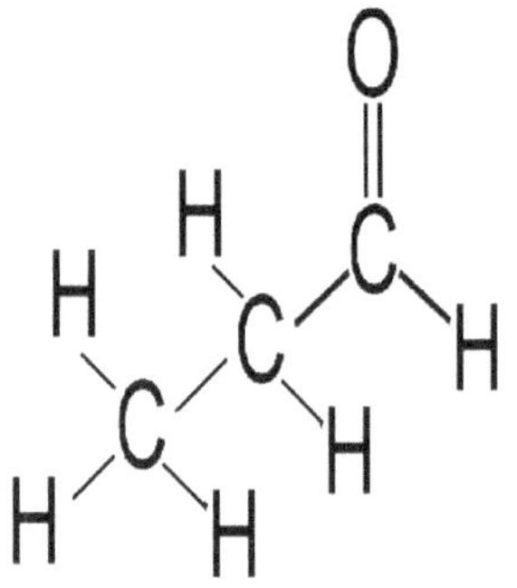

Aldehyde 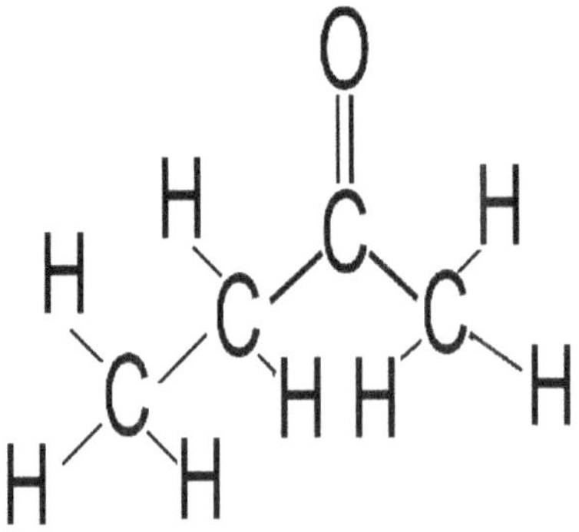   ketone

If the carbon is attached to two carbon chains, the molecule is a ketone.

The double bonded oxygen atom is highly electronegative so it creates a polar molecule and will exhibit properties of polar molecules.

Carboxyl group:

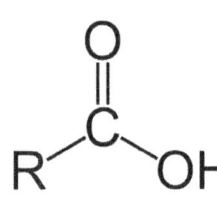

The –COOH group has the ability to donate a proton or H^+ ion giving the molecule acidic properties.

Amino group:

An amino group contains an ammonia-like functional group composed of a nitrogen and two hydrogen atoms covalently bonded. The nitrogen atom has unshared electrons and can add H^+ ions (proton). This gives the molecule basic properties. An organic compound that contains an amino group is called an amine. the amines are weak bases because the unshared electron pair of the nitrogen atom can form a coordinate bond with a proton. Another molecule that contains an amino group is an amino acid. It consists of the $-NH_2$ group of an amine and the –COOH group of an acid.

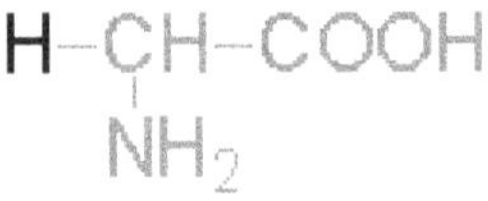

H–CH–COOH   This is the amino acid glycine.
   |
   NH_2

Sulfhydryl group:

R—S—H

A **thiol** is a compound that contains the functional group composed of a sulfur atom and a hydrogen atom (-SH). This functional group is referred to either as a *thiol group* or a *sulfhydryl group*. More traditionally, thiols have been referred to as *mercaptans*.

The small difference in electronegativity between the sulfur and the hydrogen atom produces a non-polar covalent bond. This in turn provides for no hydrogen bonding giving thiols lower boiling points and less solubility in water than alcohols of a similar molecular mass.

Phosphate group:

$$-O-\overset{\overset{O}{\parallel}}{\underset{\underset{O}{|}}{P}}-O$$

The phosphate ion is contained in a hydrocarbon chain making a phosphate group present in the molecule. This molecule is ideal for energy transfer reactions (ATP) because of its symmetry and rotating double bond.

In biological systems, phosphates are most commonly found in the form of adenosine phosphates, (AMP, ADP and ATP) and in DNA and RNA and can be released by the hydrolysis of ATP or ADP.

The IUPAC is the **International Union of Pure and Applied Chemistry**. **Organic compounds contain carbon,** and have their own branch of chemistry because of the huge number of carbon compounds in nature, including nearly all the molecules in living things. The 1979 IUPAC organic nomenclature is used and taught most often today, and it is the nomenclature described here.

The simplest organic compounds are called **hydrocarbons** because they **contain only carbon and hydrogen**. Hydrocarbon molecules may be divided into the classes of **cyclic** and **open-chain** depending on whether they contain a ring of carbon atoms. Open-chain molecules may be divided into **branched** or **straight-chain** categories.

Hydrocarbons are also divided into classes called **aliphatic** and **aromatic**. Aromatic hydrocarbons are related to benzene and are always cyclic. Aliphatic hydrocarbons may be open-chain or cyclic. Aliphatic cyclic hydrocarbons are called **alicyclic**. Aliphatic hydrocarbons are one of three types: alkanes, alkenes, and alkynes.

See also Skill 19.6.

Skill 29.2 **Demonstrate an understanding of the concepts and mechanisms of the substitution, addition, elimination, and other reactions of organic molecules**

Organic reactions can be grouped into basic classes of addition, substitution, elimination, and polymerization along with combustion and oxidation reactions.

An **addition reaction** is a reaction in which two atoms or ions react with a double bond of an alkene, forming a compound with two new functional groups bonded to the carbons of the original double bond. In these reactions, the existing pi bond is broken and in its place, sigma bonds form to two new atoms.

Examples of Simple Addition Reactions

$$C=C + H-Cl \longrightarrow -C-C- \quad \text{hydrochlorination}$$

$$C=C + H_2O \longrightarrow -C-C- \quad \text{hydration}$$

$$C=C + H_2 \longrightarrow -C-C- \quad \text{hydrogenation}$$

The mechanisms for these types of reactions depend on nucleophilicity/electrophilicity of both the alkene and adding group, and the presence of solvent or catalyst. In many cases, the first step of the reaction is the attack of a positively charged proton by the pi electrons, causing a proton transfer across the double bond. This is followed by addition of the nucleophile to the remaining cation.

Mechanism for Electrophilic Addition of HCl to 2-Butene

$$H_3CHC=CHCH_3 + H-Cl: \xrightleftharpoons[]{\text{slow, rate determining}} H_3CHC-\overset{+}{C}HCH_3 + :Cl:^-$$

$$:Cl:^- + H_3CHC-\overset{+}{C}H_2CH_3 \xrightarrow{\text{fast}} H_3CHC(Cl)-CH_2CH_3$$

A **substitution reaction** is a reaction in which an atom or group of atoms is replaced by another atom or group of atoms. The most common types of these reactions are S_N1 and S_N2 reactions.

Examples of Substitution Reactions

$$HO^- + CH_3Br \longrightarrow CH_3OH + :Br:^-$$

(CH$_3$)$_3$CH + Br$_2$ $\longrightarrow$ (CH$_3$)$_3$CBr + HBr

On of the most important types of substitution reaction is a nucleophilic substitution, an S_N2 reaction in which a halide is added to a molecule. These reactions can lead to a variety of new functional groups. The mechanism for these reactions involves the attack of a nucleophile on a central carbon atom. Simultaneously, β-elimination of a leaving group occurs.

Mechanism for Nucleophilic Substitution of OH⁻ to Bromomethane (S_N2 Reaction)

[Diagram: HO⁻ attacks CH₃Br → transition state with bond breaking and forming → HOCH₃ + :Br:⁻]

The mechanism for an S_N1 reaction is a multi-step mechanism, where the leaving group is eliminated in the first step to leave a positively charged carbocation (an electrophile). The cation is then attacked by a nucleophile, followed by the final step of proton transfer to afford a neutral molecule.

An **elimination reaction** is a reaction in which a functional group is split (eliminated) from adjacent carbons. This is a reaction that can often compete with nucleophilic substitution and is highly dependant on the leaving group present in the molecule. Elimination reactions are favored by the presence of strong bases.

SCIENCE: CHEMISTRY

Examples of Elimination Reactions

There are two types of elimination reactions, E1 and E2 reactions. The mechanism for E1 is a multistep reaction that involves the formation of a carbocation intermediate. The E2 mechanism is a series of steps, bond breaking and bond formation, that occurs simultaneously. Similar to the S_N2 case outlined above, both the haloalkane and the base are involved in the transition state.

Mechanism for Elimination of 2-Bromo-2-methylpropane (E1 Reaction)

Examples of Polymerization Reactions

Polymers are substances whose molecules have high molar masses and are composed of a large number of repeating units called monomers. For example, polyethylene is many ethylene molecules put together, much like you would link paper clips together to make a long chain.

$$-[CH_2CH_2CH_2CH_2CH_2CH_2CH_2CH_2]_n$$

Polymers are made from the repeating units through two process. One process simply adds each succeeding monomer onto the chain through various methods, called addition polymerization. Condensation polymerization is the second process of adding monomers onto the chain to make large molecules. In condensation polymerization, small molecules like water are removed as the monomer unit is added onto the chain.

It isn't difficult to form addition polymers from monomers containing C=C double bonds; many of these compounds polymerize spontaneously unless polymerization is actively inhibited.

The simplest way to catalyze the polymerization reaction that leads to an addition polymer is to add a source of a **free radical** to the monomer. The term

Ethylene has two carbon atoms and four hydrogen atoms, and the polyethylene repeat structure has two carbon atoms and four hydrogen atoms. None gained, none lost.

free radical is used to describe a family of very reactive, short-lived components of a reaction that contain one or more unpaired electrons. In the presence of a free radical, addition polymers form by a chain-reaction mechanism that contains chain-initiation, chain-propagation, and chain- termination steps.

Chain Initiation
A source of free radicals is needed to initiate the chain reaction. These free radicals are usually produced by decomposing a peroxide such as di-*tert*-butyl peroxide or benzoyl peroxide, shown below. In the presence of either heat or light, these peroxides decompose to form a pair of free radicals that contain an unpaired electron.

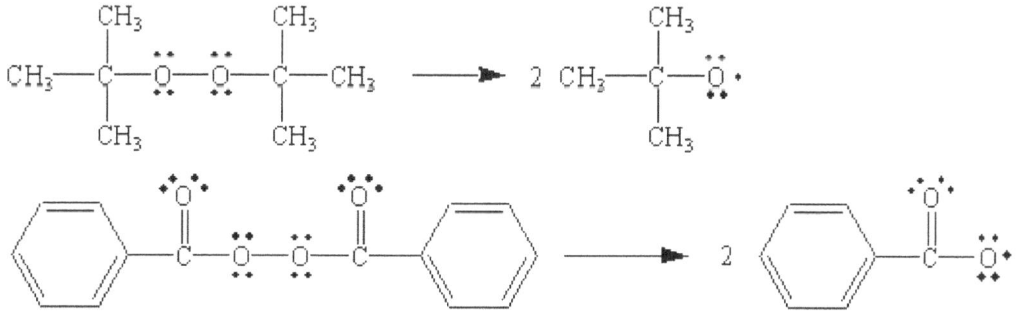

Chain Propagation

The free radical produced in the chain-initiation step adds to an alkene to form a new free radical.

$$(CH_3)_3C-O\cdot + CH_2=CH_2 \longrightarrow (CH_3)_3C-O-CH_2-CH_2\cdot$$

The product of this reaction can then add additional monomers in a chain reaction.

$$(CH_3)_3C-O-CH_2-CH_2\cdot + CH_2=CH_2 \longrightarrow (CH_3)_3C-O-CH_2-CH_2-CH_2-CH_2\cdot$$

Chain Termination

Whenever pairs of radicals combine to form a covalent bond, the chain reactions carried by these radicals are terminated.

$$(CH_3)_3C-O-(CH_2CH_2)_n\cdot + \cdot(CH_2CH_2)_m-O-C(CH_3)_3 \longrightarrow$$

$$(CH_3)_3C-O-(CH_2CH_2)_{n+m}-O-C(CH_3)_3$$

Condensation Polymerization

Monomers involved in condensation polymerization are not like those involved in addition polymerization. These monomers have functional groups like alcohols (-OH), amine ($-NH_2$) or carboxylic acid (-COOH) instead of double bonds. Each monomer also has at least two active sites at which it can bond.

$$Cl-\overset{O}{\underset{\|}{C}}-CH_2-CH_2-CH_2-CH_2-\overset{O}{\underset{\|}{C}}-Cl \quad + \quad \overset{H}{\underset{H}{\diagdown}}N-CH_2-CH_2-CH_2-CH_2-CH_2-CH_2-N\overset{H}{\underset{H}{\diagup}} \longrightarrow$$

This Chlorine atom and this hydrogen atom don't end up in the polymer. They split off to form HCl gas.

$$+\overset{O}{\underset{\|}{C}}-CH_2-CH_2-CH_2-CH_2-\overset{O}{\underset{\|}{C}}-\underset{H}{N}-CH_2-CH_2-CH_2-CH_2-CH_2-CH_2-\underset{H}{N}\underset{n}{]} \quad + \quad HCl$$

When an organic acid and an amine react, a water molecule is removed and an amide forms. This is called an amide linkage because of the amide that forms.

When a and an water removed, molecule is referred to due to the

$$R-\overset{O}{\underset{\|}{C}}-OH + H-\underset{H}{N}-R' \longrightarrow R-\overset{O}{\underset{\|}{C}}-\underset{H}{N}-R' + H_2O$$
Carboxylic acid Amine Amide Water

$$R-\overset{O}{\underset{\|}{C}}-OH + H-OR'' \longrightarrow R-\overset{O}{\underset{\|}{C}}-OR'' + H_2O$$
Carboxylic acid Alcohol Ester Water

carboxylic acid alcohol react, a molecule is and an ester formed. This is as an ester linkage ester that forms.

Mechanism for the formation of polyester

A carboxylic acid monomer and an alcohol monomer can join in an ester linkage.

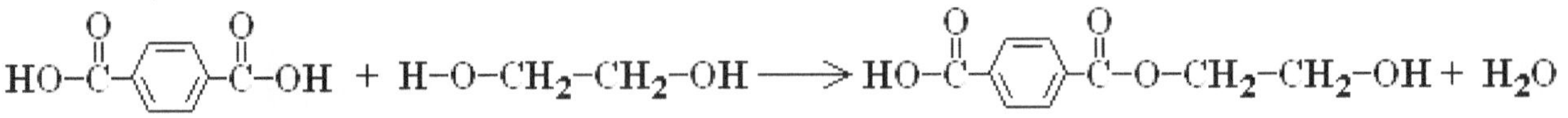

$$HO-\overset{O}{\underset{}{C}}-\underset{}{\bigcirc}-\overset{O}{\underset{}{C}}-OH + H-O-CH_2-CH_2-OH \longrightarrow HO-\overset{O}{\underset{}{C}}-\underset{}{\bigcirc}-\overset{O}{\underset{}{C}}-O-CH_2-CH_2-OH + H_2O$$

Terephthalic acid   **Ethylene glycol**   **Water**

A water molecule is removed as the ester linkage is formed. Notice the acid and the alcohol groups that are still available for bonding.

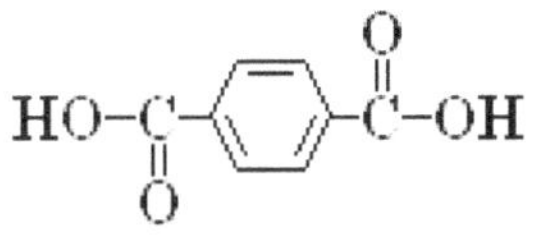

$$HO-\overset{O}{\underset{O}{C}}-\bigcirc-\overset{O}{\underset{}{C}}-OH$$

Because the monomers above are all joined by ester linkages, the polymer chain is a polyester. This one is called PET, which stands for poly(ethylene terephthalate). (PET is used to make soft-drink bottles, magnetic tape, and many other plastic products.)

Skill 29.3 Demonstrate knowledge of appropriate separation, purification, and identification schemes for organic molecules (e.g., chromatography, spectroscopy).

When presented with a mixture of unknown organic compounds to identify, the modern chemist has an arsenal of tools available to assist her. The fist task is typically to separate the mixture into pure substances. Many **separation processes** have been developed for this purpose. These techniques may utilize differences in the molecules to separate them. Such differences may be in **size, charge, chemical affinity, or physical properties**. By repeatedly applying separation techniques, compounds can also be made increasingly pure. A few of the more common laboratory separation process are listed below:

Distillation involves heating the mixture slowly such that those compounds with the lowest boiling point become gas first. The gas can then be collected and condensed.

Fractional freezing utilizes differences in freezing point by lowering the temperature of a liquid mixture until one substance becomes a solid.

Extraction involves introducing another solvent to the mixture (typically an aqueous solvent to an organic mixture). The compounds will then separate between the two phases, depending on their relative solubilities.

Centrifugation relies on differences in density. When the mixture is rapidly spun, centrifugal forces draw the more dense components to the bottom.

Gel electrophoresis uses an electrical gradient to separate compounds by size or charge; this is a very gentle separation technique that is typically used for proteins and other biomolecules.

Precipitation and filtration involves introducing another substance that will bind with one or more of the compounds in the mixture and form a solid. These solids can then be filtered out of the solution.

Chromatography techniques include many specific technologies, but all involve passing the mixture through a stationary phase. The various components in the mixture will have different degrees of affinity for this stationary phase and will thus be separated. This affinity may be based upon charge, relative solubility, or adsorption. The major types of chromatography are capillary-action (paper and thin layer), column, gas-liquid, and counter-current.

Once the components are fully separated, they can be further investigated. To determine the identity of an unknown, **chemical and physical properties can be used as important clues**. However, the fastest and surest way to do this is through spectroscopy. **Spectroscopy studies matter by analyzing the light, sound, or particles that are emitted, absorbed, or scattered by a sample**. The results of spectroscopy must be carefully interpreted, but give much information about the elements and bonding structures in a molecule. The main types of spectroscopy are:

Absorption spectroscopy technologies use particular parts of the electromagnetic (EM) spectra. The sample's absorption of the EM waves reveals its molecular make-up. Examples of this type include atomic absorption spectroscopy, ultraviolet/visible absorption spectroscopy, and infrared spectroscopy.

Emission spectroscopy also utilizes the range of EM spectra, but the sample's *emission* of EM waves, rather than its absorption is studied. Typically, the sample is allowed to absorb energy and then the resulting emissions are studied. This type of spectroscopy includes plasma emission spectroscopy, atomic emission spectroscopy, and fluorescence spectroscopy.

Scattering spectroscopy measures the light that a sample scatters at a certain wavelength, incident angle, or polarization angle. This technique is somewhat similar to emission spectroscopy, but scattering occurs much more quickly than the absorption/emission process. Raman spectroscopy is the most useful example of this type.

Skill 29.4   Recognize the general structure, properties, and uses of organic polymers, pharmaceuticals, pesticides, and other practical products.

The number of naturally occurring organic compounds is mind-boggling and even more **compounds can be creating using the tools of organic synthesis**. Organic compounds are especially important to humankind because they are **involved in all biochemical reactions**. Not only does this mean we must study organic compounds to understand natural phenomena, but that we **can subtly alter biological reactions by introducing or changing the concentrations of organic molecules**. Finally, organic compounds **exhibit wide varieties of chemical and physical properties** and small alterations in structure allow us to "tweak" these properties to suit our needs. For these reasons, organic molecules are important in the production of plastics, fabrics, paint, pharmaceuticals, fertilizers, petrochemicals, explosives, foods, and many other goods.

Polymers are large organic molecules consisting of repeated units linked by covalent bonds. There are many naturally occurring polymers such as proteins and starches. Additionally, many artificial polymers have been developed. The repeated unit in a polymer is known as a monomer. Thus, the monomer in a protein is an amino acid and the monomer in the manmade polymer polyethene (better known as polyethelyene) is ethene. Copolymers may be created by using two or more different monomers. Both the physical and chemical properties of polymers vary widely and are a function of the monomer, the molecular weight or length of the polymer, and intermolecular forces. Polymers range from low viscosity liquids to extremely hard, crystalline solids and from biologically degradable to nearly inert. The structure of polymers can be changed and this allows very tight control of these physical properties. Therefore, polymers have been used in a large variety of medical, construction, clothing, packaging, and industrial applications. Just a few of the many examples of products made from polymers are: poly-styrene food containers, poly-vinyl-chloride (PVC) pipes, poly-lactic acid (absorbable) sutures, neoprene wetsuits, polyethylene grocery bags, and polytetrafluoro-ethylene lined cooking pans (Teflon).

Pharmaceuticals

Pharmaceuticals are organic molecules with therapeutic benefit. Not all pharmaceuticals are organic chemicals, but the vast majority are. Often these compounds are synthetically produced versions of naturally occurring molecules such as hormones, enzymes, or vitamins. Other drugs have structures that have been specifically developed to block the action of natural compounds (for example, a molecule that stops the action of an enzyme by permanently occupying its binding site). Delivery and dosage are important considerations for all pharmaceuticals since it is necessary that they reach their target tissue intact and at a therapeutic concentration. Pharmaceuticals have been developed and marketed to treat of vast array of physical and mental diseases and degenerative conditions, to fight infections and allergies, for contraception, to diminish pain, and for diagnostic purposes.

Pesticides

A pesticide is any substance designed to prevent, repel, or destroy a pest. Pesticides include insecticides, herbicides, fungicides, and rodenticides. While biologic (i.e., beneficial viruses and bacteria) and inorganic pesticides exist, the majority are organic compounds. Like pharmaceuticals, many pesticides work by disrupting natural biochemical pathways. Extreme care must be taken with pesticides, as they are dangerous to people and the environment. While pesticides are in use in residential, commercial, and industrial settings, it is in agricultural endeavors that they are most utilized. Pesticides are helpful in that they minimize crop damage and loss, but they have a negative effect on the environment, can lead to the evolution of resistant organisms, and may leave residue on foods.

Skill 29.5 Demonstrate an understanding of the structure, properties, and function of common biological molecules (carbohydrates, lipids, proteins, and nucleic acids) and how these biomolecules are involved in life processes.

Lipids

Lipids typically have **large hydrocarbons** as part of their structure and are **insoluble in water**. Animal fats and vegetable oils are **complex lipids** called **triacylglycerides** These molecules contain three estergroups.

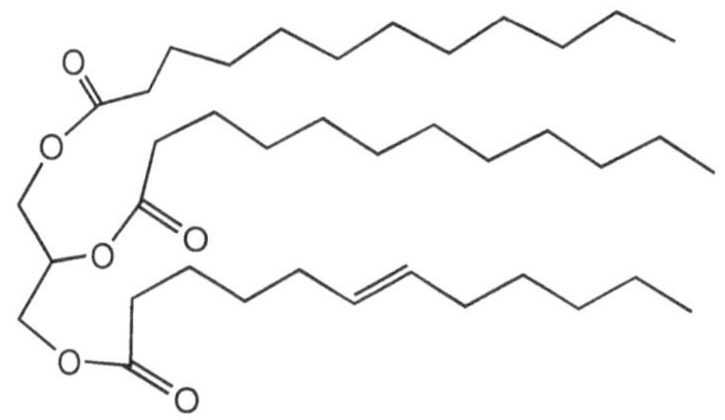

Fats such as the molecule above may be broken apart to yield **glycerol** and long-chain carboxylic acids known as **fatty acids**. Glycerol is shown to the right and two fatty acids are shown below.

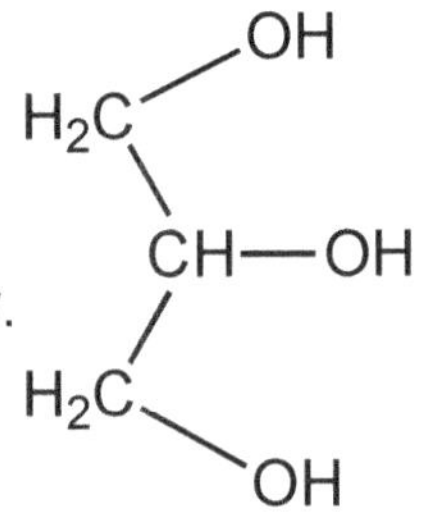

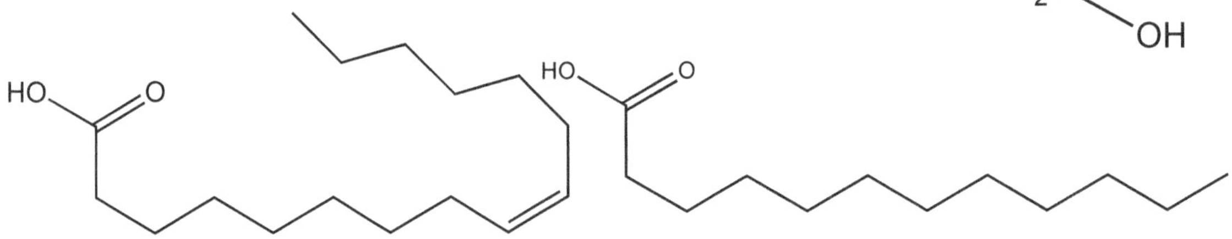

Classes of hydrocarbons are often applied to the corresponding fatty acid. **Saturated fat** refers to fatty acids containing a hydrocarbon chain with only single bonds as shown above on the right. **Unsaturated fat** refers to fatty acids containing one or more alkene group. If one alkene linkage is present on the hydrocarbon, it is **monounsaturated**. If more than one is present, it is **polyunsaturated**. Unsaturated fats are also described as *cis–* or *trans–* and may be conjugated. The molecule above on the left is a monounsaturated *cis-*fatty acid. Unsaturated fat in processed food is often converted to saturated fat by **hydrogenation**.

Simple lipids such as cholesterol (shown below) do not contain ester groups:

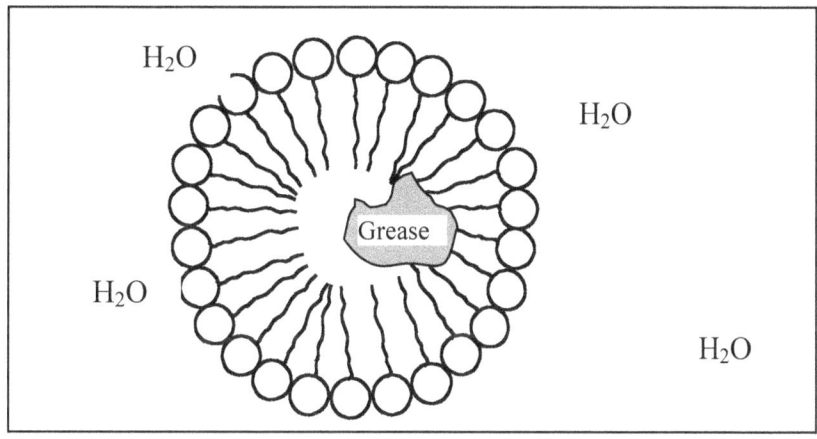

Many lipids like the fatty acids above have a long non-polar hydrocarbon "tail" region and a small polar "head" region. In water, the hydrocarbon is **hydrophobic** and the polar region is **hydrophilic**. Hydrophobic means water hating while hydrophilic means water loving.

Soaps and synthetic **detergents** clean materials because their molecules have these two regions. When they are dispersed in water, the hydrophilic heads face the water in an attempt to dissolve, but the hydrophobic tails are attracted to each other and surround any grease particulates. These spherical clusters are called **micelles**. The net effect is to disperse grease in water where it can be washed away.

Lipid molecules in the membranes of cells form a **lipid bilayer** by lining up tail-to-tail in order to separate the space inside the cell from the extracellular environment.

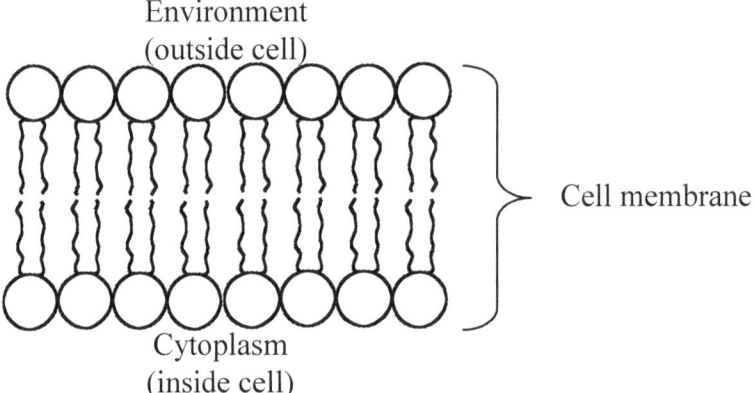

Proteins

Proteins play a role in nearly every process in living organisms and are the most important and diverse molecules in living things. **Amino acids form the building blocks of proteins**. Amino acids contain both an amine and a carboxylic acid

Each of the 20 different common amino acids uses a different **side chain** for R. Side chains may be nonpolar or polar. The polar side chains may be acidic or basic. Side chains may also be aromatic or aliphatic.

The carbonyl carbon atom of one amino acid bonds to the amine nitrogen of another to form an amide group. This bond is called a peptide bond:

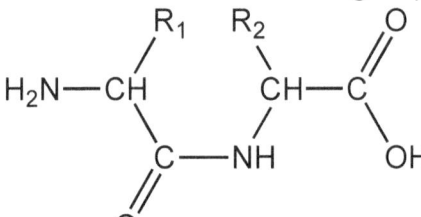

The molecule to the left is a **dipeptide** because it contains two amino acids. Many amino acids strung together form a **polypeptide**, and the term **protein** is used for these larger chains.

Interactions among specific sequences of side chains give each protein a certain shape with unique chemical properties. A common shape found within many proteins is an ☐-**helix** shown to the right. Physical properties of the protein follow from the way individual protein molecules interact with water and with each other.

A protein called **keratin** is insoluble in water but binds to other keratin molecules to form hard structures. Proteins like keratin are known as **structural proteins** or **fibrous proteins**. Keratin is the main component in hair and fingernails. A different protein called **insulin** is soluble in water and achieves a certain shape as an individual molecule. Proteins like insulin are known as **globular proteins**Insulin in the bloodstream regulates glucose metabolism.

Globular proteins called **enzymes** act as catalysts to increase the rate of biochemical reactions. The names of enzymes often end with the suffix *–ase*. Many other protein names end with the suffix *–in*. Heating a protein or changing its chemical environment may cause it to lose its shape without breaking any covalent bonds. This loss of structure is called **denaturation**.

Carbohydrates

Monosaccharides (also known as **simple sugars**) **form the building blocks of carbohydrates**. The empirical formula for simple sugars is CH_2O. The name *carbohydrate* is derived from "hydrate of carbon" based on this formula. The names of monosaccharides use the suffix *–ose*. A monosaccharide contains multiple hydroxyl groups and may be an **aldose** or a **ketose** depending on whether it contains an aldehyde or a ketone group.

Organisms use the bonds in carbohydrates to store energy in chemical form. The most important monosaccharide is glucose. Glucose is a **hexose** because it contains six carbon atoms. Like all **hexoses**, glucose has the formula $C_6H_{12}O_6$. It is also an aldose. Like many monosaccharides, the carbonyl group of glucose may react with one of its hydroxyl groups. This creates an **equilibrium between open chain and ring forms**. These two forms of glucose are shown below:

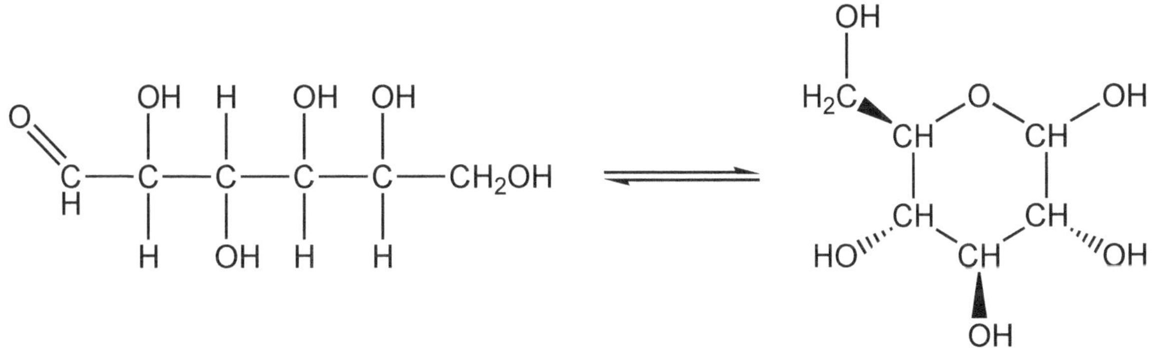

Two simple sugars may be joined together by a **glycosidic bond**.

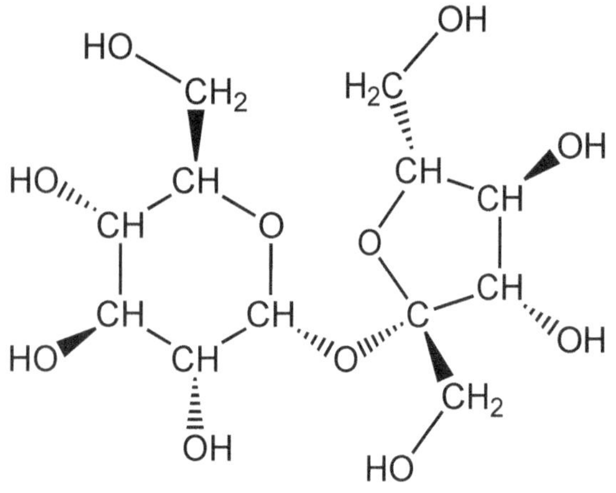

The molecule to the left is the **disaccharide** sucrose. Many sugars linked together form a **polysaccharide**, and the term **complex carbohydrate** is used for these structures. More than two glycosidic bonds may attach to a simple sugar, so complex carbohydrates often contain branch-like structures. This is in contrast to proteins where building blocks are strung together in a linear fashion.

Starch and **cellulose** are two examples of glucose complex carbohydrates.

Nucleic Acids
Nucleotides form the building blocks of nucleic acids. A nucleotide is made up of a phosphate a sugar, and an amine "base." An example is shown below:

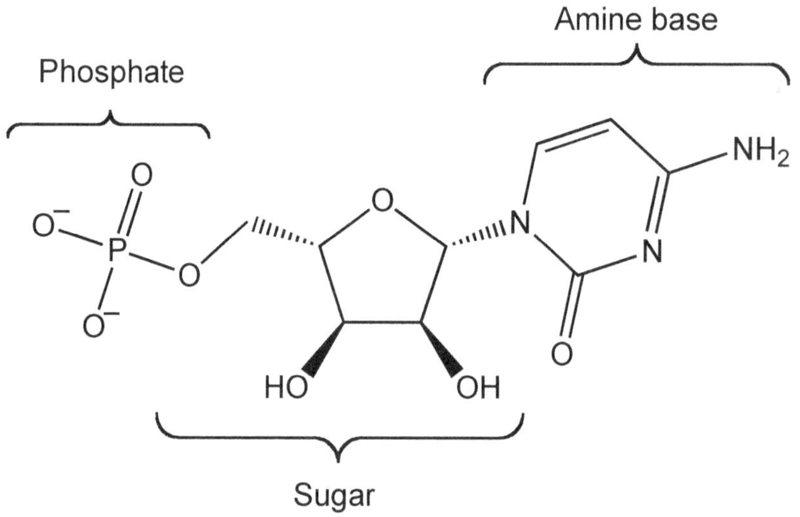

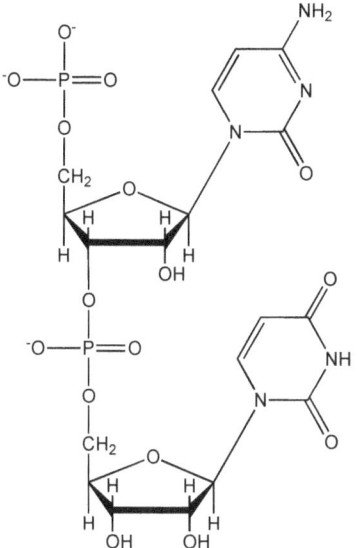

Living things use nucleic acids to carry genetic information based on the identity of the amine base present. This information is used to determine the amino acid sequence of every protein in the organism and it provides a blueprint for how the organism is made.

The phosphate of one nucleotide may form a covalent bond with the sugar residue of another to form a **dinucleotide** as shown on the left. Sugar-phosphate groups link to each other to form a helix "backbone" with the amine bases protruding outwards. Many nucleotides linked together in this way form **ribonucleic acid (RNA)** if the sugar is ribose and **deoxyribonucleic acid (DNA** if the sugar is ribose lacking a hydroxyl group .

Amine bases on one nucleic acid molecule may form hydrogen bonds with bases on a second strand. For DNA, these two strands form the familiar **double-helix**

Skill 29.6 Recognize the general features of three-dimensional structures, bonding, molecular properties, and reactivity of organic molecules.

The hundreds of thousands of organic molecules have various chemical and physical properties and three-dimensional structures. However, certain similarities exist. Organic compounds, of course, are **covalently bonded, carbon based molecules**. The ability of carbon atoms to bond with one another allows the formation of **long chains, double and triple bonds, and even rings**.

Among organic molecules, isomers, or molecules with the same molecular formulas but different structures, are very common. **Structural isomers** actually have the atoms joined in different ways. **Stereoisomers**, on the other hand, have the same bond structures, but with different geometrical positioning. Enantiomers are stereoisomers are mirror images of one another but diastereomers are stereoisomers that are not mirror images. Diastereomers can exist in either *cis* or *trans* form, depending on the relative location of functional groups. **Diastereomers are common in biochemical reactions where the reactivity between *cis* and *trans* isomers can vary substantially**. Even when isomerism is not a concern, the three-dimensional structure of organic molecules is important to their reactivity. This is because large functional groups can actually physically prevent two molecules from coming into close enough contact for a reaction to occur. This phenomenon is referred to as **steric hindrance**.

Trends also exist in physical properties. Organic compounds tend to melt, boil, sublimate, or decompose below 300 °C. Typically, they are highly flammable. Further, most organic molecules are only slightly soluble in water and dissolve better in organic solvents such as acetones or ethyl alcohol. However, **solubility and physical properties of organic compounds largely depend on their functional groups**. These **functional groups, such as hydroxyl or amine groups, also determine the chemical properties of these molecules**.

Organic reactions tend to be complex processes that depend on relative electron affinity, bond strength and polarity, and steric hindrance. Furthermore, reactions between organic molecules typically lead to reactive intermediates. The stability of such possible intermediates determines how and whether a reaction occurs.

Sample Test

Directions: Read each item and select the best response.

1. A piston compresses a gas at constant temperature. Which gas properties increase?

   I. Average speed of molecules
   II. Pressure
   III. Molecular collisions with container walls per second

   A. I and II
   B. I and III
   C. II and III
   D. I, II, and III

2. The temperature of a liquid is raised at atmospheric pressure. Which liquid property increases?

   A. critical pressure
   B. vapor pressure
   C. surface tension
   D. viscosity

3. Potassium crystallizes with two atoms contained in each unit cell. What is the mass of potassium found in a lattice 1.00×10^6 unit cells wide, 2.00×10^6 unit cells high, and 5.00×10^6 unit cells deep?

   A. 85.0 ng
   B. 32.5 μg
   C. 64.9 μg
   D. 130. μg

4. A gas is heated in a sealed container. Which of the following occur?

   A. gas pressure rises
   B. gas density decreases
   C. the average distance between molecules increases
   D. all of the above

5. How many molecules are in 2.20 pg of a protein with a molecular weight of 150. kDa?

   A. 8.83×10^9
   B. 1.82×10^9
   C. 8.83×10^6
   D. 1.82×10^6

6. At STP, 20. μL of O_2 contain 5.4×10^{16} molecules. According to Avogadro's hypothesis, how many molecules are in 20. μL of Ne?

   A. 5.4×10^{15}
   B. 1.0×10^{16}
   C. 2.7×10^{16}
   D. 5.4×10^{16}

SCIENCE: CHEMISTRY

7. An ideal gas at 50.0 °C and 3.00 atm is in a 300. cm³ cylinder. The cylinder volume changes by moving a piston until the gas is at 50.0 °C and 1.00 atm. What is the final volume?

   A. 100. cm³
   B. 450. cm³
   C. 900. cm³
   D. 1.20 dm³

8. Which gas law may be used to solve the previous question?

   A. Charles's law
   B. Boyle's law
   C. Graham's law
   D. Avogadro's law

9. A blimp is filled with 5000. m³ of helium at 28.0 °C and 99.7 kPa. What is the mass of helium used?

   $R = 8.3144 \dfrac{J}{mol \cdot K}$

   A. 797 kg
   B. 810. kg
   C. 879 kg
   D. 8.57×10^3 kg

10. Which of the following are able to flow from one place to another?

    I. Gases
    II. Liquids
    III. Solids
    IV. Supercritical fluids

    A. I and II
    B. II only
    C. I, II, and IV
    D. I, II, III, and IV

11. One mole of an ideal gas at STP occupies 22.4 L. At what temperature will one mole of an ideal gas at one atm occupy 31.0 L?

    A. 34.6 °C
    B. 105 °C
    C. 378 °C
    D. 442 °C

12. Why does $CaCl_2$ have a higher normal melting point than NH_3?

    A. Covalent bonds are stronger than London dispersion forces.
    B. Covalent bonds are stronger than hydrogen bonds.
    C. Ionic bonds are stronger than London dispersion forces.
    D. Ionic bonds are stronger than hydrogen bonds.

13. Which intermolecular attraction explains the following trend in straight-chain alkanes?

Condensed structural formula	Boiling point (°C)
CH_4	-161.5
CH_3CH_3	-88.6
$CH_3CH_2CH_3$	-42.1
$CH_3CH_2CH_2CH_3$	-0.5
$CH_3CH_2CH_2CH_2CH_3$	36.0
$CH_3CH_2CH_2CH_2CH_2CH_3$	68.7

A. London dispersion forces
B. Dipole-dipole interactions
C. Hydrogen bonding
D. Ion-induced dipole interactions

14. List the substances NH_3, PH_3, $MgCl_2$, Ne, and N_2 in order of increasing melting point.

A. N_2 < Ne < PH_3 < NH_3 < $MgCl_2$
B. N_2 < NH_3 < Ne < $MgCl_2$ < PH_3
C. Ne < N_2 < NH_3 < PH_3 < $MgCl_2$
D. Ne < N_2 < PH_3 < NH_3 < $MgCl_2$

15. 1-butanol, ethanol, methanol, and 1-propanol are all liquids at room temperature. Rank them in order of increasing viscosity.

A. 1-butanol < 1-propanol < ethanol < methanol
B. methanol < ethanol < 1-propanol < 1-butanol
C. methanol < ethanol < 1-butanol < 1-propanol
D. 1-propanol < 1-butanol < ethanol < methanol

16. Which gas has a diffusion rate of 25% the rate for hydrogen?

A. helium
B. methane
C. nitrogen
D. oxygen

17. 2.00 L of an unknown gas at 1500. mm Hg and a temperature of 25.0 °C weighs 7.52 g. Assuming the ideal gas equation, what is the molecular mass of the gas?

**760 mm Hg=1 atm
R=0.08206 L-atm/(mol-K)**

A. 21.6 u
B. 23.3 u
C. 46.6 u
D. 93.2 u

18. Which substance is most likely to be a gas at room temperature?

A. SeO_2
B. F_2
C. $CaCl_2$
D. I_2

19. What pressure is exerted by a mixture of 2.7 g of H_2 and 59 g of Xe at STP on a 50. L container?

A. 0.69 atm
B. 0.76 atm
C. 0.80 atm
D. 0.97 atm

20. A few minutes after opening a bottle of perfume, the scent is detected on the other side of the room. What law relates to this phenomenon?

A. Graham's law
B. Dalton's law
C. Boyle's law
D. Avogadro's law

21. Which of the following are true?

A. Solids have no vapor pressure.
B. Dissolving a solute in a liquid increases its vapor pressure.
C. The vapor pressure of a pure substance is characteristic of that substance and its temperature.
D. All of the above

22. Find the partial pressure of N_2 in a container at 150. kPa holding H_2O and N_2 at 50 °C. The vapor pressure of H_2O at 50 °C is 12 kPa.

A. 12 kPa
B. 138 kPa
C. 162 kPa
D. The value cannot be determined.

23. The normal boiling point of water on the Kelvin scale is closest to:

A. 112 K
B. 212 K
C. 273 K
D. 373 K
E.

24. Which phase may be present at the triple point of a substance?

I. Gas
II. Liquid
III. Solid
IV. Supercritical fluid

A. I, II, and III
B. I, II, and IV
C. II, III, and IV
D. I, II, III, and IV

25. In the following phase diagram, _____ occurs as P is decreased from A to B at constant T and _____ occurs as T is increased from C to D at constant P.

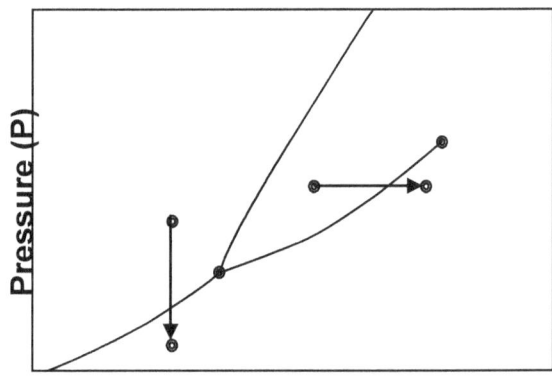

A. deposition, melting
B. sublimation, melting
C. deposition, vaporization
D. sublimation, vaporization

26. Heat is added to a pure solid at its melting point until it all becomes liquid at its freezing point. Which of the following occur?

   A. Intermolecular attractions are weakened.
   B. The kinetic energy of the molecules does not change.
   C. The freedom of the molecules to move about increases.
   D. All of the above.

27. Which of the following occur when NaCl dissolves in water?

   A. Heat is required to break bonds in the NaCl crystal lattice.
   B. Heat is released when hydrogen bonds in water are broken.
   C. Heat is required to form bonds of hydration.
   D. The oxygen end of the water molecule is attracted to the Cl^- ion.

28. The solubility of $CoCl_2$ is 54 g per 100 g of ethanol. Three flasks each contain 100 g of ethanol. Flask #1 also contains 40 g $CoCl_2$ in solution. Flask #2 contains 56 g $CoCl_2$ in solution. Flask #3 contains 5 g of solid $CoCl_2$ in equilibrium with 54 g $CoCl_2$ in solution. Which of the following describe the solutions present in the liquid phase of the flasks?

   A. #1-saturated, #2-supersaturated, #3-unsaturated.
   B. #1-unsaturated, #2-miscible, #3-saturated.
   C. #1-unsaturated, #2-supersaturated, #3-saturated.
   D. #1-unsaturated, #2-not at equilibrium, #3-miscible.

29. The solubility at 1.0 atm of pure CO_2 in water at 25 °C is 0.034 M. According to Henry's law, what is the solubility at 4.0 atm of pure CO_2 in water at 25 °C? Assume no chemical reaction occurs between CO_2 and H_2O.

   A. 0.0085 M
   B. 0.034 M
   C. 0.14 M
   D. 0.25 M

30. Carbonated water is bottled at 25 °C under pure CO_2 at 4.0 atm. Later the bottle is opened at 4 °C under air at 1.0 atm that has a partial pressure of 3×10^{-4} atm CO_2. Why do CO_2 bubbles form when the bottle is opened?

   A. CO_2 falls out of solution due to a drop in solubility at the lower total pressure.
   B. CO_2 falls out of solution due to a drop in solubility at the lower CO_2 pressure.
   C. CO_2 falls out of solution due to a drop in solubility at the lower temperature.
   D. CO_2 is formed by the decomposition of carbonic acid.

31. When KNO_3 dissolves in water, the water grows slightly colder. An increase in temperature will _____ the solubility of KNO_3.

   A. increase
   B. decrease
   C. have no effect on
   D. have an unknown effect with the information given on

32. An experiment requires 100. mL of a 0.500 M solution of $MgBr_2$. How many grams of $MgBr_2$ will be present in this solution?

   A. 9.21 g
   B. 11.7 g
   C. 12.4 g
   D. 15.6 g

33. 500. mg of RbOH are added to 500. g of ethanol (C_2H_6O) resulting in 395 mL of solution. Determine the molarity and molality of RbOH.

   A. 0.0124 M, 0.00488 m
   B. 0.0124 M, 0.00976 m
   C. 0.0223 M, 0.00488 m
   D. 0.0223 M, 0.00976 m

34. 20.0 g H_3PO_4 in 1.5 L of solution are intended to react with KOH according to the following reaction:
   $$H_3PO_4 + 3 KOH \rightarrow K_3PO_4 + 3 H_2O$$
   What is the molarity and normality of the H_3PO_4 solution?

   A. 0.41 M, 1.22 N
   B. 0.41 M, 0.20 N
   C. 0.14 M, 0.045 N
   D. 0.14 M, 0.41 N

35. Aluminum sulfate is a strong electrolyte. What is the concentration of all species in a 0.2 M solution of aluminum sulfate?

   A. 0.2 M Al^{3+}, 0.2 M SO_4^{2-}
   B. 0.4 M Al^{3+}, 0.6 M SO_4^{2-}
   C. 0.6 M Al^{3+}, 0.4 M SO_4^{2-}
   D. 0.2 M $Al_2(SO_4)_3$

36. 15 g of formaldehyde (CH_2O) are dissolved in 100. g of water. Calculate the weight percentage and mole fraction of formaldehyde in the solution.

   A. 13%, 0.090
   B. 15%, 0.090
   C. 13%, 0.083
   D. 15%, 0.083

37. Which of the following would make the best solvent for Br_2?

   A. H_2O
   B. CS_2
   C. NH_3
   D. molten NaCl

38. Which of the following is most likely to dissolve in water?

   A. H_2
   B. CCl_4
   C. SF_6
   D. CH_3OH

39. Which of the following is not a colligative property?

   A. Viscosity lowering
   B. Freezing point lowering
   C. Boiling point elevation
   D. Vapor pressure lowering

40. $BaCl_2(aq) + Na_2SO_4(aq) \rightarrow BaSO_4(s) + 2NaCl(aq)$

   is an example of a _____ reaction.

   A. acid-base
   B. precipitation
   C. redox
   D. nuclear

41. List the following aqueous solutions in order of increasing boiling point.

   I. 0.050 m $AlCl_3$
   II. 0.080 m $Ba(NO_3)_2$
   III. 0.090 m NaCl
   IV. 0.12 m ethylene glycol ($C_2H_6O_2$)

   A. I < II < III < IV
   B. I < III < IV < II
   C. IV < III < I < II
   D. IV < III < II < I

42. Osmotic pressure is the pressure required to prevent _____ flowing from low to high _____ concentration across a semipermeable membrane.

   A. solute, solute
   B. solute, solvent
   C. solvent, solute
   D. solvent, solvent

43. A solution of NaCl in water is heated on a mountain in an open container until it boils at 100. °C. The air pressure on the mountain is 0.92 atm. According to Raoult's law, what mole fraction of Na^+ and Cl^- are present in the solution?

A. 0.04 Na^+, 0.04 Cl^-
B. 0.08 Na^+, 0.08 Cl^-
C. 0.46 Na^+, 0.46 Cl^-
D. 0.92 Na^+, 0.92 Cl^-

44. Write a balanced nuclear equation for the emission of an alpha particle by polonium-209.

A. $^{209}_{84}Po \rightarrow ^{205}_{81}Pb + ^{4}_{2}He$
B. $^{209}_{84}Po \rightarrow ^{205}_{82}Bi + ^{4}_{2}He$
C. $^{209}_{84}Po \rightarrow ^{209}_{85}At + ^{0}_{-1}e$
D. $^{209}_{84}Po \rightarrow ^{205}_{82}Pb + ^{4}_{2}He$

45. Write a balanced nuclear equation for the decay of calcium-45 to scandium-45.

A. $^{45}_{20}Ca \rightarrow ^{41}_{18}Sc + ^{4}_{2}He$
B. $^{45}_{20}Ca + ^{0}_{1}e \rightarrow ^{45}_{21}Sc$
C. $^{45}_{20}Ca \rightarrow ^{45}_{21}Sc + ^{0}_{-1}e$
D. $^{45}_{20}Ca + ^{0}_{1}p \rightarrow ^{45}_{21}Sc$

46. $^{3}_{1}H$ decays with a half-life of 12 years. 3.0 g of pure $^{3}_{1}H$ were placed in a sealed container 24 years ago. How many grams of $^{3}_{1}H$ remain?

A. 0.38 g
B. 0.75 g
C. 1.5 g
D. 3.0 g

47. Oxygen-15 has a half-life of 122 seconds. What percentage of a sample of oxygen-15 has decayed after 300. seconds?

A. 18.2%
B. 21.3%
C. 78.7%
D. 81.8%

48. Which of the following isotopes is commonly used for medical imaging in the diagnose of diseases?

A. cobalt-60
B. technetium-99m
C. tin-117m
D. plutonium-238

49. Carbon-14 dating would be useful in obtaining the age of which object?

A. a 20th century Picasso painting
B. a mummy from ancient Egypt
C. a dinosaur fossil
D. all of the above

SCIENCE: CHEMISTRY

50. Which of the following isotopes can create a chain reaction of nuclear fission?

A. uranium-235
B. uranium-238
C. plutonium-238
D. all of the above

51. List the following scientists in chronological order from earliest to most recent with respect to their most significant contribution to atomic theory:

I. John Dalton
II. Niels Bohr
III. J. J. Thomson
IV. Ernest Rutherford

A. I, III, II, IV
B. I, III, IV, II
C. I, IV, III, II
D. III, I, II, IV

52. Match the theory with the scientist who first proposed it:

I. Electrons, atoms, and all objects with momentum also exist as waves.
II. Electron density may be accurately described by a single mathematical equation.
III. There is an inherent indeterminacy in the position and momentum of particles.
IV. Radiant energy is transferred between particles in exact multiples of a discrete unit.

A. I-de Broglie, II-Planck, III-Schrödinger, IV-Thomson
B. I-Dalton, II-Bohr, III-Planck, IV-de Broglie
C. I-Henry, II-Bohr, III-Heisenberg, IV-Schrödinger
D. I-de Broglie, II-Schrödinger, III-Heisenberg, IV-Planck

53. How many neutrons are in $^{60}_{27}Co$?

A. 27
B. 33
C. 60
D. 87

54. The terrestrial composition of an element is: 50.7% as an isotope with an atomic mass of 78.9 u and 49.3% as an isotope with an atomic mass of 80.9 u. Both isotopes are stable. Calculate the atomic mass of the element.
   A. 79.0 u
   B. 79.8 u
   C. 79.9 u
   D. 80.8 u

55. Which of the following is a correct electron arrangement for oxygen?

   A.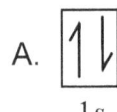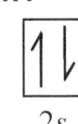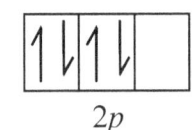
       1s   2s   2p

   B. $1s^2 1p^2 2s^2 2p^2$
   C. 2, 2, 4
   D. none of the above

56. Which of the following statements about radiant energy is **not** true?

   A. The energy change of an electron transition is directly proportional to the wavelength of the emitted or absorbed photon.
   B. The energy of an electron in a hydrogen atom depends only on the principle quantum number.
   C. The frequency of photons striking a metal determines whether the photoelectric effect will occur.
   D. The frequency of a wave of electromagnetic radiation is inversely proportional to its wavelength

57. Match the orbital diagram for the ground state of carbon with the rule/principle it violates:

   I.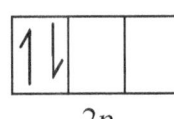

   II.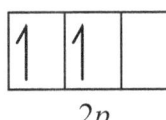

   III.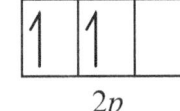

   IV.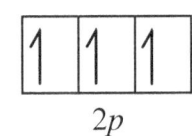

   A. I-Pauli exclusion, II-Aufbau, III-no violation, IV-Hund's
   B. I-Aufbau, II-Pauli exclusion, III-no violation, IV-Hund's
   C. I-Hund's, II-no violation, III-Pauli exclusion, IV-Aufbau
   D. I-Hund's, II-no violation, III-Aufbau, IV-Pauli exclusion

58. Select the list of atoms that are arranged in order of increasing *size*.

   A. Mg, Na, Si, Cl
   B. Si, Cl, Mg, Na
   C. Cl, Si, Mg, Na
   D. Na, Mg, Si, Cl

59. Based on trends in the periodic table, which of the following properties would you expect to be greater for Rb than for K?

   I. Density
   II. Melting point
   III. Ionization energy
   IV. Oxidation number in a compound with chlorine

   A. I only
   B. I, II, and III
   C. II and III
   D. I, II, III, and IV

60. Which oxide forms the strongest acid in water?

   A. Al_2O_3
   B. Cl_2O_7
   C. As_2O_5
   D. CO_2

61. Rank the following bonds from least to most polar:

   C-H, C-Cl, H-H, C-F

   A. C-H < H-H < C-F < C-Cl
   B. H-H < C-H < C-F < C-Cl
   C. C-F < C-Cl < C-H < H-H
   D. H-H < C-H < C-Cl < C-F

62. At room temperature, $CaBr_2$ is expected to be:

   A. a ductile solid
   B. a brittle solid
   C. a soft solid
   D. a gas

63. Which of the following is a proper Lewis dot structure of CHClO?

   A., 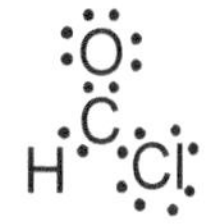 B., 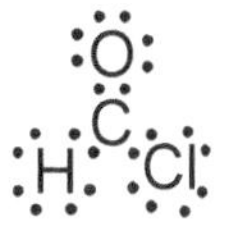 C., 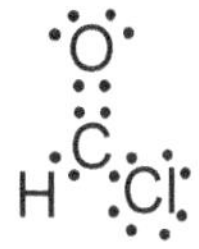 D. 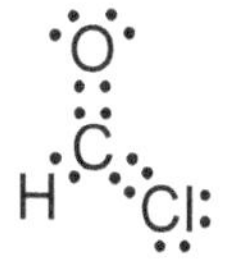 (Lewis structures shown)

64. In C_2H_2, each carbon atom contains the following valence orbitals:

   A. p only
   B. p and sp hybrids
   C. p and sp^2 hybrids
   D. sp^3 hybrids only

65. Which statement about molecular structures is false?

   A. 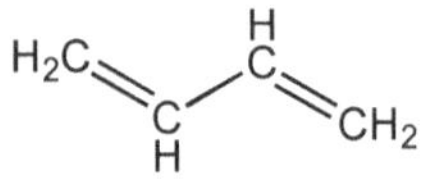 H₂C=CH−CH=CH₂ is a conjugated molecule
   B. A bonding σ orbital connects two atoms by the straight line between them.
   C. A bonding π orbital connects two atoms in a separate region from the straight line between them.
   D. The anion with resonance forms

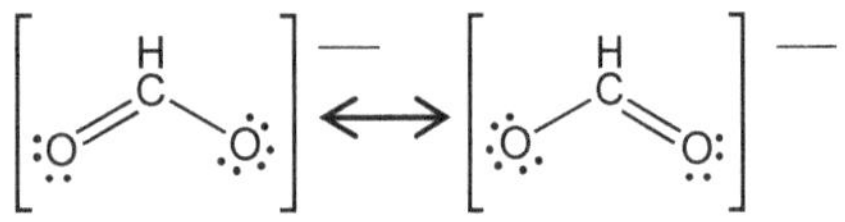

   [formate resonance structures]

   will always exist in one form or the other.

66. What is the shape of the PH₃ molecule? Use the VSEPR model.

   A. Trigonal pyramidal
   B. Trigonal bipyramidal
   C. Trigonal planar
   D. Tetrahedral

67. What is the chemical composition of magnesium nitrate?

   A. 11.1% Mg, 22.2% N, 66.7% O
   B. 16.4% Mg, 18.9% N, 64.7% O
   C. 20.9% Mg, 24.1% N, 55.0% O
   D. 28.2% Mg, 16.2% N, 55.7% O

68. The IUPAC name for Cu₂SO₃ is:

   A. Dicopper sulfur trioxide
   B. Copper (II) sulfate
   C. Copper (I) sulfite
   D. Copper (II) sulfite

69. Which name or formula is not represented properly?

   A. Cl₄S
   B. KClO₃
   C. Calcium dihydrogen phosphate
   D. Sulfurous acid

70. Household "chlorine bleach" is sodium hypochlorite. Which of the following best represent the production of sodium hypochlorite, sodium chloride, and water by bubbling chlorine gas through aqueous sodium hydroxide?

   A. $4Cl(g) + 4NaOH(aq) \rightarrow NaClO_2(aq) + 3NaCl(aq) + 2H_2O(l)$

   B. $2Cl_2(g) + 4NaOH(aq) \rightarrow NaClO_2(aq) + 3NaCl(aq) + 2H_2O(l)$

   C. $2Cl(g) + 2NaOH(aq) \rightarrow NaClO(aq) + NaCl(aq) + H_2O(l)$

   D. $Cl_2(g) + 2NaOH(aq) \rightarrow NaClO(aq) + NaCl(aq) + H_2O(l)$

71. Balance the equation for the neutralization reaction between phosphoric acid and calcium hydroxide by filling in the blank stoichiometric coefficients.

__H_3PO_4 + __$Ca(OH)_2$ → __$Ca_3(PO_4)_2$ + __H_2O

A. 4, 3, 1, 4
B. 2, 3, 1, 8
C. 2, 3, 1, 6
D. 2, 1, 1, 2

72. Write an equation showing the reaction between calcium nitrate and lithium sulfate in aqueous solution. Include all products.

A. $CaNO_3(aq) + Li_2SO_4(aq) \rightarrow CaSO_4(s) + Li_2NO_3(aq)$

B. $Ca(NO_3)_2(aq) + Li_2SO_4(aq) \rightarrow CaSO_4(s) + 2LiNO_3(aq)$

C. $Ca(NO_3)_2(aq) + Li_2SO_4(aq) \rightarrow 2LiNO_3(s) + CaSO_4(aq)$

D. $Ca(NO_3)_2(aq) + Li_2SO_4(aq) + 2H_2O(l) \rightarrow 2LiNO_3(aq) + Ca(OH)_2(aq) + H_2SO_4(aq)$

73. Find the mass of CO_2 produced by the combustion of 15 kg of isopropyl alcohol in the reaction:

$2C_3H_7OH + 9O_2 \rightarrow 6CO_2 + 8H_2O$

A. 33 kg
B. 44 kg
C. 50 kg
D. 60 kg

74. What is the density of nitrogen gas at STP? Assume an ideal gas and a value of 0.08206 L•atm/(mol•K) for the gas constant.

A. 0.62 g/L
B. 1.14 g/L
C. 1.25 g/L
D. 2.03 g/L

75. Find the volume of methane that will produce 12 m³ of hydrogen in the reaction:

$CH_4(g) + H_2O(g) \rightarrow CO(g) + 3H_2(g)$

Assume temperature and pressure remain constant.

A. 4.0 m³
B. 32 m³
C. 36 m³
D. 64 m³

SCIENCE: CHEMISTRY

76. A 100. L vessel of pure O_2 at 500. kPa and 20. °C is used for the combustion of butane:
$2C_4H_{10} + 13O_2 \rightarrow 8CO_2 + 10H_2O$

Find the mass of butane to consume all the O_2 in the vessel. Assume O_2 is an ideal gas and use a value of $R =$ 8.314 J/(mol·K).

A. 183 g
B. 467 g
C. 1.83 kg
D. 7.75 kg

77. Consider the reaction between iron and hydrogen chloride gas:
$Fe(s) + 2HCl(g) \rightarrow FeCl_2(s) + H_2(g)$

7 moles of iron and 10 moles of HCl react until the limiting reagent is consumed. Which statements are true?

I. HCl is the excess reagent
II. HCl is the limiting reagent
III. 7 moles of H_2 are produced
IV. 2 moles of the excess reagent remain

A. I and III
B. I and IV
C. II and III
D. II and IV

78. 32.0 g of hydrogen and 32.0 grams of oxygen react to form water until the limiting reagent is consumed. What is present in the vessel after the reaction is complete?

A. 16.0 g O_2 and 48.0 g H_2O
B. 24.0 g H_2 and 40.0 g H_2O
C. 28.0 g H_2 and 36.0 g H_2O
D. 28.0 g H_2 and 34.0 g H_2O

79. Three experiments were performed at the same initial temperature and pressure to determine the rate of the reaction
$2ClO_2(g) + F_2(g) \rightarrow 2ClO_2F(g)$

Results are shown in the table below. Concentrations are given in millimoles per liter (mM).

Exp.	Initial $[ClO_2]$ (mM)	Initial $[F_2]$ (mM)	Initial rate of $[ClO_2F]$ increase (mM/sec)
1	5.0	5.0	0.63
2	5.0	20	2.5
3	10	10	2.5

What is the rate law for this reaction?

A. Rate = $k[F_2]$
B. Rate = $k[ClO_2][F_2]$
C. Rate = $k[ClO_2]^2[F_2]$
D. Rate = $k[ClO_2][F_2]^2$

80. The reaction

$(CH_3)_3CBr(aq) + OH^-(aq) \rightarrow$

$(CH_3)_3COH(aq) + Br^-(aq)$

occurs in three elementary steps:

$(CH_3)_3CBr \rightarrow (CH_3)_3C^+ + Br^-$ is slow

$(CH_3)_3C^+ + H_2O \rightarrow (CH_3)_3COH_2^+$ is fast

$(CH_3)_3COH_2^+ + OH^- \rightarrow (CH_3)_3COH + H_2O$ is fast

What is the rate law for this reaction?

A. Rate $= k\left[(CH_3)_3CBr\right]$
B. Rate $= k\left[OH^-\right]$
C. Rate $= k\left[(CH_3)_3CBr\right]\left[OH^-\right]$
D. Rate $= k\left[(CH_3)_3CBr\right]^2$

81. Which statement about equilibrium is not true?

A. Equilibrium shifts to minimize the impact of changes.
B. Forward and reverse reactions have equal rates at equilibrium.
C. A closed container of air and water is at a vapor-liquid equilibrium if the humidity is constant.
D. The equilibrium between solid and dissolved forms is maintained when salt is added to an unsaturated solution.

82. Which statements about reaction rates are true?

I. Catalysts shift an equilibrium to favor product formation.
II. Catalysts increase the rate of forward and reverse reactions.
III. A greater temperature increases the chance that a molecular collision will overcome a reaction's activation energy.
IV. A catalytic converter contains a homogeneous catalyst.

A. I and II
B. II and III
C. II, III, and IV
D. I, III, and IV

83. Write the equilibrium expression K_{eq} for the reaction

$CO_2(g) + H_2(g) \rightleftharpoons CO(g) + H_2O(l)$

A. $\dfrac{[CO][H_2O]}{[CO_2][H_2]^2}$

B. $\dfrac{[CO_2][H_2]}{[CO][H_2O]}$

C. $\dfrac{[CO][H_2O]}{[CO_2][H_2]}$

D. $\dfrac{[CO]}{[CO_2][H_2]}$

84. What could cause this change in the energy diagram of a reaction?

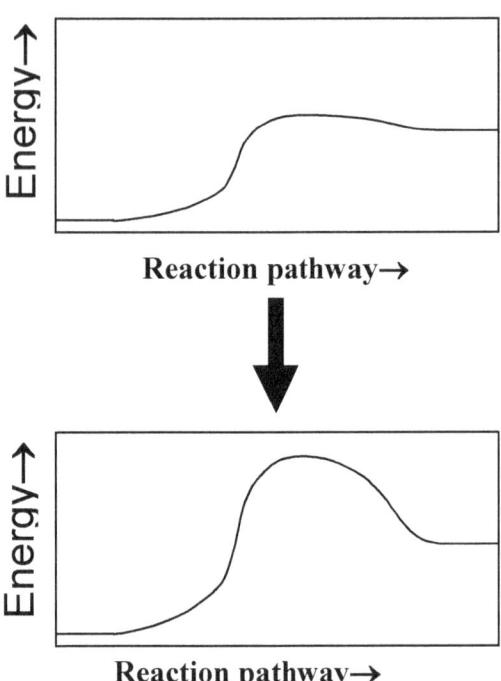

Reaction pathway→

Reaction pathway→

A. Adding catalyst to an endothermic reaction
B. Removing catalyst from an endothermic reaction
C. Adding catalyst to an exothermic reaction
D. Removing catalyst from an exothermic reaction

85. BaSO$_4$ (K_{sp} = 1X10^{-10}) is added to pure H$_2$O. How much is dissolved in 1 L of saturated solution?

A. 2 mg
B. 10 μg
C. 2 μg
D. 100 pg

86. The exothermic reaction $2NO(g) + Br_2(g) \rightleftharpoons 2NOBr(g)$ is at equilibrium. According to LeChatelier's principle:

A. Adding Br$_2$ will increase [NO].
B. An increase in container volume (with T constant) will increase [NOBr].
C. An increase in pressure (with T constant) will increase [NOBr].
D. An increase in temperature (with P constant) will increase [NOBr].

87. At a certain temperature, T, the equilibrium constant for the reaction $2NO(g) \rightleftharpoons N_2(g) + O_2(g)$ is K_{eq} = 2X10^3. If a 1.0 L container at this temperature contains 90 mM N$_2$, 20 mM O$_2$, and 5 mM NO, what will occur?

A. The reaction will make more N$_2$ and O$_2$.
B. The reaction is at equilibrium.
C. The reaction will make more NO.
D. The temperature, T, is required to solve this problem.

88. Which statement about acids and bases is not true?

A. All strong acids ionize in water.
B. All Lewis acids accept an electron pair.
C. All Brønsted bases use OH$^-$ as a proton acceptor
D. All Arrhenius acids form H$^+$ ions in water.

89. Which of the following are listed from weakest to strongest acid?

   A. $H_2SO_3, H_2SeO_3, H_2TeO_3$
   B. $HBrO, HBrO_2, HBrO_3, HBrO_4$
   C. HI, HBr, HCl, HF
   D. $H_3PO_4, H_2PO_4^-, HPO_4^{2-}$

90. NH_4F is dissolved in water. Which of the following are conjugate acid/base pairs present in the solution?

   I. NH_4^+/NH_4OH
   II. HF/F^-
   III. H_3O^+/H_2O
   IV. H_2O/OH^-

   A. I, II, and III
   B. I, III, and IV
   C. II and IV
   D. II, III, and IV

91. What are the pH and the pOH of 0.010 M $HNO_3(aq)$?

   A. pH = 1.0, pOH = 9.0
   B. pH = 2.0, pOH = 12.0
   C. pH = 2.0, pOH = 8.0
   D. pH = 8.0, pOH = 6.0

92. What is the pH of a buffer made of 0.128 M sodium formate (HCOONa) and 0.072 M formic acid (HCOOH)? The pK_a of formic acid is 3.75.

   A. 2.0
   B. 3.0
   C. 4.0
   D. 5.0

93. A sample of 50.0 ml KOH is titrated with 0.100 M $HClO_4$. The initial buret reading is 1.6 ml and the reading at the endpoint is 22.4 ml. What is [KOH]?

   A. 0.0416 M
   B. 0.0481 M
   C. 0.0832 M
   D. 0.0962 mM

94. Rank the following from lowest to highest pH. Assume a small volume for the component given in moles:

   I. 0.01 mol HCl added to 1 L H_2O
   II. 0.01 mol HI added to 1 L of an acetic acid/sodium acetate solution at pH 4.0
   III. 0.01 mol NH_3 added to 1 L H_2O
   IV. 0.1 mol HNO_3 added to 1 L of a 0.1 M $Ca(OH)_2$ solution

   A. I < II < III < IV
   B. I < II < IV < III
   C. II < I < III < IV
   D. II < I < IV < III

95. The curve below resulted from the titration of a _____ _____ with a _____ _____ titrant.

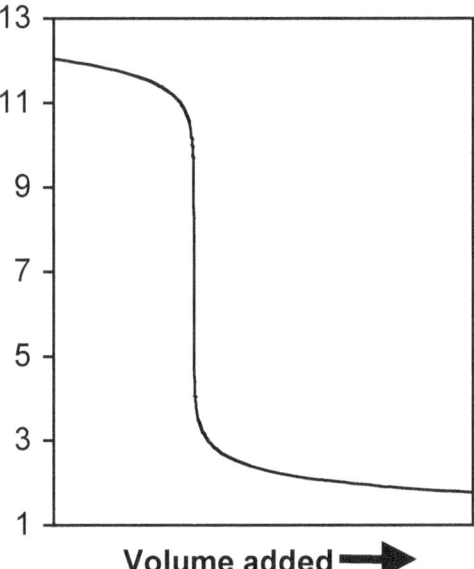

A. weak acid, strong base
B. weak base, strong acid
C. strong acid, strong base
D. strong base, strong acid

96. Which statement about thermochemistry is true?

A. Particles in a system move about less freely at high entropy
B. Water at 100 °C has the same internal energy as water vapor at 100°C
C. A decrease in the order of a system corresponds to an increase in entropy.
D. At its sublimation temperature, dry ice has a higher entropy than gaseous CO_2

97. What is the heat change of 36.0 g H_2O at atmospheric pressure when its temperature is reduced from 125 °C to 40. °C? Use the following data:

Values for water

Heat capacity of solid	37.6 J/mol•°C
Heat capacity of liquid	75.3 J/mol•°C
Heat capacity of gas	33.1 J/mol•°C
Heat of fusion	6.02 kJ/mol
Heat of vaporization	40.67 kJ/mol

A. −92.0 kJ
B. −10.8 kJ
C. 10.8 kJ
D. 92.0 kJ

98. What is the standard heat of combustion of $CH_4(g)$? Use the following data:

Standard heats of formation

$CH_4(g)$	−74.8 kJ/mol
$CO_2(g)$	−393.5 kJ/mol
$H_2O(l)$	−285.8 kJ/mol

A. −890.3 kJ/mol
B. −604.6 kJ/mol
C. −252.9 kJ/mol
D. −182.5 kJ/mol

99. Which reaction creates products at a lower total entropy than the reactants?

A. Dissolution of table salt:
$NaCl(s) \rightarrow Na^+(aq) + Cl^-(aq)$
B. Oxidation of iron:
$4Fe(s) + 3O_2(g) \rightarrow 2Fe_2O_3(s)$
C. Dissociation of ozone:
$O_3(g) \rightarrow O_2(g) + O(g)$
D. Vaporization of butane:
$C_4H_{10}(l) \rightarrow C_4H_{10}(g)$

100. Which statement about reactions is true?

A. All spontaneous reactions are both exothermic and cause an increase in entropy.
B. An endothermic reaction that increases the order of the system cannot be spontaneous.
C. A reaction can be non-spontaneous in one direction and also non-spontaneous in the opposite direction.
D. Melting snow is an exothermic process.

101. 10. kJ of heat are added to one kilogram of Iron at 10. °C. What is its final temperature? The specific heat of iron is 0.45 J/g•°C.

A. 22 °C
B. 27 °C
C. 32 °C
D. 37 °C

102. Which reaction is not a redox process?

A. Combustion of octane:
$2C_8H_{18} + 25O_2 \rightarrow 16CO_2 + 18H_2O$
B. Depletion of a lithium battery:
$Li + MnO_2 \rightarrow LiMnO_2$
C. Corrosion of aluminum by acid:
$2Al + 6HCl \rightarrow 2AlCl_3 + 3H_2$
D. Taking an antacid for heartburn:
$CaCO_3 + 2HCl \rightarrow CaCl_2 + H_2CO_3$
$\rightarrow CaCl_2 + CO_2 + H_2O$

103. Given the following heats of reaction:

$\Delta H = -0.3$ kJ/mol for
$Fe(s) + CO_2(g) \rightarrow FeO(s) + CO(g)$
$\Delta H = 5.7$ kJ/mol for
$2Fe(s) + 3CO_2(g) \rightarrow Fe_2O_3(s) + 3CO(g)$
and $\Delta H = 4.5$ kJ/mol for
$3FeO(s) + CO_2(g) \rightarrow Fe_3O_4(s) + CO(g)$

use Hess's Law to determine the heat of reaction for:

$3Fe_2O_3(s) + CO(g) \rightarrow 2Fe_3O_4(s) + CO_2(g)$

A. −10.8 kJ/mol
B. −9.9 kJ/mol
C. −9.0 kJ/mol
D. −8.1 kJ/mol

104. What is the oxidant in the reaction:
$2H_2S + SO_2 \rightarrow 3S + 2H_2O$?

A. H_2S
B. SO_2
C. S
D. H_2O

105. Molten NaCl is subjected to electrolysis. What reaction takes place at the cathode?

A. $2Cl^-(l) \rightarrow Cl_2(g) + 2e^-$
B. $Cl_2(g) + 2e^- \rightarrow 2Cl^-(l)$
C. $Na^+(l) + e^- \rightarrow Na(l)$
D. $Na^+(l) \rightarrow Na(l) + e^-$

106. What is the purpose of the salt bridge in an electrochemical cell?

A. To receive electrons from the oxidation half-reaction
B. To relieve the buildup of positive charge in the anode half-cell
C. To conduct electron flow
D. To permit positive ions to flow from the cathode half-cell to the anode half-cell

107. Given:
$E°=-2.37V$ for $Mg^{2+}(aq)+2e^- \rightarrow Mg(s)$
and
$E°=0.80$ V for $Ag^+(aq)+e^- \rightarrow Ag(s)$,
what is the standard potential of a voltaic cell composed of a piece of magnesium dipped in a 1 M Ag^+ solution and a piece of silver dipped in 1 M Mg^{2+}?

A. 0.77 V
B. 1.57 V
C. 3.17 V
D. 3.97 V

108.

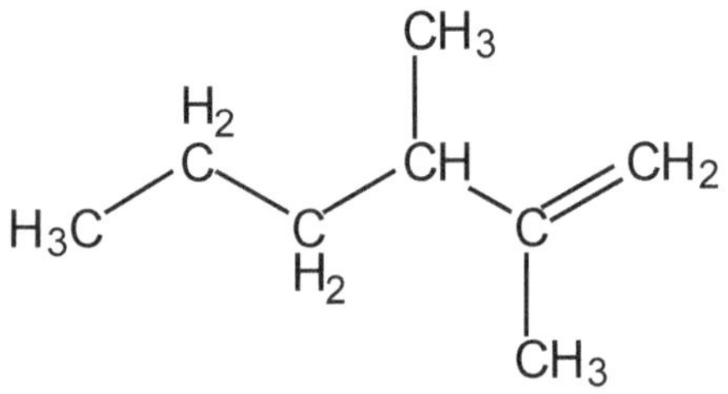

A proper name for this hydrocarbon is:

A. 4,5-dimethyl-6-hexene
B. 2,3-dimethyl-1-hexene
C. 4,5-dimethyl-6-hexyne
D. 2-methyl-3-propyl-1-butene

109. An IUPAC approved name for this molecule is:

   A. butanal
   B. propanal
   C. butanoic acid
   D. propanoic acid

110. Which molecule has a systematic name of methyl ethanoate?

   A. 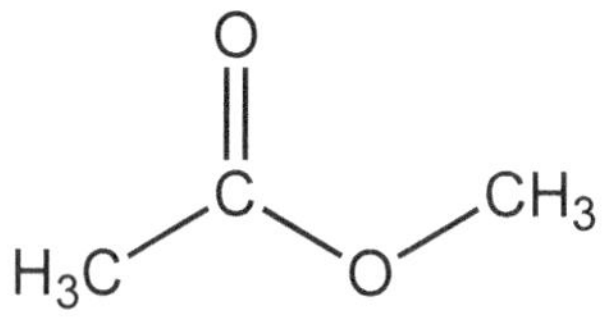 [structure: H₃C–C(=O)–O–CH₃]

   B. [structure: HC(=O)–CH₂–O–CH₂–C(=O)–CH₂OH with H₃C and CH₃ groups]

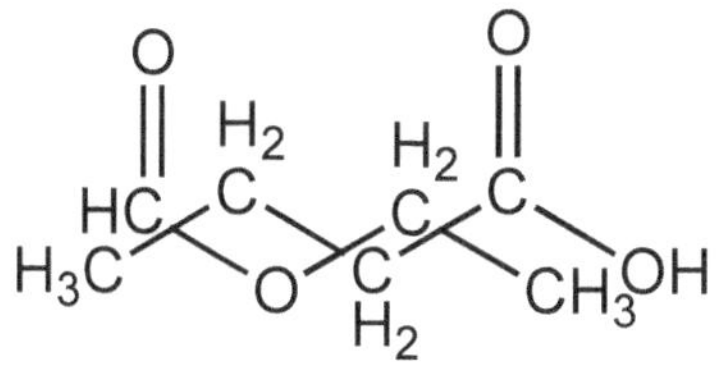

   C. [structure: H₃C–C(=O)–CH₂–CH₃]

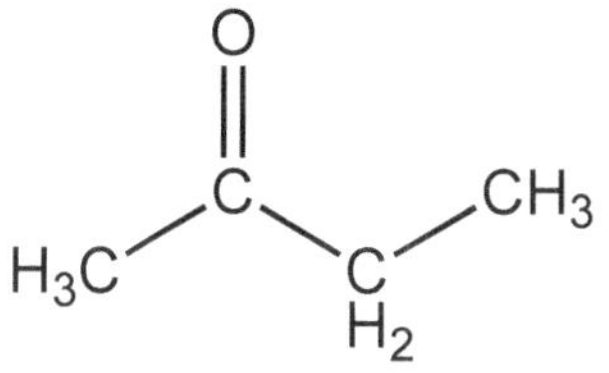

   D. 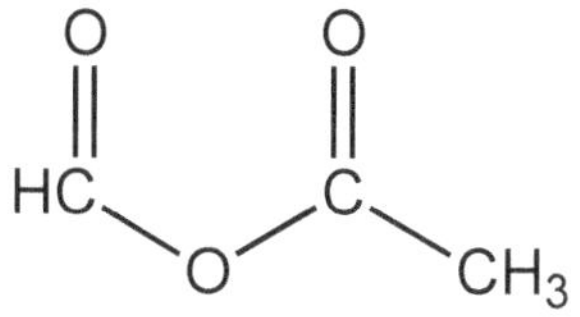 [structure: HC(=O)–O–C(=O)–CH₃]

111.

[structure of a bicyclic compound containing a lactone ring fused to a cyclohexene, with a –CH₂–CHO substituent and a –COOH group]

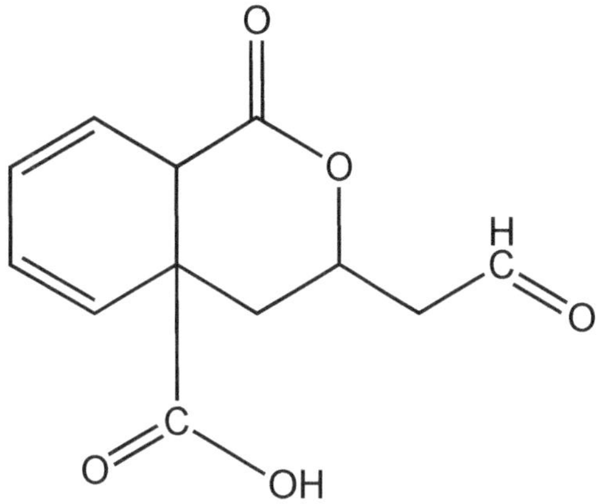

This compound contains an:

   A. alkene, carboxylic acid, ester, and ketone
   B. aldehyde, alkyne, ester, and ketone
   C. aldehyde, alkene, carboxylic acid, and ester
   D. acid anhydride, aldehyde, alkene, and amine

112. Which group of scientists made contributions in the same area of chemistry?

   A. Volta, Kekulé, Faraday, London
   B. Hess, Joule, Kelvin, Gibbs
   C. Boyle, Charles, Arrhenius, Pauli
   D. Davy, Mendeleev, Ramsay, Galvani

113. Which of the following pairs are isomers?

I. 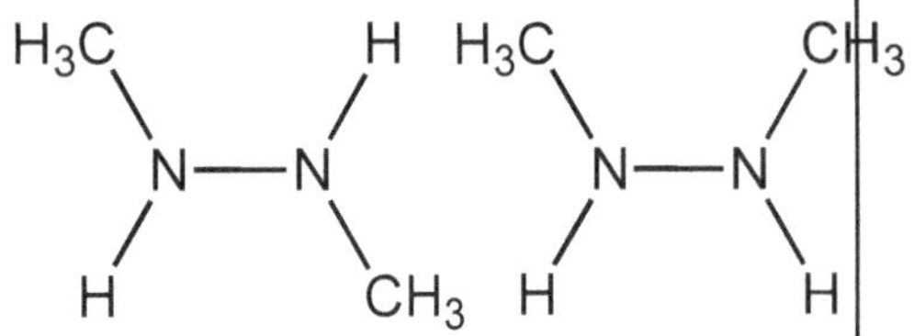 H₃C–NH–N(CH₃)–H   and   H₃C–N(CH₃)–NH–H (hydrazine isomers)

II. pentanal 2-pentanone

III. 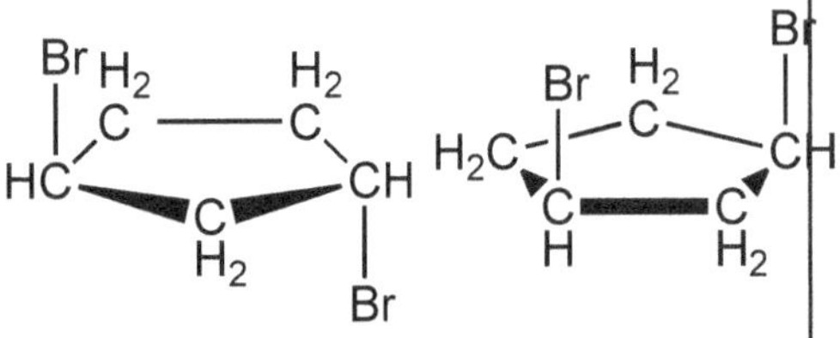 (two brominated cyclopentane structures)

IV. 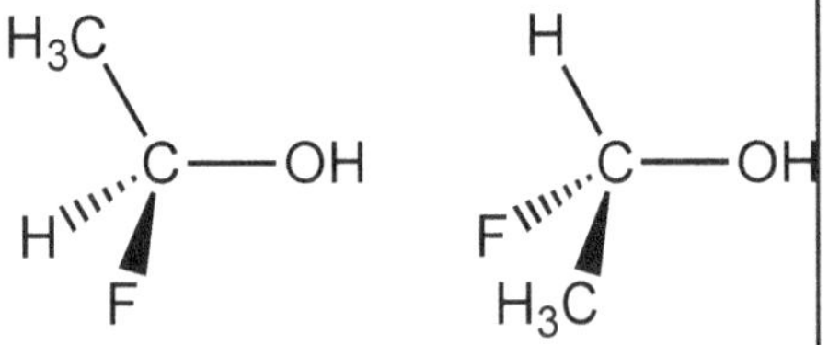 (two stereochemistry structures with H₃C, OH, H, F)

A. I and IV
B. II and III
C. I, II, and III
D. I, II, III, and IV

114. Which instrument would be most useful for separating two different proteins from a mixture?

A. UV/Vis spectrophotometer
B. Mass spectrometer
C. Gas chromatograph
D. Liquid chromatograph

115. Classify these biochemicals.

I. 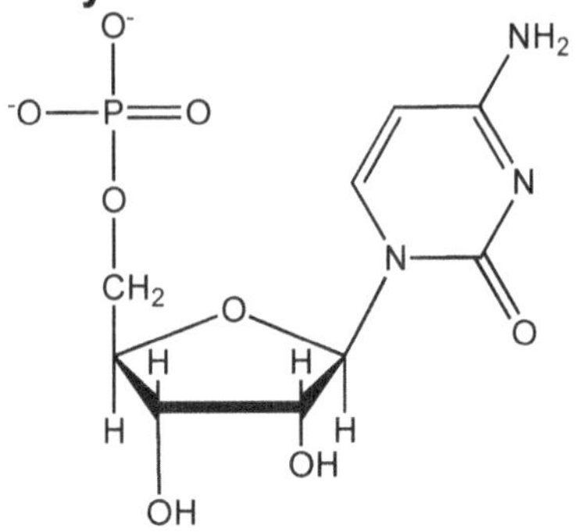 (phosphorylated nucleoside structure)

II. 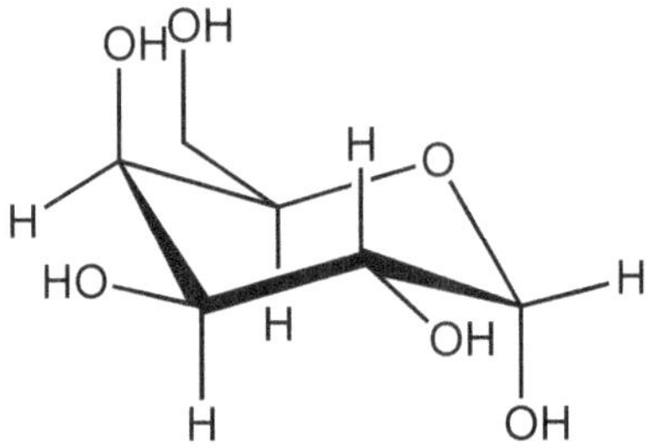 (cyclic sugar structure)

III. 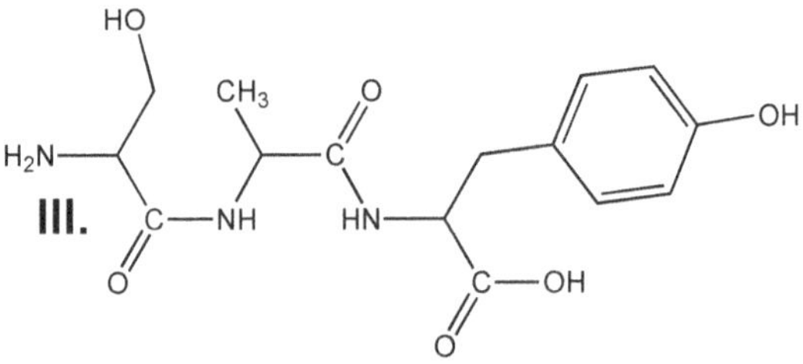 (tripeptide structure)

IV.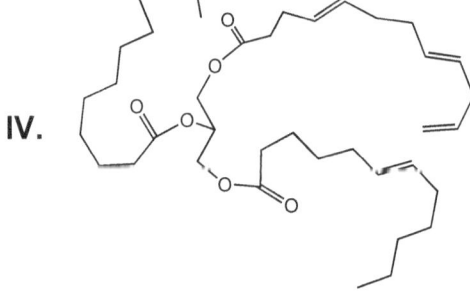

A. I-nucleotide, II-sugar, III-peptide, IV-fat
B. I-disaccharide, II-sugar, III-fatty acid, IV-polypeptide
C. I-disaccharide, II-amino acid, III-fatty acid, IV-polysaccharide
D. I I-nucleotide, II-sugar, III-triacylglyceride, and IV-DNA

116. You create a solution of 2.00 µg/ml of a pigment and divide the solution into 12 samples. You give four samples each to three teams of students. They use a spectrophotometer to determine the pigment concentration. Here is their data:

Team	Concentration (µg/ml)			
	sample 1	sample 2	sample 3	sample 4
1	1.98	1.93	1.92	1.88
2	1.70	1.72	1.69	1.70
3	1.78	1.99	2.87	2.20

Which of the following are true?

A. Team 1 has the most precise data
B. Team 3 has the most accurate data in spite of it having low precision
C. The data from team 2 is characteristic of a systematic error
D. The data from team 1 is more characteristic of random error than the data from team 3.

117. Which pair of measurements have an identical meaning?

A. 32 micrograms and 0.032 g
B. 26 nm and 2.60×10^{-8} m
C. 3.01×10^{-5} m^3 and 30.1 ml
D. 0.0020 L and 20 cm^3

118. Match the instrument with the quantity it measures

II. eudiometer
III. calorimeter
IV. manometer
V. hygrometer

A. I-volume, II-mass, III-radioactivity, IV-humidity
B. I-volume, II-heat, III-pressure, IV-humidity
C. I-viscosity, II-mass, III-pressure, IV-surface tension
D. I-viscosity, II-heat, III-radioactivity, IV-surface tension

119. Four nearly identical gems from the same mineral are weighed using different balances. Their masses are:

3.4533 g, 3.459 g, 3.4656 g, 3.464 g

The four gems are then collected and added to a volumetric cylinder containing 10.00 ml of liquid, and a new volume of 14.97 ml is read. What is the average mass of the four stones and what is the density of the mineral?

A. 3.460 g, and 2.78 g/ml
B. 3.460 g and 2.79 g/ml
C. 3.4605 g and 2.78 g/ml
D. 3.461 g and 2.79 g/ml

120. Which list includes equipment that would not be used in vacuum filtration.

    A. Rubber tubing, Florence flask, Büchner funnel
    B. Vacuum pump, Hirsch funnel, rubber stopper with a single hole
    C. Aspirator, filter paper, filter flask
    D. Lab stand, clamp, filter trap

121. Which of the following statements about lab safety is not true?

    A. Corrosive chemicals should be stored below eye level.
    B. A chemical splash on the eye or skin should be rinsed for 15 minutes in cold water.
    C. MSDS means "Material Safety Data Sheet."
    D. A student should "stop, drop, and roll" if their clothing catches fire in the lab.

122. Which of the following lists consists entirely of chemicals that are considered safe enough to be in a high school lab?

    A. hydrochloric acid, lauric acid, potassium permanganate, calcium hydroxide
    B. ethyl ether, nitric acid, sodium benzoate, methanol
    C. cobalt (II) sulfide, ethylene glycol, benzoyl peroxide, ammonium chloride
    D. picric acid, hydrofluoric acid, cadmium chloride, carbon disulfide.

123. The following procedure was developed to find the specific heat capacity of metals:

    1. Place pieces of the metals in an ice-water bath so their initial temperature is 0 °C.
    2. Weigh a styrofoam cup.
    3. Add water at room temperature to the cup and weigh it again
    4. Add a cold metal from the bath to the cup and weigh the cup a third time.
    5. Monitor the temperature drop of the water until a final temperature at thermal equilibrium is found.

    _____ is also required as additional information in order to obtain heat capacities for the metals. The best control would be to follow the same protocol except to use _____ in step 4 instead of a cold metal.

    A. The heat capacity of water / a metal at 100 °C
    B. The heat of formation of water / ice from the 0 °C bath
    C. The heat of capacity of ice / glass at 0 °C
    D. The heat capacity of water / water from the 0 °C bath

SCIENCE: CHEMISTRY

124. Which statement about the impact of chemistry on society is **not** true?

   A. Partial hydrogenation creates *trans* fat.
   B. The Haber Process incorporates nitrogen from the air into molecules for agricultural use.
   C. The CO_2 concentration in the atmosphere has decreased in the last ten years.
   D. The concentration of ozone-destroying chemicals in the stratosphere has decreased in the last ten years.

125. Which statement about everyday applications of chemistry is **true**?

   A. Rainwater found near sources of air pollution will most likely be basic.
   B. Batteries run down more quickly at low temperatures because chemical reactions are proceeding more slowly.
   C. Benzyl alcohol is a detergent used in shampoo.
   D. Adding salt decreases the time required for water to boil.

Answer Key

1. C	26. D	51. B	76. A	101. C
2. B	27. A	52. D	77. D	102. D
3. D	28. C	53. B	78. C	103. B
4. A	29. C	54. C	79. B	104. B
5. C	30. B	55. D	80. A	105. C
6. D	31. A	56. A	81. D	106. D
7. C	32. A	57. C	82. B	107. C
8. B	33. B	58. C	83. D	108. B
9. A	34. D	59. A	84. B	109. C
10. C	35. B	60. B	85. A	110. A
11. B	36. C	61. D	86. C	111. C
12. D	37. B	62. B	87. A	112. B
13. A	38. D	63. C	88. C	113. B
14. D	39. A	64. B	89. B	114. D
15. B	40. B	65. D	90. D	115. A
16. D	41. C	66. A	91. B	116. C
17. C	42. C	67. B	92. C	117. C
18. B	43. A	68. C	93. A	118. B
19. C	44. D	69. A	94. A	119. B
20. A	45. C	70. D	95. D	120. A
21. C	46. B	71. C	96. C	121. D
22. B	47. D	72. B	97. A	122. A
23. D	48. B	73. A	98. A	123. D
24. A	49. B	74. C	99. B	124. C
25. D	50. A	75. A	100. B	125. B

Rationales with Sample Questions

Note: The first insignificant digit should be carried through intermediate calculations. This digit is shown using *italics* in the solutions below.

1. **A piston compresses a gas at constant temperature. Which gas properties increase?**

   II. Average speed of molecules
   III. Pressure
   IV. Molecular collisions with container walls per second

   A. I and II
   B. I and III
   C. II and III
   D. I, II, and III

C. A decrease in volume (V) occurs at constant temperature (T). Average molecular speed is determined only by temperature and will be constant. V and P are inversely related, so pressure will increase. With less wall area and at higher pressure, more collisions occur per second.

2. **The temperature of a liquid is raised at atmospheric pressure. Which liquid property increases?**

   A. critical pressure
   B. vapor pressure
   C. surface tension
   D. viscosity

B. The critical pressure of a liquid is its vapor pressure at the critical temperature and is always a constant value. A rising temperature increases the kinetic energy of molecules and decreases the importance of intermolecular attraction. More molecules will be free to escape to the vapor phase (vapor pressure increases), but the effect of attractions at the liquid-gas interface will fall (surface tension decreases) and molecules will flow against each other more easily (viscosity decreases).

3. **Potassium crystallizes with two atoms contained in each unit cell. What is the mass of potassium found in a lattice 1.00×10^6 unit cells wide, 2.00×10^6 unit cells high, and 5.00×10^5 unit cells deep?**

   A. 85.0 ng
   B. 32.5 μg
   C. 64.9 μg
   D. 130. μg

D. First we find the number of unit cells in the lattice by multiplying the number in each row, stack, and column:

1.00×10^6 unit cell lengths $\times$ 2.00×10^6 unit cell lengths $\times$ 5.00×10^5 unit cell lengths
$= 1.00 \times 10^{18}$ unit cells

Avogadro's number and the molecular weight of potassium (K) are used in the solution:

$$1.00 \times 10^{18} \text{ unit cells} \times \frac{2 \text{ atoms of K}}{\text{unit cell}} \times \frac{1 \text{ mole of K}}{6.02 \times 10^{23} \text{ atoms of K}} \times \frac{39.098 \text{ g K}}{1 \text{ mole of K}}$$
$$= 1.30 \times 10^{-4} \text{ g}$$
$$= 130. \text{ μg}$$

4. **A gas is heated in a sealed container. Which of the following occur?**

   A. gas pressure rises
   B. gas density decreases
   C. the average distance between molecules increases
   D. all of the above

A. The same material is kept in a constant volume, so neither density nor the distance between molecules will change. Pressure will rise because of increasing molecular kinetic energy impacting container walls.

5. How many molecules are in 2.20 pg of a protein with a molecular weight of 150. kDa?

   A. 8.83×10^9
   B. 1.82×10^9
   C. 8.83×10^6
   D. 1.82×10^6

C. The prefix "p" for "pico-" indicates 10^{-12}. A kilodalton is 1000 atomic mass units.

$$2.20 \text{ pg protein} \times \frac{10^{-12} \text{ g}}{1 \text{ pg}} \times \frac{1 \text{ mole protein}}{150 \times 10^3 \text{ g protein}} \times \frac{6.02 \times 10^{23} \text{ molecules protein}}{1 \text{ mole protein}} =$$
$$= 8.83 \times 10^6 \text{ molecules}$$

6. At STP, 20. μL of O_2 contain 5.4×10^{16} molecules. According to Avogadro's hypothesis, how many molecules are in 20. μL of Ne at STP?

   A. 5.4×10^{15}
   B. 1.0×10^{16}
   C. 2.7×10^{16}
   D. 5.4×10^{16}

D. Avogadro's hypothesis states that equal volumes of different gases at the same temperature and pressure contain equal numbers of molecules.

7. An ideal gas at 50.0 °C and 3.00 atm is in a 300. cm³ cylinder. The cylinder volume changes by moving a piston until the gas is at 50.0 °C and 1.00 atm. What is the final volume?

   A. 100. cm³
   B. 450. cm³
   C. 900. cm³
   D. 1.20 dm³

C. A three-fold decrease in pressure of a constant quantity of gas at constant temperature will cause a three-fold increase in gas volume.

8. Which gas law may be used to solve the previous question?

   A. Charles's law
   B. Boyle's law
   C. Graham's law
   D. Avogadro's law

B. The inverse relationship between volume and pressure is Boyle's law.

9. A blimp is filled with 5000. m^3 of helium at 28.0 °C and 99.7 kPa. What is the mass of helium used?

   $R = 8.3144 \dfrac{J}{mol\text{-}K}$

   A. 797 kg
   B. 810. kg
   C. 1.99×10^3 kg
   D. 8.57×10^3 kg

A. First the ideal gas law is manipulated to solve for moles.

$$PV = nRT \quad \Rightarrow \quad n = \dfrac{PV}{RT}$$

Temperature must be expressed in Kelvin: $T = (28.0 + 273.15)\,K = 301.15\,K$.

The ideal gas law is then used with the knowledge that joules are equivalent to Pa-m^3:

$$n = \dfrac{PV}{RT} = \dfrac{(99.7 \times 10^3\,Pa)(5000.\,m^3)}{\left(8.3144\,\dfrac{m^3\text{-}Pa}{mol\text{-}K}\right)(301.15\,K)} = 1.991 \times 10^3\,mol\,He.$$

Moles are then converted to grams using the molecular weight of helium:

$$1.991 \times 10^3\,mol\,He \times \dfrac{4.0026\,g\,He}{1\,mol\,He} = 797 \times 10^3\,g\,He = 797\,kg\,He.$$

10. Which of the following are able to flow from one place to another?

   I. Gases
   II. Liquids
   III. Solids
   IV. Supercritical fluids

   A. I and II
   B. II only
   C. I, II, and IV
   D. I, II, III, and IV

C. Gases and liquids both flow. Supercritical fluids have some traits in common with gases and some in common with liquids, and so they flow also. Solids have a fixed volume and shape.

11. One mole of an ideal gas at STP occupies 22.4 L. At what temperature will one mole of an ideal gas at one atm occupy 31.0 L?

   A. 34.6 °C
   B. 105 °C
   C. 378 °C
   D. 442 °C

B. Either Charles's law, the combined gas law, or the ideal gas law may be used with temperature in Kelvin.

Charles's law or the combined gas law with $P_1 = P_2$ may be manipulated to equate a ratio between temperature and volume when P and n are constant.

$$V \propto T \text{ or } \frac{P_1 V_1}{T_1} = \frac{P_2 V_2}{T_2} \Rightarrow \frac{T_1}{V_1} = \frac{T_2}{V_2} \Rightarrow T_2 = V_2 \frac{T_1}{V_1}$$

$$T_2 = 31.0 \text{ L} \frac{273.15 \text{ K}}{22.4 \text{ L}} = 378 \text{ K} = 105 \text{ °C}.$$

The ideal gas law may also be used with the appropriate gas constant:

$$PV = nRT \Rightarrow T = \frac{PV}{nR}$$

$$T = \frac{(1 \text{ atm})(31.0 \text{ L})}{(1 \text{ mol})\left(0.08206 \frac{\text{L-atm}}{\text{mol-K}}\right)} = 378 \text{ K} = 105 \text{ °C}.$$

12. Why does $CaCl_2$ have a higher normal melting point than NH_3?

   A. London dispersion forces in $CaCl_2$ are stronger than covalent bonds in NH_3.
   B. Covalent bonds in NH_3 are stronger than dipole-dipole bonds in $CaCl_2$.
   C. Ionic bonds in $CaCl_2$ are stronger than London dispersion forces in NH_3.
   D. Ionic bonds in $CaCl_2$ are stronger than hydrogen bonds in NH_3.

D. London dispersion forces are weaker than covalent bonds, eliminating choice A. A higher melting point will result from stronger intermolecular bonds, eliminating choice B. $CaCl_2$ is an ionic solid resulting from a cation on the left and an anion on the right of the periodic table. The dominant attractive forces between NH_3 molecules are hydrogen bonds.

13. Which intermolecular attraction explains the following trend in straight-chain alkanes?

Condensed structural formula	Boiling point (°C)
CH_4	-161.5
CH_3CH_3	-88.6
$CH_3CH_2CH_3$	-42.1
$CH_3CH_2CH_2CH_3$	-0.5
$CH_3CH_2CH_2CH_2CH_3$	36.0
$CH_3CH_2CH_2CH_2CH_2CH_3$	68.7

   A. London dispersion forces
   B. Dipole-dipole interactions
   C. Hydrogen bonding
   D. Ion-induced dipole interactions

A. Alkanes are composed entirely of non-polar C-C and C-H bonds, resulting in no dipole interactions or hydrogen bonding. London dispersion forces increase with the size of the molecule, resulting in a higher temperature requirement to break these bonds and a higher boiling point.

14. List NH₃, PH₃, MgCl₂, Ne, and N₂ in order of increasing melting point.

   A. N_2 < Ne < PH_3 < NH_3 < $MgCl_2$
   B. N_2 < NH_3 < Ne < $MgCl_2$ < PH_3
   C. Ne < N_2 < NH_3 < PH_3 < $MgCl_2$
   D. Ne < N_2 < PH_3 < NH_3 < $MgCl_2$

D. Higher melting points result from stronger intermolecular forces. $MgCl_2$ is the only material listed with ionic bonds and will have the highest melting point. Dipole-dipole interactions are present in NH_3 and PH_3 but not in Ne and N_2. Ne and N_2 are also small molecules expected to have very weak London dispersion forces and so will have lower melting points than NH_3 and PH_3. NH_3 will have stronger intermolecular attractions and a higher melting point than PH_3 because hydrogen bonding occurs in NH_3. Ne has a molecular weight of 20 and a spherical shape and N_2 has a molecular weight of 28 and is not spherical. Both of these factors predict stronger London dispersion forces and a higher melting point for N_2. Actual melting points are: Ne (25 K) < N_2 (63 K) < PH_3 (140 K) < NH_3 (195 K) < $MgCl_2$ (987 K).

15. 1-butanol, ethanol, methanol, and 1-propanol are all liquids at room temperature. Rank them in order of increasing viscosity.

   A. 1-butanol < 1-propanol < ethanol < methanol
   B. methanol < ethanol < 1-propanol < 1-butanol
   C. methanol < ethanol < 1-butanol < 1-propanol
   D. 1-propanol < 1-butanol < ethanol < methanol

B. Higher viscosities result from stronger intermolecular attractive forces. The molecules listed are all alcohols with the -OH functional group attached to the end of a straight-chain alkane. In other words, they all have the formula $CH_3(CH_2)_{n-1}OH$. The only difference between the molecules is the length of the alkane corresponding to the value of *n*. With all else identical, larger molecules have greater intermolecular attractive forces due to a greater molecular surface for the attractions. Therefore the viscosities are ranked: methanol (CH_3OH) < ethanol (CH_3CH_2OH) < 1-propanol ($CH_3CH_2CH_2OH$) < 1-butanol ($CH_3CH_2CH_2CH_2OH$).

16. Which gas has a diffusion rate of 25% the rate for hydrogen?

   A. helium
   B. methane
   C. nitrogen
   D. oxygen

D. Graham's law of diffusion states:

$$\frac{r_1}{r_2} = \sqrt{\frac{M_2}{M_1}}.$$

Hydrogen (H_2) has molecular weight of 2.0158 u. Using the unknown for material #1 and hydrogen for material #2 in the equation for Graham's law, the ratio of rates is:

$\frac{r_{unknown}}{r_{hydrogen}} = \sqrt{\frac{2.0158 \text{ u}}{M_{unknown}}} = 0.25.$ Squaring both sides yields $\frac{2.0158 \text{ u}}{M_{unknown}} = 0.0625.$

Solving for $M_{unknown}$ gives:

$$M_{unknown} = \frac{2.0158 \text{ u}}{0.0625} = 32 \text{ u}.$$

The given possibilities are: He (4.0 u), CH_4 (16 u), N_2 (28 u), and O_2 (32 u).

17. 2.00 L of an unknown gas at 1500. mm Hg and a temperature of 25.0 °C weighs 7.52 g. Assuming the ideal gas equation, what is the molecular weight of the gas?

$$760 \text{ mm Hg} = 1 \text{ atm}$$
$$R = 0.08206 \text{ L-atm/(mol-K)}$$

- A. 21.6 u
- B. 23.3 u
- C. 46.6 u
- D. 93.2 u

C. Pressure and temperature must be expressed in the proper units. Next the ideal gas law is used to find the number of moles of gas.

$$P = 1500 \text{ mm Hg} \times \frac{1 \text{ atm}}{760 \text{ mm Hg}} = 1.974 \text{ atm and } T = 25.0 + 273.15 = 298.15 \text{ K}$$

$$PV = nRT \implies n = \frac{PV}{RT}$$

$$n = \frac{(1.974 \text{ atm})(2.00 \text{ L})}{\left(0.08206 \frac{\text{L-atm}}{\text{mol-K}}\right)(298.15 \text{ K})} = 0.1613 \text{ mol.}$$

The molecular mass may be found from the mass of one mole.

$$\frac{7.52 \text{ g}}{0.1613 \text{ mol}} = 46.6 \frac{\text{g}}{\text{mol}} \implies 46.6 \text{ u}$$

18. Which substance is most likely to be a gas at STP?

- A. SeO_2
- B. F_2
- C. $CaCl_2$
- D. I_2

B. A gas at STP has a normal boiling point under 0 °C. The substance with the lowest boiling point will have the weakest intermolecular attractive forces and will be the most likely gas at STP. F_2 has the lowest molecular weight, is not a salt, metal, or covalent network solid, and is non-polar, indicating the weakest intermolecular attractive forces of the four choices. F_2 actually is a gas at STP, and the other three are solids.

19. What pressure is exerted by a mixture of 2.7 g of H2 and 59 g of Xe at 0 °C on a 50. L container?

   A. 0.69 atm
   B. 0.76 atm
   C. 0.80 atm
   D. 0.97 atm

C. Grams of gas are first converted to moles:

$$2.7 \text{ g H}_2 \times \frac{1 \text{ mol H}_2}{2 \times 1.0079 \text{ g H}_2} = 1.33 \text{ mol H}_2 \quad \text{and} \quad 59 \text{ g Xe} \times \frac{1 \text{ mol H}_2}{131.29 \text{ g H}_2} = 0.449 \text{ mol Xe}$$

Dalton's law of partial pressures for an ideal gas is used to find the pressure of the mixture:

$$P_{total}V = (n_{H_2} + n_{Xe})RT \Rightarrow P_{total} = \frac{(n_{H_2} + n_{Xe})RT}{V}$$

$$P_{total} = \frac{(1.33 \text{ mol} + 0.449 \text{ mol})\left(0.08206 \frac{\text{L-atm}}{\text{mol-K}}\right)(273.15 \text{ K})}{50. \text{ L}} = 0.80 \text{ atm.}$$

20. A few minutes after opening a bottle of perfume, the scent is detected on the other side of the room. What law relates to this phenomenon?

   A. Graham's law
   B. Dalton's law
   C. Boyle's law
   D. Avogadro's law

A. Graham's law describes the rate of diffusion (or effusion) of a gas, in this instance, the rate of diffusion of molecules in perfume vapor.

21. Which of the following statements are true of vapor pressure at equilibrium?

    A. Solids have no vapor pressure.
    B. Dissolving a solute in a liquid increases its vapor pressure.
    C. The vapor pressure of a pure substance is characteristic of that substance and its temperature.
    D. All of the above

C. Only temperature and the identity of the substance determine vapor pressure. Solids have a vapor pressure, and solutes decrease vapor pressure.

22. Find the partial pressure of N_2 in a container holding H_2O and N_2 at 150. kPa and 50 °C. The vapor pressure of H_2O at 50 °C is 12 kPa.

    A. 12 kPa
    B. 138 kPa
    C. 162 kPa
    D. The value cannot be determined.

B. The partial pressure of H_2O vapor in the container is its vapor pressure. The partial pressure of N_2 may be found by manipulating Dalton's law:
$$P_{total} = P_{H_2O} + P_{N_2} \Rightarrow P_{N_2} = P_{total} - P_{H_2O}$$
$$P_{N_2} = P_{total} - P_{H_2O} = 150.\ \text{kPa} - 12\ \text{kPa} = 138\ \text{kPa}$$

23. The normal boiling point of water on the Kelvin scale is closest to:

    A. 112 K
    B. 212 K
    C. 273 K
    D. 373 K

D. Temperature in Kelvin are equal to Celsius temperatures plus 273.15. Since the normal boiling point of water is 100 °C, it will boil at 373.15 K, corresponding to answer D.

24. Which phase may be present at the triple point of a substance?

   I. Gas
   II. Liquid
   III. Solid
   IV. Supercritical fluid

   A. I, II, and III
   B. I, II, and IV
   C. II, III, and IV
   D. I, II, III, and IV

A. Gas, liquid and solid may exist together at the triple point.

25. In the following phase diagram, _____ occurs as P is decreased from A to B at constant T and _____ occurs as T is increased from C to D at constant P.

   A. deposition, melting
   B. sublimation, melting
   C. deposition, vaporization
   D. sublimation, vaporization

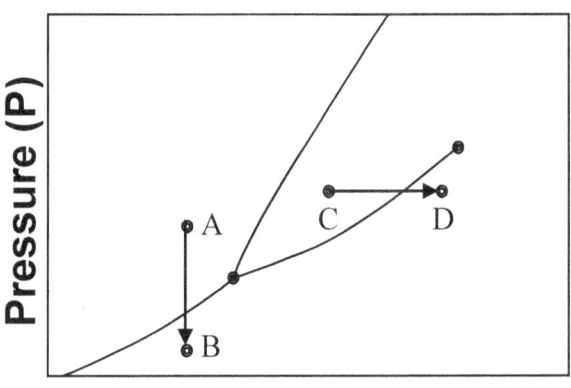

D. Point A is located in the solid phase, point C is located in the liquid phase. Points B and D are located in the gas phase. The transition from solid to gas is sublimation and the transition from liquid to gas is vaporization.

26. Heat is added to a pure solid at its melting point until it all becomes liquid at its freezing point. Which of the following occur?

   A. Intermolecular attractions are weakened.
   B. The kinetic energy of the molecules does not change.
   C. The freedom of the molecules to move about increases.
   D. All of the above

D. Intermolecular attractions are lessened during melting. This permits molecules to move about more freely, but there is no change in the kinetic energy of the molecules because the temperature has remained the same.

27. Which of the following occur when NaCl dissolves in water?

   A. Heat is required to break bonds in the NaCl crystal lattice.
   B. Heat is released when hydrogen bonds in water are broken.
   C. Heat is required to form bonds of hydration.
   D. The oxygen end of the water molecule is attracted to the Cl⁻ ion.

A. The lattice does break apart, H-bonds in water are broken, and bonds of hydration are formed, but the first and second process require heat while the third process releases heat. The oxygen end of the water molecule has a partial negative charge and is attracted to the Na^+ ion.

28. The solubility of $CoCl_2$ is 54 g per 100 g of ethanol. Three flasks each contain 100 g of ethanol. Flask #1 also contains 40 g $CoCl_2$ in solution. Flask #2 contains 56 g $CoCl_2$ in solution. Flask #3 contains 5 g of solid $CoCl_2$ in equilibrium with 54 g $CoCl_2$ in solution. Which of the following describe the solutions present in the liquid phase of the flasks?

   A. #1-saturated, #2-supersaturated, #3-unsaturated.
   B. #1-unsaturated, #2-miscible, #3-saturated.
   C. #1-unsaturated, #2-supersaturated, #3-saturated.
   D. #1-unsaturated, #2-not at equilibrium, #3-miscible.

C. Flask #1 contains less solute than the solubility limit, and is unsaturated. Flask #2 contains more solute than the solubility limit, and is supersaturated and also not at equilibrium. Flask #3 contains the solubility limit and is a saturated solution. The term "miscible" applies only to liquids that mix together in all proportions.

29. The solubility at 1.0 atm of pure CO_2 in water at 25 °C is 0.034 M. According to Henry's law, what is the solubility at 4.0 atm of pure CO_2 in water at 25 °C? Assume no chemical reaction occurs between CO_2 and H_2O.

   A. 0.0085 M
   B. 0.034 M
   C. 0.14 M
   D. 0.25 M

C. Henry's law states that CO_2 solubility in M (mol/L) will be proportional to the partial pressure of the gas. A four-fold increase in pressure from 1.0 atm to 4.0 atm will increase solubility four-fold from 0.034 M to 0.14 M.

TEACHER CERTIFICATION STUDY GUIDE

30. Carbonated water is bottled at 25 °C under pure CO_2 at 4.0 atm. Later the bottle is opened at 4 °C under air at 1.0 atm that has a partial pressure of 3×10^{-4} atm CO_2. Why do CO_2 bubbles form when the bottle is opened?

   A. CO_2 leaves the solution due to a drop in solubility at the lower total pressure.
   B. CO_2 leaves the solution due to a drop in solubility at the lower CO_2 pressure.
   C. CO_2 leaves the solution due to a drop in solubility at the lower temperature.
   D. CO_2 is formed by the decomposition of carbonic acid.

B. A is incorrect because if the water were bottled under a different gas at a high pressure, it would not be carbonated. CO_2 partial pressure is the important factor in solubility. C is incorrect because a decrease in temperature will increase solubility, and the chance from 298 K to 277 K is relatively small. D may occur, but this represents a small fraction of the gas released.

31. When KNO_3 dissolves in water, the water grows slightly colder. An increase in temperature will _____ the solubility of KNO_3.

   A. increase
   B. decrease
   C. have no effect on
   D. have an unknown effect with the information given on

A. The decline in water temperature indicates that the net solution process is endothermic (requiring heat). A temperature increase supplying more heat will favor the solution and increase solubility according to Le Chatelier's principle.

32. An experiment requires 100. mL of a 0.500 M solution of $MgBr_2$. How many grams of $MgBr_2$ will be present in this solution?

   A. 9.21 g
   B. 11.7 g
   C. 12.4 g
   D. 15.6 g

A.

$$0.100 \text{ L solution} \times \frac{0.500 \text{ mol } MgBr_2}{L} \times \frac{(24.305 + 2 \times 79.904) \text{ g } MgBr_2}{\text{mol } MgBr_2} = 9.21 \text{ g } MgBr_2$$

33. 500. mg of RbOH are added to 500. g of ethanol (C_2H_6O) resulting in 395 mL of solution. Determine the molarity and molality of RbOH.

   A. 0.0124 M, 0.00488 *m*
   B. 0.0124 M, 0.00976 *m*
   C. 0.0223 M, 0.00488 *m*
   D. 0.0223 M, 0.00976 *m*

B. First we determine the moles of solute present:

$$0.500 \text{ g RbOH} \times \frac{1 \text{ mol RbOH}}{(85.468 + 15.999 + 1.0079) \text{ g RbOH}} = 0.004879 \text{ mol RbOH}.$$

This value is used to calculate molarity and molality:

$$\frac{0.04879 \text{ mol RbOH}}{0.395 \text{ L solution}} = 0.0124 \text{ M RbOH}$$

and

$$\frac{0.04879 \text{ mol RbOH}}{0.500 \text{ kg ethanol}} = 0.00976 \text{ } m \text{ RbOH}.$$

34. 20.0 g H₃PO₄ in 1.5 L of solution are intended to react with KOH according to the following reaction: $H_3PO_4 + 3\,KOH \rightarrow K_3PO_4 + 3\,H_2O$. What is the molarity and normality of the H₃PO₄ solution?

A. 0.41 M, 1.22 N
B. 0.41 M, 0.20 N
C. 0.14 M, 0.045 N
D. 0.14 M, 0.41 N

D. We use two methods to solve this problem. In the first method, we determine the moles of solute present and use it to calculate molarity and normality:

$$20.0 \text{ g } H_3PO_4 \times \frac{1 \text{ mol } H_3PO_4}{(3 \times 1.0079 + 30.974 + 4 \times 15.999) \text{ g } H_3PO_4} = 0.204 \text{ mol } H_3PO_4.$$

$$\frac{0.204 \text{ mol } H_3PO_4}{1.5 \text{ L solution}} = 0.136 \frac{\text{mol } H_3PO_4}{\text{L}} = 0.14 \text{ M } H_3PO_4$$

and

$$\frac{0.204 \text{ mol } H_3PO_4}{1.5 \text{ L solution}} \times \frac{3 \text{ reaction equivalents}}{1 \text{ mol } H_3PO_4} = 0.408 \frac{\text{reaction equivalents}}{\text{L}} = 0.41 \text{ N } H_3PO_4.$$

Alternatively, molarity may be found in one step and normality may be determined from the molarity:

$$\frac{20.0 \text{ g } H_3PO_4}{1.5 \text{ L}} \times \frac{1 \text{ mol } H_3PO_4}{(3 \times 1.0079 + 30.974 + 4 \times 15.999) \text{ g } H_3PO_4} = 0.136 \frac{\text{mol } H_3PO_4}{\text{L}} = 0.14 \text{ M } H_3PO_4$$

and

$$0.136 \frac{\text{mol } H_3PO_4}{\text{L}} \times \frac{3 \text{ reaction equivalents}}{1 \text{ mol } H_3PO_4} = 0.408 \frac{\text{reaction equivalents}}{\text{L}} = 0.41 \text{ N}.$$

TEACHER CERTIFICATION STUDY GUIDE

35. Aluminum sulfate is a strong electrolyte. What is the concentration of all species in a 0.2 M solution of aluminum sulfate?

   A. 0.2 M Al^{3+}, 0.2 M SO_4^{2-}
   B. 0.4 M Al^{3+}, 0.6 M SO_4^{2-}
   C. 0.6 M Al^{3+}, 0.4 M SO_4^{2-}
   D. 0.2 M $Al_2(SO_4)_3$

B. A strong electrolyte will completely ionize into its cation and anion. Aluminum sulfate is $Al_2(SO_4)_3$. Each mole of aluminum sulfate ionizes into 2 moles of Al^{3+} and 3 moles of SO_4^{2-}:

$$0.2 \frac{\text{mol } Al_2(SO_4)_3}{L} \times \frac{2 \text{ mol } Al^{3+}}{\text{mol } Al_2(SO_4)_3} = 0.4 \frac{\text{mol } Al^{3+}}{L} \text{ and}$$

$$0.2 \frac{\text{mol } Al_2(SO_4)_3}{L} \times \frac{3 \text{ mol } SO_4^{2-}}{\text{mol } Al_2(SO_4)_3} = 0.6 \frac{\text{mol } SO_4^{2-}}{L}.$$

36. 15 g of formaldehyde (CH_2O) are dissolved in 100. g of water. Calculate the weight percentage and mole fraction of formaldehyde in the solution.

   A. 13%, 0.090
   B. 15%, 0.090
   C. 13%, 0.083
   D. 15%, 0.083

C. Remember to use the total amounts in the denominator.

For weight percentage: $\frac{15 \text{ g } CH_2O}{(15+100) \text{ g total}} = 0.13 = 13\%$.

For mole fraction, first convert grams of each substance to moles:

$$15 \text{ g } CH_2O \times \frac{\text{mol } CH_2O}{(12.011 + 2 \times 1.0079 + 15.999) \text{ g } CH_2O} = 0.4996 \text{ mol } CH_2O$$

$$100 \text{ g } H_2O \times \frac{\text{mol } H_2O}{(2 \times 1.0079 + 15.999) \text{ g } H_2O} = 5.551 \text{ mol } H_2O.$$

Again use the total amount in the denominator $\frac{0.4996 \text{ mol } CH_2O}{(0.4996 + 5.551) \text{ mol total}} = 0.083$.

37. Which of the following would make the best solvent for Br_2?

   A. H_2O
   B. CS_2
   C. NH_3
   D. molten NaCl

B. The best solvents for a solute have intermolecular bonds of similar strength to the solute ("like dissolves like"). Bromine is a non-polar molecule with intermolecular attractions due to weak London dispersion forces. The relatively strong hydrogen bonding in H_2O and NH_3 and the very strong electrostatic attractions in molten NaCl would make each of them a poor solvent for Br_2 because these molecules would prefer to remain attracted to one another. CS_2 is a fairly small non-polar molecule.

38. Which of the following is most likely to dissolve in water?

   A. H_2
   B. CCl_4
   C. $(SiO_2)_n$
   D. CH_3OH

D. The best solutes for a solvent have intermolecular bonds of similar strength to the solvent. H_2O molecules are connected by fairly strong hydrogen bonds. H_2 and CCl_4 are molecules with intermolecular attractions due to weak London dispersion forces. $(SiO_2)_n$ is a covalent network solid and is essentially one large molecule with bonds that much stronger than hydrogen bonds. CH_3OH (methanol) is miscible with water because it contains hydrogen bonds between molecules.

39. Which of the following is not a colligative property?

   A. Viscosity lowering
   B. Freezing point lowering
   C. Boiling point elevation
   D. Vapor pressure lowering

A. Vapor pressure lowering, boiling point elevation, and freezing point lowering may all be visualized as a result of solute particles interfering with the interface between phases in a consistent way. This is not the case for viscosity.

TEACHER CERTIFICATION STUDY GUIDE

40. $BaCl_2(aq) + Na_2SO_4(aq) \rightarrow BaSO_4(s) + 2NaCl(aq)$ is an example of a _____ reaction.

A. acid-base
B. precipitation
C. redox
D. nuclear

B. $BaSO_4$ falls out of the solution as a precipitate, but the charges on Ba^{2+} and SO_4^{2-} remain unchanged, so this is not a redox reaction. Neither $BaCl_2$ nor Na_2SO_4 are acids or bases, and the nuclei involved also remain unaltered

41. List the following aqueous solutions in order of increasing boiling point.

I. 0.050 *m* $AlCl_3$
II. 0.080 *m* $Ba(NO_3)_2$
III. 0.090 *m* NaCl
IV. 0.12 *m* ethylene glycol ($C_2H_6O_2$)

A. I < II < III < IV
B. I < III < IV < II
C. IV < III < I < II
D. IV < III < II < I

C. Particles in solution determine colligative properties. The first three materials are strong electrolyte salts, and $C_2H_6O_2$ is a non-electrolyte.

$AlCl_3(aq)$ is $Al^{3+} + 3\ Cl^-$. So $0.050 \dfrac{\text{mol } AlCl_3}{\text{kg } H_2O} \times \dfrac{4 \text{ mol particles}}{\text{mol } AlCl_3} = 0.200\ m$ particles

$Ba(NO_3)_2(aq)$ is $Ba^{2+} + 2\ NO_3^-$. So $0.080 \dfrac{\text{mol } Ba(NO_3)_2}{\text{kg } H_2O} \times \dfrac{3 \text{ mol particles}}{\text{mol } Ba(NO_3)_2} = 0.240\ m$ particles

NaCl(aq) is $Na^+ + Cl^-$. So $0.090 \dfrac{\text{mol NaCl}}{\text{kg } H_2O} \times \dfrac{2 \text{ mol particles}}{\text{mol NaCl}} = 0.180\ m$ particles

$C_2H_6O_2(aq)$ is not an electrolyte. So $0.12 \dfrac{\text{mol } C_2H_6O_2}{\text{kg } H_2O} \times \dfrac{1 \text{ mol particles}}{\text{mol } C_2H_6O_2} = 0.12\ m$ particles

The greater the number of dissolved particles, the greater the boiling point elevation.

SCIENCE: CHEMISTRY

42. Osmotic pressure is the pressure required to prevent _____ flowing from low to high _____ concentration across a semipermeable membrane.

   A. solute, solute
   B. solute, solvent
   C. solvent, solute
   D. solvent, solvent

C. Osmotic pressure is the pressure required to prevent osmosis, which is the flow of solvent across the membrane from low to high solute concentration. This is also the direction from high to low solvent concentration.

TEACHER CERTIFICATION STUDY GUIDE

43. A solution of NaCl in water is heated on a mountain in an open container until it boils at 100. °C. The air pressure on the mountain is 0.92 atm. According to Raoult's law, what mole fraction of Na^+ and Cl^- are present in the solution?

   A. 0.04 Na^+, 0.04 Cl^-
   B. 0.08 Na^+, 0.08 Cl^-
   C. 0.46 Na^+, 0.46 Cl^-
   D. 0.92 Na^+, 0.92 Cl^-

A. The vapor pressure of H_2O at 100. °C is exactly 1 atm. Boiling point decreases with external pressure, so the boiling point of pure H_2O at 0.9 atm will be less than 100. °C. Adding salt raises the boiling point at 0.92 atm to 100. °C by decreasing vapor pressure to 0.92 atm. According to Raoult's law:

$$P^{vapor}_{solution} = P^{vapor}_{pure\ solvent} (\text{mole fraction})_{solvent} \Rightarrow (\text{mole fraction})_{solvent} = \frac{P^{vapor}_{solution}}{P^{vapor}_{pure\ solvent}}.$$

Therefore, $(\text{mole fraction})_{H_2O} = \frac{0.92 \text{ atm at } 100. °C}{1.0 \text{ atm at } 100. °C} = 0.92 \frac{\text{mol } H_2O}{\text{mol total}}.$

The remaining 0.08 mole fraction of solute is evenly divided between the two ions:

$(\text{mole fraction})_{solute} = 1 - (\text{mole fraction})_{H_2O} = 1 - 0.92 = 0.08 \frac{\text{mol solute particles}}{\text{mol total}}$

$(\text{mole fraction})_{Na^+} = 0.08 \frac{\text{mol solute particles}}{\text{mol total}} \times \frac{1 \text{ mol } Na^+}{2 \text{ mol solute particles}} = 0.04 \frac{\text{mol } Na^+}{\text{mol total}}$

$(\text{mole fraction})_{Cl^-} = 0.08 \frac{\text{mol solute particles}}{\text{mol total}} \times \frac{1 \text{ mol } Cl^-}{2 \text{ mol solute particles}} = 0.04 \frac{\text{mol } Cl^-}{\text{mol total}}.$

44. Write a balanced nuclear equation for the emission of an alpha particle by polonium-209.

   A. $^{209}_{84}Po \rightarrow\ ^{205}_{81}Pb +\ ^{4}_{2}He$
   B. $^{209}_{84}Po \rightarrow\ ^{205}_{82}Bi +\ ^{4}_{2}He$
   C. $^{209}_{84}Po \rightarrow\ ^{209}_{85}At +\ ^{0}_{-1}e$
   D. $^{209}_{84}Po \rightarrow\ ^{205}_{82}Pb +\ ^{4}_{2}He$

   D. The periodic table before skill 1.1 shows that polonium has an atomic number of 84. The emission of an alpha particle, $^{4}_{2}He$ (eliminating choice C), will leave an atom with an atomic number of 82 and a mass number of 205 (eliminating choice A). The periodic table identifies this element as lead, $^{205}_{82}Pb$, not bismuth (eliminating choice B).

45. Write a balanced nuclear equation for the decay of calcium-45 to scandium-45.

   A. $^{45}_{20}Ca \rightarrow\ ^{41}_{18}Sc +\ ^{4}_{2}He$
   B. $^{45}_{20}Ca +\ ^{0}_{1}e \rightarrow\ ^{45}_{21}Sc$
   C. $^{45}_{20}Ca \rightarrow\ ^{45}_{21}Sc +\ ^{0}_{-1}e$
   D. $^{45}_{20}Ca +\ ^{0}_{1}p \rightarrow\ ^{45}_{21}Sc$

   C. All four choices are balanced mathematically. "A" leaves scandium-41 as a decay product, not scandium-45. "B" and "D" require the addition of particles not normally present in the atom. If these reactions do occur, they are not decay reactions because they are not spontaneous. "C" involves the common decay mechanism of beta emission.

46. $^{3}_{1}H$ decays with a half-life of 12 years. 3.0 g of pure $^{3}_{1}H$ were placed in a sealed container 24 years ago. How many grams of $^{3}_{1}H$ remain?

   A. 0.38 g
   B. 0.75 g
   C. 1.5 g
   D. 3.0 g

   B. Every 12 years, the amount remaining is cut in half. After 12 years, 1.5 g will remain. After another 12 years, 0.75 g will remain.

47. Oxygen-15 has a half-life of 122 seconds. What percentage of a sample of oxygen-15 has decayed after 300. seconds?

   A. 18.2%
   B. 21.3%
   C. 78.7%
   D. 81.8%

D. We may assume a convenient number (like 100.0 g) for a sample size. The amount remaining may be found from:

$$A_{remaining} = A_{initially}\left(\frac{1}{2}\right)^{\frac{t}{t_{halflife}}}$$

$$= 100.0 \text{ g } ^{15}O \left(\frac{1}{2}\right)^{\frac{300.\text{ seconds}}{122 \text{ seconds}}} = 18.2 \text{ g } ^{15}O$$

We are asked to determine the percentage that has decayed. This will be 100.0 g − 18.2 g = 81.8 g or 81.8% of the initial sample.

48. Which of the following isotopes is commonly used for medical imaging in the diagnose of diseases?

   A. cobalt-60
   B. technetium-99m
   C. tin-117m
   D. plutonium-238

B. The other three isotopes have limited medical applications (tin-117m has been used for the relief of bone cancer pain), but only Tc-99m is used routinely for imaging.

49. Carbon-14 dating would be useful in obtaining the age of which object?

   A. a 20th century Picasso painting
   B. a mummy from ancient Egypt
   C. a dinosaur fossil
   D. all of the above

B. C-14 is used in archeology because its half-life is 5730 years. Too little C-14 would have decayed from the painting and nearly all of the C-14 would have decayed from the fossil. In both cases, an estimate of age would be impossible with this isotope.

50. Which of the following isotopes can create a chain reaction of nuclear fission?

   A. uranium-235
   B. uranium-238
   C. plutonium-238
   D. all of the above

A. Uranium-235 and plutonium-239 are the two fissile isotopes used for nuclear power. ^{238}U is the most common uranium isotope. ^{238}Pu is used as a heat source for energy in space probes and some pacemakers.

51. List the following scientists in chronological order from earliest to most recent with respect to their most significant contribution to atomic theory:

   I. John Dalton
   II. Niels Bohr
   III. J. J. Thomson
   IV. Ernest Rutherford

   A. I, III, II, IV
   B. I, III, IV, II
   C. I, IV, III, II
   D. III, I, II, IV

B. Dalton founded modern atomic theory. J.J. Thomson determined that the electron is a subatomic particle but he placed it in the center of the atom. Rutherford discovered that electrons surround a small dense nucleus. Bohr determined that electrons may only occupy discrete positions around the nucleus.

52. Match the theory with the scientist who first proposed it:

   I. Electrons, atoms, and all objects with momentum also exist as waves.
   II. Electron density may be accurately described by a single mathematical equation.
   III. There is an inherent indeterminacy in the position and momentum of particles.
   IV. Radiant energy is transferred between particles in exact multiples of a discrete unit.

   A. I-de Broglie, II-Planck, III-Schrödinger, IV-Thomson
   B. I-Dalton, II-Bohr, III-Planck, IV-de Broglie
   C. I-Henry, II-Bohr, III-Heisenberg, IV-Schrödinger
   D. I-de Broglie, II-Schrödinger, III-Heisenberg, IV-Planck

D. Henry's law relates gas partial pressure to liquid solubility.

53. How many neutrons are in $^{60}_{27}Co$?

   A. 27
   B. 33
   C. 60
   D. 87

B. The number of neutrons is found by subtracting the atomic number (27) from the mass number (60).

54. The terrestrial composition of an element is: 50.7% as an isotope with an atomic mass of 78.9 u and 49.3% as an isotope with an atomic mass of 80.9 u. Both isotopes are stable. Calculate the atomic mass of the element.

   A. 79.0 u
   B. 79.8 u
   C. 79.9 u
   D. 80.8 u

C.

Atomic mass of element = (Fraction as 1st isotope) (Atomic mass of 1st isotope)
+
(Fraction as 2nd isotope) (Atomic mass of 2nd isotope)
= (0.507) (78.9 u) + (0.493) (80.9 u) = 79.89 u = 79.9 u

55. Which of the following is a correct electron arrangement for oxygen?

A.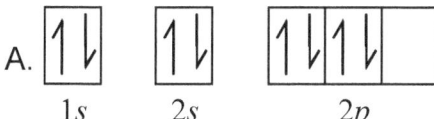
    1s   2s   2p

B. $1s^21p^22s^22p^2$
C. 2, 2, 4
D. none of the above

D. Choice A violates Hund's rule. The two electrons on the far right should occupy the final two orbitals. B should be $1s^22s^22p^4$. There is no $1p$ subshell. C should be 2, 6. Number lists indicate electrons in shells.

56. Which of the following statements about radiant energy is <u>not</u> true?

    A. The energy change of an electron transition is directly proportional to the wavelength of the emitted or absorbed photon.
    B. The energy of an electron in a hydrogen atom depends only on the principle quantum number.
    C. The frequency of photons striking a metal determines whether the photoelectric effect will occur.
    D. The frequency of a wave of electromagnetic radiation is inversely proportional to its wavelength.

A. The energy change (ΔE) is <u>inversely</u> proportional to the wavelength (λ) of the photon according the equations:

$$\Delta E = \frac{hc}{\lambda}.$$

where h is Planck's constant and c is the speed of light.

Choice B is true for hydrogen. Atoms with more than one electron are more complex. The frequency of individual photons, not the number of photons determines whether the photoelectric effect occurs, so choice C is true. Choice D is true. The proportionality constant is the speed of light according to the equation:

$$\nu = \frac{c}{\lambda}.$$

57. Match the orbital diagram for the ground state of carbon with the rule/principle it violates:

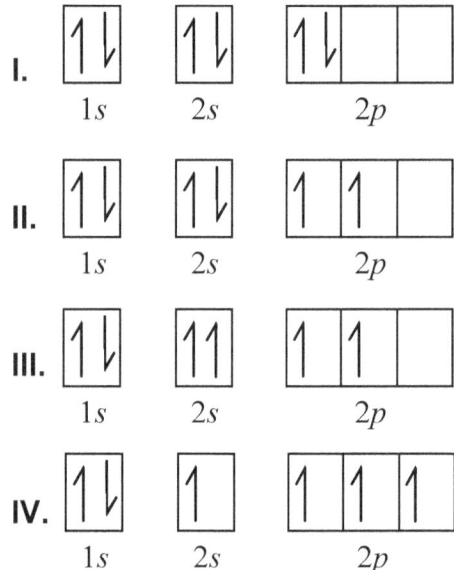

A. I-Pauli exclusion, II-Aufbau, III-no violation, IV-Hund's
B. I-Aufbau, II-Pauli exclusion, III-no violation, IV-Hund's
C. I-Hund's, II-no violation, III-Pauli exclusion, IV-Aufbau
D. I-Hund's, II-no violation, III-Aufbau, IV-Pauli exclusion

C. Diagram I violates Hund's rule because a second electron is added to a degenerate orbital before all orbitals in the subshell have one electron. Diagram III violates the Pauli exclusion principle because both electrons in the 2s orbital have the same spin. They would have the same 4 quantum numbers. Diagram IV violates the Aufbau principle because an electron occupies the higher energy 2p orbital before 2s orbital has been filled; this configuration is not at the ground state.

58. Select the list of atoms that are arranged in order of increasing size.

A. Mg, Na, Si, Cl
B. Si, Cl, Mg, Na
C. Cl, Si, Mg, Na
D. Na, Mg, Si, Cl

C. These atoms are all in the same row of the periodic table. Size increases further to the left for atoms in the same row.

59. Based on trends in the periodic table, which of the following properties would you expect to be greater for Rb than for K?

   I. Density
   II. Melting point
   III. Ionization energy
   IV. Oxidation number in a compound with chlorine

   A. I only
   B. I, II, and III
   C. II and III
   D. I, II, III, and IV

A. Rb is underneath K in the alkali metal column (group 1) of the periodic table. There is a general trend for density to increase lower on the table for elements in the same row, so we select choice I. Rb and K experience metallic bonds for intermolecular forces and the strength of metallic bonds decreases for larger atoms further down the periodic table resulting in a lower melting point for Rb, so we do not choose II. Ionization energy decreases for larger atoms further down the periodic table, so we do not choose III. Both Rb and K would be expected to have a charge of +1 and therefore an oxidation number of +1 in a compound with chlorine, so we do not choose IV.

60. Which oxide forms the strongest acid in water?

   A. Al_2O_3
   B. Cl_2O_7
   C. As_2O_5
   D. CO_2

B. The strength of acids formed from oxides increases with electronegativity and with oxidation state. We know Cl has a greater electronegativity than Al, As, and C because it is closer to the top right of the periodic table. The oxidation numbers of our choices are +3 for Al, +7 for Cl, +5 for As, and +4 for C. Both its electronegativity and its oxidation state indicate Cl_2O_7 will form the strongest acid.

61. Rank the following bonds from least to most polar:

C-H, C-Cl, H-H, C-F

A. C-H < H-H < C-F < C-Cl
B. H-H < C-H < C-F < C-Cl
C. C-F < C-Cl < C-H < H-H
D. H-H < C-H < C-Cl < C-F

D. Bonds between atoms of the same element are completely non-polar, so H-H is the least polar bond in the list, eliminating choices A and C. The C-H bond is considered to be non-polar even though the electrons of the bond are slightly unequally shared. C-Cl and C-F are both polar covalent bonds, but C-F is more strongly polar because F has a greater electronegativity.

62. At room temperature, $CaBr_2$ is expected to be:

A. a ductile solid
B. a brittle solid
C. a soft solid
D. a gas

B. Ca is a metal because it is on the left of the periodic table, and Br is a non-metal because it is on the right. The compound they form together will be an ionic salt, and ionic salts are brittle solids (choice B) at room temperature. NaCl is another example.

63. Which of the following is a proper Lewis dot structure of CHClO?

A.   B.   C.   D.

C. C has 4 valence shell electrons, H has 1, Cl has 7, and O has 6. The molecule has a total of 18 valence shell electrons. This eliminates choice B which has 24. Choice B is also incorrect because has an octet around a hydrogen atom instead of 2 electrons and because there are only six electrons surrounding the central carbon. A single bond connecting all atoms would give choice A. This is incorrect because there are only 6 electrons surrounding the central carbon. A double bond between C and O gives the correct answer, C. A double bond between C and O and also between C and Cl would give choice D. This is incorrect because there are 10 electrons surrounding the central carbon.

64. In C_2H_2, each carbon atom contains the following valence orbitals:

A. *p* only
B. *p* and *sp* hybrids
C. *p* and *sp²* hybrids
D. *sp³* hybrids only

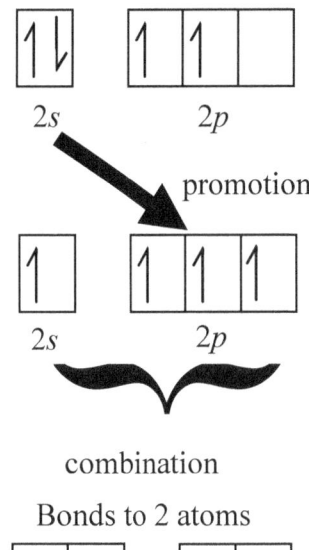

B. An isolated C has the valence electron configuration $2s^2 2p^2$. Before bonding, one *s* electron is promoted to an empty *p* orbital. In C_2H_2, each C atom bonds to 2 other atoms. Bonding to two other atoms is achieved by combination into two *p* orbitals and two *sp* hybrids.

65. Which statement about molecular structures is false?

A. 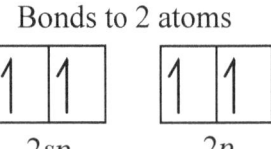 is a conjugated molecule.

B. A bonding σ orbital connects two atoms by the straight line between them.
C. A bonding π orbital connects two atoms in a separate region from the straight line between them.
D. The anion with resonance forms will always exist in one form or the other.

D. A conjugated molecule is a molecule with double bonds on adjacent atoms such as the molecule shown in A. Choice B and C give the definition of sigma and pi molecular orbitals. D is false because a resonance form is one of multiple equivalent Lewis structures, but these structures do not describe the actual state of the molecule. The anion will exist in a state between the two forms.

66. What is the shape of the PH₃ molecule? Use the VSEPR model.

   A. Trigonal pyramidal
   B. Trigonal bipyramidal
   C. Trigonal planar
   D. Tetrahedral

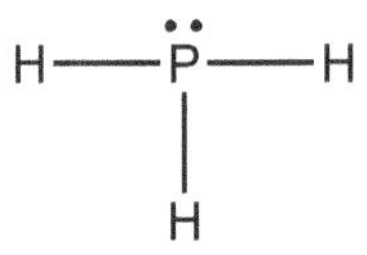

A. The Lewis structure for PH₃ is given to the right. This structure contains 4 electron pairs around the central atom, so the geometral arrangement is tetrahedral. However, the shape of a molecule is given by its atom locations, and there are only three atoms so choice D is not correct. Four electrons pairs with one unshared pair (3 bonds and one lone pair) give a trigonal pyramidal shape as shown to the left.

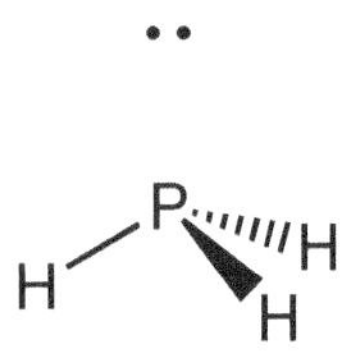

TEACHER CERTIFICATION STUDY GUIDE

67. What is the chemical composition of magnesium nitrate?

A. 11.1% Mg, 22.2% N, 66.7% O
B. 16.4% Mg, 18.9% N, 64.7% O
C. 20.9% Mg, 24.1% N, 55.0% O
D. 28.2% Mg, 16.2% N, 55.7% O

B. First find the formula for magnesium nitrate. Mg is an alkali earth metal (**Skill 3.1**) and will always have a 2+ charge. The nitrate ion is NO_3^- (**Skill 5.2**). Two nitrate ions are required for each Mg^{2+} ion. Therefore the formula is $Mg(NO_3)_2$

Skill 5.1 describes determination chemical composition.
1) Determine the number of atoms for elemen in $Mg(NO_3)_2$: 1 Mg, 2 N, 6 O.
2) Multiply by the molecular weight of the elements to determine the grams of each in one mole of the formula.

$$\frac{1 \text{ mol Mg}}{\text{mol Mg(NO}_3)_2} \times \frac{24.3 \text{ g Mg}}{\text{mol Mg}} = 24.3 \text{ g Mg/mol Mg(NO}_3)_2$$

$$2(14.0) = 28.0 \text{ g N/mol Mg(NO}_3)_2$$

$$6(16.0) = 96.0 \text{ g O/mol Mg(NO}_3)_2$$

3) Determine formula mass $\quad$ 148.3 g $Mg(NO_3)_2$/mol $Mg(NO_3)_2$
4) Divide to determine % composition

$$\%Mg = \frac{24.3 \text{ g Mg/mol Mg(NO}_3)_2}{148.3 \text{ g Mg(NO}_3)_2/\text{mol Mg(NO}_3)_2} = 0.164 \text{ g Mg/g Mg(NO}_3)_2 \times 100\% = 16.4\%$$

$$\%N = \frac{28.0}{148.3} \times 100\% = 18.9\% \qquad \%O = \frac{96.0}{148.3} \times 100\% = 64.7\%$$

Answer A is the fractional representation of the presence of each atom in the formula. Composition is based on mass percentage. Answer C is the chemical composition of $Mg(NO_2)_2$, magnesium nitrite. Answer D is the chemical composition of "$MgNO_3$", a formula that results from not balancing charges.

TEACHER CERTIFICATION STUDY GUIDE

68. The IUPAC name for Cu_2SO_3 is:

    A. Dicopper sulfur trioxide
    B. Copper (II) sulfate
    C. Copper (I) sulfite
    D. Copper (II) sulfite

C. Cu_2SO_3 is an ionic compound containing copper cation and the SO_3 anion. Choice A is wrong because it uses the naming system for molecular compounds. The SO_3 anion is 2– and is named sulfite. It takes two copper cations in to neutralize this charge, so Cu has a charge of 1+, and the name is copper (I) sulfite.

69. Which name or formula is not represented properly?

    A. Cl_4S
    B. $KClO_3$
    C. Calcium dihydrogen phosphate
    D. Sulfurous acid

A A is the answer because the atoms in the sulfur tetrachloride molecule are placed in order of increasing electronegativity. This formla is properly written as SCl_4. B is a proper formula for potassium chlorate. Calcium dihydrogen phosphate is $Ca(H_2PO_4)_2$. It derives its name from the Ca^{2+} cation in combination with an anion composed of a phosphate anion (PO_4^{3-}) that is doubly protonated to give a $H_2PO_4^-$ ion. Sulfurous acid is $H_2SO_3(aq)$.

70. Household "chlorine bleach" is sodium hypochlorite. Which of the following best represent the production of sodium hypochlorite, sodium chloride, and water by bubbling chlorine gas through aqueous sodium hydroxide?

    A. $4Cl(g) + 4NaOH(aq) \rightarrow NaClO_2(aq) + 3NaCl(aq) + 2H_2O(l)$
    B. $2Cl_2(g) + 4NaOH(aq) \rightarrow NaClO_2(aq) + 3NaCl(aq) + 2H_2O(l)$
    C. $2Cl(g) + 2NaOH(aq) \rightarrow NaClO(aq) + NaCl(aq) + H_2O(l)$
    D. $Cl_2(g) + 2NaOH(aq) \rightarrow NaClO(aq) + NaCl(aq) + H_2O(l)$

D. Chlorine gas is a diatomic molecule, eliminating choices A and C. The hypochlorite ion is ClO^- eliminating choices A and B. All of the equations are properly balanced.

71. Balance the equation for the neutralization reaction between phosphoric acid and calcium hydroxide by filling in the blank stoichiometric coefficients.

$$\_H_3PO_4 + \_Ca(OH)_2 \rightarrow \_Ca_3(PO_4)_2 + \_H_2O$$

A. 4, 3, 1, 4
B. 2, 3, 1, 8
C. 2, 3, 1, 6
D. 2, 1, 1, 2

C. We are given the unbalanced equation (**step 1**).

Next we determine the number of atoms on each side (**step 2**). For reactants (left of the arrow): 5H, 1P, 6O, and 1Ca. For products: 2H, 2P, 9O, and 3Ca.

We assume that the molecule with the most atoms—i.e. $Ca_3(PO_4)_2$—has a coefficient of one, and find the other coefficients required to have the same number of atoms on each side of the equation (**step 3**). Assuming $Ca_3(PO_4)_2$ has a coefficient of one means that there will be 3 Ca and 2 P on the right because H_2O has no Ca or P. A balanced equation would also have 3 Ca and 2 P on the left. This is achieved with a coefficient of 2 for H_3PO_4 and 3 for $Ca(OH)_2$. Now we have:

$$2H_3PO_4 + 3Ca(OH)_2 \rightarrow Ca_3(PO_4)_2 + ?H_2O$$

The coefficient for H_2O is found by a balance on H or on O. Whichever one is chosen, the other atom should be checked to confirm that a balance actually occurs. For H, there are 6 H from $2H_3PO_4$ and 6 from $3Ca(OH)_2$ for a total of 12 H on the left. There must be 12 H on the right for balance. None are accounted for by $Ca_3(PO_4)_2$, so all 12 H must occur on H_2O. It has a coefficient of 6.

$$2H_3PO_4 + 3Ca(OH)_2 \rightarrow Ca_3(PO_4)_2 + 6H_2O$$

This is choice C, but if time is available, it is best to check that the remaining atom is balanced. There are 8 O from $2H_3PO_4$ and 6 from $3Ca(OH)_2$ for a total of 14 on the left, and 8 O from $Ca_3(PO_4)_2$ and 6 from $6H_2O$ for a total of 14 on the right. The equation is balanced.

Mulitplication by a whole number (**step 4**) is not required because the stoichiometric coefficients from step 3 already are whole numbers.

An alternative method would be to try the coefficients given for answer A, answer B, etc. until we recognize a properly balanced equation.

72. Write an equation showing the reaction between calcium nitrate and lithium sulfate in aqueous solution. Include all products.

A. $CaNO_3(aq) + Li_2SO_4(aq) \rightarrow CaSO_4(s) + Li_2NO_3(aq)$
B. $Ca(NO_3)_2(aq) + Li_2SO_4(aq) \rightarrow CaSO_4(s) + 2LiNO_3(aq)$
C. $Ca(NO_3)_2(aq) + Li_2SO_4(aq) \rightarrow 2LiNO_3(s) + CaSO_4(aq)$
D. $Ca(NO_3)_2(aq) + Li_2SO_4(aq) + 2H_2O(l) \rightarrow 2LiNO_3(aq) + Ca(OH)_2(aq) + H_2SO_4(aq)$

B. When two ionic compounds are in solution, a precipitation reaction should be considered. We can determine from their names that the two reactants are the ionic compounds $Ca(NO_3)_2$ and Li_2SO_4. The compounds are present in aqueous solution as their four component ions Ca^{2+}, NO_3^-, Li^+, and SO_4^{2-}. Solubility rules indicate that nitrates are always soluble but sulfate will form a solid precipitate with Ca^{2+} forming $CaSO_4(s)$. Choice A results from assuming that the nitrate anion has a 2– charge instead of its 1– charge. B is correct. C assumes lithium nitrate is the precipitate. Choice D includes the reverse of a neutralization reaction. Water would not decompose due to the addition of these salts.

73. Find the mass of CO_2 produced by the combustion of 15 kg of isopropyl alcohol in the reaction:

$$2C_3H_7OH + 9O_2 \rightarrow 6CO_2 + 8H_2O$$

A. 33 kg
B. 44 kg
C. 50 kg
D. 60 kg

A Remember "grams to moles to moles to grams." Step 1 converts mass to moles for the known value. In this case, kg and kmol are used. Step 2 relates moles of the known value to moles of the unknown value by their stoichiometry coefficients. Step 3 converts moles off the unknown value to a mass.

$$15 \times 10^3 \text{ g } C_4H_8O \times \underbrace{\frac{1 \text{ mol } C_4H_8O}{60 \text{ g } C_4H_8O}}_{\text{step 1}} \times \underbrace{\frac{6 \text{ mol } CO_2}{2 \text{ mol } C_4H_8O}}_{\text{step 2}} \times \underbrace{\frac{44 \text{ g } CO_2}{1 \text{ mol } CO_2}}_{\text{step 3}} = 33 \times 10^3 \text{ g } CO_2$$

$$= 33 \text{ kg } CO_2$$

74. What is the density of nitrogen gas at STP? Assume an ideal gas and a value of 0.08206 L-atm/(mol-K) for the gas constant.

   A. 0.62 g/L
   B. 1.14 g/L
   C. 1.25 g/L
   D. 2.03 g/L

C The molecular mass M of N_2 is 28.0 g/mol.

$$d = \frac{nM}{V} = \frac{PM}{RT} = \frac{(1\,\text{atm})\left(28.0\,\frac{g}{mol}\right)}{\left(0.08206\,\frac{L\cdot atm}{mol\cdot K}\right)(273.15\,K)} = 1.25\,\frac{g}{L}$$

Choice A results from forgetting that nitrogen is a diatomic gas. Choice B results from using a value of 25 °C for standard temperature. This is the thermodynamic standard temperature, but not STP.

A faster method is to recall that one mole of an ideal gas at STP occupies 22.4 L.

$$d\,(\text{in }\frac{g}{L}) = \frac{M\,(\text{in }\frac{g}{mol})}{22.4\,\frac{L}{mol}} = \frac{28.0\,\frac{g}{mol}}{22.4\,\frac{L}{mol}} = 1.25\,\frac{g}{L}.$$

75. Find the volume of methane that will produce 12 m³ of hydrogen in the reaction: $CH_4(g) + H_2O(g) \rightarrow CO(g) + 3H_2(g)$. Assume temperature and pressure remain constant.

   A. 4.0 m³
   B. 32 m³
   C. 36 m³
   D. 64 m³

A Stoichiometric coefficients may be used directly for ideal gas volumes at constant T and P because of Avogadro's Law.

$$12\,m^3\,H_2 \times \frac{1\,m^3\,CH_4}{3\,m^3\,H_2} = 4.0\,m^3\,CH_4$$

12 g of H_2 will be produced from 32 g of CH_4 (incorrect choice B).

76. A 100. L vessel of pure O_2 at 500. kPa and 20. °C is used for the combustion of butane:

$$2C_4H_{10} + 13O_2 \rightarrow 8CO_2 + 10H_2O.$$

Find the mass of butane to consume all the O_2 in the vessel. Assume O_2 is an ideal gas and use a value of R = 8.314 J/(mol•K).

A. 183 g
B. 467 g
C. 1.83 kg
D. 7.75 kg

A We are given a volume and asked for a mass. The steps will be "volume to moles to moles to mass."

"Volume to moles..." requires the ideal gas law, but first several units must be altered.
  Units of joules are identical to $m^3 \cdot Pa$.
  500 kPa is 500×10^3 Pa.
  100 L is 0.100 m^3.
  20 °C is 293.15 K.
$PV = nRT$ is rearranged to give:

$$n = \frac{PV}{RT} = \frac{(500 \times 10^3 \text{ Pa})(0.100 \text{ m}^3 \text{ O}_2)}{\left(8.314 \frac{\text{m}^3 \cdot \text{Pa}}{\text{mol} \cdot \text{K}}\right)(293.15 \text{ K})} = 20.51 \text{ mol O}_2$$

"...to moles to mass" utilizes stoichiometry. The molecular weight of butane is 58.1 u.

$$20.51 \text{ mol O}_2 \times \frac{2 \text{ mol C}_4\text{H}_{10}}{13 \text{ mol O}_2} \times \frac{58.1 \text{ g C}_4\text{H}_{10}}{1 \text{ mol C}_4\text{H}_{10}} = 183 \text{ g C}_4\text{H}_{10}$$

77. Consider the reaction between iron and hydrogen chloride gas:
$$Fe(s) + 2HCl(g) \rightarrow FeCl_2(s) + H_2(g).$$

7 moles of iron and 10 moles of HCl react until the limiting reagent is consumed. Which statements are true?

I. HCl is the excess reagent
II. HCl is the limiting reagent
III. 7 moles of H_2 are produced
IV. 2 moles of the excess reagent remain

A. I and III
B. I and IV
C. II and III
D. II and IV

D The limiting reagent is found by dividing the number of moles of each reactant by its stoichiometric coefficient. The lowest result is the limiting reagent.

$$7 \text{ mol Fe} \times \frac{1 \text{ mol reaction}}{1 \text{ mol Fe}} = 7 \text{ mol reaction if Fe is limiting}$$

$$10 \text{ mol HCl} \times \frac{1 \text{ mol reaction}}{2 \text{ mol HCl}} = 5 \text{ mol reaction if HCl is limiting.}$$

Therefore, HCl is the limiting reagent (II is true) and Fe is the excess reagent.

5 moles of the reaction take place, so 5 moles of H_2 are produced, and of the 7 moles of Fe supplied, 5 are consumed, leaving 2 moles of the excess reagent (IV is true).

78. **32.0 g of hydrogen and 32.0 grams of oxygen react to form water until the limiting reagent is consumed. What is present in the vessel after the reaction is complete?**

A. 16.0 g O_2 and 48.0 g H_2O
B. 24.0 g H_2 and 40.0 g H_2O
C. 28.0 g H_2 and 36.0 g H_2O
D. 28.0 g H_2 and 34.0 g H_2O

C   First the equation must be constructed:
$$2H_2 + O_2 \rightarrow 2H_2O$$

A fast and intuitive solution would be to recognize that:
1) One mole of H_2 is about 2.0 g, so about 16 moles of H_2 are present.
2) One mole of O_2 is 32.0 g, so one mole of is O_2 is present
3) Imagine the 16 moles of H_2 reacting with one mole of O_2. 2 moles of H_2 will be consumed before the one mole of O_2 is gone. O_2 is limiting. (Eliminate choice A.)
4) 16 moles less 2 leaves 14 moles of H_2 or about 28 g. (Eliminate choice B.)
5) The reaction began with 64.0 g total. Conservation of mass for chemical reactions forces the total final mass to be 64.0 g also. (Eliminate choice D.)

A more standard solution is presented next. First, mass is converted to moles:

$$32.0 \text{ g } H_2 \times \frac{1 \text{ mol } H_2}{2.016 \text{ g } H_2} = 15.87 \text{ mol } H_2 \quad \text{and} \quad 32.0 \text{ g } O_2 \times \frac{1 \text{ mol } O_2}{32.00 \text{ g } O_2} = 1.000 \text{ mol } O_2$$

Dividing by stoichiometric coefficients give

$$15.87 \text{ mol } H_2 \times \frac{1 \text{ mol reaction}}{2 \text{ mol } H_2} = 7.935 \text{ mol reaction if } H_2 \text{ is limiting}$$

$$1.000 \text{ mol } O_2 \times \frac{1 \text{ mol reaction}}{1 \text{ mol } O_2} = 1.000 \text{ mol reaction if } O_2 \text{ is limiting.}$$

O_2 is the limiting reagent, so no O_2 will remain in the vessel.

$$1.000 \text{ mol } O_2 \text{ consumed} \times \frac{2 \text{ mol } H_2O \text{ produced}}{1 \text{ mol } O_2} \times \frac{18.016 \text{ g } H_2O}{1 \text{ mol } H_2O} = 36.0 \text{ g } H_2O \text{ produced}$$

$$1.000 \text{ mol } O_2 \text{ consumed} \times \frac{2 \text{ mol } H_2 \text{ consumed}}{1 \text{ mol } O_2} \times \frac{2.016 \text{ g } H_2}{1 \text{ mol } H_2} = 4.03 \text{ g } H_2 \text{ consumed}$$

Remaining H_2 is found from:
  32.0 g H_2 initially − 4.03 g H_2 consumed = 28.0 g H_2 remain.

79. Three experiments were performed at the same initial temperature and pressure to determine the rate of the reaction

$$2ClO_2(g) + F_2(g) \rightarrow 2ClO_2F(g).$$

Results are shown in the table below. Concentrations are given in millimoles per liter (mM).

Exp.	Initial $[ClO_2]$ (mM)	Initial $[F_2]$ (mM)	Initial rate of $[ClO_2F]$ increase (mM/sec)
1	5.0	5.0	0.63
2	5.0	20	2.5
3	10	10	2.5

What is the rate law for this reaction?

A. Rate = $k[F_2]$

B. Rate = $k[ClO_2][F_2]$

C. Rate = $k[ClO_2]^2[F_2]$

D. Rate = $k[ClO_2][F_2]^2$

B A four-fold increase in [F₂] at constant [ClO₂] between experiment one and two caused a four-fold increase in rate. Rate is therefore proportional to [F₂] at constant [ClO₂], eliminating choice D (Choice D predicts rate to increase by a factor of 16).

Between experiment 1 and 3, [F₂] and [ClO₂] both double in value. Once again, there is a four-fold increase in rate. If rate were only dependent on [F₂] (choice A), there would be a two-fold increase. The correct answer, B, attributes a two-fold increase in rate to the doubling of [F₂] and a two-fold increase to the doubling of [ClO₂], resulting in a net four-fold increase. Choice C predicts a rate increase by a factor of 8.

If this were an elementary reaction describing a collision event between three molecules, choice C would be expected, but stoichiometry cannot be used to predict a rate law.

80. The reaction
$$(CH_3)_3CBr(aq) + OH^-(aq) \rightarrow (CH_3)_3COH(aq) + Br^-(aq)$$
occurs in three elementary steps:
$$(CH_3)_3CBr \rightarrow (CH_3)_3C^+ + Br^- \text{ is slow}$$
$$(CH_3)_3C^+ + H_2O \rightarrow (CH_3)_3COH_2^+ \text{ is fast}$$
$$(CH_3)_3COH_2^+ + OH^- \rightarrow (CH_3)_3COH + H_2O \text{ is fast}$$

What is the rate law for this reaction?

A. Rate $= k\left[(CH_3)_3CBr\right]$

B. Rate $= k\left[OH^-\right]$

C. Rate $= k\left[(CH_3)_3CBr\right]\left[OH^-\right]$

D. Rate $= k\left[(CH_3)_3CBr\right]^2$

A The first step will be rate-limiting. It will determine the rate for the entire reaction because it is slower than the other steps. This step is a unimolecular process with the rate given by answer A. Choice C would be correct if the reaction as a whole were one elementary step instead of three, but the stoichiometry of a reaction composed of multiple elementary steps cannot be used to predict a rate law.

81. Which statement about equilibrium is <u>not</u> true?

A. Equilibrium shifts to minimize the impact of changes.
B. Forward and reverse reactions have equal rates at equilibrium.
C. A closed container of air and water is at a vapor-liquid equilibrium if the humidity is constant.
D. The equilibrium between solid and dissolved forms is maintained when salt is added to an unsaturated solution.

D Choice A is a restatement of Le Chatelier's Principle. B is a definition of equilibrium. A constant humidity (Choice C) occurs if the rate of vaporization and condensation are equal, indicating equilibrium. No solid is present in an **un**saturated solution. If solid is added, all of it dissolves indicating a lack of equilibrium. D would be true for a saturated soution.

82. Which statements about reaction rates are true?

   I. A catalyst will shift an equilibrium to favor product formation.
   II. Catalysts increase the rate of forward and reverse reactions.
   III. A greater temperature increases the chance that a molecular collision will overcome a reaction's activation energy.
   IV. A catalytic converter contains a homogeneous catalyst.

   A. I and II
   B. II and III
   C. II, III and IV
   D. I, III, and IV

B Catalysts provide an alternate mechanism in both directions, but do not alter equilibrium (I is false, II is true). The kinetic energy of molecules increases with temperature, so the energy of their collisions increases also (III is true). Catalytic converters contain a heterogeneous catalyst (IV is false).

83. Write the equilibrium expression K_{eq} for the reaction
$CO_2(g) + H_2(g) \rightleftharpoons CO(g) + H_2O(l)$

   A. $\dfrac{[CO][H_2O]}{[CO_2][H_2]^2}$

   B. $\dfrac{[CO_2][H_2]}{[CO][H_2O]}$

   C. $\dfrac{[CO][H_2O]}{[CO_2][H_2]}$

   D. $\dfrac{[CO]}{[CO_2][H_2]}$

D Product concentrations are multiplied together in the numerator and reactant concentrations in the denominator, eliminating choice B. The stoichiometric coefficient of H_2 is one, eliminating choice A. For heterogeneous reactions, concentrations of pure liquids or solids are absent from the expression because they are constant, eliminating choice C. D is correct.

84. What could cause this change in the energy diagram of a reaction?

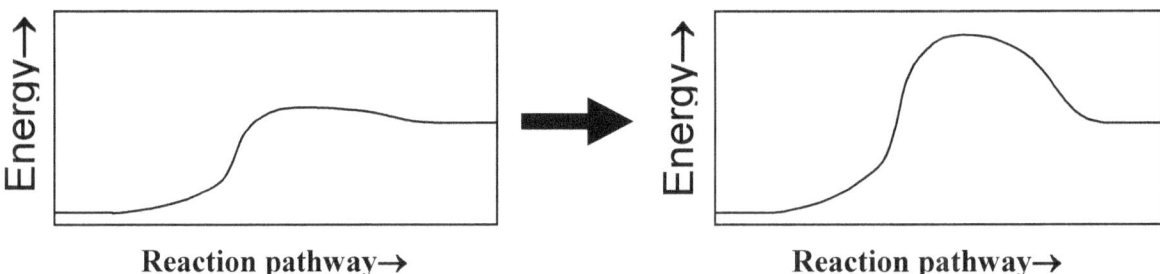

A. Adding catalyst to an endothermic reaction
B. Removing catalyst from an endothermic reaction
C. Adding catalyst to an exothermic reaction
D. Removing catalyst from an exothermic reaction

B The products at the end of the reaction pathway are at a greater energy than the reactants, so the reaction is endothermic (narrowing down the answer to A or B). The maximum height on the diagram corresponds to activation energy. An increase in activation energy could be caused by removing a heterogeneous catalyst.

85. $BaSO_4$ (K_{sp} = 1X10^{-10}) is added to pure H_2O. How much is dissolved in 1 L of saturated solution?

A. 2 mg
B. 10 μg
C. 2 μg
D. 100 pg

A $BaSO_4(s) \rightleftharpoons Ba^{2+}(aq) + SO_4^{2-}(aq)$, therefore: $K_{sp} = [Ba^{2+}][SO_4^{2-}]$.

In a saturated solution: $[Ba^{2+}] = [SO_4^{2-}] = \sqrt{1 \times 10^{-10}} = 1 \times 10^{-5}$ M.

The mass in one liter is found from the molarity:

$$1 \times 10^{-5} \frac{\text{mol Ba}^{2+} \text{ or SO}_4^{2-}}{\text{L}} \times \frac{1 \text{ mol dissolved BaSO}_4}{1 \text{ mol Ba}^{2+} \text{ or SO}_4^{2-}} \times \frac{(137+32+4 \times 16)\text{g BaSO}_4}{1 \text{ mol BaSO}_4}$$

$$= 0.002 \frac{\text{g}}{\text{L}} \text{ BaSO}_4 \times 1 \text{ L solution} \times \frac{1000 \text{ mg}}{\text{g}} = 2 \text{ mg BaSO}_4$$

TEACHER CERTIFICATION STUDY GUIDE

86. The exothermic reaction $2NO(g) + Br_2(g) \rightleftharpoons 2NOBr(g)$ is at equilibrium. According to LeChatelier's principle:

   A. Adding Br_2 will increase [NO].
   B. An increase in container volume (with T constant) will increase [NOBr].
   C. An increase in pressure (with T constant) will increase [NOBr].
   D. An increase in temperature (with P constant) will increase [NOBr].

C LeChatelier's principle predicts that equilibrium will shift to partially offset any change. Adding Br_2 will be partially offset by reducing $[Br_2]$ and [NO] via a shift to the right (not choice A). For the remaining possibilities, we may write the reaction as: 3 moles $\rightleftharpoons$ 2 moles + heat. An increase in container volume will decrease pressure. This change will be partially offset by increasing the number of moles present, shifting the reaction to the left (not choice B). An increase in pressure will be offset by a decrease the number of moles present, shifting the reaction to the right (choice C, correct). Raising the temperature by adding heat will shift the reaction to the left (not choice D).

87. At a certain temperature, T, the equilibrium constant for the reaction $2NO(g) \rightleftharpoons N_2(g) + O_2(g)$ is $K_{eq} = 2 \times 10^3$. If a 1.0 L container at this temperature contains 90 mM N_2, 20 mM O_2, and 5 mM NO, what will occur?

   A. The reaction will make more N_2 and O_2.
   B. The reaction is at equilibrium.
   C. The reaction will make more NO.
   D. The temperature, T, is required to solve this problem.

A Calculate the reaction quotient at the actual conditions:

$$Q = \frac{[N_2][O_2]}{[NO]^2} = \frac{(0.090 \text{ M})(0.020 \text{ M})}{(0.005 \text{ M})^2} = 72$$

This value is less than K_{eq}: $72 < 2 \times 10^3$, therefore $Q < K_{eq}$. To achieve equilibrium, the numerator of Q must be larger relative to the denominator. This occurs when products turn into reactants. Therefore NO will react to make more N_2 and O_2.

88. Which statement about acids and bases is not true?

A. All strong acids ionize in water.
B. All Lewis acids accept an electron pair.
C. All Brønsted bases use OH⁻ as a proton acceptor.
D. All Arrhenius acids form H⁺ ions in water.

C Choice A is the definition of a strong acid, choice B is the definition of a Lewis acid, and choice D is the definition of an Arrhenius acid. By definition, all Arrhenius bases form OH⁻ ions in water, and all Brønsted bases are proton acceptors. But not all Brønsted bases use OH⁻ as a proton acceptor. NH₃ is a Brønsted base for example.

89. Which of the following are listed from weakest to strongest acid?

A. H_2SO_3, H_2SeO_3, H_2TeO_3
B. $HBrO$, $HBrO_2$, $HBrO_3$, $HBrO_4$
C. HI, HBr, HCl, HF
D. H_3PO_4, $H_2PO_4^-$, HPO_4^{2-}

B The electronegativity of the central atom decreases from S to Se to Te as period number increases in the same periodic table group. The acidity of the oxide also decreases. Choice B is correct because acid strength increases with the oxidation state of the central atom. C is wrong because HI, HBr, and HCl are all strong acids but HF is a weak acid. D is wrong because acid strength is greater for polyprotic acids.

90. NH₄F is dissolved in water. Which of the following are conjugate acid/base pairs present in the solution?

   I. NH_4^+/NH_4OH
   II. HF/F^-
   III. H_3O^+/H_2O
   IV. H_2O/OH^-

   A. I, II, and III
   B. I, III, and IV
   C. II and IV
   D. II, III, and IV

D NH₄F is soluble in water and completely dissociates to NH_4^+ and F^-. F^- is a weak base with HF as its conjugate acid (II). NH_4^+ is a weak acid with NH_3 as its conjugate base. A conjugate acid/base pair must have the form HX/X (where X is one lower charge than HX). NH_4^+/NH_4OH (I) is not a conjugate acid/base pair, eliminating choice A and B. H_3O^+/H_2O and H_2O/OH^- (III and IV) are always present in water and in all aqueous solutions as conjugate acid/base pairs. All of the following equilibrium reactions occur in NH₄F(aq):

$$NH_4^+(aq) + OH^-(aq) \rightleftharpoons NH_3(aq) + H_2O(l)$$
$$F^-(aq) + H_3O^+(aq) \rightleftharpoons HF(aq) + H_2O(l)$$
$$2H_2O(l) \rightleftharpoons H_3O^+(aq) + OH^-(aq)$$

91. What are the pH and the pOH of 0.010 M HNO₃(aq)?

   A. pH = 1.0, pOH = 9.0
   B. pH = 2.0, pOH = 12.0
   C. pH = 2.0, pOH = 8.0
   D. pH = 8.0, pOH = 6.0

B HNO₃ is a strong acid, so it completely dissociates:
$$\left[H^+\right] = 0.010 \text{ M} = 1.0 \times 10^{-2} \text{ M}.$$
$$pH = -\log_{10}\left[H^+\right] = -\log_{10}\left(1.0 \times 10^{-2}\right) = 2.0 \text{ (choices B or C)}.$$
From pH + pOH = 14: pOH = 12.0 (choice B).

92. What is the pH of a buffer made of 0.128 M sodium formate (HCOONa) and 0.072 M formic acid (HCOOH)? The pK_a of formic acid is 3.75.

   A. 2.0
   B. 3.0
   C. 4.0
   D. 5.0

C From the pK_a, we may find the K_a of formic acid:
$$K_a = 10^{-pK_a} = 10^{-3.75} = 1.78 \times 10^{-4}$$

This is the equilibrium constant:
$$K_a = \frac{[H^+][HCOO^-]}{[HCOOH]} = 1.78 \times 10^{-4} \text{ for the dissociation:}$$
$$HCOOH \rightleftharpoons H^+ + HCOO^-.$$

The pH is found by solving for the H^+ concentration:
$$[H^+] = K_a \frac{[HCOOH]}{[HCOO^-]} = (1.78 \times 10^{-4})\frac{0.072}{0.128} = 1.0 \times 10^{-4} \text{ M}$$
$$pH = -\log_{10}[H^+] = -\log_{10}(1.0 \times 10^{-4}) = 4.0 \text{ (choice C)}$$

93. A sample of 50.0 ml KOH is titrated with 0.100 M HClO$_4$. The initial buret reading is 1.6 ml and the reading at the endpoint is 22.4 ml. What is [KOH]?

   A. 0.0416 M
   B. 0.0481 M
   C. 0.0832 M
   D. 0.0962 M

A HClO$_4$ and KOH are both strong electrolytes. If you are good at memorizing formulas, solve the problem this way:
$$C_{unknown} = \frac{C_{known}(V_{final} - V_{initial})}{V_{unknown}} = \frac{0.100 \text{ M }(22.4 \text{ ml} - 1.6 \text{ ml})}{50.0 \text{ ml}} = 0.0416 \text{ M}.$$

The problem may also be solved by finding the moles of known substance:
$$0.100 \frac{\text{mol}}{\text{L}} \times \frac{1 \text{ L}}{1000 \text{ mL}} \times (22.4 \text{ mL} - 1.6 \text{ mL}) = 0.00208 \text{ mol HClO}_4$$

This will neutralize 0.00208 mol KOH, and $\frac{0.00208 \text{ mol}}{0.0500 \text{ L}} = 0.0416 \text{ M}$

94. Rank the following from lowest to highest pH. Assume a small volume for the added component:

I. 0.01 mol HCl added to 1 L H_2O
II. 0.01 mol HI added to 1 L of an acetic acid/sodium acetate solution at pH 4.0
III. 0.01 mol NH_3 added to 1 L H_2O
IV. 0.1 mol HNO_3 added to 1 L of a 0.1 M $Ca(OH)_2$ solution

A. I < II < III < IV
B. I < II < IV < III
C. II < I < III < IV
D. II < I < IV < III

A HCl is a strong acid. Therefore solution I has a <u>pH of 2</u> because $pH = -\log_{10}\left[H^+\right] = -\log_{10}(0.01) = 2$.

HI is also a strong acid and would have a pH of 2 at this concentration in water, but the buffer will prevent pH from dropping this low. Solution II will have a pH <u>above 2</u> and below 4, eliminating choices C and D.

If a strong base were in solution III, its pOH would be 2. Using the equation pH + pOH = 14, its pH would be 12. Because NH_3 is a weak base, the pH of solution III will be greater than 7 and <u>less than 12</u>.

A neutralization reaction occurs in solution IV between 0.1 mol of H^+ from the strong acid HNO_3 and <u>0.2 mol of OH^-</u> from the strong base $Ca(OH)_2$. Each mole of $Ca(OH)_2$ contributes two base equivalents for the neutralization reaction. The base is the excess reagent, and 0.1 mol of OH^- remain after the reaction. This resulting solution will have a pOH of 1 and a <u>pH of 13</u>.

A is correct because: 2 < between 2 and 4 < betweeen 7 and 12 < 13

95. The curve below resulted from the titration of a _____ _____ with a _____ _____ titrant.

A. weak acid, strong base
B. weak base, strong acid
C. strong acid, strong base
D. strong base, strong acid

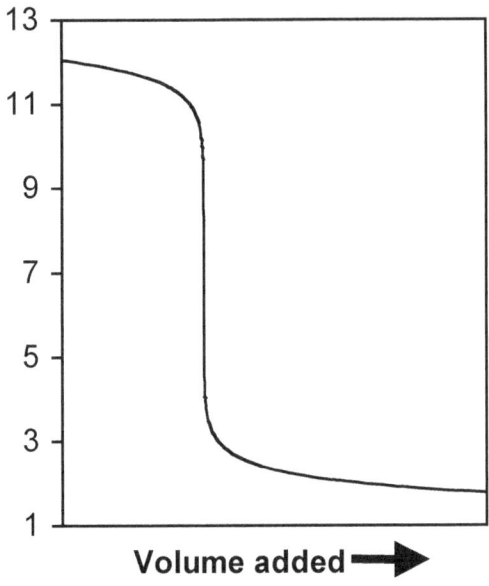
Volume added ➤

D   The pH is above 7 initially and decreases, so an acid titrant is neutralizing a base. This eliminates A and C. The maximum slope (equivalence point) at the neutral pH of 7 indicates a strong base titrated with a strong acid, D.

96. Which statement about thermochemistry is true?

A. Particles in a system move about less freely at high entropy
B. Water at 100 °C has the same internal energy as water vapor at 100°C
C. A decrease in the order of a system corresponds to an increase in entropy.
D. At its sublimation temperature, dry ice has a higher entropy than gaseous CO_2

C   At high entropy, particles have a large freedom of molecular motion (A is false). Water and water vapor at 100 °C contain the same translational kinetic energy, but water vapor has additional internal energy in the form of resisting the intermolecular attractions between molecules (B is false). We also know water vapor has a higher internal energy because heat must be added to boil water. Entropy may be thought of as the disorder in a system (C is correct). Sublimation is the phase change from solid to gas, and there is less freedom of motion for particles in solids than in gases. Solid CO_2 (dry ice) has a lower entropy than gaseous CO_2 because entropy decreases during a phase change that prevents molecular motion (D is false).

97. What is the heat change of 36.0 g H₂O at atmospheric pressure when its temperature is reduced from 125 °C to 40. °C? Use the following data:

A. −92.0 kJ
B. −10.8 kJ
C. 10.8 kJ
D. 92.0 kJ

Values for water

Heat capacity of solid	37.6 J/mol·°C
Heat capacity of liquid	75.3 J/mol·°C
Heat capacity of gas	33.1 J/mol·°C
Heat of fusion	6.02 kJ/mol
Heat of vaporization	40.67 kJ/mol

A Heat is evolved from the substance as it cools, so the heat change will be negative, eliminating choices C and D. Data in the table are given using moles, so the first step is to convert the mass of water to moles:

$$36.0 \text{ g H}_2\text{O} \times \frac{1 \text{ mol H}_2\text{O}}{18.02 \text{ g H}_2\text{O}} = 2.00 \text{ mol H}_2\text{O}$$

There are three contributions to the heat evolved. First, the heat evolved when cooling the vapor from 125 °C to 100 °C is found from the heat capacity of the gas:

$$q_1 = n \times C \times \Delta T = 2.00 \text{ mol H}_2\text{O}(g) \times 33.1 \frac{\text{J}}{\text{mol °C}} \times (100 \text{ °C} - 125 \text{ °C})$$

$$= -1655 \text{ J to cool vapor}$$

Next, the heat evolved during condensation is found from the heat of vaporization:

$$q_2 = n \times (-\Delta H_{vaporization}) = 2.00 \text{ mol H}_2\text{O} \times (-40.67 \frac{\text{kJ}}{\text{mol}})$$

$$= -81.34 \text{ kJ to condense vapor}$$

Incorrect answer B results from using a heat of vaporization of 40.67 J/mol instead of kJ/mol.

Finally, the heat evolved when cooling the liquid from 100 °C to 40 °C is found from the heat capacity of the liquid:

$$q_3 = n \times C \times \Delta T = 2.00 \text{ mol H}_2\text{O}(g) \times 75.3 \frac{\text{J}}{\text{mol °C}} \times (40 \text{ °C} - 100 \text{ °C})$$

$$= -9036 \text{ J to cool liquid}$$

The total heat change is the sum of these contributions:

$$q = q_1 + q_2 + q_3 = -1.655 \text{ kJ} + (-81.34 \text{ kJ}) + (-9.036 \text{ kJ}) = -92.03 \text{ kJ}$$

$$= -92.0 \text{ kJ (Choice A)}$$

TEACHER CERTIFICATION STUDY GUIDE

98. **What is the standard heat of combustion of CH₄(g)? Use the following data:**

    A. −890.3 kJ/mol
    B. −604.5 kJ/mol
    C. −252.9 kJ/mol
    D. −182.5 kJ/mol

    Standard heats of formation

CH₄(g)	−74.8 kJ/mol
CO₂(g)	−393.5 kJ/mol
H₂O(l)	−285.8 kJ/mol

A First we must write a balanced equation for the combustion of CH₄. The balanced equation is:

$$CH_4(g) + 2O_2(g) \rightarrow CO_2(g) + 2H_2O(l).$$

The heat of combustion may be found from the sum of the productions minus the sum of the reactants of the heats of formation:

$$\Delta H_{rxn} = H_{product\ 1} + H_{product\ 2} + \ldots - (H_{reactant\ 1} + H_{reactant\ 2} + \ldots)$$

$$= \Delta H_f^\circ(CO_2) + 2\Delta H_f^\circ(H_2O) - \left(\Delta H_f^\circ(CH_4) + 2\Delta H_f^\circ(O_2)\right)$$

The heat of formation of an element in its most stable form is zero by definition, so $\Delta H_f^\circ(O_2(g)) = 0 \ \frac{kJ}{mol}$, and the remaining values are found from the table:

$$\Delta H_{rxn} = -393.5 \ \frac{kJ}{mol} + 2(-285.8 \ \frac{kJ}{mol}) - \left(-74.8 \ \frac{kJ}{mol} + 2(0)\right) = -890.3 \ \frac{kJ}{mol} \ \text{(choice A)}$$

99. **Which reaction creates products at a lower total entropy than the reactants?**

    A. Dissolution of table salt: $NaCl(s) \rightarrow Na^+(aq) + Cl^-(aq)$
    B. Oxidation of iron: $4Fe(s) + 3O_2(g) \rightarrow 2Fe_2O_3(s)$
    C. Dissociation of ozone: $O_3(g) \rightarrow O_2(g) + O(g)$
    D. Vaporization of butane: $C_4H_{10}(l) \rightarrow C_4H_{10}(g)$

B Choice A is incorrect because two particles are at a greater entropy than one and because ions in solution have more freedom of motion than a solid. For B (the correct answer), the products are at a lower entropy than the reactants because there are fewer product molecules and they are all in the solid form but one of the reactants is a gas. Reaction B is still spontaneous because it is highly exothermic. For C, there are more product molecules than reactants, and for D, the gas phase is always at a higher entropy than the liquid.

100. Which statement about reactions is true?

   A. All spontaneous reactions are both exothermic and cause an increase in entropy.
   B. An endothermic reaction that increases the order of the system cannot be spontaneous.
   C. A reaction can be non-spontaneous in one direction and also non-spontaneous in the opposite direction.
   D. Melting snow is an exothermic process

B All reactions that are both exothermic and cause an increase in entropy will be spontaneous, but the converse (choice A) is not true. Some spontaneous reactions are exothermic but decrease entropy and some are endothermic and increase entropy. Choice B is correct. The reverse reaction of a non-spontaneous reaction (choice C) will be spontaneous. Melting snow (choice D) requires heat. Therefore it is an endothermic process

101. 10. kJ of heat are added to one kilogram of Iron at 10. °C. What is its final temperature? The specific heat of iron is 0.45 J/g•°C.

- A. 22 °C
- B. 27 °C
- C. 32 °C
- D. 37 °C

C The expression for heat as a function of temperature change:
$$q = n \times C \times \Delta T$$
may be rearranged to solve for the temperature change:
$$\Delta T = \frac{q}{n \times C}.$$
In this case, n is a mass and C is the specific heat of iron:
$$\Delta T = \frac{10000 \text{ J}}{1000 \text{ g} \times 0.45 \frac{\text{J}}{\text{g °C}}} = 22 \text{ °C}.$$
This is not the final temperature (choice A is incorrect). It is the temperature difference between the initial and final temperature.
$$\Delta T = T_{final} - T_{initial} = 22 \text{ °C}$$
Solving for the final temperature gives us:
$$T_{final} = \Delta T + T_{initial} = 22 \text{ °C} + 10 \text{ °C} = 32 \text{ °C (Choice C)}$$

TEACHER CERTIFICATION STUDY GUIDE

102. Which reaction is **not** a redox process?

    A. Combustion of octane: $2C_8H_{18} + 25O_2 \rightarrow 16CO_2 + 18H_2O$
    B. Depletion of a lithium battery: $Li + MnO_2 \rightarrow LiMnO_2$
    C. Corrosion of aluminum by acid: $2Al + 6HCl \rightarrow 2AlCl_3 + 3H_2$
    D. Taking an antacid for heartburn:
       $CaCO_3 + 2HCl \rightarrow CaCl_2 + H_2CO_3 \rightarrow CaCl_2 + CO_2 + H_2O$

D The oxidation state of atoms is altered in a redox process. During combustion (choice A), the carbon atoms are oxidized from an oxidation number of –4 to +4. Oxygen atoms are reduced from an oxidation number of 0 to –2. All batteries (choice B) generate electricity by forcing electrons from a redox process through a circuit. Li is oxidized from 0 in the metal to +1 in the LiMnO$_2$ salt. Mn is reduced from +4 in manganese(IV) oxide to +3 in lithium manganese(III) oxide salt. Corrosion (choice C) is due to oxidation. Al is oxidized from 0 to +3. H is reduced from +1 to 0. Acid-base neutralization (choice D) transfers a proton (an H atom with an oxidation state of +1) from an acid to a base. The oxidation state of all atoms remains unchanged (Ca at +2, C at +4, O at –2, H at +1, and Cl at –1), so D is correct. Note that choices C and D both involve an acid. The availability of electrons in aluminum metal favors electron transfer but the availability of CO_3^{2-} as a proton acceptor favors proton transfer.

SCIENCE: CHEMISTRY

103. Given the following heats of reaction:

$\Delta H = -0.3$ kJ/mol for $\quad Fe(s) + CO_2(g) \rightarrow FeO(s) + CO(g)$

$\Delta H = 5.7$ kJ/mol for $\quad 2Fe(s) + 3CO_2(g) \rightarrow Fe_2O_3(s) + 3CO(g)$

and $\Delta H = 4.5$ kJ/mol for $\quad 3FeO(s) + CO_2(g) \rightarrow Fe_3O_4(s) + CO(g)$

use Hess's Law to determine the heat of reaction for:

$3Fe_2O_3(s) + CO(g) \rightarrow 2Fe_3O_4(s) + CO_2(g)$?

A. −10.8 kJ/mol
B. −9.9 kJ/mol
C. −9.0 kJ/mol
D. −8.1 kJ/mol

B We are interested in $3Fe_2O_3$ as a reactant. Only the second reaction contains this molecule, so we will take three times the opposite of the second reaction. We are interested in $2Fe_3O_4$ as a product, so we will take two times the third reaction. An intermediate result is:

$3Fe_2O_3(s) + 9CO(g) \rightarrow 6Fe(s) + 9CO_2(g) \quad\quad \Delta H = -3 \times 5.7$ kJ/mol $= -17.1$ kJ/mol

$6FeO(s) + 2CO_2(g) \rightarrow 2Fe_3O_4(s) + 2CO(g) \quad\quad \Delta H = 2 \times 4.5$ kJ/mol $= 9.0$ kJ/mol

---

$3Fe_2O_3(s) + 6FeO(s) + 7CO(g) \rightarrow$
$\quad 2Fe_3O_4(s) + 6Fe(s) + 7CO_2(g)$

$\Delta H = (-17.1 + 9.0)$ kJ/mol $= -8.1$ kJ/mol

However, D is not the correct answer because it is not ΔH for the reaction of the problem statement. We may use six times the first reaction to eliminate both FeO and Fe from the intermediate result and obtain the reaction of interest:

$3Fe_2O_3(s) + 6FeO(s) + 7CO(g) \rightarrow$
$\quad 2Fe_3O_4(s) + 6Fe(s) + 7CO_2(g)$ $\quad\quad \Delta H = -8.1$ kJ/mol

$6Fe(s) + 6CO_2(g) \rightarrow 6FeO(s) + 6CO(g) \quad\quad \Delta H = 6 \times (-0.3$ kJ/mol$) = -1.8$ kJ/mol

---

$3Fe_2O_3(s) + CO(g) \rightarrow 2Fe_3O_4(s) + CO(g)$

$\Delta H = (-8.1 + -1.8)$ kJ/mol
$\quad\quad = -9.9$ kJ/mol (choice B)

104. What is the oxidant in the reaction: $2H_2S + SO_2 \rightarrow 3S + 2H_2O$?

A. H_2S
B. SO_2
C. S
D. H_2O

B The S atom in H_2S has an oxidation number of –2 and is oxidized by SO_2 (the oxidant, choice B) to elemental sulfer (oxidation number = 0). The S atom in SO_2 has an oxidation number of +4 and is reduced. The two half-reactions are:

$$SO_2 + 4e^- + 4H^+ \xrightarrow{\text{reduction}} S + 2H_2O$$

$$2H_2S \xrightarrow{\text{oxidation}} 2S + 4e^- + 4H^+$$

105. Molten NaCl is subjected to electrolysis. What reaction takes place at the cathode?

A. $2Cl^-(l) \rightarrow Cl_2(g) + 2e^-$
B. $Cl_2(g) + 2e^- \rightarrow 2Cl^-(l)$
C. $Na^+(l) + e^- \rightarrow Na(l)$
D. $Na^+(l) \rightarrow Na(l) + e^-$

C Reduction (choices B and C) always occurs at the cathode. Molten NaCl is composed of ions in liquid form before electrolysis (answer C). A and D are oxidation reactions, and D is also not properly balanced because a +1 charge is on the left and a –1 charge is on the right. The two half-reactions are:

$$Na^+(l) + e^- \xrightarrow{\text{reduction at cathode}} Na(l)$$

$$2Cl^-(l) \xrightarrow{\text{oxidation at anode}} Cl_2(g) + 2e^-$$

The net reaction is:

$$2NaCl(l) \rightarrow 2Na(l) + Cl_2(g)$$

106. What is the purpose of the salt bridge in a voltaic cell?

    A. To receive electrons from the oxidation half-reaction
    B. To relieve the buildup of positive charge in the anode half-cell
    C. To conduct electron flow
    D. To permit positive ions to flow from the cathode half-cell to the anode half-cell

D The anode receives electrons from the oxidation half-reaction (choice A) and the circuit conducts electron flow (choice C) to the cathode which supplies electrons for the reduction half-reaction. This flow of electrons from the anode to the cathode is relieved by a flow of ions through the salt bridge from the cathode to the anode (answer D). The salt bridge relieves the buildup of positive charge in the cathode half-cell (choice B is incorrect).

107. Given $E°=-2.37$ V for $Mg^{2+}(aq)+2e^-\rightarrow Mg(s)$ and $E°=0.80$ V for $Ag^+(aq)+e^-\rightarrow Ag(s)$, what is the standard potential of a voltaic cell composed of a piece of magnesium dipped in a 1 M Ag^+ solution and a piece of silver dipped in 1 M Mg^{2+}?

A. 0.77 V
B. 1.57 V
C. 3.17 V
D. 3.97 V

C $Ag^+(aq)+e^-\rightarrow Ag(s)$ has a larger value for $E°$ (reduction potential) than $Mg^{2+}(aq)+2e^-\rightarrow Mg(s)$. Therefore, in the cell described, reduction will occur at the Ag electrode and it will be the cathode. Using the equation:

$$E^o_{cell} = E^o(\text{cathode}) - E^o(\text{anode}),\text{ we obtain:}$$

$$E^o_{cell} = 0.80 \text{ V} - (-2.37 \text{ V}) = 3.17 \text{ V (Answer C)}.$$

Choice D results from the incorrect assumption that electrode potentials depend on the amount of material present. The balanced net reaction for the cell is:

$$Mg(s) \rightarrow Mg^{2+}(aq) + 2e^- \qquad E^o_{ox} = 2.37 \text{ V}$$
$$\underline{2Ag^+(aq) + 2e^- \rightarrow 2Ag(s) \qquad E^o_{red} = 0.80 \text{ V (\textbf{not} 1.60 V)}}$$
$$Mg(s) + 2Ag^+(aq) \rightarrow 2Ag(s) + Mg^{2+}(aq) \qquad E^o_{cell} = 3.17 \text{ V (\textbf{not} 3.97 V)}$$

108. A proper name for this hydrocarbon is:

A. 4,5-dimethyl-6-hexene
B. 2,3-dimethyl-1-hexene
C. 4,5-dimethyl-6-hexyne
D. 2-methyl-3-propyl-1-butene

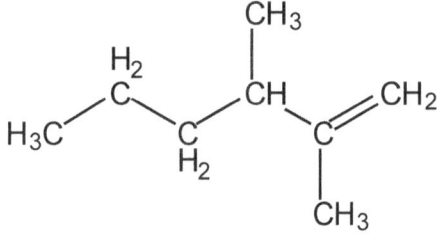

B The hydrocarbon contains a double bond and no triple bonds, so it is an alkene. Choice C describes an alkyne. The longest carbon chain is six carbons long, corresponding to a parent molecule of 1-hexene (circled to the left). Choice D is an improper name because it names the molecule as a substituted butane, using a shorter chain as the parent molecule.

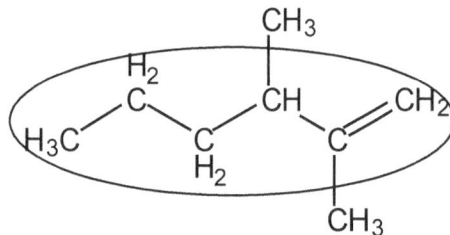

Finally, the lowest possible set of locant numbers must be used. Choice A is an improper name because the larger possible set of locant numbers is chosen.

109. An IUPAC approved name for this molecule is:

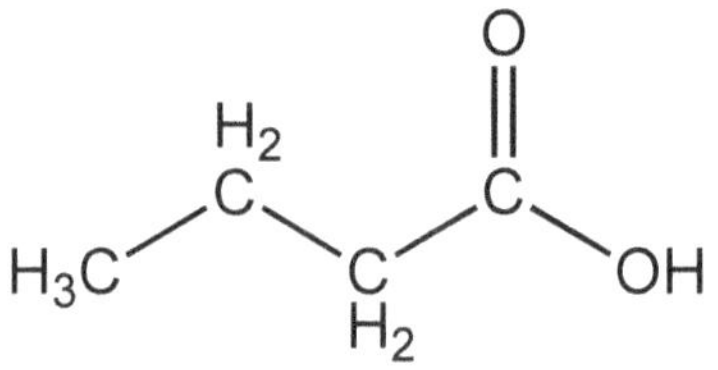

A. butanal
B. propanal
C. butanoic acid
D. propanoic acid

C The COOH group means that the molecule is a carboxylic acid and its name will use the suffix –*oic acid*. The presence of 4 carbon atoms means the prefix *butan-* will be used. An alternate name for the molecule is butyric acid. Choices A and B would be used for aldehydes (CHO group). Choices B and D would be used for 3 carbon atoms:

butanal (also called butyraldehyde):

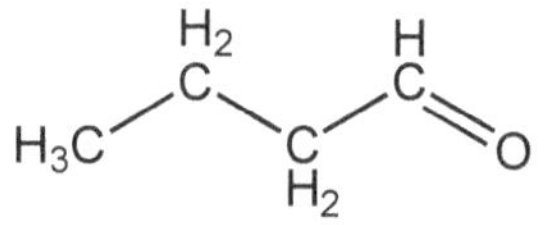

propanal (also called propionaldehyde):

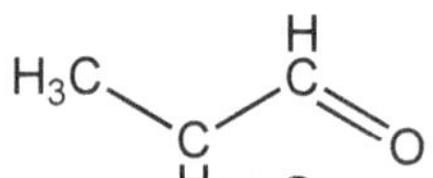

propanoic acid (also called propionic acid):

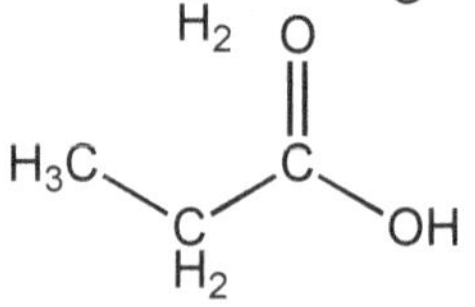

110. Which molecule has a systematic name of methyl ethanoate?

A. 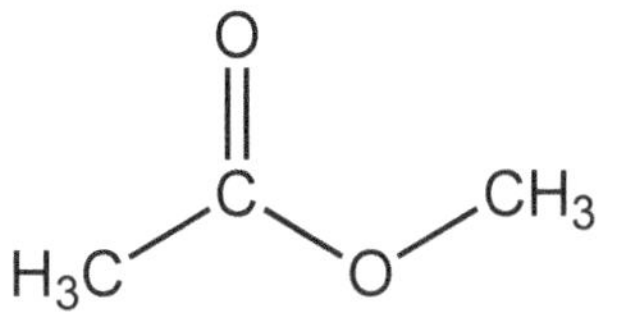 ![structure A]
B. ![structure B] 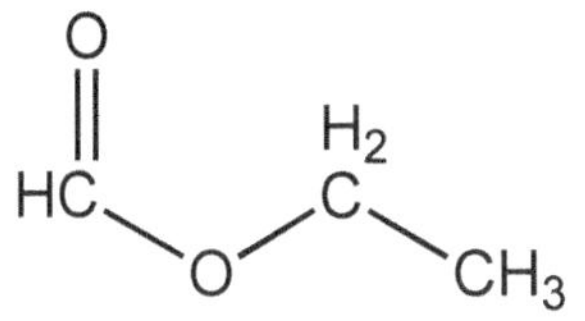
C. 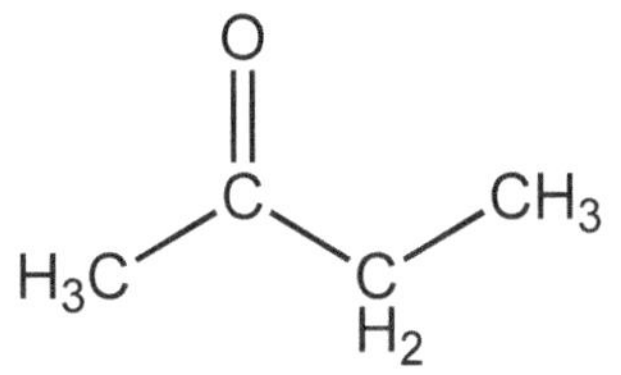 ![structure C]
D. ![structure D]

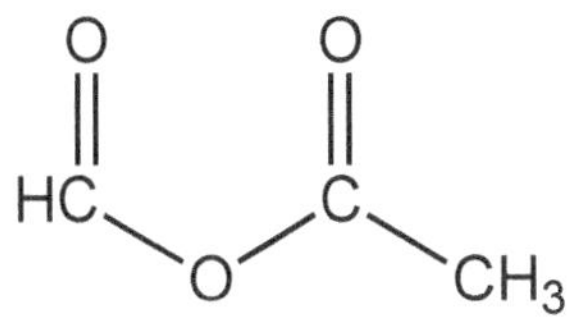

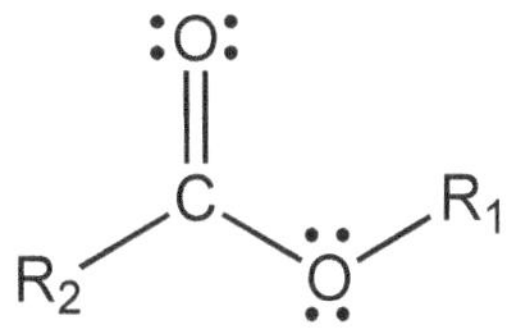

A The suffix *–oate* is used for esters. The ester group is shown to the right. Choice C is a ketone (ethyl methyl ketone or 2-butanone). The ketone group is shown to the left. Choice D is an acid anhydride (ethanoic methanoic anhydride). The acid anhydride group is shown below to the right. A and B are both esters. The hydrocarbon R_2 with the carbonyl group receives the *–oate* suffix and the hydrocarbon R_1 with the *-yl* suffix is attached to the other oxygen. Choice B is ethyl methanoate and A is correct.

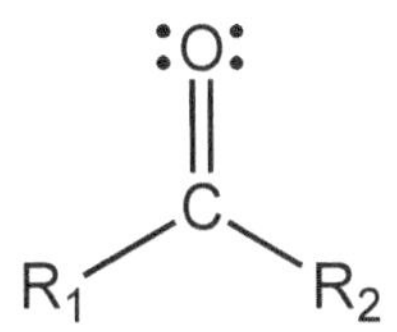

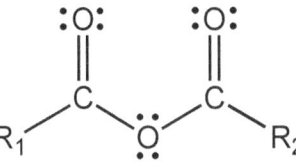

111. This compound contains an:

A. alkene, carboxylic acid, ester, and ketone
B. aldehyde, alkyne, ester, and ketone
C. aldehyde, alkene, carboxylic acid, and ester
D. acid anhydride, aldehyde, alkene, and amine

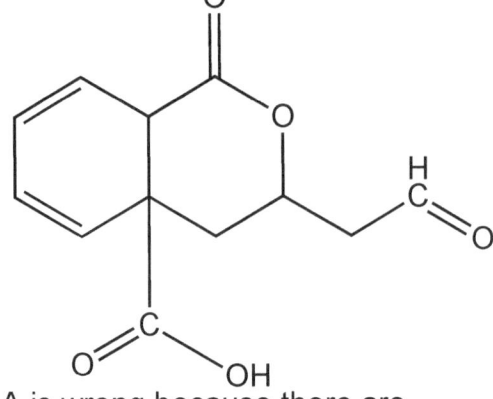

C The derivatives are circled below:

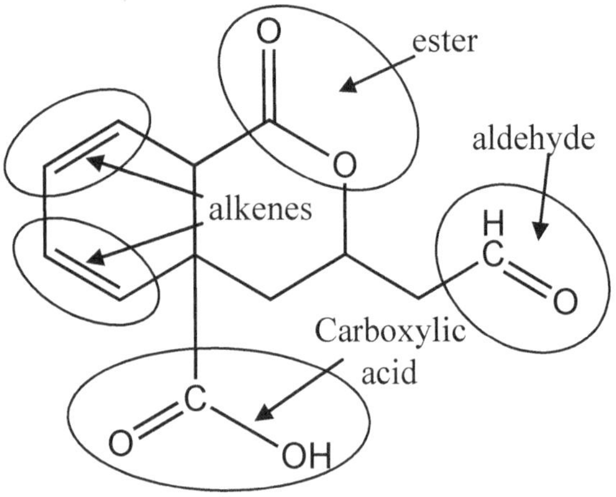

Choice A is wrong because there are no ketones in the molecule. A ketone has a carbonyl group linked to two hydrocarbons as shown to the right. All the carbonyls in the molecule are linked to at least one oxygen atom. Choice B is wrong because there are no ketones and no alkynes in the molecule. An alkyne contains a C≡C triple bond. Choice D is wrong because there are no acid anhydrides (shown to the left) and no amines (shown to the right). Amines require at least one N-C bond and there are no nitrogen atoms in the molecule.

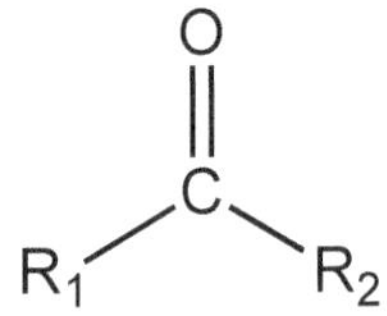

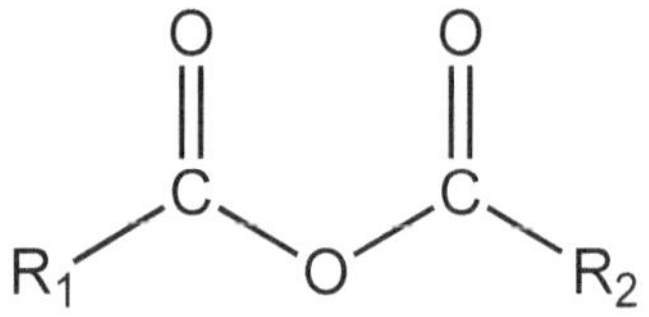

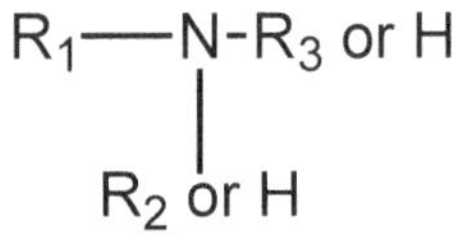

112. Which group of scientists made contributions in the same area of chemistry?

A. Volta, Kekulé, Faraday, London
B. Hess, Joule, Kelvin, Gibbs
C. Boyle, Charles, Arrhenius, Pauli
D. Davy, Mendeleev, Ramsay, Galvani

B Hess, Joule, Kelvin, and Gibbs all contributed to thermochemistry and have thermodynamic entities named after them. Volta, Faraday, and Galvani (choice D) contributed to electrochemistry, Kekulé to organic chemistry, London to chemical bonding, Boyle and Charles to gas laws, Arrhenius to acid/base chemistry and thermochemstry, Pauli to quantum theory, Davy and Ramsay to element isolation, and Mendeleev to the periodic table.

113. Which of the following pairs are isomers?

I. 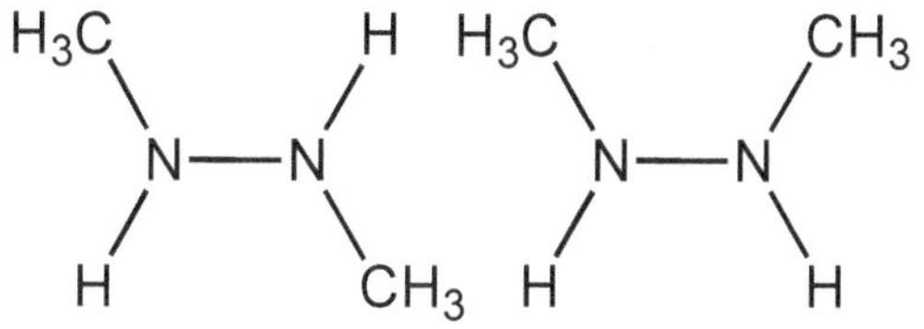 [structures showing H₃C-N(H)-N(CH₃)-H and H₃C-N(H)-N(H)-CH₃]

II. pentanal 2-pentanone

III. 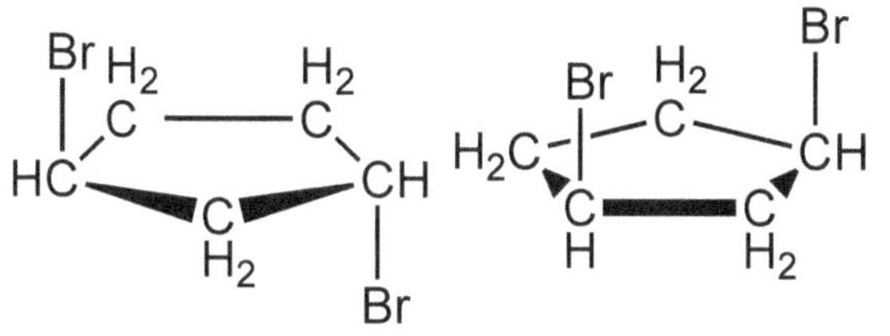 [two structures of 1,3-dibromocyclopentane, trans and cis]

IV. 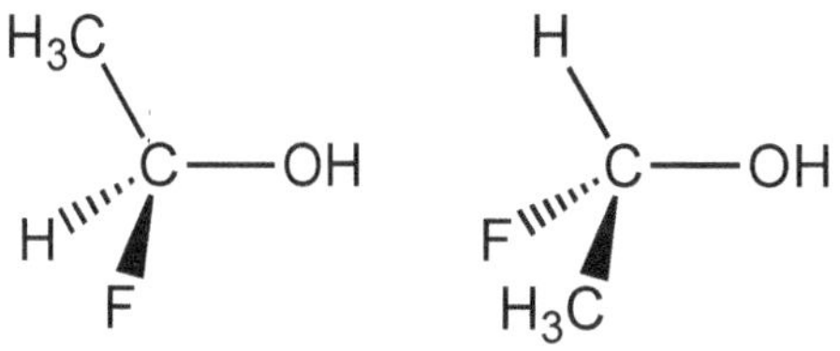 [two structures of 1-fluoroethanol stereoisomer depictions]

A. I and IV
B. II and III
C. I, II, and III
D. I, II, III, and IV

B In pair I, the N—N bond may freely rotate in the molecule because it is not a double bond. The identical molecule is represented twice.

For pair II, pentanal is 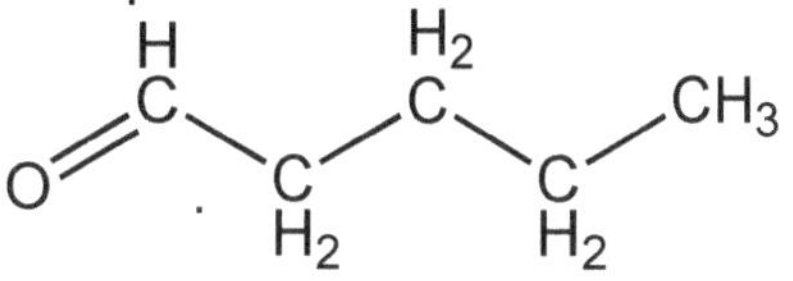 and 2-pentanone is:

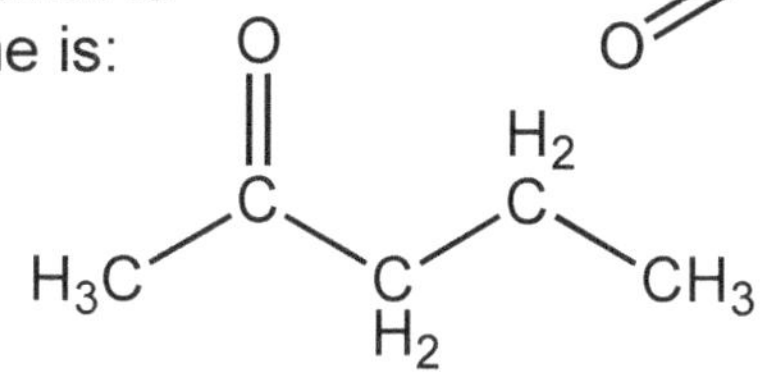

[structures of pentanal and 2-pentanone]

Both molecules are $C_5H_{10}O$, and they are isomers because they have the same formula with a different arrangement of atoms.

In pair III, both molecules are 1,3-dibromocyclopentane, $C_5H_8Br_2$. In the first molecule, the bromines are in a *trans* configuration, and in the second molecule, they are *cis*. The two molecules are also viewed from different perspectives. Unlike pair I, no bond rotation may occur because the intervening atoms are locked into place by the ring, so they are different arrangements and are isomers.

In pair IV (1-fluoroethanol), there is a chiral center, so stereoisomers are possible, but as in pair I, the same molecule is represented twice. Rotating the C-O bond indicates that the two structures are superimposable. This molecule: to the right is a stereoisomer to the molecule represented in IV. The answer is B (pairs II and III).

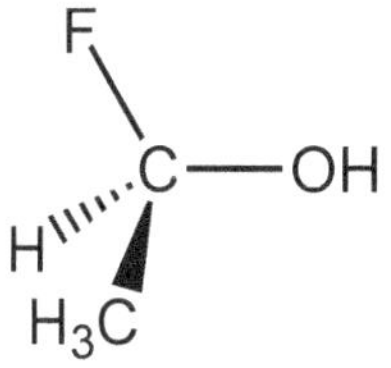

114. Which instrument would be most useful for separating two different proteins from a mixture?

A. UV/Vis spectrophotometer
B. Mass spectrometer
C. Gas chromatograph
D. Liquid chromatograph

D UV/Vis spectrophotometry measures the light at ultraviolet and visible wavelengths that can pass through the mixture, and mass spectrometry determines molecular weights. Both might be used to find the concentration of each protein, but neither is a separation technique. Gas chromatography is used for small molecules in the gas phase. Proteins are too large to exist in the gas phase. Liquid chromatography (answer D) is used to separate large molecules.

115. Classify these biochemicals.

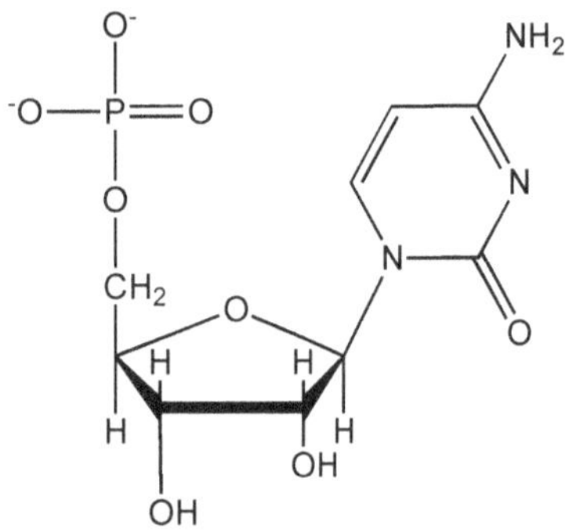

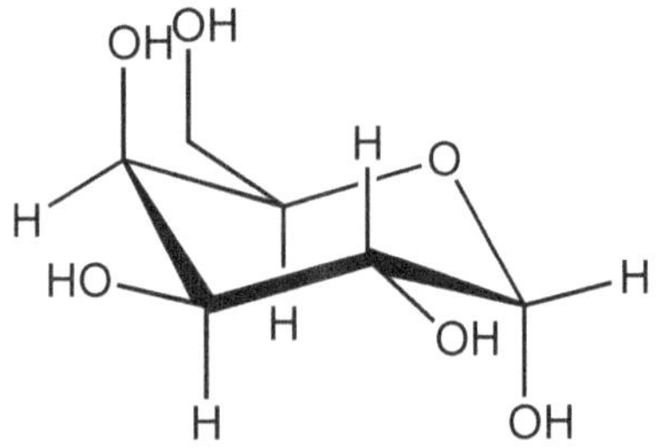

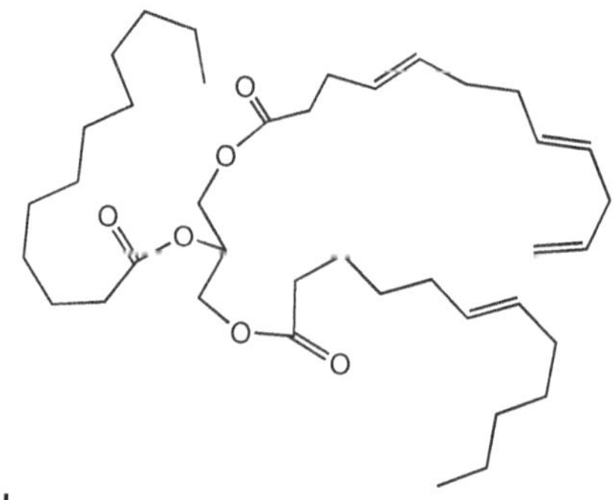

A. I-nucleotide, II-sugar, III-peptide, IV-fat
B. I-disaccharide, II-sugar, III-fatty acid, IV-polypeptide
C. I-disaccharide, II-amino acid, III-fatty acid, IV- polysaccharide
D. I-nucleotide, II-sugar, III-triacylglyceride, and IV-DNA

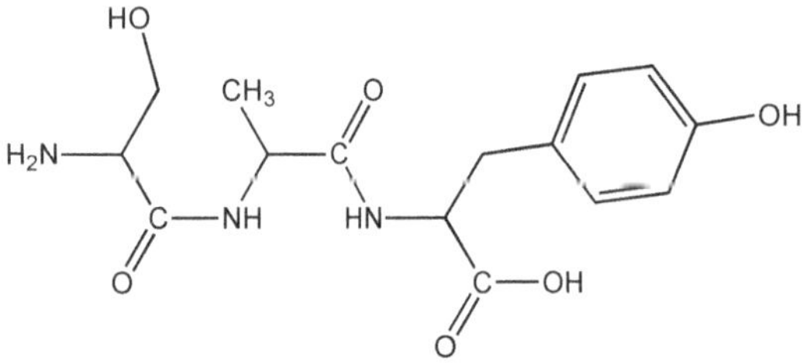

A I is a phosphate (PO_4) linked to a sugar and an amine: a nucleotide. II has the formula $C_nH_{2n}O_n$, indicative of a sugar. III contains three amino acids linked with peptide bonds. It is a tripeptide. IV is a triacylglyceride, a fat molecule.

116. You create a solution of 2.00 µg/ml of a pigment and divide the solution into 12 samples. You give four samples each to three teams of students. They use a spectrophotometer to determine the pigment concentration. Here is their data:

Team	Concentration (µg/ml)			
	sample 1	sample 2	sample 3	sample 4
1	1.98	1.93	1.92	1.88
2	1.70	1.72	1.69	1.70
3	1.78	1.99	2.87	2.20

Which of the following are true?

A. Team 1 has the most precise data
B. Team 3 has the most accurate data in spite of it having low precision
C. The data from team 2 is characteristic of a systematic error
D. The data from team 1 is more characteristic of random error than the data from team 3.

C For choice A, the data from team 2 are closer to the mean for team 2 than the data from team 1 are to its mean. Therefore, team 1's data does not have the most precision.

For choice B, the mean from team 1 is near 1.9 µg/ml (we don't need to calculate exact values). It differs from the actual value by 0.1 µg/ml. The mean from team 2 is near 1.7 µg/ml and is inaccurate by 0.3 µg/ml. The mean from team 3 is not obvious, but it may be calculated as 2.21 µg/ml, differing from the actual value by about 0.2 µg/ml. Team 3's data is less accurate than the data from team 1.

The data from team 2 is clustered close to a central value but this value is wrong. Low accuracy with high precision is indicative of a systematic error. (C is correct).

For choice D, a lack of precision is indicative of random error, and the data from team 1 is more precise than the data from team 3.

117. Which pair of measurements have an identical meaning?

A. 32 micrometers and 0.032 g
B. 26 nm and 2.60×10^{-8} m
C. 3.01×10^{-5} m^3 and 30.1 ml
D. 0.0020 L and 20 cm^3

C For A, the prefix *micro*— indicates 10^{-6}. 32 micrograms is 0.000032 g. For B, the two measurements do not have the same meaning because they differ in the number of significant figures. 26 nm is 2.6×10^{-8} m. The symbol "n" for *nano*— indicates 10^{-9}. For C and D, unit conversions between cubic meters and liters are required.

For C: 3.01×10^{-5} m$^3 \times \dfrac{1000 \text{ L}}{1 \text{ m}^3} \times \dfrac{1000 \text{ ml}}{1 \text{ L}} = 30.1$ ml (C is correct).

For D: 0.0020 L $\times \dfrac{1 \text{ m}^3}{1000 \text{ L}} \times \dfrac{(100)^3 \text{ cm}^3}{1 \text{ m}^3} = 2.0$ cm^3 (D is incorrect).

118. Match the instrument with the quantity it measures

I. eudiometer
II. calorimeter
III. manometer
IV. hygrometer

A. I-volume, II-mass, III-radioactivity, IV-humidity
B. I-volume, II-heat, III-pressure, IV-humidity
C. I-viscosity, II-mass, III-pressure, IV-surface tension
D. I-viscosity, II-heat, III-radioactivity, IV-surface tension

B A eudiometer is a straight tube used to measure gas volume by liquid exclusion. A calorimeter is a device used to measure changes in heat. A manometer is a U-shaped tube used to measure pressure. A hygrometer measures humidity (Answer B). Mass is measured with a balance, radioactivity is measured with a Geiger counter or scintillation counter. Viscosity is measured with a viscometer, surface tension is measured by several different techniques.

119. Four nearly identical gems from the same mineral are weighed using different balances. Their masses are:

3.4533 g, 3.459 g, 3.4656 g, 3.464 g.

The four gems are then collected and added to a volumetric cylinder containing 10.00 ml of liquid, and a new volume of 14.97 ml is read. What is the average mass of the four stones and what is the density of the mineral?

A. 3.460 g, and 2.78 g/ml
B. 3.460 g and 2.79 g/ml
C. 3.4605 g and 2.78 g/ml
D. 3.461 g and 2.79 g/ml

B The average mass is the sum of the four readings divided by four:
(3.4533 g + 3.459 g + 3.4656 g + 3.464 g)/4 = 3.460475 g (caculator value)

This value must be rounded off to three significant digits <u>after the decimal point</u> because this is the lowest precision of the added values. The four is an exact number. This means rounding downwards to 3.460 g, eliminating choices C and D. The volume of the collected stones is found from the increase in the level read off the cylinder:
14.97 ml − 10.00 ml = 4.97 ml

The density is found by dividing the sum of the masses by this volume:
$$\frac{3.4533 \text{ g} + 3.459 \text{ g} + 3.4656 \text{ g} + 3.464 \text{ g}}{4.97 \text{ ml}} = \frac{13.8419 \text{ g}}{4.97 \text{ ml}} = 2.7850905 \text{ g/ml (caculator value)}$$

This value must be rounded off to three <u>total</u> significant digits because this is the lower precision of the numerator and the denominator. The first insignificant digit is a 5. In this case there are additional non-zero digits after the 5, so rounding occurs upwards to 2.79 g/ml (answer B).

120. Which list includes equipment that would not be used in vacuum filtration.

   A. Rubber tubing, Florence flask, Büchner funnel
   B. Vacuum pump, Hirsch funnel, rubber stopper with a single hole
   C. Aspirator, filter paper, filter flask
   D. Lab stand, clamp, filter trap

A Florence flasks are round-bottomed and are used for uniform heating. They do not have the hose barb or the thick wall needed to serve as a filter flask during vacuum filtration. Only a designated filter flask should be used during vacuum filtration. Every other piece of equipment could be used in filtration. A spatula is often used to scrape dried product off of filter paper.

121. Which of the following statements about lab safety is not true?

   A. Corrosive chemicals should be stored below eye level.
   B. A chemical splash on the eye or skin should be rinsed for 15 minutes in cold water.
   C. MSDS means "Material Safety Data Sheet."
   D. A student should "stop, drop, and roll" if their clothing catches fire in the lab.

D In the lab, the safety shower should be used.

122. Which of the following lists consists entirely of chemicals that are considered safe enough to be in a high school lab?

   A. hydrochloric acid, lauric acid, potassium permanganate, calcium hydroxide
   B. ethyl ether, nitric acid, sodium benzoate, methanol
   C. cobalt (II) sulfide, ethylene glycol, benzoyl peroxide, ammonium chloride
   D. picric acid, hydrofluoric acid, cadmium chloride, carbon disulfide.

A Hydrochloric acid (HCl) is a common acid reagent in high school chemistry. Lauric acid is the fatty acid $CH_3(CH_2)_{10}COOH$ also known as dodecanoic acid. Potassium permanganate ($KMnO_4$) is a strong oxidizer. Calcium hydroxide ($Ca(OH)_2$) is a strong base. These chemicals in their pure state are hazardous, but they are considered safe enough to be in high schools. Ethyl ether (Choice B) should not be in high schools because it may form highly explosive organic peroxides over time. Benzoyl peroxide (choice C) at low concentrations in gel form is an acne medication, but the pure compound is highly explosive. Choice D consists entirely of chemicals that are too dangerous for high schools. Picric acid is highly explosive, hydrofluoric acid is very corrosive and very toxic, all cadmium compounds are highly toxic, and carbon disulfide is explosive and toxic.

123. The following procedure was developed to find the specific heat capacity of metals:

   1. Place pieces of the metals in an ice-water bath so their initial temperature is 0 °C.
   2. Weigh a styrofoam cup.
   3. Add water at room temperature to the cup and weigh it again
   4. Add a cold metal from the bath to the cup and weigh the cup a third time.
   5. Monitor the temperature drop of the water until a final temperature at thermal equilibrium is found.

   _____ is also required as additional information in order to obtain heat capacities for the metals. The best control would be to follow the same protocol except to use _____ in step 4 instead of a cold metal.

   A. The heat capacity of water / a metal at 100 °C
   B. The heat of formation of water / ice from the 0 °C bath
   C. The heat of capacity of ice / glass at 0 °C
   D. The heat capacity of water / water from the 0 °C bath

D The equation:

$$q = n \times C \times \Delta T$$

is used to determine what additional information is needed. The specific heat, C, of the metals may be found from the heat added, the amount of material, and the temperature change. The amount of metal is found from the difference in weight between steps 3 and 4, and the temperature change is found from the difference between the final temperature and 0 °C. The additional value required is the heat added, q. This may be found from the heat removed from the water if the amount of water, the heat capacity of water, and the temperature change of water are known. The amount of water is found from the difference in weight between step 2 and 3, and the temperature change is found from the difference between the final temperature and room temperature. The only additional information required is the heat capacity of water, eliminating choices B and C. Heat of formation (choice B) is only used for chemical reactions.

A good control simplifies only the one aspect under study without adding anything new. Metal at 100 °C (choice A) would alter the temperature of the experiment and glass (choice C) would add an additional material to the study. Ice (choice B) would require consideration of the heat of fusion. Choice D is an ideal control because the impact of water at 0 °C on room temperature water is simpler than the impact of metals at 0 °C on room temperature water, and nothing new is added.

TEACHER CERTIFICATION STUDY GUIDE

124. Which statement about the impact of chemistry on society is <u>not</u> true?

A. Partial hydrogenation creates *trans* fat.
B. The Haber Process incorporates nitrogen from the air into molecules for agricultural use.
C. The CO_2 concentration in the atmosphere has decreased in the last ten years.
D. The concentration of ozone-destroying chemicals in the stratosphere has decreased in the last ten years.

C CO_2 concentrations in the atmospehere continue to increase (answer C), but the concentration of ozone destroying chemicals has fallen (answer D) due to international agreements.

125. Which statement about everyday applications of chemistry is <u>true</u>?

A. Rainwater found near sources of air pollution will most likely be basic.
B. Batteries run down more quickly at low temperatures because chemical reactions are proceeding more slowly.
C. Benzyl alcohol is a detergent used in shampoo.
D. Adding salt decreases the time required for water to boil.

B Souces of air pollution (choice A) will most likely cause acid rain.

Low temperatures decrease reaction rates, and this is also true of electrochemical reactions in batteries. At low temperature, less current is supplied and the effect will be a short life for applications that demand current. (Answer B is correct).

Benzyl alcohol (choice C) has the formula shown to the right. Like detergents, this molecule has a non-polar region (the benzene ring) and a polar region (the hydroxyl group). But, unlike detergents, the non-polar region for benzyl alcohol is small and short. Detergents have long, "tail-like" non-polar regions that can surround oils and grease. Benzyl alcohol is sometimes included in shampoo to prevent itching and bacterial growth.

Adding salt (choice D) increases the boiling point of water, thus increasing the time required for water to boil. It decreases the time required to cook food once boiling occurs.

TEACHER CERTIFICATION STUDY GUIDE

Sample Open-Response Questions

Directions: Read the information below and complete the given exercise. Explain your reasoning and show your work.

126. Level: Challenging.

A teapot containing 675 g of water at 25.0 °C is placed on a kitchen stove and heated to 100.0 °C until just before it begins to boil. Natural gas is delivered to the stove at a rate of 135 mL per second at 25.0 °C and a constant total pressure of 1.13 atm. Natural gas is supplied with the following composition:

Weight percentage		
Methane	Ethane	Carbon dioxide
94.9%	4.4 %	0.7%

a. How much energy is required to heat the water in the teapot? The specific heat of water is $4.18 \text{ J/(g} \cdot ^\circ\text{C)}$.

b. Write balanced equations for the combustion of methane and of ethane.

c. How many moles of gas are supplied to the stove each second? Assume that the gas behaves as an ideal gas.
$R = 0.08205 \text{ L} \cdot \text{atm/(mol} \cdot \text{K)}$.

d. How many moles of methane and ethane are supplied to the stove each second?

e. How much heat is produced by hydrocarbon combustion each second? Assume complete combustion and use the following values:

Heat of combustion (kJ/mol)	
Methane	Ethane
890	2900

f. What is the mass of carbon dioxide released into the atmosphere each second? Assume complete combustion.

g. Using only the answers from A and E, estimate a length of time for the water to reach 100.0 °C. An experiment was performed and the water was observed to reach 100.0 °C in 258 seconds. Provide a reason why this value differs from the estimated value.

SCIENCE: CHEMISTRY

127. Level: Intermediate.

Students are learning about equilibrium in a chemistry laboratory exercise. The relevant materials include: an aqueous solution of $CoCl_2$, concentrated HCl, water, a hot water bath, an ice-water bath, and all necessary glassware. $CoCl_2$ dissociates in water into Cl^- ions and Co^{2+} ions which form the hydrated complex $[Co(H_2O)_6]^{2+}$. This ionic complex turns the solution pink. When HCl is added, the additional Cl^- reacts with $[Co(H_2O)_6]^{2+}$ in a mildly endothermic reversible reaction to form $[CoCl_4]^{2-}$. This ion turns the solution blue.

Write an essay describing a qualitative (not quantitative) investigation to explore the effects of both concentration and temperature on equilibrium. In your essay:

a. Describe an appropriate experimental design.

b. Describe the kind of data that will need to be gathered and how the data will be analyzed.

c. Describe the expected results of the study and relate the results to the reactions involved and the relevant concepts of chemical equilibrium.

TEACHER CERTIFICATION STUDY GUIDE

Sample Open-Response Answers

Note: Many chemistry essays on certification exams consist of quantitative problem solving with the requirement to show your work. The first of the two sample essays is of this type. For additional practice, I recommend solving quantitative problems from the multiple choice sample test with an "essay mindset" and comparing your essays to the solutions shown in the "Answers with Solutions" section. Some chemistry essays require little or no quantitative problem solving, but they ask for an experimental design or analysis of a design. The second of the two sample essays is of this type. These essays usually have no single correct solution.

126.

A) The energy required to heat the water in the teapot may be found from the mass, specific heat, and temperature change of the water by utilizing the expression:

$$q = m \times C \times \Delta T \quad \text{where } q \Rightarrow \text{heat added}$$
$$m \Rightarrow \text{mass of water}$$
$$C \Rightarrow \text{specific heat of water}$$
$$\Delta T \Rightarrow \text{change in temperature } T_{final} - T_{initial}$$

Substituting values yields:

$$q = 675 \text{ g} \times 4.18 \frac{J}{g \cdot °C} \times (100.0 \text{ °C} - 25.0 \text{ °C}) = 211 \times 10^3 \text{ J}$$
$$= 211 \text{ kJ}$$

211 kJ of energy are required.

B) The chemical formula for methane is CH_4 and the formula for ethane is C_2H_6. During combustion reactions, the substance reacts with oxygen, and products consist of compounds with oxygen with each atom at its highest possible oxidation state. For C, this product is CO_2, and for H it is H_2O. The unbalanced equations are:

$$CH_4 + O_2 \rightarrow CO_2 + H_2O \quad \text{for methane and}$$
$$C_2H_6 + O_2 \rightarrow CO_2 + H_2O \quad \text{for ethane}$$

The most complex molecule in both cases is the hydrocarbon, and so a stoichiometric coefficient of one will be assumed for now.

SCIENCE: CHEMISTRY

For methane, this results in 1 C atom on both the left and right, so C is balanced. There are 4 H atoms on the left side of the equation and 2 on the right. A stoichiometric coefficient of 2 for H_2O corrects this imbalance:

$$CH_4 + ?O_2 \rightarrow CO_2 + 2H_2O.$$

Finally, there are 2 O atoms on the left and 4 on the right. A stoichiometric coefficient of 2 for O_2 balances the equation:

$$CH_4 + 2O_2 \rightarrow CO_2 + 2H_2O.$$

For ethane, there are 2 C atoms on the left and one on the right, so a coefficient of 2 will initially be given to CO_2. There are 6 H atoms on the left and 2 on the right, so H_2O will have a coefficient of 3:

$$C_2H_6 + ?O_2 \rightarrow 2CO_2 + 3H_2O.$$

There are 2 O atoms on the left and 7 on the right. A fractional stoichiometric coefficient describes the combustion of one mole of ethane:

$$C_2H_6 + \frac{7}{2}O_2 \rightarrow 2CO_2 + 3H_2O$$

Finally, the fractional coefficient could be eliminated by multiplying the entire expression by 2:

$$2C_2H_6 + 7O_2 \rightarrow 4CO_2 + 6H_2O$$

A final check confirms that there are now 4 C atoms, 12 H atoms, and 14 O atoms on both sides of the equation.

C) The problem states that 135 mL of an ideal gas are supplied to the stove each second. The pressure and temperature are also known. The ideal gas equation, $PV = nRT$, may be rearranged to solve for the number of moles of gas flowing in a second:

$$n = \frac{PV}{RT}.$$

135 mL is converted to 0.135 L to correspond to the given units of the ideal gas constant. . 25.0 °C is converted to Kelvin before using the ideal gas law:

273.15 + 25.0 = 298.15 K (the last digit isn't significant)

Plugging these values into the equation for one second of gas flow yields:

$$n = \frac{1.13 \text{ atm} \times 0.135 \frac{L}{s}}{0.08205 \frac{L \cdot atm}{mol \cdot K} \times 298.15 \text{ K}} = 6.24 \times 10^{-3} \frac{mol}{s}.$$

0.00624 moles of gas are supplied to the stove each second.

D) Weight percentages of methane and ethane must first be converted to mole fractions using the molecular weights of all three species. These fractions will then be used with the answer to part C to determine the number of moles of each hydrocarbon supplied to the stove every second.

The molecular weights of the three components are:
For methane: $12.011 + 4 \times 1.0079 = 16.043$ g/mole CH_4
For ethane: $2 \times 12.011 + 6 \times 1.0079 = 30.069$ g/mole C_2H_6.
For carbon dioxide: $12.011 + 2 \times 15.999 = 44.009$ g/mole CO_2

The molecular weights and weight percentages given in the table will be used to find the number of moles of each component using a basis of exactly 1 g of natural gas:

$$\frac{0.949 \text{ g } CH_4}{\text{g gas}} \times \frac{\text{mole } CH_4}{16.043 \text{ g } CH_4} = \frac{0.05915 \text{ mole } CH_4}{\text{g gas}}$$

$$\frac{0.044 \text{ g } C_2H_6}{\text{g gas}} \times \frac{\text{mole } C_2H_6}{30.069 \text{ g } C_2H_6} = \frac{0.00146 \text{ mole } C_2H_6}{\text{g gas}}.$$

$$\frac{0.007 \text{ g } CO_2}{\text{g gas}} \times \frac{\text{mole } CO_2}{44.009 \text{ g } CO_2} = \frac{0.00016 \text{ mole } CO_2}{\text{g gas}}$$

These intermediate results contain an extra, insignificant digit. The three values above are added together to give the total number of moles in a gram of gas:

$$0.05915 + 0.00146 + 0.00016 = 0.06077 \frac{\text{mole gas}}{\text{g gas}}.$$

The mole fractions of the hydrocarbon components may then be found:

$$\frac{0.05915 \text{ mole } CH_4}{0.06077 \text{ mole gas}} = 0.9733 \frac{\text{mole } CH_4}{\text{mole gas}}$$

$$\frac{0.00146 \text{ mole } C_2H_6}{0.06077 \text{ mole gas}} = 0.0240 \frac{\text{mole } C_2H_6}{\text{mole gas}}.$$

Finally, these values are multiplied by the result from part C to give the moles of hydrocarbons supplied each second. The extra insignificant digit for the ethane problem is removed from this final result.

$$0.00624 \frac{\text{mole gas}}{\text{s}} \times 0.9733 \frac{\text{mole } CH_4}{\text{mole gas}} = 0.00607 \frac{\text{mole } CH_4}{\text{s}}$$

$$0.00624 \frac{\text{mole gas}}{\text{s}} \times 0.0240 \frac{\text{mole } C_2H_6}{\text{mole gas}} = 0.00015 \frac{\text{mole } C_2H_6}{\text{s}}.$$

E). The heats of combustion are multiplied by the rate of supply for each gas:

$$0.00607 \frac{\text{mole CH}_4}{\text{s}} \times 890 \frac{\text{kJ}}{\text{mole CH}_4} = 5.4 \frac{\text{kJ}}{\text{s}} \text{ from methane combustion}$$

$$0.00015 \frac{\text{mole C}_2\text{H}_6}{\text{s}} \times 2900 \frac{\text{kJ}}{\text{mole C}_2\text{H}_6} = 0.44 \frac{\text{kJ}}{\text{s}} \text{ from ethane combustion}$$

The total heat produced from hydrocarbon combustion is the sum of these two values: 5.8 kJ each second.

F) There are three sources of carbon dioxide in this problem. CO_2 already in the natural gas before combustion is released into the atmosphere. This value is found from its weight percentage and values calculated in parts C and D:

$$\frac{0.007 \text{ g CO}_2}{\text{g gas}} \times \frac{\text{g gas}}{0.06077 \text{ mole gas}} \times \frac{0.00624 \text{ mole gas}}{\text{s}} = 0.0007 \frac{\text{g CO}_2}{\text{s}}$$

CO_2 from combustion is found from the values calculated in part D and the stoichiometry of the chemical equations from part B.

For methane:
$$0.00607 \frac{\text{mole CH}_4}{\text{s}} \times \frac{1 \text{ mole CO}_2}{1 \text{ mole CH}_4} \times \frac{44.009 \text{ g CO}_2}{1 \text{ mole CO}_2} = 0.267 \frac{\text{g CO}_2}{\text{s}}.$$

For ethane:
$$0.00015 \frac{\text{mole C}_2\text{H}_6}{\text{s}} \times \frac{4 \text{ mole CO}_2}{2 \text{ mole C}_2\text{H}_6} \times \frac{44.009 \text{ g CO}_2}{1 \text{ mole CO}_2} = 0.013 \frac{\text{g CO}_2}{\text{s}}.$$

The mass of CO_2 released is found from the sum of these three contributions:

$$0.0007 + 0.267 + 0.013 = 0.281 \frac{\text{g CO}_2}{\text{s}}.$$

G) From A, 211 kJ are required to heat the water. From E, the rate of heat produced by combustion is 5.8 kJ per second. An estimate of the number of seconds to heat the water may be found by dividing the heat required by the rate at which it is supplied:

$$211 \text{ kJ} \times \frac{1 \text{ s}}{5.8 \text{ kJ}} = 36 \text{ seconds}.$$

One reason why this value differs from the observed value of 258 seconds is because the heat supplied by combustion does not transfer perfectly into the heating of water in an insulated, adiabatic process. Heat from combustion will also be used to raise the temperature of the teapot, the stovetop, and nearby air. Heat from the hot water is also lost to the air.

127. The dissociation of $CoCl_2$ in water and the formation of the pink-colored complex is described by the reaction:

$$CoCl_2(s) + 6H_2O(l) \rightarrow [Co(H_2O)_6]^{2+}(aq)_{PINK} + 2Cl^-(aq)$$

The dissociation of HCl is described by the reaction:

$$HCl(aq) \rightarrow H^+(aq) + Cl^-(aq).$$

When these two solutions are combined, the pink solution is expected to turn blue due to the formation of $[CoCl_4]^{2-}$. The equilibrium reaction under study is:

$$[Co(H_2O)_6]^{2+}(aq)_{PINK} + 4Cl^-(aq) + \text{heat} \rightleftharpoons [CoCl_4]^{2-}(aq)_{BLUE} + 6H_2O(l)$$

The relevant concept under study is Le Chatelier's principle and its application to the impact of concentration and temperature on equilibrium.

The only data that will be gathered in this qualitative study is an observation of color changes. Every color change should be recorded in the students' lab notebooks. A color change from pink to blue indicates the reaction above is occurring from left to right. A color change from blue to pink indicates the reaction is occurring from right to left.

The first step will provide a large volume of uniform experimental material for the students. This step will utilize concentrated HCl, so it should be performed by the instructor while the students watch. The instructor should wear gloves. Concentrated HCl should be slowly added to the cobalt(II) chloride solution until the entire solution changes color. Students should note the color before and after the change takes place. This should be a change from pink to blue because the equilibrium reaction under study has shifted to the right to partially offset the impact of added chloride ion. A sufficient volume should be prepared to provide every student or team of students with an aliquot of 10 mL of this blue solution. Even though these volumes are small, the students are still handling a corrosive acid at moderate concentration and should wear gloves to minimize their risk of contact. The students should perform the following procedure and answer the following questions:

1. Label six test tubes 1 through 6.
2. Place half of your blue solution in tube 1 and half in tube 2.
3. Add water to tube 2 until a change in color takes place. Which direction does the equilibrium shift when water is added? (Answer: Adding water shifted equilibrium from right to left)
4. Divide the solution in tube 1 in half. Place half in tube 3 and half in tube 4.

5. Divide the solution in tube 2 in half. Place half in tube 5 and half in tube 6.
6. Test tube 3 and 4 should contain blue solution and the solution in tubes 5 and 6 should be pink.
7. Place tubes 3 and 5 in the hot water bath. Which solution changes color? (Answer: solution in tube 5 turns blue) Which direction did the equilibrium shift? (Answer: Adding heat shifted equilibrium from left to right).
8. Place tubes 4 and 6 in the ice-water bath. Which test tube changes color? (Answer: solution in tube 4 turns pink) Which direction did the equilibrium shift? (Answer: Removing heat shifted equilibrium from right to left).

The following table summarizes the experimental study in terms of predictions from Le Chatelier's principle and the expected results in the lab:

$$[Co(H_2O)_6]^{2+}(aq)_{PINK} + 4Cl^-(aq) + heat \rightleftharpoons [CoCl_4]^{2-}(aq)_{BLUE} + 6H_2O(l)$$

Test tube	Treatment	Prediction	Result
1	Instructor added Cl^-	Shift to the right	Pink to blue (moved to 3 and 4)
2	Add H_2O	Shift to the left	Blue to pink (moved to 5 and 6)
3	Add heat	Shift to the right	No change (or deeper blue)
4	Remove heat	Shift to the left	Blue to pink
5	Add heat	Shift to the right	Pink to blue
6	Remove heat	Shift to the left	No change (or deeper pink)

www.ingramcontent.com/pod-product-compliance
Lightning Source LLC
Chambersburg PA
CBHW080532300426
44111CB00017B/2691